Mindfulness
at Work

FOR

DUMMIES®

A Wiley Brand

Mindfulness at Work

FOR

DUMMIES®

A Wiley Brand

by Shamash Alidina
and
Juliet Adams

FOR

DUMMIES®

A Wiley Brand

Mindfulness at Work For Dummies®

Published by: **John Wiley & Sons, Ltd.,** The Atrium, Southern Gate, Chichester, www.wiley.com

This edition first published 2014

© 2014 John Wiley & Sons, Ltd, Chichester, West Sussex.

Registered office

John Wiley & Sons Ltd, The Atrium, Southern Gate, Chichester, West Sussex, PO19 8SQ, United Kingdom

For details of our global editorial offices, for customer services and for information about how to apply for permission to reuse the copyright material in this book please see our website at www.wiley.com.

The right of the author to be identified as the author of this work has been asserted in accordance with the Copyright, Designs and Patents Act 1988.

Wiley publishes in a variety of print and electronic formats and by print-on-demand. Some material included with standard print versions of this book may not be included in e-books or in print-on-demand. If this book refers to media such as a CD or DVD that is not included in the version you purchased, you may download this material at http://booksupport.wiley.com. For more information about Wiley products, visit www.wiley.com.

Designations used by companies to distinguish their products are often claimed as trademarks. All brand names and product names used in this book are trade names, service marks, trademarks or registered trademarks of their respective owners. The publisher is not associated with any product or vendor mentioned in this book.

For general information on our other products and services, please contact our Customer Care Department within the U.S. at 877-762-2974, outside the U.S. at (001) 317-572-3993, or fax 317-572-4002. For technical support, please visit www.wiley.com/techsupport.

For technical support, please visit www.wiley.com/techsupport.

A catalogue record for this book is available from the British Library.

ISBN 978-1-118-72799-7 (paperback) ISBN 978-1-118-72797-3 (ebk)
ISBN 978-1-118-72790-4 (ebk)

Printed in Great Britain by Bell & Bain, Ltd., Glasgow.

10 9 8 7 6 5 4 3 2 1

Contents at a Glance

Table of Contents

Introduction

Mindfulness is a mental discipline and way of being that has been practiced for thousands of years. Modern science has researched mindfulness as a secular practice and discovered its tremendous power-creating positive changes in the brain that have never been seen before in brain scans.

Mindfulness was initially used in medical settings in the late 1970s. In the decades that followed, the use of mindfulness throughout western society began to rapidly increase. Nowadays, hundreds of corporate organisations, from Google to General Mills, use mindfulness to help their employees boost their resilience, productivity, emotional intelligence, focus or even just to make them feel happier!

This book, *Mindfulness at Work For Dummies*, offers an accessible and fairly comprehensive look at the ways of bringing greater mindfulness into the workplace setting, whatever your motivation.

This book is for anyone with any sort of role in the workplace. Employees, small business owners, managers and corporate executives and leaders will find practical application from this book, we hope. We even explore mindful leadership in some depth, a leadership theory that's now taught in the finest business schools in the world.

We wrote this book because we're passionate about mindfulness! Having practiced mindfulness both in our personal and professional lives, we can see the massive positive benefits of a workforce that is trained to use mindfulness – greater creativity, improved communication and higher levels of productivity and wellbeing.

We also feel mindfulness can help manage the negative consequences of the demanding modern workplace environment. High levels of pressure, tight deadlines and overly demanding managers can take their toll on the toughest individuals. With stress now one of the leading causes of absence from work according to the World Health Organization, the need to find ways of building mental resilience is huge. We like to think that mindfulness offers a powerful way of raising resilience in the workplace setting, and the science agrees.

With hundreds of organisations, big and small, now offering mindfulness at work, this book offers a systematic and evidence-based way to integrate mindfulness in the workplace. We tried to simplify the concepts without losing their subtle essence, and include lots of exercises for everyone to try out, from the boardroom to the shop floor. We hope *Mindfulness at Work For Dummies* will offer something for you too – and offers you a fresh approach to your work.

About This Book

Mindfulness at Work For Dummies provides you with practical techniques to integrate mindfulness into the workplace. Each chapter is jam packed with insights about the art of mindfulness, how to be mindful quickly and easily, and how to work with mindful awareness. This book has been written for beginners to the idea of mindfulness and those looking for ways to introduce mindfulness into their organisation in a scientifically proven way.

This book comes with access to downloadable mindfulness exercises designed specifically for the workplace. The audio is in MP3 format so you can listen on your computer, phone, MP3 player or burn onto a CD for your personal use.

Within this book, you may note that some Web addresses break across two lines of text. If you're reading this book in print and want to visit one of these Web pages, simply key in the Web address exactly as it's noted in the text, pretending as though the line break doesn't exist. If you're reading this as an e-book, you've got it easy – just click the Web address to be taken directly to the Web page.

Foolish Assumptions

In writing this book, we made a few assumptions about who you are:

- You work on a regular basis, or are actively seeking work.
- You are looking for an approach to improve you and your staff's success in the workplace.
- You want be more mindful at work, but don't know where to start.
- You are willing to try the various mindfulness exercises and strategies we have suggested several times before judging if they could work for you or your staff.
- You're looking for long-term ways of improving your effectiveness in the workplace rather that just a quick fix.

Beyond those, we've not assumed too much, we hope. This book is for you whether you're male or female, eighteen upwards.

Icons Used in This Book

Scattered through the book you'll see various icons to guide you on your way. Icons are a *For Dummies* way of drawing your attention to important stuff, interesting stuff, and stuff you really need to know not to do.

This icon indicates an activity that's specifically tied in to the Mindfulness At Work Training (MAWT) you can find in Chapters 6 and 7.

Shoot over to www.dummies.com/go/mindfulnessatworkuk and download the audio that goes along with this book.

This is stuff you need to know: whatever else you carry away from this book, note these bits with care.

Look out for these icons if you like science and want to learn about the evidence behind the mindfulness exercises and approaches.

Handy tidbits to help you get you nice and mindful at work.

An activity for you to try out for yourself.

Beyond the Book

We offer further resources that go with this book. Firstly, visit http://mawt.co.uk – register your email to get free resources, links to recommended videos and access to research material mentioned in this book. Also, visit that website if you'd like to get in touch with us about our own trainings.

In addition to the material in the print or e-book you're reading right now, this book comes with some access-anywhere content on the Web. Check out the free Cheat Sheet at www.dummies.com/cheatsheet/mindfulnessatworkuk.

We also specially recorded a set of guided mindfulness exercises for you to use along with this book. You can download the content whenever you wish. Go to www.dummies.com/go/mindfulnessatworkuk to access the guided mindfulness audio.

Where to Go from Here

We've compiled this book so that you can dip in and out as you please. We invite you to make good use of the Table of Contents (or the index) and jump straight into the section you fancy. You're in charge and it's up to you. If you're a total beginner to mindfulness, or not sure where to start, begin with Part I and you'll have a better idea how to proceed.

We wish you all the best in your quest to be mindful or to bring mindfulness to others at work, and hope you find something of use within these pages.

Part I
Getting Started with Mindfulness at Work

getting started with

Mindfulness at Work

For Dummies can help you get started with a huge range of subjects. Visit www.dummies.com to learn more and do more with *For Dummies*.

In this part . . .

- ✔ Find out exactly what mindfulness is – and isn't.
- ✔ Discover the genuine impact that practising mindfulness can have on your brain.
- ✔ Understand the real benefits that mindfulness can bring to both individuals and organisations.
- ✔ Begin your mindfulness at work journey.
- ✔ Develop a sense of perspective in the workplace.

Chapter 1

Exploring Mindfulness in the Workplace

In This Chapter

▶ Identifying what mindfulness is and is not

▶ Retraining your brain

▶ Getting started

*I*n tough economic times, many organisations are looking for new ways to deliver better products and services to customers while simultaneously reducing costs. Carrying on as normal is not isn't an option. Organisations are looking for sustainable ways to be more innovative. Leaders must really engage staff, and everyone needs to become more resilient in the face of ongoing change. For these reasons, more and more organisations are offering staff training in mindfulness.

Major corporations in the USA, like General Mills, and major employers in the UK, such as the National Health Service, have offered staff mindfulness training in recent years. Google and eBay are among the many companies that now provide rooms for staff to practise mindfulness in work time. Business schools including Harvard Business School in the USA and Ashridge Business School in the UK now include mindfulness principles in their leadership programmes.

So what is mindfulness, and why are so many leading organisations investing in it?

Becoming More Mindful at Work

In this section you will discover what mindfulness is. More importantly, you'll also discover what mindfulness is not! You'll find out how mindfulness evolved and why it's become so important in the modern day workplace.

Clarifying what mindfulness is

Have you ever driven somewhere and arrived at your destination remembering nothing about your journey? Or grabbed a snack and noticed a few moments later that all you have left is an empty packet? Most people have! These examples are common ones of 'mindlessness', or 'going on automatic pilot'.

Like many humans, you're probably 'not present' for much of your own life. You may fail to notice the good things in your life or hear what your body is telling you. You probably also make your life harder than it needs to be by poisoning yourself with toxic self-criticism.

Mindfulness can help you to become more aware of your thoughts, feelings and sensations in a way that suspends judgement and self-criticism. Developing the ability to pay attention to and see clearly whatever is happening moment by moment does not eliminate life's pressures, but it can help you respond to them in a more productive, calmer manner.

Learning and practising mindfulness can help you to recognise and step away from habitual, often unconscious emotional and physiological reactions to everyday events. Practising mindfulness allows you to be fully present in your life and work and improves your quality of life.

Mindfulness can help you to:

- Recognise, slow down or stop automatic and habitual reactions
- Respond more effectively to complex or difficult situations
- See situations with greater focus and clarity
- Become more creative
- Achieve balance and resilience at both work and home

Mindfulness at work is all about developing awareness of thoughts, emotions and physiology and how they interact with one another. Mindfulness is also about being aware of your surroundings, helping you better understand the needs of those around you.

Mindfulness training is like going to the gym. In the same way as training a muscle, you can train your brain to direct your attention to where you want it to be. In simple terms, mindfulness is all about managing your mind.

Taking a look at the background

Mindfulness has its origins in ancient Eastern meditation practices. Jon Kabat-Zinn developed Mindfulness-Based Stress Reduction (MBSR) in the USA in the late 1970s, which became the foundation for modern-day mindfulness. Figure 1-1 shows how it developed.

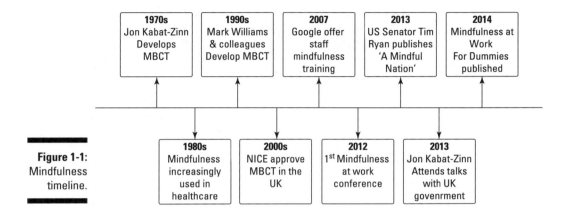

1970s	1990s	2007	2013	2014
Jon Kabat-Zinn Develops MBCT	Mark Williams & colleagues Develop MBCT	Google offer staff mindfulness training	US Senator Tim Ryan publishes 'A Mindful Nation'	Mindfulness at Work For Dummies published

1980s	2000s	2012	2013
Mindfulness increasingly used in healthcare	NICE approve MBCT in the UK	1st Mindfulness at work conference	Jon Kabat-Zinn Attends talks with UK govenrment

Figure 1-1: Mindfulness timeline.

In the 1990s Mark Williams, John Teasdale and Zindel Segal further developed MBSR to help people suffering from depression. Mindfulness Based Cognitive Therapy (MBCT) combined cognitive behavioural therapy (CBT) with mindfulness. In 2004, MBCT was clinically approved in the UK by the National Institute for Clinical Excellence (NICE) as a 'treatment of choice' for recurrent depression.

Since the late 1970s, research into the benefits of mindfulness has steadily increased. Recent studies have examined, for example, the impact of practising mindfulness on the immune system and its effects on those working in high pressure environments.

Advances in brain scanning technology have demonstrated that as little as eight weeks of mindfulness training can positively alter brain structures, including the amygdala (the fear centre) and the left prefrontal cortex (an area associated with happiness and well-being). Other studies show benefits in even shorter periods of time.

Busy leaders who practise mindfulness have long extolled its virtues, but little research has existed to back up their claims. Fortunately, researchers are now increasingly focusing their attention on the benefits of mindfulness from a workplace perspective.

MBSR and MBCT are taught using a standard eight-week curriculum, and all teachers follow a formalised development route. The core techniques are the same for both courses. Most workplace mindfulness courses are based around MBCT or MBSR, but tailored to meet the needs of the workplace.

Although MBSR and MBCT were first developed to help treat a range of physical and mental health conditions, new applications for the techniques have been established. Mindfulness is now being taught in schools and universities, and has even been introduced to prisoners. Many professional education programmes, such as MBAs, now include mindfulness training.

Researchers have linked the practice of mindfulness to skills that are highly valuable in the workplace. Research suggests that practising mindfulness can enhance:

- Emotional intelligence
- Creativity and innovation
- Employee engagement
- Interpersonal relationships
- Ability to see the bigger picture
- Resilience
- Self-management
- Problem solving
- Decision making
- Focus and concentration

In addition, mindfulness is valuable in the workplace because it has a positive impact on immunity and general well-being. It has been demonstrated to relieve the symptoms of depression, anxiety and stress. See www.mawt.co.uk for a list of some of the research papers on mindfulness at work.

ACT

In the late 1980s, research began by Steven Hayes and colleagues for another form training called Acceptance and Commitment Theraphy (ACT). ACT combines mindfulness and acceptance with action-based strategies. In the last few years, ACT has begun to been adapted to meet the modern workplace, sometimes called Acceptance and Commitment Training.

Recognising what mindfulness isn't

Misleading myths about mindfulness abound. Here are a few:

Myth 1: 'I will need to visit a Buddhist centre, go on a retreat or travel to the Far East to learn mindfulness.'

Experienced mindfulness instructors are operating all over the world. Many teachers now teach mindfulness to groups of staff in the workplace. One-to-one mindfulness teaching can be delivered in the office, in hotel meeting rooms or even via the web. Some people do attend retreats after learning mindfulness if they wish to deepen their knowledge, experience peace and quiet or gain further tuition, but doing so isn't essential.

Myth 2: 'Practising mindfulness will conflict with my religious beliefs.'

Mindfulness isn't a religion. For example, MBSR, MBCT are entirely secular – as are most workplace programs. No religious belief of any kind is necessary. Mindfulness can help you step back from your mental noise and tune into your own innate wisdom. Mindfulness is practised by people of all faiths and by those with no spiritual beliefs. Practising mindfulness won't turn you into a hemp-clad tofu eater, a tree-hugging hippie or a monk sitting on top of a mountain – unless you want to be one of these people, of course!

Myth 3: 'I'm too busy to sit and be quiet for any length of time.'

When you're busy, the thought of sitting and 'doing nothing' may seem like the last thing you want to do. In 2010 researchers at Harvard University gathered evidence from a quarter of a million people suggesting that, on average, the mind wanders for 47 per cent of the working day. Just 15 minutes a day spent practising mindfulness can help you to become more productive and less distracted. Then you'll be able to make the most of your busy day and get more done in less time. When you first start practising mindfulness, you'll almost certainly experience mental distractions, but if you persevere you'll find it easier to tune out distractions and to manage your mind. As time goes on, your ability to concentrate increases as does your sense of well-being and feeling of control over your life.

Myth 4: 'Practising mindfulness will reduce my ambition and drive.'

Practising mindfulness can help you become more focused on your goals and better able to achieve them. It can help you become more creative and to gain new perspectives on life. If your approach to work is chaotic, mindfulness can make you more focused and centred, which in turn enables you to channel your energy more productively. Coupled with an improved sense of well-being, this ability to focus helps you achieve your career ambitions and goals.

Myth 5: 'If I practise mindfulness, people will take me less seriously and my career prospects will be damaged.'

Some of the most successful and influential people in the world practise mindfulness. US Senator Tim Ryan, Goldie Hawn, Joanna Lumley and Ruby Wax are all keen advocates of mindfulness. Practising mindfulness doesn't involve sitting cross-legged on the floor – an office chair is fine. If you find it impossible to sit quietly and focus because you work in an open-plan office, or you're concerned about what others think, plenty of other everyday activities are available that can become opportunities to practise mindfulness that nobody will notice. Walking, eating, waiting for your computer to boot up or even exercising at the gym are all good opportunities to practise mindfulness. Mindfulness can be practising with your eyes open, whilst you're moving around during the day.

Myth 6: 'Mindfulness and meditation are one and the same. Mindfulness is just a trendy new name.'

Fact: Mindfulness often involves specific meditation practices. Fiction: All meditation is the same. Many popular forms of meditation are all about relaxation – leaving your troubles behind and imagining yourself in a calm and tranquil 'special place'. Mindfulness helps you to find out how to live with your life in the present moment – warts and all – rather than run away from it. Mindfulness is about approaching life and things that you find difficult and exploring them with openness, rather than avoiding them. Most people find that practising mindfulness does help them to relax, but that this relaxation is a welcome by-product, not the objective!

Training your attention: the power of focus

Are you one of the millions of workers who routinely put in long hours, often for little or no extra pay? In the current climate of cutbacks, job losses and 'business efficiencies', many people feel the need to work longer hours just to keep on top of their workload. However, research shows that working longer hours does not mean that you get more done. Actually, if you continue to work when past your peak, your performance slackens off and continues to do so as time goes on (see Chapter 5).

Imagine your job is to chop logs. After a while, your axe needs sharpening and your muscles need resting. If you keep going, you'll become very inefficient and are more likely to have an accident. By taking a break, and sharpening your axe, you can return to the job and get more done in less time. You'll probably enjoy the job more too. Mindfulness practice is like taking that break – you both re-energise yourself and sharpen your mind, ready for your next activity.

Discovering how to focus and concentrate better is the key to maintaining peak performance. Recognising when you've slipped past peak performance and then taking steps to bring yourself back to peak is also vital. Mindfulness comes in at this point. Over time, it helps you focus your attention to where you want it to be.

Focusing your attention may sound easy, but try thinking of just one thing for 90 seconds. It could be an object on your desk, a specific sound or the sensation of your own breathing.

Focus your full attention on your chosen object, sound or sensation and nothing else. Then consider these questions:

- ✔ Did you manage to focus your complete attention for the full 90 seconds, or did your mind wander and random thoughts arise?
- ✔ Did you become distracted by a bodily pain or ache?
- ✔ Did you find yourself getting annoyed with yourself, or annoyed with a sound such as a ticking clock or traffic?

You're not alone! Most people find this activity really difficult at first. In truth, you're unlikely to ever be able to shut out all of your mental chatter, but you can turn the volume right down. Doing so enables you to see things more clearly, reduce time wasted on duplicated work and stop your mind wandering. Mindfulness offers you a way of getting more done in less time without burning yourself out.

Applying mindful attitudes

Practising mindfulness involves more than just training your brain to focus. It also teaches you some alternative mindful attitudes to life's challenges. You discover the links between your thoughts, emotions and physiology. You find out that what's important isn't what happens to you, but how you choose to respond that matters. This statement may sound simple, but most people respond to situations based on their mental programming (past experiences and predictions of what will happen next). Practising mindfulness makes you more aware of how your thoughts, emotions and physiology impact on your responses to people and situations. This awareness then enables you to choose how to respond rather than reacting on auto-pilot. You may well find that you respond in a different manner.

By gaining a better understanding of your brain's response to life events, you can use mindfulness techniques to reduce your 'fight or flight' response and regain your bodies 'rest and relaxation' state. You will see things more clearly and get more done.

Mindfulness also brings you face to face with your inner bully – the voice in your head that says you are not talented enough, not smart enough or not good enough. By learning to treat thoughts like these ones as 'just mental processes and not facts', the inner bully loses its grip on your life and you become free to reach your full potential.

These examples are just a few of the many ways that a mindful attitude can have a positive impact on your life and career prospects.

Finding Out Why Your Brain Needs Mindfulness

Recent advances in brain scanning technology are helping us to understand why our brain needs mindfulness. In this section you discover powerful things about your brain – its evolution, its hidden rules, how thoughts shape your brain structure and the basics of how your brain operates at work.

Your brain's technical specifications

Size:

- Around 1,300 grams – that's over three times the size of a chimpanzee's, our closest animal relative.

- The human brain accounts for 2 per cent of the body's weight, but it uses around 20 per cent of its energy.

Energy consumption:

- A typical adult human brain runs on around 12 watts – a fifth of the power required by a standard 60 watt light bulb.

- Compared with most other organs, the brain is energy-hungry; but compared to man-made electronics, the brain is extremely efficient. IBM's Watson supercomputer depends on 90 IBM Power 750 servers, each of which requires around 1,000 watts.

Operating system:

- Energy travels to the brain via blood vessels in the form of glucose.

- The brain contains billions of nerve cells that send and receive information around the body.

- The brain never sleeps! It provides instant access to information on demand.

Performance:

- Neurons (brain cells that process and transmit information through electrical and chemical signals) fire around 5 to 50 times a second (or faster).

- Signals cross your brain in a tenth or hundredth of a second.

Evolving from lizard to spaceman

In order to understand how mindfulness works, you need to know some basics about the human brain. Over millions of years, the human brain has evolved to become the most sophisticated on the planet (see Figure 1-2).

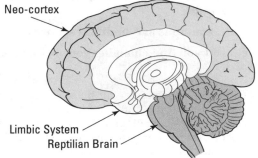

Neo-cortex

Limbic System

Reptilian Brain

Figure 1-2: Evolution of the human brain.

The oldest part of the brain is known as the reptilian brain. It controls your body's vital functions such as heart rate, breathing, body temperature and balance. Your reptilian brain includes the main structures found in a reptile's brain: the brainstem and the cerebellum.

The middle part of your brain is known as the limbic brain. It emerged in the first mammals. It records memories of behaviours that produced agreeable and disagreeable experiences for you. The limbic system is responsible for your emotions and value judgements. The reptilian brain and limbic system are quite rigid and inflexible in how they operate. We call these two areas the primitive brain.

The newest part of our brain consists is the neo-cortex. It has deep grooves and wrinkles that allow the surface area to increase far beyond what could otherwise fit in the same size skull. It accounts for around 85 per cent of the human brain's total mass. Some say that the neo-cortex is what makes us human. The neo-cortex is responsible for your abstract thoughts, imagination and consciousness. For simplicity, we call it the 'higher brain'. The higher brain is highly flexible and has an almost infinite ability to learn.

The primitive brain deals with routine tasks and needs little energy to operate quickly. The higher brain is incredibly powerful, but requires a lot of energy to run and operates more slowly than the primitive brain. These differences in the different parts of the brain explain why you often experience strong emotions or take action long before logic starts to kick in. It also explains the human tendency to work on auto-pilot (based on responses stored in the primitive brain) for much of the time.

Because you spend much of your time work on auto-pilot, you're often unaware of your thoughts, emotions and physiology in the present moment. The short activity below is designed to help you recognise your routine responses and how changing them just slightly can make you more aware of them.

1. **Sit in a different chair from usual in a meeting, park in a different spot in the car park, sleep on the other side of the bed or use a different hand to write with.**

2. **Observe your thoughts, emotions and bodily responses.**

3. **Identify how you felt. Did you find changing your behaviour difficult? Did you feel awkward?**

Doing things differently can be hard because your mental programming is probably screaming, 'You've got it wrong; that's not how you do it.' Carrying out an activity in a new way involves conscious thought, and thus engages your higher brain, which needs more energy to function. This explains why even small changes can feel difficult or uncomfortable.

Discovering your brain's hidden rules

Imagine yourself as one of your ancient ancestors – a cave dweller. In ancient times you had to make life or death decisions every day. You had to decide whether it was best to approach a reward (such as killing a deer) or avoid a threat (such as a fierce predator charging at you). If you failed to gain your reward, in this example a deer to eat, you'd probably live to hunt another day. But, if you failed to avoid the threat, you'd be dead, never to hunt again.

As a result of facing these daily dangers, your brain has evolved to minimise threat. Unfortunately, this has led to the brain spending much more time looking for potential risks and problems than seeking rewards and embracing new opportunities. This tendency is called 'the human negativity bias'.

1. **Think of six bad things that have happened recently.**

2. **Think of six good things that have happened recently.**

3. **Identify which task you found easiest.**

Most people readily conjure up six bad things, but struggle to think of six good things. The bad things dominate because the brain is primed to expend more energy looking for potential threats (bad things) than looking for opportunities (good things).

When your brain detects a potential threat, it floods your system with powerful hormones designed to help you evade mortal danger. The sudden flood of dozens of hormones into your body results in your heart rate speeding up, blood pressure increasing, pupils dilating and veins in skin constricting to send more blood to major muscle groups to help you sprint away from danger. More oxygen is pumped into your lungs, and non-essential systems (such as digestion, the immune system and routine body repair and maintenance) shut down to provide more energy for emergency functions. Your brain starts to have trouble focusing on small tasks because it's trying to maintain focus on the big picture to anticipate and avoid further threat.

Threat or risk avoidance is controlled by the primitive areas of your brain, which operate fast. This speed explains why, when you unexpectedly encounter a snake in the woods, your primitive brain decides on the best way to keep you safe from harm with no conscious thought and you jump out of the way long before your higher brain engages to find a rational solution.

This process is great from an evolutionary perspective, but can be bad news in modern-day life. Many people routinely overestimate the potential threat involved in everyday work such as a critical boss, a failed presentation or social humiliation. These modern-day 'threats' are treated by the brain in exactly the same way as your ancestor's response to mortal danger. This 'fight or flight' response was designed to be used for short periods of time. Unfortunately, when under pressure at work it can remain activated for long periods of time. This activation can lead to poor concentration, inability to focus, low immunity and even serious illness.

Mindfulness training helps you to recognise when you're in this heightened state of arousal and be able to reduce or even switch off the 'fight or flight' response. It also helps you develop the skill to trigger at will your 'rest and relaxation' response, bringing your body back to normal, allowing it to repair itself and increasing both your sense of well-being and ability to focus on work.

Recognising that you are what you think

For many years it was thought that once you reached a certain age your brain became fixed. We now know that the adult brain retains impressive powers of 'neuroplasticity'; that is, the ability to change its structure and function in response to experience. It was also believed that, if you damaged certain areas of the brain (as a result of a stroke or other brain injury), you'd no longer be capable of performing certain brain functions. We now know that in some cases the brain can re-wire itself and train a different area to undertake the functions that the damaged part previously carried out. The brain's hard wiring (neural pathways) change constantly in response to thoughts and experiences.

Neuroplasticity offers amazing opportunities to re-invent yourself and change the way you do and think about things. Your unique brain wiring is a result of your thoughts and experiences in life. Blaming your genes or upbringing; saying 'it's not my fault, that's how I was born' isn't no longer a good excuse!

In order to take advantage of this knowledge, you need to develop awareness of your thoughts, and the impact that these thoughts have on your emotions and physiology. The problem is that, if you're like most people, you're probably rarely aware of the majority of your thoughts. Let's face it; you'd be exhausted if you were! Mindfulness helps you to develop the ability to passively observe your thoughts as mental processes. In turn, this allows you to observe patterns of thought and decide whether these patterns are appropriate and serve you well. If you decide that they're not, your awareness of them gives you the opportunity to replace them with better ways of thinking and behaving.

For example, if you arrive at work and think 'Oh no, I've got so much to do on my to-do list. I'm never going to get them all done! I'm so inefficient . . .' and so on, your brain is on a negative thought stream. Mindfulness helps you to catch yourself doing that, and instead, simply and more calmly move your attention to the first priority on your list of things to do.

Another common problem you may encounter is that, although you may *think* that your decisions and actions are always based on present-moment facts, in reality they rarely are. Making decisions based on your brain's prediction of the future (which is usually based on your past experiences and unique brain wiring) is common. In addition, you see with your brain; in other words, your brain acts as a filter to incoming information from the eyes and picks out what it thinks is important. The problem with all the above is that you routinely make decisions and act without full possession of the facts. What happened in the past will not necessarily happen now; your predictions about the future could be inaccurate, leading to inappropriate responses and actions.

So, going back to the above example of the long to-do list, if you're mindful, you can choose to do what's most important, rather than just automatically reacting to the last email that pings you.

Practising mindfulness helps you to see the bigger picture and make decisions based on present-moment facts rather than self-generated assumptions and fiction.

Here's another example. When you're under pressure, falling into a thought spiral, with one thought driving the next, is all too easy. In the process, you develop your own story of what's going on around you, which can be wildly different from reality. For example, if you fail to get an invite to a meeting at work you think you should be at, your thoughts might follow this pattern:

> Why haven't they invited me?
>
> They obviously think that my team and I have nothing to contribute.
>
> Maybe they're discussing redundancies.
>
> Maybe they haven't invited me because they're discussing making me redundant!

At my age I'll never get another job!

How will I pay off the remainder of the mortgage?

This may mean my son has to drop out of university.

I'll ruin my son's life. I'm a dreadful father. I'm such a loser.

In reality, the failure to invite you was an administrative error, but your mind has created a detailed story, which your brain has treated as reality. As a result your brain has triggered emotions (anger or fear), your body has become tense and your heart rate has speeded up. Your emotions and physiology have a further impact on your thoughts and behaviour, and so on.

Many people fall into this trap. Mindfulness helps you to notice when your thoughts begin to spiral and to take action to stop them spiralling down even further. You can observe what's going on in the present moment, and separate present-moment facts from self-created fiction. This ability gives you choices and a world of new possibilities.

Think of a person or situation that triggers your primitive brain's threat system. (Don't pick anything too scary or threatening!)

1. **Observe what's going on in your head.** Identify patterns of thoughts, as if you were a spectator observing from the outside. What is it specifically that has triggered your primitive brain?

2. **Acknowledge your emotional response without judgement or self-blame.** Try to observe from a distance and see if you can reduce or prevent a strong emotional reaction by observing the interplay of your thoughts and emotions as if you were a bystander.

3. **Be kind to yourself.** You're human, and just responding according to your mental wiring. Observe both your thoughts and emotions as simply 'mental processes', without the need to respond to them. Regarding them as 'thoughts not facts' and being kind to yourself helps to encourage your primitive brain to let go of the steering wheel and allow your higher brain to become the driver once more.

When developing new neural pathways, practice makes perfect. Changing your behaviour or learning to do something new takes awareness, intention, action and practice – no short cuts exist! Understanding a few simple facts about how your brain works and making small adjustments to your responses can help you to create new, more productive, neural pathways.

Exploring your brain at work

Before diving into more detail about mindfulness, and how it could be of benefit to your work, you need to discover a little more about how your brain processes everyday work tasks.

Let's look at a real-life example. A friend of mine (Juliet) – let's call her Jen – is a senior manager working within a police training organisation, where she is responsible for leading a team who develop doctrine (guidance and standards) for police forces across the UK. Her job description includes the following desirable characteristics:

- ✔ Organisational skills
- ✔ Communication skills
- ✔ Ability to manage conflicting priorities
- ✔ Problem-solving skills
- ✔ Decision-making skills
- ✔ Relationship building skills
- ✔ Ability to manage change

One of the most challenging aspects of Jen's work is managing multiple, often conflicting, demands. As her role is national, she is responsible to multiple stakeholders working in different police forces and affiliate organisations across the UK. Problems sometimes arise when stakeholders think that their project is more important than other projects, and completion of that project by a certain date takes on an almost 'life or death' importance in their minds. This elevated importance is often compounded by senior stakeholders taking sides and applying pressure. When this situation arises, Jen uses negotiation skills to try to resolve the issue. She gives the stakeholders a reality check, often along the lines of, 'If I prioritise this, then I can't do that' or 'If I do this first, that will be late'.

At times like these, Jen notices her body tensing. She sometimes wakes at 2 a.m. trying to find a solution that resolves the conflict for all concerned. Emotionally she sometimes experiences irritation and frustration at the inability of others to see the bigger picture. Her thoughts run along the following lines: 'Either I'm not explaining it right or they're being obtuse'; 'We're all supposed to be professionals, why can't they behave as such?'; 'No one will die if we're a few days late with this project'; 'Why are they acting so selfishly?'

What Jen is unaware of is the impact of one of the foundations of mindfulness training: non-judgemental observation of the interplay between her thoughts, emotions and physiology. Her thoughts are triggering emotions, which are triggering a bodily response. Her bodily response (which she is largely unaware of) is having a tangible impact on her thoughts and decisions. Although she thinks that she's fully rational and in control when making decisions, in reality her emotions are also impacting on her thoughts. If Jen was practising mindfulness, she'd be much more aware of what's going on, and able to choose alternative strategies that were better for her well-being and that may lead to wiser decisions.

Despite the fact that Jen is an experienced leader, calm, organised and highly intelligent, her primitive brain has detected a possible threat to her social and professional status. Status – your place in the pecking order – is important to humans. Jen's amygdala (part of the limbic system in her primitive brain) triggers a fight or flight response. Her primitive brain is now in charge. Hijacked by emotions, her higher brain becomes helpless. In an attempt to keep her safe from harm, her primitive brain hijacks the driver's seat and she is reduced to being a passenger sitting in the back seat, hanging on for dear life. Jen is in this position because her primitive brain switches off her higher brain, including the prefrontal cortex (PFC), shown in Figure 1-3. This vital part of your brain plays a huge role in decision making. The prefrontal cortex allows you to plan ahead and create strategies, pay attention, learn and focus on goals.

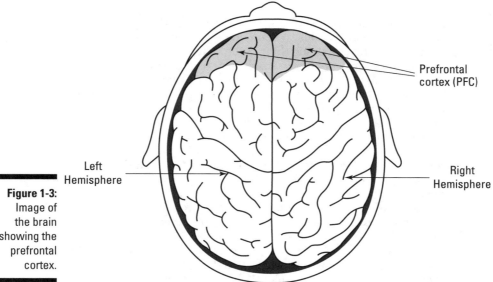

Prefrontal
cortex (PFC)

Left
Hemisphere

Right
Hemisphere

Figure 1-3:
Image of
the brain
showing the
prefrontal
cortex.

When finding out about mindfulness, you discover the interplay between your primitive brain's desire to keep you safe from harm, and the impact of your sympathetic nervous system (which mobilises your parasympathetic fight-or-flight response) on both your body and ability to think clearly.

At times like this, Jen would benefit from a mindfulness exercise. She should focus her full attention on taking slow, deep breaths for a few minutes. Focusing her attention fully on the sensation of breathing will slow down or stop her mental chatter, which in turn will reduce the feeling of threat and trigger a lessening of her fight-or-flight response. In addition, her brain's PFC will get the oxygen it needs to regain control, and her primitive brain will hand back control to her PFC.

Of course, the rational PFC can't always prevent the primitive brain from engaging. This inability is because the primitive brain is more evolved and responds much more quickly than the highly powerful, but slower, less-evolved higher brain. Mindfulness does not stop your rational higher brain from getting hijacked by your primitive brain, but it does make you much more aware of what's going on, much earlier. This awareness gives you choices in how to respond. You won't be forced to unconsciously default to primitive brain auto-pilot responses and actions. You have a choice!

Now, we need to look at other elements of the brain that impact on Jen's work and explore how mindfulness could be beneficial.

At times Jen feels as if she's hitting a brick wall when she's trying to find new solutions to old problems. When under pressure, defaulting to well-used, comfortable ways of doing things stored in the primitive brain is all too easy. Giving 'stock' answers to questions may result. Mindfulness teaches you the benefits of taking time out to calm your mind and centre yourself. Doing so can take as little as three minutes and can produce dramatic results. Allowing the brain to relax and let go of its frantic activity to solve the problem can deactivate the primitive brain's grip, and allow the higher brain to apply creativity and innovation to the problem.

Jen often multi-tasks, flitting from one project to another and juggling project work with phone calls and emails as they arise. She often finds herself becoming tired and having difficulty concentrating. The ability to multi-task is a myth. Many research studies show that regular multi-taskers get less done than those who focus on one thing at a time – even the people that think they're good at mulit-tasking. Multi-tasking actually means that the brain is switching backwards and forwards from task to task, which wastes a huge amount of valuable energy, and details are invariably lost with each switch. No wonder that Jen feels tired! She's making her life much harder than it needs to be.

Mindfulness shows you how to mentally stand back and observe what's going on around you and in your brain. It also helps you to develop different approaches to life that are kinder to you and usually more productive. Mindfulness helps you observe and reduce the mental chatter that distracts you from your work, allowing you to focus on it more fully. By intentionally taking steps to recognise and avoid distractions and focusing your full attention on one task at a time, you can get things done more quickly, with fewer mistakes and less repetition. Using mindfulness techniques when you feel your attention waning can help you to restart work feeling refreshed and focused.

Mindfulness can also be useful in high-level meetings when emotions can sometimes be charged. Training in mindfulness would help Jen to observe the dynamics at play in such meetings more clearly. She'd probably recognise that in this situation people are commonly motivated by the need to avoid potential threat (to status and social standing) and are unlikely to approach the task with an open mind and look for the best possible solution. Jen would also be aware of the two possible states of mind that people could be operating in. In avoidance mode, people are motivated by the desire to avoid something happening. With their threat system activated, they may fail to see the bigger picture, be less able to think clearly and be less creative in their ideas and solutions. Avoidance mode tends to be associated with increased activation of the right PFC. Excessive right PFC activation is associated with depression and anxiety. Mindfulness cultivates an approach state of mind. Often the effort taken to avoid something happening is disproportionate to dealing with the thing you seek to avoid. An approach mode of mind is associated with increased left brain PFC activation, which is connected with positivity and an upbeat approach to life. In approach mode, you're able to explore new possibilities and opportunities with an open mind.

When working in avoidance mode, cognitive thinking resources are diminished, making it harder to think and work things through. You're also likely to feel less positive and engaged. If Jen applied mindfulness to her work life, she'd be able to better manage her own emotions and subtly take steps to help reduce the sense of threat often permeating business meetings.

The brain can have a significant impact on how you work. Finding out about and practising mindfulness gives you the tools you need to harness this knowledge to manage your mind better.

Starting Your Mindful Journey

Congratulations! The fact that you've picked up this book and started reading it means that you've already started your mindful journey. The chapters in this book describe lots of ways to learn mindfulness, one of which is sure to suit your learning style and fit in with your busy life. You'll also discover that mindfulness involves much more than sitting down and focusing on your breath. In this book, you should find a number of mindfulness techniques that work for you.

A good book is a great starting point, but nothing can replace experiencing mindfulness for yourself. As with learning anything new, you may find it difficult to know where to start. Learning mindfulness from an experienced teacher who can help you to overcome obstacles and guide your development is advisable. The idea behind this book is to demonstrate *how* and *why* mindfulness can benefit you at work, and provide suggestions of how to apply simple mindfulness techniques to everyday work challenges.

Being mindful at work yourself

Getting caught up in the manic pace of everyday work life is common. You, like many workers, may feel under pressure to deliver more with fewer resources. You may also be keen to demonstrate what an asset you are to your company by working longer and longer hours, and being contactable round the clock.

Being mindful at work can involve as little or as much change as you're able to accommodate at this moment in time. At one end of the scale, you may simply apply knowledge of how the brain works and some mindful principles to your work. To gain maximum benefit, you need to practise mindfulness regularly and apply quick mindfulness techniques in the workplace when you need to regain focus or encounter difficulties. The choice is yours! The benefits you gain increase in line with the effort you put in. You should see a real difference after practising mindfulness for as little as ten minutes a day for about six weeks.

At times, being mindful at work can involve an act of bravery – swimming against the tide by doing things differently. If the way you're currently working is leading to stress, anxiety, tiredness or exhaustion, then maybe you need to try something different. If you're tasked with being innovative and finding new ways of doing things, what makes you think that carrying on as you've always done will make this creativity possible? As this book constantly reiterates, humans dislike uncertainty and crave certainty. Defaulting to doing things as you've always done them is always easier, especially if they've become stored as habits in the primitive brain and can be repeated with little or no conscious thought.

As you discover in Chapter 7, changing habits takes time and effort. For this reason, most mindfulness courses are taught weekly, over a five- to eight-week period. Each week you learn something new, practise it for a week and then build new knowledge onto it the following week. When first learning to be mindful, most people find it easier to practise at home than at work. Practising at home is simpler because controlling noise and disturbances at home is obviously easier.

Following these initial practice sessions, most people then introduce a few short mindfulness techniques at work. Over time, as mindfulness becomes second nature to you, you'll develop the ability to practise wherever and whenever the opportunity arises. As your confidence builds and you apply mindfulness to your work further, others will probably notice changes in you. You may appear calmer, more poised and better focused. Possibly your work relationships have improved. If you're lucky enough to be offered mindfulness sessions in work time, don't be surprised if people are curious, and ask you for tips and techniques to try out for themselves. Organisations that offer mindfulness classes often have a long waiting list of staff eager to attend.

Overcoming common challenges

Probably the most common challenges you face when learning mindfulness are: concerns about what others think; finding the right time and place to practise; and breaking down habits and mindsets in order to do things differently.

You now need to address each of these challenges in turn.

Dealing with concerns about what others think

In the past mindfulness was often associated with Buddhism, spirituality and new age ideas. This association was compounded by the fact that mindfulness was often only taught in Buddhist centres or local village halls. And, although MBSR had existed for over 40 years, and MBCT and ACT for about 20, they were only used in clinical settings and the general public was unaware of them. In addition, the media often confused mindfulness with other forms of meditation. Articles about mindfulness were often accompanied by pictures of people sitting cross-legged in the lotus position, their hands in prayer. This misleading image was almost certainly one of the reasons behind professionals' reluctance to 'come out of the mindfulness closet'.

In recent years, mindfulness has been discussed in the White House and 10 Downing Street. Mindfulness has been sampled at the World Economic Forum and is taught by major business schools. The press now feature mindfulness on a regular basis, and the pictures that accompany the articles are slowly becoming more representative of real-life mindfulness practice! As a result, more and more people are giving mindfulness a try, and integrating it into their work day.

Finding the right time and place to practise

If you're lucky enough to be offered mindfulness training by your organisation, you quickly discover that mindfulness is unlike any other courses you've attended. Unlike most courses that employers routinely offer to staff, simply attending isn't enough. Classes help you understand the principles that underpin mindfulness and how mindfulness techniques work. They also provide you with a safe environment and guidance to try out different mindfulness techniques. However, the real learning usually happens outside work, as you practise it. You can't get fit without exercising, can you? The same applies to mindfulness. Think of mindfulness as a good work out for your brain; the more you practise, the easier it becomes.

On a typical workplace mindfulness course, you're taught a different technique each week, which you need to practise for at least six days before moving on to the next one. This process can prove to be one of the most challenging aspects of learning mindfulness. For many busy workers, their entire day is scheduled, and sometimes extends into their home life. With a mindset of 'so much to do and so little time', even finding 15 minutes a day can feel daunting. The question to ask yourself is, 'Why am I doing this?' For many people, the answer is 'because I cannot continue working in the way I do'. If this is your reply, re-arranging your life to make time for mindfulness is certainly worthwhile. Try not to think about mindfulness as just another thing that needs to be fitted into your busy life; rather, view it as a new way to live your life. Think of the time you spend practising mindfulness as 'me time' – after all, this time is one of the rare moments in which you have nothing to do but focus on yourself. Chapters 6 and 7 take you through a five-week mindfulness at work course to try at home.

Breaking down habits and mindsets in order to do things differently

Habits are formed when you repeat the same thoughts or behaviours many times. Habits are highly efficient from a brain perspective because they're stored in the primitive brain, which can repeat them quickly without any conscious thought, using very little energy.

Learning mindfulness may take effort, especially if you start to challenge your habits and patterns of thinking. Make sure that you remember that, just as it takes time to form habits, so it takes time to replace old habits with different ways of thinking and being. With a little time and perseverance you can find new ways of working that are more productive and better for your health and sense of well-being.

Creating a mindful workplace

Every great journey starts with just one step. A young single mother of three I (Juliet) know was once given the opportunity to climb Mount Everest. Three-quarters of the way up the mountain she became exhausted, felt overwhelmed by the whole journey and declared that she could go no further. The trek leader calmly stood in front of her and asked whether she could see his footsteps in the snow ahead. She nodded in agreement. He told her that all she needed to do was put one foot in front of another, following his footsteps.

By focusing on the present moment action of her feet, she was able to avoid worrying about the remainder of the journey. She made it to the summit – one of the greatest achievements of her life.

Getting caught up in planning the journey ahead is common and at times you may feel overwhelmed by all the things you need to do and think about. When finding out about and practising mindfulness for the first time, focus only on the next footstep, rather than the journey as a whole, is often the best approach. Try to let your mindful journey unfold, day by day, moment by moment. If you truly want your organisation to become more mindful, you need to start by focusing on yourself. As you gain a deeper understanding of what mindfulness is, and start to experiment with integrating mindfulness into your life and work, you discover for yourself what works and what doesn't. Only then are you equipped to make a real difference to your organisation. The building blocks of a mindful organisation are mindful employees who start to transform their organisations one step at a time. Chapter 15 deals with mindful organisations.

Living the dream: Mindfulness at work

Sometimes the hardest part of a journey is taking the first step. In this book, you can find a wealth of information about mindfulness. You also discover mindful techniques for different situations that you may encounter at work and for different occupations (see Chapter 10).

The potential of mindfulness to transform the way you work and live your life is immense. The extent to which you benefit from it is entirely up to you and the effort that you're able to put into it.

When discovering how to become more mindful, remember ABC:

- ✔ A is for **awareness** – becoming more aware of what you're thinking and doing and what's going on in your mind and body.

- ✔ B is for 'just **being**' with your experiences – avoiding the tendency to respond on auto-pilot and feed problems by creating your own story.

- ✔ C is for choice – by seeing things as they are you can **choose** to respond more wisely – by creating a gap between an experience and your reaction you can step out pilot which opens up a world of new possibilities.

As with all new skills, the more you practise mindfulness, the easier it becomes. Canadian psychologist Donald Hebb coined the phrase 'neurones that fire together, wire together'. In other words, the more you practise mindfulness, the more you develop the neural pathways in the brain associated with being mindful.

Your first taste of mindfulness

If you're new to mindfulness, perhaps now is a good time to actually try a little mindfulness exercise. You can either use these instructions below or listen to the guided audio that comes with this book.

1. Sit on a chair in a comfortable posture. Try to sit upright rather than slouching, but you don't need to be tense or rigid.

2. Allow your eyes to close. If that's uncomfortable for you at the moment, simply cast your gaze downwards.

3. Take three deep in and out breaths. As you breathe in, feel the sensation of your breath through your nose and into your body. As you breathe out, again feel the sensation of your breath leaving your body through your nose.

4. Now focus your attention on the sounds that surround you. They might be sounds in the room, sounds elsewhere in the building, outside the building or sounds of nature. Try to treat them simply as sounds, using them as an anchor for your attention. There is no need to judge or categorise them, they are simply sounds.

5. Each time you notice that your mind has wandered off on a train of thoughts, which will certainly happen, turn your attention back to focussing your attention on sounds. It's important not to criticise or judge yourself for having a wandering mind – everyone has a wild mind! Just accept mind wandering as part and parcel of the process of mindfulness.

6. After a few minutes, focus your attention on any thoughts that may, or may not be going round your head. See if you can observe your thoughts simply as mental processes that come and go.

7. Finish with another three deep breaths – again, let those breaths be mindful by feeling each breath as it enters and leaves your body.

8. Slowly open your eyes if they've been closed and take a few moments to reflect on your experience. Notice how you feel having done this mindfulness exercise.

Mindfulness exercises like this can be difficult at first. Don't worry if you did not end the exercise relaxed and calm, everyone's experience is different and unique. Like anything worth doing, mindfulness takes a little effort, but regular practice will pay dividends.

Chapter 2

Exploring the Benefits of Mindfulness in the Workplace

In This Chapter

▶ Looking at mindfulness from the employees' perspective

▶ Discovering that mindfulness is good for your organisation

▶ Making employees happier and more productive

Mindfulness may appear to the 'in thing' at the moment, but does it have any substance? What are the actually benefits of mindfulness at work?

In this chapter you uncover the positive effects of mindfulness for yourself. You discover the impact of the many positive changes that take place in your own brain as a result of mindfulness practice. And you find out why so many organisations are training their leaders and employees in mindfulness, and explore organisational ways of integrating mindfulness into the workplace to increase staff performance and well-being.

Discovering the Benefits for Employees

Being a mindful employee has many benefits. In this section you find out how mindfulness changes your brain and how those changes make you more resilient, emotionally intelligent and focused. If you're in a leadership position, you discover how mindfulness can make you more effective in your work, too.

Increased mental resilience

Resilience is the process of adapting well when you experience adversity, trauma or a major source of stress. Resilience is sometimes described as the ability to 'bounce back' from difficult experiences.

In the average workplace, mental resilience is essential. If you're resilient, you're able to deal with rapid changes and serious challenges rather than spiralling downwards when faced with difficulties.

Resilience isn't a trait. You're not born with a certain amount of resilience and stuck with it. Instead, resilience involves a combination of thoughts, behaviours and actions that you can learn. That's what makes resilience such an exciting concept.

Let's imagine you've been working on securing a bid for a huge project. You've been developing the presentation and report for months. You're under tremendous pressure to succeed and, when the day comes, your nerves get the better of you. You struggle to answer questions, as your mind goes blank. You lose the contract and your manager shouts at you in frustration and may even fire you. How would you feel? What would you think?

These thoughts are the kind that could arise from such a situation: 'I failed. I'm so stupid. I messed up. What if I get fired? How will I pay my bills? I should have practised more. What's wrong with me? I'm pathetic.'

These thoughts emerge from the soup of emotions that's ignited by the stress you experienced. If you're unmindful, these thoughts persist and you're less able to bounce back from the experience. You feel increasingly worse and things can spiral downwards.

From a mindful perspective, you notice that you're having these self-judgemental thoughts. You're then able to step back from them and see that, yes, the presentation didn't go well, but all the other things you're telling yourself are just thoughts arising from your negative feelings about the event – they aren't necessarily true. By acknowledging that feelings affect your thoughts, you can avoid reacting to the imagined threat and deal with the situation in a reasoned manner. You may choose to talk to your boss, explain what happened and ask how to proceed – maybe you can give a presentation for a smaller project, or shift into a different role for the time being, or attend training in presentation skills. Over time, practising mindfulness builds up your resilience to such workplace experiences and you'll be better able to deal with them.

Even the US army is using mindfulness to help build resilience in its recruits. Initial studies show that mindfulness helps to develop soldiers' mental fitness so that they're more able to make good decisions in stressful situations and less likely to suffer post-traumatic stress disorder.

Some people mistakenly think that resilient people don't experience distress – that's not true. When adversity strikes, experiencing mental and emotional pain is normal. Developing resilience, however, ensures that, over time, you're able to rebuild your life.

But, you may be wondering, how does mindfulness increase resilience in your brain? Research by Professor Richard Davidson and colleagues has discovered how mindfulness may help build resilience. They looked at people's brains when faced with a stressor and found that their amygdala (the part of the brain responsible for processing emotions and responding to fear) became activated, releasing stress hormones. The research participants also experienced negative, cyclical thoughts long after the stressor had passed away. In those participants who practised mindfulness, however, the activity of the amygdala reduced soon after the stressor was removed. Davidson states that better control of the amygdala may be the *key* to resilience.

Psychologist Barbara Fredrickson believes that mindfulness offers other ways to build resilience too. They are:

- ✓ **Acceptance:** You have the capacity to see what you can change and what you can't. In the above example, you can't change your presentation, but you can change your relationship to your thoughts that follow.

- ✓ **Self-compassion:** Allows you to be kind to yourself in the face of adversity. You find out how to be your own best friend rather than harshly criticise yourself. You see your difficulties as part and parcel of humanity's struggle with life's challenges, rather than a sense of you suffering alone. There's over 200 studies showing the positive benefits of self-compassion alone.

- ✓ **Growth:** You are open to seeing difficulties as opportunities to learn and grow. Your mindset is open rather than fixed.

- ✓ **Creativity:** In a more mindful state, the part of your brain geared towards creative thinking is active. You can come up with more novel solutions by visualising different choices you could make, with consequent positive outcomes.

So, following an unsuccessful outcome to months of hard work, you may say to yourself: 'Beating myself up is pointless. I worked hard but I wasn't successful this time. I'm sure there are things I can discover from this experience. Perhaps I could ask for feedback and tips from others and, after a few days of well-deserved rest, I can have a go at a different project.'

Working in a resilient way isn't just for challenging circumstances. Mindfulness is a whole different way of being with your everyday experiences. You discover ways of living with awareness no matter what you're doing, seeking new challenges and looking forward to learning that may arise from them and drawing upon your insights for everything you do.

Here are five steps you can take to use mindfulness to help build your resilience:

- ✔ **Help others.** Be mindful of the needs of others rather than just yourself. By seeking ways to help others when you're not so busy, you're more likely to be supported when going through difficulties yourself. For example, help John with his report, Michelle with her difficult team or Jane with moving house at the weekend.

- ✔ **Look after yourself.** In addition to helping others, help yourself too! Be mindful of how much sleep you're getting, how much exercise you're doing and if you're taking regular breaks. Muscles strengthen only if they have time to rest between activities. Your brain is the same.

- ✔ **Nudge your mindset.** In any given moment, your brain receives far more information than it can actively be conscious of. So, rather than focusing the spotlight of your attention on what's not going well, focus it on the positives. What went well today? What are you grateful for? Think about it, make a note of it or email someone close to you and share your appreciation. Your brain will thank you for it.

- ✔ **Expect change.** If you practise mindfulness, you know that change is the only constant. When you try to focus on your breathing, your mind comes up with all sorts of thoughts. If you can see that the nature of the world is change, and you seek to adapt to the change rather than avoid or run away from it, you're being more mindful and more resilient.

- ✔ **Seek meaning.** When adversity strikes, as it inevitably does, after the initial period of sadness or anger, you do have a choice. You can sink into feeling sorry for yourself or look for an opportunity for growth. Post-traumatic growth obviously takes time but does usually happen. So, look out for what you can find out from the challenges you're currently facing. For example, losing your job isn't nice but may allow you to decide on a new career path. Be mindful of the opportunities that arise for you.

Improved relationships

You've probably had to work with someone difficult to get on with. Maybe they're rude, critical and rarely offer praise. They say the wrong thing at the wrong time. You wonder how they managed to get on in the company in the first place. You may even think that you're better off avoiding certain colleagues altogether.

Relationships matter. A lot. In fact, the human brain is designed to be social. Learning, emotional processing, creativity and insight are often enhanced when in conversation with others. If that's the case, why are workplace relationships so often fraught with difficulty? And how does mindfulness improve workplace relationships?

When you're mindful, you're better able to regulate your emotions. For example, Frank works for a large oil company and is responsible for the refining division. He talks to Samantha about her recent lateness at work. She starts giving excuses. This pattern repeats over several days. Eventually, in a fit of anger, Frank starts shouting at her. She shouts back. In the weeks that follow, Samantha does come into work early but refuses to do more than the minimum that's required of her. Behind Frank's back, she gossips about his ineffectiveness as a manager. Frank does the same to her. How could mindfulness have helped?

If Frank were more mindful, he'd have noticed the anger building up in him. As a result, he could have used mindfulness to acknowledge the feeling and make a choice. He could have chosen to speak to Samantha later in the day when he was more composed. At that time, he could go over the issue, explain why the company needs Samantha to be in work on time and the consequences of lateness. Listening to Samantha's reasons, he may discover a bigger underlying issue – maybe she's been working late on a particular project and feels she deserves a rest, or perhaps the pressure of deadlines makes it harder for her to both fall asleep at night and wake up in the morning. Seen in this bigger context, Frank is less likely to react with anger next time, and more likely to develop positive working relationships with colleagues.

The second way that mindfulness improves relationships is by enhancing the ability to listen both to the words being said and the emotions behind them. Good communication is the very heart of relationships. With greater levels of mindful awareness, you become more adept at listening to both the words being spoken and how the person is feeling. You can also pick up someone's emotional signals by observing their body posture. If you're checking your text messages while someone's talking to you, you're multitasking – you're effectively saying to the other person that what they have to say isn't important and, as a result, the relationship slightly deteriorates. If you give that person your full attention, the relationship can develop instead.

Consider someone you know who is mindful. How do they listen, talk and move about? When you're in their company, do you feel comfortable? Most people enjoy being with someone mindful because they give them the time to speak. They listen non-judgementally to your views and don't criticise. They understand the challenges you face. Being with someone like that makes you more mindful – mindfulness spreads.

You're better able to listen because mindfulness enhances focus. Research shows that the more you practise mindful exercises, the better your brain becomes at focusing on whatever it chooses to. Being better able to focus has obvious benefits when you're trying to listen to someone at work.

Mindfulness also helps you to step outside of yourself. Rather than just thinking about yourself and what you need, you think about others more. We coached one corporate executive whose brain was so frantically busy that his life was a blur. He had no chance of caring for others because he could hardly pay attention to what he had to do to look after himself. His relentless streams of thought made him see the world through cloudy glasses. Mindfulness helped him to step back from those thoughts, a bit like removing those glasses. The thoughts were still there, but not so close and not so relentless. He was then better able to offer attention and care to his colleagues. He now finds colleagues often come to see him for personal advice. He's better able to see things from the perspective of other people – a vital skill in all relationships.

Use the following tips to be more mindful in your workplace relationships:

- **Really connect.** Make a conscious effort to look people in the eye when they're speaking to you. Listen to their words and try to pick up on their emotions too. If you have the tendency to interrupt, resist it. Listen more and ask questions to clarify what the other people is saying.

- **Take a mindful pause.** Stop and think before speaking to someone you find difficult. Notice whether you react emotionally to that person and, if you do, try to step back from your habitual emotions and thoughts. If you carry on doing what you've always done, you carry on getting what you've always got. Use the mindful pause and see what effect it has on the relationship.

- **See things from their viewpoint.** Use mindful awareness to step back and see things from the other person's point of view. Maybe the person you're dealing with doesn't have the necessary social skills to cope with her staff. Possibly she makes rash decisions because she's anxious. Seen in this way, her behaviour appears far less threatening and you may feel sorry for her rather than annoyed.

- **Wish them well.** As you walk about in your workplace, rather than negatively judging people, or even being neutral towards them, you can wish them well. As you encounter people, think 'May you be well, may you be happy. After all, they're human beings just like you, and want to be happy, just like you. By wishing others well, you shift your attention away from your own worries and towards a more positive and mindful mindset. This may sound like a strange exercise to do, but certainly worth trying.

Honed mental clarity and focus

Imagine lying in a darkened room and shining a torch around. What you can see is whatever that spotlight is shining on.

Your mind works in the same way. Your attention is like a spotlight, and in a moment of mindfulness you can decide where to shine it. You can focus within yourself, on a particular part of your body or even your body as a whole. You can focus on your thoughts or emotions.

Focus is one of the most overlooked skills that humans possess. Most people think that focus is something they do or don't have. But that's not true. Your attention is like a muscle – the more you flex that brain muscle, the stronger it gets. With time and effort, the regions of your brain responsible for maintaining focus grow. And these changes happen within days, not years. Mindfulness offers a way to train that muscle in your brain so you can decide where you want to focus, and stay focused for longer periods of time.

When you lack focus, you feel scattered. Your attention can get caught by another person's conversation, a thought about the event you attended yesterday or just noise outside. The more your attention snags on other things, the less able you are to complete the tasks in front of you and you begin to feel inefficient. When you practise mindful exercises, your mind gradually shifts from being frazzled to being focused. You then become more efficient and, as a result, have more time to rest and relax.

One of the other benefits of greater focus is experiencing greater levels of happiness. Research suggests that people are at their happiest when they're fully focused on something; that is, not when they're relaxing watching TV at home or eating chocolate. That focus can be on anything: skiing downhill, painting a picture or writing a sales report. When fully focused, people enter a 'flow' state of mind, which results in a heightened feeling of well-being. As mindfulness develops your ability to focus, you're therefore more likely to be able to enter this flow state when working. And if you're happier, you're immediately more creative, productive and confident.

How can you improve your focus in the workplace using mindfulness? Try these tips:

- ✔ **Start the working day with a short mindful exercise.** Try mindfulness of breath or a body scan. (Chapter 6 takes you through the steps.) Even a mindful jog in the morning can help.

- ✔ **Avoid multi-tasking as much as possible.** If you can, do one task at a time and give it your full attention. Too much multi-tasking reduces your brain's ability to focus.

- ✔ **Feel your breathing whenever you remember.** Your breath is your anchor to bring you back to the present moment. If you're on the phone and find your mind keeps wandering, feel a few of your breaths to centre you in the present.

- ✔ **Record your progress.** Keep notes on what you complete in each hour to make you more mindful of your use of time. You can then begin to focus more effectively in each hour that you use.

I passed my test, thanks to mindfulness!

A study published in 2013 in the *Mindfulness* journal (yes, a scientific journal dedicated to the subject does exist) measured the effect of a short mindfulness exercise on quiz scores following a lecture. One group of university students was taught a six-minute mindfulness exercise and another group wasn't. The mindfulness exercise predicted which students would pass the quiz! Further analysis found that the mindfulness exercise was even more effective with a group of first-year students, perhaps because more of them were likely to have trouble focusing. The researchers were impressed with the changes that occurred in students following just a short mindfulness exercise and felt that more coaching could result in even bigger improvements in scores.

Mindful leadership

A mindful leader values both inner reflection and outer action. Rather than reacting automatically to everyday challenges, mindful leaders ensure that they're consciously making the right decision with awareness, compassion and wisdom.

Mindful leadership does not mean that the leader is always practising mindful exercises and walking around in a Zen-like bubble! A mindful leader is very much a person of action, but understands the value of rest, reflection and renewal.

A mindful leader can make a positive difference to an organisation in these changing times. Because they're better able to see the bigger picture rather than just immediate threats or opportunities, an organisation with mindful leaders can create solid corporate values and a clear mission statement.

Mindful leadership begins with self-awareness. These leaders are aware of their own thoughts, ideas, opinions, beliefs and emotional state, from moment to moment. Through this self-awareness, they can challenge their interpretations to discover new solutions. And through this self-awareness, they're better able to relate and communicate with others – they have high levels of emotional intelligence.

For example, say that you're a manager in a medium-sized organisation. You've a meeting scheduled in town, arranged weeks ago, but a few hours before one of your employees says they want to shift it to a different time. You're annoyed about the last-minute change and are just about to send a scathing email to the employee. But then you stop. You take three mindful breaths and check on your inner state. You notice that you haven't had lunch, are in an irritable mood and are emailing out of frustration, not to optimise the performance of your team. Instead, you pick up the phone, have a quick chat about meeting times in a calm voice, and all is resolved. You use discipline when necessary, but out of necessity, not out of emotional anger.

Mindful leaders use the principles of mindfulness in their leadership approach; they are:

- ✔ Physically able to look after themselves and their workforce, understanding that mind and body are not separate.

- ✔ Mentally focused, clear and flexible. They use mindful exercises to train their brains to be in the moment and able to connect with others.

- ✔ Emotionally intelligent. They're aware of their own emotional state as well as that of their team members. They can sensitively make choices based on these emotional states rather than make decisions without reflection.

- ✔ Values driven. They're aware of their own values and align them with their work in an authentic way. In turn, they appreciate the importance of values in an organisation.

- ✔ Able to balance acceptance of what can't be changed and action to implement what can and needs to be changed.

- ✔ Able to make time for stillness and reflection as well as time for activity and serving others.

- ✔ Compassionate. They care for both themselves and their colleagues. They see other members of the team as equals and don't develop a false sense of superiority.

- ✔ Passionate. They're driven by will to make their values real, helping others to fulfil their potential.

Research in mindful leadership is beginning to accelerate as mindfulness rapidly moves to the mainstream. A study by Ashridge Business School, ranked as one of the top 20 business schools in the world, looked at the effect of meditation on its members. It discovered that 90 per cent of members found some form of benefit resulted from practices such as mindfulness.

Some of the benefits of mindful leadership are hard to measure but easy to see. A mindful leader is more present, exudes a sense of control and makes her employees feel more cared for..

If you're in a leadership position, whether you manage 2 people or 2,000, try the following exercise to help you be more mindful in just a few minutes:

1. **Practise a short mindful exercise.** Try mindfulness of breath for a few minutes. (See Chapter 6)

2. **Spend a couple of minutes reflecting on your own state of mind.** Consider how you're feeling. What thoughts are popping into your mind?

3. **Think about your staff for a couple of minutes.** Consider what challenges they may be facing.

4. **Ask yourself: 'How can I best look after myself now?'**

5. **Ask yourself: 'How can I best look after my staff now?'**

Write down one idea for yourself and your staff, and if appropriate, carry them out. The exercise combines mindfulness and compassion. The mindfulness part helps you to tune into your current state. And the support part is an act of self-compassion. Finally, considering ways of supporting others shows compassion and leads to staff feeling more valued. Looking after and appreciating staff can help you get far more from them than a pay rise or promotion. Mindful leadership can develop this mindful, compassionate way of operating.

Looking at the Organisational Benefits of Mindfulness

A mindful organisation is aware of and cares for its people, whether that's employees, volunteers, customers or suppliers – whoever they work with. The organisation understands the need to focus on revenue generation but in the long rather than short term. The company is based on sound ethical and sustainable values; it aims to make a positive difference to the world. When hard decisions about discipline or redundancy are necessary, the organisation can make them but only after considering all other options. The organisation encourages physical exercise and good nutrition, mental well-being through mindfulness classes and emotional well-being through social interaction and training. In order to get the best out of people, working hours are flexible, as are many of the working practices. The organisation celebrates success and fully engages staff when making major changes and decisions about the organisation's future. It helps staff to do more of what they really enjoy and to find meaning in their work in a way that benefits both the individual and organisation.

An unmindful organisation is highly short-term focused. It may want to increase its profits for this quarter rather than care for staff or customers. Its products or services may cause harm rather than provide value for its customers. Employees display a low level of interaction, communication and emotional intelligence because they work in a climate of fear. The wrong people are in the wrong positions and are unclear about their roles and responsibilities. Working hours are long and unsustainable, and the organisation frowns upon a healthy balance between work and home/social life. It does not respond effectively to changes taking place in its sector.

A mindful organisation may sound idealistic but high levels of workplace stress, burnout and inequality; lack of creativity; unethical corporate behaviour; and too much short-term focus on profit mean that creating a mindful organisation isn't a luxury but an urgent necessity.

Happier, more engaged employees

One of my favourite business books is Tony Hsieh's *Delivering Happiness* (BusinessPlusUS, 2010). The author founded a company called Zappos in 1999. Zappos grew from zero sales in 1999 to $1 billion worth of sales in 2009. Hsieh says this success was the result of making customers happy – and he achieved that by making his employees happy.

Zappos has a set of 10 core values that the staff created together. They provide the foundation of the company's culture and are a guide to how to treat customers, suppliers, employees and sales reps. These values are:

- Deliver WOW through service
- Embrace and drive change
- Create fun and a little weirdness
- Be adventurous, creative and open-minded
- Pursue growth and learning
- Build open and honest relationships with communication
- Build a positive team and family spirit
- Do more with less
- Be passionate and determined
- Be humble

Happiness isn't usually a term bandied about in a workplace environment. Traditionally, if you wanted to increase productivity, you made employees work harder or attend a time management course, or looked for ways to automate tasks.

Mindfulness does make employees happy. So much so that the effects of happiness can be seen in brain scans! Happy people show greater activation in the left pre-frontal cortex. Completing an eight-week mindfulness course has resulted in employees demonstrating greater activity in that part of the brain – the mindfulness literally made them feel happier.

But so what, you may ask. It transpires that happiness is linked to a whole host of benefits in the workplace. Happier staff are more productive, creative, take less days off sick and are more likely to be promoted. And greater happiness pays. For every employee, the New Economics Foundation predicts that an organisation can save:

✔ £250 – assuming a conservative 1 per cent increase in productivity as a result of increased happiness

✔ £104 – assuming a reduction in sickness absence by just one day

✔ £160 – assuming just a 10 per cent reduction in staff turnover

That's £514 saved for every employee, each year. And that's a *very* conservative estimate. If your organisation has 1,000 employees, you can save over half a million pounds a year!

So good work doesn't make you happy but being happy creates good work.

Try the following tips to boost your happiness in the workplace using mindfulness. Share them with your colleagues too!

✔ Spend two minutes practising mindfulness of breath (see Chapter 6), then write down three things about your workplace for which you're grateful.

✔ Go for a 15-minute mindful walk for every 1.5 hours of work you do. Master violinists were found to use this balance of work and rest to optimise their performance and well-being. Violinists who worked hard all day with fewer breaks were less successful.

✔ Have a mindful conversation with the happiest colleagues at work. Happiness is contagious. If you're consciously present with happy colleagues at lunch, in your break or over a quick drink after work, you feel happier.

✔ Commit to doing at least one task really mindfully when at work. Start small and build up from there.

✔ Spend a mindful penny, if that's the only space available at work! Or ask the company to provide a room dedicated to quiet time and mindfulness.

Greater creativity

How important do you think creativity is in your organisation? Is it important to innovate and find new ideas for products or services? Or do you simply keep doing the same thing and hope that your competitors won't catch up? Most people agree that, in the current economy, without innovation your competitors will soon overtake you. So, to be a successful organisation, you need your employees' brains to be as creative as possible. Creative solutions not only help your organisation, they also help to meet the needs of your customers.

Take a few moments to consider the stance of a creative brain – open, flexible, attentive and not too stressed. In fact, when you're in a mindful state, the creative part of your brain is activated.

Mindfulness creates the ideal conditions in your brain for creative thought. When you're unmindful, you're on auto-pilot, thinking the same old thoughts. When you're mindful, you're more awake, energised and aware of new ideas as they emerge.

I (Shamash) am currently training a professor of architecture to teach mindfulness online. She finds that the more mindful she is, the more creative her work. She ran mindfulness sessions at a creativity and design conference. The feedback was overwhelmingly positive – the designers loved the new way of using their minds to get the creative juices flowing. Even their designs are beginning to be more mindful – spacious, calming and sustainable, with areas for individual quiet time.

Personally, I (Shamash) am much more creative in the mornings. By the afternoon, I feel less energised and work better in conversation with other people. I'm more creative before midday because I'm in a more focused frame of mind. I am in the moment. My mind is relatively clear. New ideas and concepts can easily emerge. Mindfulness, a present focused state, helps me to come up with creative ideas.

Think back to the last time you had a creative idea. Were you feeling anxious or relaxed? Were you in the moment or mired in a fog of worries and concerns? Were you feeling happy or sad?

Psychologist Mihaly Csikszentmihalyi draws on 30 years' experience of researching mindfulness to identify the following five stages when engaged in the creative process:

- ✔ Preparation: Immersion in an interesting problem that requires a creative solution

- ✔ Incubation: A period of inner reflection

- ✔ Insight: The 'Aha!' moment when the solution begins to emerge

- ✔ Evaluation: Deciding whether the solution can work

- ✔ Elaboration: Turning the chosen solution into a final product

Mindfulness comes into play in all the different stages but is most important in the second, incubation. When an idea is being incubated, your mind needs to allow the problem to sink into your subconscious. The unconscious mind is far more creative than the slow logic of the conscious mind. Just think how creative and unusual dreams can be! Mindfulness helps you to gradually step back from your conscious mind so that more creative ideas and solutions can emerge from your unconscious mind.

In Figure 2-1 below, you can see how the often creative, unconscious brain struggles to offer you new solutions because of a busy or negative mindset. When your mind is more open and calm through mindfulness, creative solutions can rise up into your unconscious brain.

Figure 2-1: Diagram showing how mindfulness may work to increase your creative solutions.

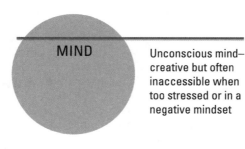

Creative solutions arising from unconscious mind when more mindful

Unconscious mind— creative but often inaccessible when too stressed or in a negative mindset

Try the following exercise to boost your own creativity at work. Then share them with your colleagues to help you develop a more mindfully creative team.

1. **Become mindful of the problem.** Be crystal clear about what you're trying to solve. As Einstein said, 'If I had an hour to solve a problem I'd spend 55 minutes thinking about the problem and 5 minutes thinking about solutions.'

2. **Incubate.** Go for a mindful walk. Try practising mindfulness of breath. At home, take a bath and just enjoy the experience. Be in the moment rather than trying hard to solve the problem with your conscious mind. Let go. Allow things to be. Reflect.

3. **Collect solutions.** Come up with as many solutions as possible, no matter how weird or wacky. They may not work, but write them all down nonetheless. Allow ideas to flow from your mind to the sheet of paper. Be utterly non-judgemental as you compile this list.

4. **Evaluate.** Consider each solution in turn and analyse whether it would work. Use mindfulness by being aware of each solution, one at a time. Avoid multi-tasking or other distractions. Take regular breaks as necessary. Keep your mind in optimal condition so you can make the right choice. Being mindful at this stage means that your brain can work in optimal conditions to achieve success.

Increased productivity

Productivity isn't just about getting things done. Productivity is also about choosing what you need to do and doing those activities at a time of day when your energy levels and focus are highest.

Productivity is about working smarter, not just harder. There's nothing wrong with working hard when at work – being lazy at work doesn't lead to a fulfilling life or an effective organisation. Sorry folks! But working smarter is about learning what you need to do and deciding how, when and where to do it.

Mindfulness improves focus. One of the direct benefits of greater focus is increased productivity. You stop being distracted by other thoughts, a text message or sounds in the office. Instead, you're able to keep your attention on whatever requires finishing.

Mindfulness of your own energy levels has a huge impact on productivity. As you become more mindful, you notice the subtle fluctuations in your energy levels. Noticing such things is an important skill. Everyone's energy rises and falls at different times of the day. When you recognise when your energy is at its peak, you can tackle your most challenging tasks. When your energy levels are naturally lower, you can use that time to chat with colleagues or take a break.

For example, if Gary knows that his energy levels peak in the morning and are lowest between 1 and 3p.m., he can make sure that he spends his time writing that important report in the office before anyone else arrives. In the afternoon, satisfied with a productive morning's work, he can call up his managers in New York and catch up with progress over there. Without this knowledge, if Gary made calls and emailed all morning, by afternoon he'd struggle to write that report, end up working late in the office, get home late – and the cycle continues.

Your energy levels also increase because you experience less emotional reactivity. Mindfulness increases your emotional awareness. So when you feel low, frustrated or angry, negative emotions don't creep up on you. You see the mood coming and you accept the feeling. You know that moods coming and going is part of being human. When something happens at work to make you feel upset or angry, you discover how to deal with your emotion before speaking. You discover how to express your emotions without losing control of yourself. This way of behaving is much more energy efficient, which means that you have energy left over to productively complete your work. Mindfulness can also make you less emotional over petty things too – so other people's comments or behaviour, which may have irritated you before, no longer do so.

Practising mindfulness also gives you more energy because you worry less. Your brain uses up 20 per cent of your energy even though it comprises only 2 per cent of your body weight. Think back to the last time you spent a few minutes worrying – did you feel energised or drained afterwards? Most people feel drained. When you're mindful, you're more focused on the moment and what needs to be done and you don't waste energy worrying. Remember: worry is like a rocking chair – it gives you something to do but never gets you anywhere. Mindfulness exercises help you to reduce your worrying.

Finally, one of the skills you develop with mindfulness is the ability to step back from whatever you're doing and see the context within which your task fits. How often have you completed a task, only to later discover that you were doing it the long way? Or that you'd already done the task before? By being mindful, your mind has the flexibility to step back from time to time to see the bird's eye view. Taking a quick overview means that you don't waste your time doing tasks that are unnecessary. Productivity isn't just about doing what needs doing, but also not doing what doesn't need doing!

The short exercise below helps you to mindfully consider the circumstances that prompted you to be particularly productive. Follow these steps:

1. **Think back to an occasion on which you were really productive.** What time of day was it? Where were you? Try to visualise yourself in that moment in time.

2. **Describe your state of mind.** Were you mindful or unfocused; in the present moment or thinking about the past or the future; judgemental or non-judgemental; curious or bored; calm or excited?

3. **Remember how much effort you were putting in to achieve that level of productivity.**

Your responses to these prompts may help you to be more productive in the future. Try to recreate those conditions and see what happens.

Here are a few tips for making your organisation more productive:

✔ Dedicate a room to quiet time, mindfulness, prayer or meditation. Taking a break in this room gives staff time to reflect and recharge their batteries.

✔ Discourage working late. Working long hours reduces efficiency and productivity and has a negative impact on employees' home life, which inevitably affects their work life too.

✔ Encourage all staff to attend a mindfulness workshop and ensure that they have access to online courses, books or e-learning. Even a 1 per cent increase in productivity more than pays back the cost of the training and resources.

Improved decision making

All CEOs know that high-quality decisions can make or break their organisation. When managers make effective decisions, staff work more efficiently, they feel more in control and the results can be seen in sustainable income for long-term growth.

Good decisions lead to:

✔ Increased opportunities for growth

✔ Higher revenue

✔ Healthier, happier employees

✔ Ability to hire the best employees for each role

✔ Improved quality of products and services for customers

You can make good decisions when your brain is functioning optimally. You can read all you like about decision theory, but if your brain isn't working optimally, you fail to take all factors into account and make bad decisions.

Think back to the last time you came home after a tough day at work. What sort of decisions did you make? Did you decide to eat a healthy fruit salad, go for a swim, meditate and phone a friend who needed cheering up? Or did you eat too much chocolate, slump in front of the TV and snap at your partner? The latter scenario is more likely – because your brain wasn't able to make good decisions. Your long-term goals of losing weight or being healthy or socialising more were overtaken by a brain starved of rest. This situation is called decision fatigue. The more decisions you make, without adequate breaks, the less effective your decisions will be. One way of countering decision fatigue is practising mindfulness exercises.

Judges are six times nicer after lunch

A study conducted in 2010 by Columbia and Ben-Gurion universities looked at 1,112 judicial rulings over 10 months. The rulings related to granting prisoners parole. An amazing pattern was found. Judges were up to six times more likely to grant parole just after lunch. About 60 per cent were granted parole at the start of the day, but this figure gradually declined. Just before lunch, prisoners had by far the lowest chance of being granted parole; and immediately after lunch, the figure went back up to about 60 per cent. The break and some food appear to refresh the judges' brains and they're more likely to make the difficult decision to set the post-lunch prisoner free.

This study demonstrates the effect of taking regular breaks and eating properly on decision-making ability. It also shows how sensitive the decision-making brain is. Through mindfulness, you can energise your brain with a mini-break during the day and improve your decision-making too. Mindfulness directly impacts on the way your brain works, activating the pre-frontal cortex. So, when faced with an important decision, take a few moments to be mindful so that your decisions are based on reason rather than emotional reaction.

Another way in which mindfulness can help with decisions is by switching off the auto-pilot response in your brain. When operating without mindfulness, all your decisions are automatic and based on previous decisions. They lack freshness and don't have access to any new information. If the employees of an organisation are more mindful, they can spot new ideas, see the activities of competitors, notice a need for, for example, younger consumers and make a different decision – and thus move the company forward successfully.

Kodak provides an example of a company's inability to see beyond habitual ideas. The company recently went bankrupt, mainly because CEO after CEO decided not to take the plunge into the digital photography market, despite all the signs showing that this was the way to go. Ironically, an engineer at Kodak actually invented the digital camera, but the company decided not to pursue the concept. Kodak's competitors jumped on the digital bandwagon, and the rest is history.

Could a more mindful management have helped Kodak? I think so. With a better ability to see the big picture and a willingness to let go of what didn't work, maybe Kodak could have gone on to be leaders in the digital photography market. But because it stuck to its habitual pattern of using chemicals to develop photographs, it lost almost everything.

For your day-to-day decisions, try the five-step approach shown in Figure 2-2.

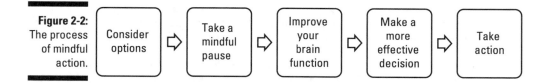

Figure 2-2: The process of mindful action.

Consider options ⇨ Take a mindful pause ⇨ Improve your brain function ⇨ Make a more effective decision ⇨ Take action

By taking a mindful minute (see Chapter 7), you can optimise your brain function, reduce decision fatigue and make better decisions.

Bear these tips in mind to improve your decision making:

✔ Ensure that you schedule meetings at a time of day when people's energy levels are high, making mindful awareness more likely.

✔ If you're chairing a meeting, take a mindful pause before you start to ensure that you're in the right state of mind. End the meeting if you notice people's attention beginning to wane.

✔ Remember that you're a human being, not a machine. You can't keep making decisions all day and expect them to be of a high standard. Take a mindful break every 90 minutes, even if just for a minute.

Reducing staff turnover

High employee turnover hits the bottom line. The cost of replacing an employee and training them can cost up to twice that employee's salary. Consider the time involved in recruitment, for carrying out interviews as you screen candidates and the loss of productivity as the new employee learns the ropes. Maybe the new employee won't even work out and you then have to repeat the process. On top of that, constant changes of staff can negatively impact staff morale.

Mindfulness can help lower staff turnover by helping employees to cope better with stress. Stress can lead to illness and ultimately result in people being on long-term sick leave. But even for staff who aren't overwhelmed by stress, mindfulness can build their resilience and improve their performance, which will make them feel more valued.

Too much stress leads to burnout. According to Professor Marie Asberg, burnout is the end of an exhaustion funnel when you gradually stop doing things that you deem 'unimportant' such as practising mindfulness, exercising and socialising, and instead obsess about your workplace outcomes. Research carried out in 2009 with doctors found that practising mindfulness decreased burnout rates in this cohort.

Prevention is better than cure. Yet most organisations focus on fixing staff after they become ill rather than preventing stress-related illness in the first place. Most employers spend 200–300 per cent more on managing ill heath than on prevention.

Research by the iOpener Institute found that increasing employee well-being in one company reduced staff turnover by 46 per cent and reduced sickness absence by 19 per cent. Mindfulness is one way of increasing well-being and reducing staff turnover.

Use the following mindful tips to help lower staff turnover:

- ✔ **Measure staff well-being and then implement means to improve it.** Search online of 'University of Pennsylvania Authentic Happiness' website for lots of wellbeing questionnaires that you could try.

- ✔ **Set up a regular mindfulness group for all staff to attend for free in the workplace.**

- ✔ **Identify staff who may be susceptible to burnout.** Ensure that they have access to more regular mindfulness courses and other forms of help.

- ✔ **Train managers in mindfulness so they're better able to listen to their staff.** Being better listened to makes employees feel more cared for and they're less likely to leave the organisation as a result. Not being appreciated and listened to is one of the causes of high staff turnover.

- ✔ **Help employees to maintain a work/life balance.** A nationwide survey found that 20 per cent of employees left their job as a result of poor work/life balance and 20 per cent because of workplace stress. Mindfulness can help improve productivity so employees can get home earlier, thus improving their work/life balance and reducing their stress levels.

Chapter 3

Applying Mindfulness in the Workplace

Mindfulness is all well and good, but how do you apply it effectively in the workplace? That's exactly what you find out in this chapter. You also discover why mindfulness is more important than ever in the modern workplace and discover lots of practical ways to start 'mindfulnessing' within minutes!

Gaining Perspective in the Modern-Day Workplace

Fifty years ago, a sizeable proportion of the population got a job and worked for that organisation until they retired. The key benefit resulting from this scenario was a sense of security and stability – you knew what to expect.

For students looking for a job today, things are very different. A recent survey of workers found that one in three remains in a job for less than two years. This massive change in people's working lives is bound to have an impact – sometimes positive, but often negative. In this section, you discover how mindfulness can help you deal with uncertainty in the workplace.

Engaging with a VUCA world

To understand the modern workplace and how mindfulness can help you deal with it, consider an acronym – VUCA. Originally used by the military, VUCA is now used in business.

VUCA stands for:

- ✓ **Volatility:** The high speed and complicated dynamics of change in modern organisations and the markets that they work in. The digital revolution, global competition and connectivity are all contributing to higher levels of volatility.

- ✓ **Uncertainty:** The lack of predictability and prospect of surprise facing many employees. In uncertain situations, forecasting becomes difficult and decision making becomes more challenging.

- ✓ **Complexity:** The wide range of ideas, information and systems that cause confusion and chaos in an organisation leads to complexity.

- ✓ **Ambiguity:** The lack of clarity about what is actually happening within the organisation as well as the environment in which the organisation operates.

To give you an idea of the VUCA world, consider the average working day of Kate, a senior executive. Her alarm goes off at 5 a.m. She turns on her phone as she wakes up and it immediately starts buzzing. She skims through and half answers emails as she gets dressed, has a quick cup of coffee and piece of toast. She jumps into her car and mentally compiles a to-do list on the journey. Half of the emails she read earlier appear urgent, so she wants to deal with them immediately. However, the complexity of the issues makes it almost impossible for her to decide which one to do first. Juggling between phone calls, emails, routine tasks and meetings, she definitely has no time for lunch. She works till late into the evening, keeping herself going with lots of cups of coffee. To ensure that she remains awake for the journey home, she blasts out music on her iPod. As she travels, her phone keeps buzzing with more emails. Kate grabs a takeaway, eats it in front of the television and then goes to bed. She answers a few more emails before turning off the light and then tries to sleep. Unsurprisingly, sleep eludes her as she tosses and turns, going over everything that's happened during the day and worrying about how she's going to function the next day if she doesn't get to sleep soon.

Kate's working day is certainly volatile, uncertain, complex and ambiguous. How can mindfulness help her? Below are a few changes that she can make to her day, that take up almost no time at all and that increase her effectiveness and efficiency:

- ✓ Over breakfast, Kate can keep her phone switched off and eat her toast being mindfully aware of its taste, perhaps looking out into her garden as she does so. The meal would be finished a bit quicker (because she isn't simultaneously dealing with emails) and the time saved can be used to check emails later in the office.

✔ She can take three mindful breaths before setting off in her car. Driving with mindful awareness, focusing solely on the road ahead rather than mentally planning her day, means that her mind is rested and ready for work.

✔ Arriving at the office, she can again take a few deep mindful breaths, instantly calming her fight-or-flight mechanism even if she's had a difficult journey.

✔ As she waits for her computer to start up, she can enjoy a mindful stretch in her chair. She can then organise her priorities for the day rather than allow her attention to be captured immediately by emails.

✔ She can allot time for dealing with emails – after she gets her most challenging task out of the way. She can then feel more in control of her day and is attending to the most difficult job while her mind is still fresh.

✔ She can mindfully walk to meetings. Rather than rushing, she can walk a little slower, feeling her feet as she does so. Walking in this way will settle her mind and her subsequent air of calmness makes attendees more willing to listen to her.

✔ She can prioritise lunch. Going to a quiet place and eating her lunch with full attention ensures that she digests the food properly. She can leave her phone on her desk to avoid the temptation of checking emails and texts while she eats.

✔ She can do her best to give her full attention to colleagues when she's talking to them. Taking subtle, deeper breaths occasionally will make her more patient because the breaths switch on her relaxation response.

✔ She can ensure that she goes home on time rather than working late. What she achieves in three hours late at night can be done in an hour when she's fresh the next morning.

Leaving work on time after a 9-to-5 day can take courage if it flies in the face of your office culture. Sheryl Sandberg, ex-Google executive and current chief operating officer of Facebook, leaves the office at 5.30 p.m. You may think that following her example is impossible but at least consider it. Leaving work earlier, despite making you feel guilty, makes you much more efficient the next day. Finishing work on time is partly a mindset.

Resilience, the ability to effective manage adversity, is the key to managing VUCA at work.

Applying mindfulness in changing times

The current rate of change in the workplace is faster than at any other time in history. The last 15 years have seen an explosion in communications technology and social networking and a rapid rise in economic growth in the emerging economies of India, China, Russia and Brazil. These changes have a big impact on the workplace and affect employees at all levels. How can mindfulness help in managing these changes?

Change isn't always easy. Sometimes change in the workplace can be met with resistance. The human brain works through habit, which creates a sense of familiarity and security. Poorly managed change can make people feel threatened and they resist it.

Mindfulness is about being aware of the emotional impact of change. You need to prepare employees in advance, providing relevant training if necessary. Following the change, you must be a good listener and respond quickly if employees express frustration or distress.

A unique way of thinking about change is provided by a deeper understanding of the principles of mindfulness. Most mindfulness teaching stresses that the world is in a constant state of flux. Mindfulness exercises demonstrate this perpetual change. Try focusing on one of your senses for more than a few minutes and notice the variety of thoughts, feelings, bodily sensations and distractions that you experience.

The universe is constantly changing. Atoms are continually moving; in fact, scientists are unable to achieve absolute zero, the temperature at which atoms stop moving. If constant change is the way of the world, you need to expect some in your own life. Resisting that change leads to pain.

You need to expect and embrace the change that is bound to come. If you find yourself reacting with sadness or anger to that change, give yourself the time and space to work through those emotions using mindfulness exercises.

To better manage change in the workplace, try these tips:

✔ **Expect change:** If you're clinging to the hope that change won't happen, you're living with greater fear and anxiety. Instead, simply expect change to happen at work. When change doesn't happen, be pleasantly surprised.

✔ **Embrace change:** Jack Welch, ex-CEO of General Electric, advises 'Change before you have to.' Try to see change as an opportunity. Write down the benefits of the change and view them as a chance to manage that change. For example, my (Shamash) new boss wanted lots of extra meetings. Initially I didn't like this change, but then I thought about ways of embracing it. I used frustrating parts of the meeting to practise mindfulness of breath; I enjoyed the extra opportunities to share my ideas. I used some of the time to identify what makes a poor meeting and what makes a good one. You, too, can see change as a chance for growth.

✔ **Anchor yourself in the present:** When you're faced with a torrent of change, you can easily feel flustered. One way of coping with that change is through mindfulness exercises. Even one deep breath taken mindfully can switch on your parasympathetic nervous system, which makes you more relaxed and grounded.

Change can be challenging. But in our experience, regular mindfulness practice makes managing external changes easier because you realise that, beyond your changing thoughts and emotions, that a deeper sense of peace, calm and spaciousness exists that is simply your own awareness. That awareness is always the same, ever present and unchanging. When faced with too much change, you can take refuge in mindfulness to rest your body, mind and emotions in your own, unchanging awareness. Figure 3-1 shows how mindfulness can help you tune in to that unchanging awareness.

Figure 3-1:
How thoughts, emotions and the world are constantly changing and how mindfulness can help you to tune into the unchanging awareness that's underneath all that.

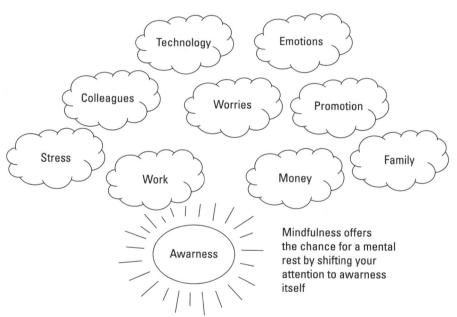

Mindfulness offers the chance for a mental rest by shifting your attention to awarness itself

Employing mindfulness for new ways of working

The essence of working with mindfulness is simple: pay attention to the task in hand. By giving work your full attention, the quality and quantity of what you do improves. But there's more to mindful working than just outcomes. Your level of focus improves, and you give less attention to your normal worries and concerns.

In addition to working with attention, you need to find moments in the day to recharge your mind. The ideal time is between the end of one task and the start of another. After spending an hour writing emails, you can spend a couple of minutes feeling the weight of your body on the chair and your feet on the floor. This mindful awareness of your bodily sensations focuses you on the present moment and is restful for your mind. You feel more energised and prepared for the next task. After a two-hour meeting, you can do a mini-mindfulness exercise (Such as a mindful minute (Chapter 7) or a three step body check (Chapter 6) after everyone has left the room.

Communication is a fundamental aspect of the workplace. On top of giving attention to your own work, and allowing yourself short periods of rest in between, you need to be able to communicate effectively with others. Businesses can be called *companies* – they involve the *companionship* of others. As you become more mindful, you're better able to simultaneously identify the emotions of others and be aware and in control of your own emotions. As a result of this heightened emotional intelligence, people feel drawn to you and are more willing to work with you. A recent survey of 2,600 managers found that 75 per cent of them were more likely to promote an employee demonstrating emotional intelligence than one with a high IQ.

Unmindful use of technology is also impacting success in the workplace. Laptops and phones mean that you can take your work home with you. If you're not in control of your behaviour, you can end up working through all of your waking hours. That's not good for you or your work. Having time away from work gives your brain a rest and an opportunity to recharge. Chapter 8 covers how to use technology in a more mindful way.

Building resilience

Too many challenges at work makes you feel overwhelmed and frustrated. In response you trigger your fight or flight mechanism. This threat response, if switched on for too long, leads to inefficient use of your brain and disease in your body. Building resilience is a way of managing challenges more effectively. For more on mindfulness for resilience, see Chapter 5.

Take the example of Thomas Edison, legendary inventor of the light bulb. He famously said that each time he failed, he didn't view the experiment as a failure; rather he saw it as another way that didn't work. Seeing failed attempts as stepping stones to success is an example of a resilient attitude. Edison bounced back from attempts that didn't work to discover what did work. He certainly thrived on success, inventing the phonograph, motion picture and telegraph.

The achievements of Edison may seem hard to emulate. He seemed to be almost born with a positive attitude and destined for success. And, as far as we know, he didn't formally practise mindfulness! How can mindfulness help you?

As you become more mindful, your tendency to ruminate declines. Rumination is how much you think about and dwell on your problems. Rumination is like a broken record that keeps replaying itself – that argument you had with your colleague, that error you made in your presentation. If you ruminate, you overthink about situations or life events.

Mindfulness may be one of the most effective ways to reduce ruminative thinking because you become more aware of your thought patterns and more skilful at stepping back from unhelpful thoughts.

An online experiment conducted in 2013 in conjunction with the BBC and the University of Liverpool and involving over 32,000 participants, found that people who didn't ruminate or self-blame demonstrated much lower levels of depression and anxiety, even though they'd experienced many negative events.

Carrots, eggs and coffee beans

Once upon a time, a daughter complained about her enormous troubles to her mother. The mother took her to the kitchen and began boiling three pots of water. In the first pot she put some carrots, in the second she put some eggs and in the third pot some coffee beans. The pots boiled away. After 10 minutes, she took the carrots, eggs and some coffee out and asked the daughter what she noticed about them.

The daughter felt the carrots – they were soft and soggy. She broke the egg and discovered it was hard inside. And she sipped the coffee – it tasted delicious. 'What does this all mean?' asked the daughter.

Her mother explained that each experienced the same adversity – boiling water. The carrots started off strong, but became soft. The egg was initially fragile, but now had become hardened on the inside. But the coffee was unique – the coffee beans had actually flavoured the water beautifully.

The mother asked the daughter 'When adversity knocks on your door, are you a carrot, egg or coffee bean?'

Consider this question yourself. Are you like the carrot – hard and strong but when faced with adversity, do you wilt? Or are you like the egg – fluid on the inside at first, but through the adversity of financial hardship or other challenges, become hard of heart on the inside, even though you look the same on the outside?

Or are you like the coffee bean? The coffee bean is actually changed by the adversity itself. When the heat of the water touches the coffee bean, it releases a rich aroma. When faced with hardship, can you rise to the challenge and either change the circumstance or your attitude to meet the difficulty? Can you use adversity to enhance what you can offer the world?

Mindfulness helps you to spot those little niggling negative thoughts before they grow too large. And mindfulness helps you to naturally see tough situations at work as challenges to be faced and overcome rather than avoided. If you're feeling overwhelmed by adversity, mindfulness won't offer a quick fix. But dealing with each challenge, step by step, combining mindfulness with help from your colleagues and/or a coach, means that you can begin to thrive at work.

Think of someone in your workplace who seems to thrive on change and whom you respect. Identify:

- ✔ His attitudes and beliefs

- ✔ The kind of language he uses to describe a change in the workplace

- ✔ The sort of hours he works and what she does to rest and recharge

- ✔ How mindful (present) he is when at work

Spending time talking with those who thrive on change in the workplace can help you to see things from their perspective.

Adjusting Your Mental Mindset

'Your living is determined not so much by what life brings to you as by the attitude you bring to life; not so much by what happens to you as by the way your mind looks at what happens.'

Kahlil Gibran

When I (Shamash) discovered mindfulness, my mindset shifted 180 degrees. Before that first lesson in mindfulness, I was completely goal-orientated. I was halfway through a degree in chemical engineering and wanted a career working for a big corporation. I was only 20 years old, but ever since I was a boy I'd striven to achieve the top grades at school so that I could get into a good university. I aimed to be among the best at university so that I could get a good job, and so on. The obsessive desire for success was draining me. But after that mindfulness class, something shifted. I discovered that life was not only to be enjoyed in the future, after attaining all my goals; life was to be enjoyed right now, here in the present moment. There's nothing wrong with achieving success and attaining goals, but not at the expense of the here and now. Ironically, by living in a more present-focused way, I've been better able to achieve success – the best way to prepare for the future is to live in the present.

Focusing on the present moment

'The secret of health for both mind and body is not to mourn for the past, worry about the future, or anticipate troubles, but to live in the present moment wisely and earnestly.'

Buddha

We know that our most successful coaching, training and writing sessions occur when we're fully in the present. Think of someone operating at the highest level of performance: an Olympic athlete. He's very much in the present moment. Have you ever seen a top Olympic athlete look as if his mind is wandering when he's performing? I haven't. He's fully present because being that way optimises his success. Take the 100-metre sprint. Once the athlete starts running, he's wholly in the here and now, which leads him to success.

Everyone experiences being fully in the moment at some point. Consider the last time you were fully present at work – what were you doing? How did you feel? How productive were you?

Here are a few tips to help you be more mindfully present at work:

- ✔ **Do something different:** Work can be filled with habits and routines. You sit at the same desk, open the same program, speak to the same people about the same issues. Shake things up a bit. Take a different route to work. Eat something different for lunch or speak to someone on the phone who you normally email. Doing something new makes you switch from auto-pilot to a more present-moment awareness.

- ✔ **Savour:** Living in the present moment can be highly enjoyable. Present-moment living means that you can stop waiting for success in the future. Instead, enjoy the simple pleasures in each moment – the taste of your sandwich, the colour of the autumn leaves on your route to work, the simple smooth feeling of your breath. Don't dismiss these everyday pleasures – they boost your mood and mental well-being.

- ✔ **Know that you can always find out more:** No matter what you do, room for improvement always exists. Professor of Psychology at Harvard University, Ellen Langer, says we stop paying attention to something when we think that we know it all. Musicians in an orchestra who are told to make their performance subtly different not only enjoy the performance more themselves, so do the audience. By noticing something new, you've space to explore, discover and grow – and you shift straight back into the moment. Make work an adventure by seeking to discover subtly new ways to perform your tasks.

Treating thoughts as mental processes

Some people estimate that they have up to 60,000 thoughts a day. If you've tried practising mindfulness exercises already, you probably think that's an underestimate. In the East, the brain's tendency to constantly go from one thought to another is called the 'monkey mind' because it resembles a monkey swinging from branch to branch.

Thoughts can be great. Through the power of thinking, humans have managed to achieve feats way beyond what any other animal on earth has done. We've created cities, designed planes and landed on the moon. Unfortunately, we've also designed nuclear weapons and heavily polluted the planet.

Thoughts have another disadvantage on a personal level too. If all your thoughts are taken to be true, and if those thoughts are self-critical, your mental well-being suffers. As a result, your performance at work declines too.

Try this thought bubble exercise:

1. **Picture bubbles floating away in the sky.** Maintain this image for one minute.

2. **Imagine that every thought you have can float away in one of those bubbles.**

3. **Let your mind wander.** Each time a thought pops into your head, imagine it drifting away in a bubble. Continue to do this for a few minutes. You may have lots of thoughts or very few. It doesn't matter.

How did you find this exercise? Did your thoughts float away? More importantly, were you able to observe your thoughts? If you were, you've demonstrated that you are not your thoughts – you can observe them from a distance.

The thought bubble and similar exercises help to show you an important mindfulness skill: the ability to step back from your thoughts. You may have all sorts of thoughts popping into your head in the workplace, such as:

- ✔ I'm useless in meetings.

- ✔ I can't handle this project. It's too big for me.

- ✔ What if Mike tells Michelle about my report? I'll miss my chance at promotion.

- ✔ I hate working with David. He's too slow for me.

These types of thoughts have an effect on your emotions, bodily sensations and ability to get your work done.

Mindfulness offers a solution. As you become more mindful, you notice these thoughts more often. You are then able to step back from them, seeing them as mental processes in your mind rather than absolute truths.

Being able to step back from your thoughts takes practice, especially in the hustle and bustle of the workplace. For this reason, we recommend that you try out some of these exercises when you're not under too much pressure. Once your brain gets the hang of how to watch and step back from unhelpful thoughts, you've a powerful and life-changing skill.

In the old days of personal development, self-help gurus promoted 'positive thinking'. For most people, slapping positive thoughts on top of negative beliefs means they just slip off! Instead, you need to become aware of those negative beliefs and see them for what they are – just thoughts.

Use the exercise below to deal with your thoughts and mind state when you're judging things negatively. It's a simple process but has long-lasting effects once it becomes a habit for you.

You can deal with your negative thoughts by following these three simple steps:

1. **Notice your thoughts:** Focus particularly on unhelpful thoughts about yourself, others or your workplace.

2. **Step back from your thoughts:** See them as simply mental processes arising in your mind that aren't necessarily true. You can imagine them on clouds, in bubbles or floating away like leaves on a stream. The idea is to create a sense of distance between you and your thoughts – not to just get rid of them.

3. **Refocus your attention on the task or person in front of you:** The more mindfulness exercises you practise, the better your brain gets at dealing with negative thoughts.

The importance of stepping back from your negative thoughts, and the way they cloud your judgement, is shown in Figure 3-2.

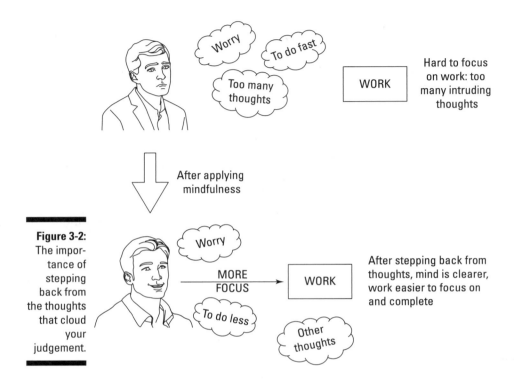

Figure 3-2:
The importance of stepping back from the thoughts that cloud your judgement.

Approaching rather than avoiding difficulties

I (Shamash) love the taste of chocolate and don't like the taste of cauliflower. So I tend to approach chocolate more positively than I do cauliflower. If you could scan my brain when I see these two different foods, you'd probably see different patterns emerging.

Say that work causes you anxiety. You worry about all the meetings you have to attend, the deadlines you have to meet and the colleagues you have to deal with. How do you cope with that feeling of anxiety? Should you continue to face up to the challenges at work and just get on with the uncomfortable feeling of anxiety, or should you avoid anything that makes you feel that way?

You can avoid the feeling by working even harder so that your attention is completely focused on the task in hand and not on your anxiety. Or you can go for a drink every evening after work, causing the emotional sensation to reduce. Or you can start eating every time that feeling arises, so your attention is focused on the food instead of your anxiety.

All these strategies help you to avoid the feeling of anxiety in the workplace. Unfortunately, however, none of them work over the long term. The feeling of anxiety is still there and requires an increasing number of avoidant strategies to help you supress it.

Mindfulness is about approach rather than avoidance. It helps you to approach unpleasant feelings at a pace that's right for you.

Approaching difficult emotions when you've always found a way to avoid them isn't easy at first. To help you get better at doing so, you need to approach your feeling as you'd approach a kitten. You don't rush towards a kitten because it gets frightened and runs away. You approach a kitten slowly. First you walk towards it and then you crouch down so that you don't look too big. Next, you reach out and gently stroke it. Hopefully, the kitten begins to trust you and eventually you can pick it up.

Treat whatever emotion you're dealing with in the same way. Notice where you're holding the feeling in your body. Approach the feeling slowly and tentatively, with a sense of curiosity. Gradually you come to fully feel the sensation, just as it is. This experience is like having a kitten in your hand. Unlike a kitten, however, the feeling is likely to change as you approach it.

Sometimes it grows, sometimes it dissolves. But that's not the point. The point is that you're *willing* to feel that emotion and approach rather than avoid it. This empowering move leads to greater emotional regulation – you've control over your emotion rather than the emotion controlling you.

Approaching emotions involves a process of non-judgemental acceptance – a key aspect of mindfulness. When you're practising mindfulness, you're endeavouring to experience thoughts, emotions, sensations and events as they are in the moment, without trying to judge them as good or bad, desirable or undesirable.

Approach a challenge rather than avoid it, if you can, and discover how to accept the sensations that it produces. Being able to approach your difficulties makes you feel more confident and you're less likely to let your emotions control your life.

Have a go at this five- to ten-minute mindful exercise on managing difficulties. Follow these steps:

1. **Sit comfortably and spend a couple of minutes focusing your attention on your breathing or the sounds around you.**

2. **Think of something in the workplace that scares you a little. Bring to mind a difficult presentation, an aggressive colleague or the thought of losing your job, for example.**

3. Notice any tension in your body resulting from your sense of anxiety.

4. Approach that sensation in your body slowly and gently.

5. Try feeling the sensation together with your breathing.

6. Be aware that you're approaching rather than avoiding the feeling – a mindful step. Notice whether the feeling changes or stays the same from one breath to the next.

7. Refocus on your breathing alone for a couple of minutes before ending the exercise.

Try this exercise whenever you find yourself using avoidant strategies to deal with difficult emotions.

Rewiring Your Brain

Your brain is made up of neurons, which are like wires that carry electrical current from one place to another. Each neuron is connected to many others. The brain is the most complex organism in the known universe and scientists still have very little idea about how it works.

If you were at school in the 1970s, you were probably taught that your brain gradually deteriorates as you get older. The prevailing view was that the brain can't improve itself and that neurons die off as you age. That view was incorrect! We now know that you can create new connections in your brain at any age.

Your brain is unique and shaped by your daily experiences and what you pay attention to. If you're a violinist, the part of your brain that maps touch in your fingers is actually larger. If you're a taxi driver in London, the part of your brain responsible for spatial awareness is more pronounced. And if you're a mindfulness practitioner, the area of your brain that controls focus is more powerful, as is that part which manages emotions. Finally, if you're a mindfulness practitioner, the area of the brain responsible for higher levels of well-being is more active – the left prefrontal cortex.

Getting to grips with the science of mindfulness

An explosion of interest in the study of mindfulness has recently occurred. Centres for mindfulness have been established at numerous universities (see Chapter 20), both in the UK and all over the world. US examples include the University of Massachusetts Center for Mindfulness, UCLA's Mindful Awareness Research Center and the UCSD Center for Mindfulness. Figure 3-3 shows the growth in publications on Mindfulness between 1980 and 2011.

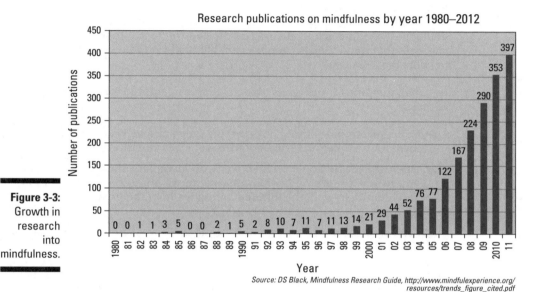

Source: DS Black, Mindfulness Research Guide, http://www.mindfulexperience.org/resources/trends_figure_cited.pdf

Figure 3-3: Growth in research into mindfulness.

Throughout this book we share insights about the effects of mindfulness on the brain. In this section we describe findings from the world of neuroscience. (Chapter 20 provides a list of research articles that you may find interesting.)

Resculpting your brain to make you more productive at work

Most people feel that their mind is all over the place. In fact, some people who practise mindfulness even think that the exercises make them less focused! Studies show that the opposite is actually true. When you sit down to be mindful, you're much more likely to notice each time your mind gets distracted. Usually, your mind is even less focused – so much so that you don't even realise it.

Brain scans reveal that even after just a week or so of daily mindfulness practice, the parts of the brain dedicated to the paying attention (which include the parietal and prefrontal structures), become more activated. In other words you are actively improving your brains ability to pay attention.

Longer-term practitioners appear to have more permanent changes in the brain, showing a greater propensity to be in the present moment even when in a resting state.

In his most recent book, *Focus,* psychologist Daniel Goleman argues that incessant use of technology, such as emails and text messages, has rendered young people increasingly distracted. He goes on to say that current research suggests that mindfulness exercises enable the brain to rewire itself and become more focused.

Goleman identifies three types of focus that are required for different types of tasks:

- ✔ **Concentration:** Focusing on one thing only and blocking out distractions – ideal for completing tasks requiring your full attention.
- ✔ **Open presence:** You are receptive to all incoming information – ideal if you're in a leadership position that requires you to see the big picture and identify how all the different activities help the organisation achieve its goals.
- ✔ **Free association:** Letting go of your old ideas and allowing your mind to drift – ideal when tapping into your creativity.

Mindfulness directly helps to strengthen the networks in your brain associated with concentration and open presence, and allows you to choose to engage in free association when you need to.

If you want to know more about focus, you can find my interview with Goleman on shamashalidina.com

Using mindfulness to increase your present-moment circuitry

Children love stories. Adults love stories. Have you ever wondered why? The brain is designed to be hooked by stories. Stories switch on the visual part of your brain. Because stories are formed of connecting ideas, they tune into the connections in your own brain.

Some people refer to the brain as a story-telling machine. Think about when you first wake up in the morning. Your mind is blank and then, suddenly, whoosh! Who you are and where you live and that long to-do list come to mind.

Your storytelling mind is the 'default' network in your brain. In other words, your brain's normal mode is to tell you stories about yourself and others. For example, 'I need to finish this project by noon, then I need to have a chat with Paul before I get dressed to meet my editor. I must make sure that I'm on time. That hotel we're meeting in looks very big. I hope we can find a table. I wonder if my co-author can join us . . . ?'

That's the storytelling brain at work – not always terribly exciting and often repetitive. But mindfulness is different and much more interesting. If your brain is in a more mindful state, you're focused on the present moment, which engages a different circuitry in your brain. You can access the present moment right now by noticing the sensations that your body is experiencing as it sits on a chair. Do you start to become aware of your poor posture or notice tension in your neck? You can now start to notice information from the world around you: the coolness of the book you're holding, the size of the tree outside, the wispy clouds and hints of a blue sky beyond. That's present focused attention.

When you're more present-moment focused, rather than running on your default network all the time, you're more in control of your life. Instead of finding yourself aimlessly surfing the web, you can catch yourself and choose to get on and finish your work. If you're lost in thought after thought, you can't make a choice about what you're doing until you snap out of the dream. Mindfulness offers you that choice.

Try this exercise to help you become more present-moment focused:

1. **Make a concerted effort to engage your present-moment focus for the next 24 hours.**

2. **Use any free moments in the day to focus your attention on your bodily sensations and breathing or smells, tastes and sights.** In any given moment when you'd usually let your mind wander, choose one of the above and observe. Focus your attention on just that one thing.

3. **Record your observations.** What did you discover or notice? Is your mind more clear and focused? How did you cope with the distractions that your mind created? If 24 hours was too challenging, try one hour.

Developing Mindfulness at Work

This book is filled to the brim with mindfulness exercises to do on your own and ways to integrate mindfulness into your workplace. This section describes some of the key principles of true mindfulness, which are important both in the workplace and beyond. Some of these principles have emerged from ancient practices, developed by millions of people over thousands of years. Take a few moments to consider the key aspects of mindfulness at work and whether these ideas resonate with you.

Examining intentions and attitudes

Mindfulness is much more than just paying attention in the present moment. Mindfulness has three aspects: intention, attention and attitude.

Intention is clarifying what you hope to get from mindfulness. Your intention when introducing mindfulness in the workplace may be to:

- ✔ Increase focus
- ✔ Encourage creativity
- ✔ Reduce anxiety or stress
- ✔ Improve well-being
- ✔ Increase productivity
- ✔ Generate bigger profits
- ✔ Find greater meaning in your work
- ✔ Improve your relationships at work
- ✔ Develop your resilience

Your intentions play a huge role in your mindfulness practice. You may practise mindfulness for very personal reasons or to benefit your team, your organisation or even the world!

Your intentions in everyday life may be so subtle that you don't recognise just how important they are. For example, take the example of breaking a window. A thief may break your window to enter and steal something from your home. A firefighter, however, may break your window to enter your home and rescue you from a fire. The action is exactly the same but the intention is totally different. In the same way, being clear about your intention has a big effect on your practice.

At first, you may practise mindfulness for yourself. And that's fine. But as you develop your practice, you may like to consider being mindful for the benefit of others too. For example:

- ✔ To improve relations in your work team
- ✔ To be more productive so you can serve your customers better
- ✔ To be more emotionally intelligent so you can relate more effectively with your colleagues
- ✔ To help calm the anxious atmosphere in the office

These intentions aren't right or wrong – but may help you to find greater meaning in your mindfulness practice and your working life. And people whose sense of meaning is connected to their work tend to be happier, healthier and more successful in their role – a triple whammy! See the nearby sidebar 'Job, career or calling' for more on what motivates people at work.

In addition to intention, your attitudes are also important. Jon Kabat-Zinn, co-developer of mindfulness-based approaches in the West, recommends developing the following attitudes to life.

Being non-judgemental

Your mind is constantly judging experiences as good or bad. Mindfulness practice offers time for you to let go of those internal judgements and just observe whatever you're experiencing, accepting the moment as it is.

Job, career or calling?

Amy Wrzensniewski, Associate Professor of Organizational Behaviour at Yale University's School of Management, conducted fascinating research on how you approach your work. She may have found the key to happiness and meaning in the workplace. She explored the following three orientations towards work:

✔ **Job:** If you fall into this category, you view work as a means to an end. You receive pay to support your family, hobbies or other pleasures outside of work. You seek work that doesn't interfere with your personal life. It's just a job.

✔ **Career:** In this category, you seek work where you've an opportunity to rise up the ladder. If no chance for promotion or development exists, you move to a different workplace. You're interested in success and prestige. You want new titles and the social standing that comes with the career.

Calling: If you see your work as a calling, you see work as integral to your life. Your work is a form of self-expression and personal passion. You're more likely to find work meaningful and be more satisfied in both your work and life in general. If work is your calling, you'd probably say that you'd do the work even if you didn't get paid for it.

These categories aren't exclusive – you may have a calling for your work but also seek good pay and career prospects. And no right or wrong job orientation exists – you may prefer to find more meaning outside of your work.

The incredible finding is that it doesn't matter what type of work people do – the orientations seem to be evenly spread, one third each. So a personal assistant may see his work as a job (I want to get paid and get out of here), a career (hopefully this job leads to extra training and a chance to work with the vice president) or a calling (I enjoy making my boss's life run smoothly and seeing her achieve her goals). It's the mindset that counts.

Being patient

Mindfulness requires patience. You need to bring your attention back to the present again and again. If you're naturally impatient, mindfulness is probably the best training you can undertake! But it won't be easy. You need to experience sitting with the discomfort of impatience. With time, the feeling dissolves. Being non-judgemental with your feelings helps you to accept and be with them, no matter how impatient you feel.

Adopting a beginner's mind

If you adopt a beginner's mind, you undertake each mindfulness practice as if the experience was a completely new one. And not only mindfulness – to work with a beginner's mind means that you approach your work with freshness – as if you've never done this kind of work before. Adopting this attitude helps you to switch off your habitual, automatic ways of doing things. As you become more experienced in mindfulness, the beginner's mind is particularly important. Always practise mindfulness as if you're a beginner!

Developing trust

Mindfulness takes time to show its benefits. In that time, you need to be able to trust the process. If you're going through a difficult time at work, you also need to be able to trust your own inner capacity to work through the challenge with the support of mindfulness, together with any other support that you can access. Trust is about believing that things can be better. And with that mindset, you're willing to try something new. Developing trust involves noticing and respecting your doubts, but not letting your doubts run away with you. The greatest of scientists needs to trust that her experiment may lead to new discoveries, otherwise she wouldn't bother trying it in the first place. Try to adopt the trusting and open attitude of a scientist as you learn to be more mindful.

Learning to be non-striving

To strive means trying to reach a future goal, whether that's an internal goal of feeling happier or more focused, or an external goal of achieving financial success. Striving engages the 'doing mode' in your brain. In this state, you experience a sense of inherent dissatisfaction with the way things are in the present moment. This dissatisfaction drives the action to achieve the goal.

Mindfulness is about non-striving. To be mindful, you need to let go of your constant desire to achieve. Just be with whatever experiences show up; simply observe them with curiosity and make no judgements. You don't have to feel calm or relaxed; you simply need to be present in your moment-to-moment experiences as best you can.

Being accepting

Acceptance is a fundamental aspect of mindfulness. To accept means to stop fighting with your present-moment experience and just be aware of whatever is happening. For example, if you feel discomfort in your body when you're practising mindfulness, and shifting your posture doesn't ease it, just acknowledge the sensation and let it be. Giving presentations may make you feel anxious. Mindfulness lets you acknowledge the anxiety as an interesting feeling and then ignore it.

Letting go

When I (Shamash) was writing my first book, I struggled. I wanted it to be perfect. But the more I strove for that, the longer the book took me to write. When I finally let go of the idea of perfection, the words began to flow. Letting go was the key.

Consider what you're holding on to. A job that isn't right for you? Ways of working that are no longer effective? Even more importantly, are you holding on to ideas that are limiting your potential, such as 'I can't handle this project' or 'I'll never be able to give a speech'? Perhaps you need to let go of your old ideas.

Letting go is an act of freedom. When you let go of old ideas, beliefs, people, jobs or ways of working, you create space for the new. When practising mindfulness, you need to let go of each stream of thought that you notice. The process is a continuous movement of observation and letting go.

Sometimes mindful awareness results in a complete sense of letting go and being in your moment-to-moment experience, with full acceptance, total peace and joyful effortlessness. If this experience ever happens to you, remember to let it go too!

Remembering that practice makes perfect

Monks practise mindfulness for years. Early scientific research into mindfulness investigated the effect it has on monks. Brain scans revealed that monks' brains operate far more effectively than those of people who don't practise mindfulness. The researchers also found that the more practice a monk had undertaken, the greater number of positive changes observed. Monks have an incredible ability to focus, can manage their emotions very well, experience lots of positive emotions (that's why they're always smiling!) and rarely, if ever, lose their temper.

The good news is – you don't need to become a monk to benefit from mindfulness. Positive changes have been observed in the brains of people who've been practising mindfulness for just 10–20 minutes a day for a few days.

Daily practice is the key. Consider the process of discovering how to ride a bike. If you spend just one minute a day practising, you eventually get better but doing so takes years! If you practise for 20 minutes a day with a teacher, you may be able to ride within a week or two. Once you get the hang of riding a bike, to be able to cycle faster you need regular practice. You may need to train with a coach, read books about cycling, meet other cyclists to share ideas and so on.

Mindfulness is similar. You need to practise regularly, and the more time you can dedicate to being mindful, the better you get at it. You can start slowly with short mindful exercises and gradually build up to longer sessions. If you want to get really good at mindfulness, you need to read about it, get a coach or trainer and practise diligently.

Experimenting with mindfulness in the workplace lab

What makes a good scientist? Someone who has a theory, tests it out and perseveres until it's proven.

We encourage you to think of your work as a laboratory – time to pop your lab coat on! Think of your job as a place where you can test out the effect of mindfulness on the quality of your work, your relationships with colleagues, your productivity or whatever outcome you're hoping for. You're much more likely to adopt mindfulness if you find out that the exercises work.

Use the steps below to monitor the effects of your mindfulness practice:

1. **Record how things are for you now, without mindfulness.** You can record how much work you've achieved every hour or how well you're getting on with your colleagues, how focused you are or even how much you're enjoying your work at the end of each day. Measure whatever you're interested in ultimately changing. As with any good budding scientist, keep clear records. Enter data on a spreadsheet, note data in a journal or even record findings on your phone.

2. **Integrate mindfulness into your work for a few weeks.** You can do a 10-minute mindfulness exercise at the start of the day, or enjoy three mindful pauses spread out over the day, or set reminder alarms on your phone to be mindful and focused while you're working. Continue to record your productivity or whatever else you're measuring.

3. **Analyse your results.** What effect did mindfulness have on whatever you're measuring? Notice what worked for you and stick with it. The longer you practise, the more effective your mindfulness is.

Don't take these results too seriously. It takes a lot longer than a few weeks to really reap the benefits. When they first start practising mindfulness, many people notice more of their own negative thoughts and patterns than positive ones. But after that initial dip, they're better able to focus and to ignore negative thoughts and modify unhelpful behaviours. So you may want to experiment for a few months before drawing any conclusions.

Acting ethically for the organisation and its people

To behave in an ethical manner means doing what you consider to be right. Being ethical is vital for all parts of the organisation, but especially so for its leaders. If the leaders of your company are unethical, other employees are tempted to follow suit. The example set by leaders holds far more weight than all the words in the ethics handbook.

Not only is acting ethically important in itself, it has numerous benefits:

✔ **Safeguarding assets:** If your organisation has an ethical culture, the staff respect the company's assets. So office supplies won't go missing and employees won't use the phone for personal conversations. When employees feel proud of their organisation and work with integrity, they respect the company's supplies and equipment.

✔ **Quality of decision making:** Decisions are often based on ethical choices. The more tempting decision may not be the most ethical one. Ethical decisions based on transparency and accountability lead to the long-term health of the organisation.

✔ **Public image:** An ethical organisation is far more attractive to the general public. When unethical actions come to light, a company's image can be destroyed overnight. The public would like to see you value your staff, the environment and those less fortunate rather than profits alone.

> ✔ **Teamwork:** If your organisation communicates its values and ethics to employees, they can better align their own values with those of the company. When these positive values are authentic and acted upon, employees feel proud of their organisation and what it stands for. The quality and quantity of work increase alongside increased intrinsic motivation.

Examples abound of multinationals incurring huge financial losses as a result of acting unethically. Lack of corporate integrity can bring down a whole organisation.

Mindfulness can affect the ethical stance of everyone in the organisation. Ethics are ultimately based on decisions. When mindful, you're more aware of the decision you're making and the impact that it has. As all decisions contain an element of emotion, you can use mindfulness to focus on those emotions that result in more ethically sound decisions.

Marc Lampe, Professor at University of San Diego, argues that mindfulness improves cognitive awareness and emotional regulation, positively contributing to ethical decisions.

Common sense agrees. Mindfulness is based on attitudes such as compassion, curiosity and self-awareness. The non-reactive and caregiving stance that mindfulness promotes is bound to lead to morally sensitive choices in the workplace.

Living life mindfully

To get the best results, mindfulness needs to be practised at home as well as at work. If you live mindfully when you're travelling, at home, with friends or engaging in hobbies, you're more likely to be mindful when you're at work too.

If you're training to run a marathon, you don't just eat healthily during the day and then pig out in the evening – you need to live a healthy life. To develop mindfulness, you need to *live* mindfully.

Here are a few tips for practising mindfulness at home:

- **When conversing with your partner, give them your full attention:** Notice your tendencies to interrupt, argue or ignore. Instead, make a concerted effort to step back and see your partner afresh, with a sense of gratitude for what they offer to the relationship. See relationship interactions as a chance for you to grow and develop rather than a means to fix or change others. Seeing the faults in others is often much easier than recognising your own shortcomings.

- **When you're with your children, know that love and attention go hand in hand:** When you play with them, listen to their stories about school or help them with their problems. Doing so makes your children feel more loved. You can't always give them your undivided attention, of course, but if you usually do some work in the evening and always see your kids as a distraction, redress your priorities.

- **Housework is a great way to practise mindfulness:** The work doesn't involve too much thinking, the processes are repetitive and there's a clear focus for attention. Take ironing, for example. Rather than trying to finish it as quickly as possible, take your time. Enjoy the heat coming off the shirt, the sensation of the iron gliding over the material, the smell of a freshly washed garment and the beauty of a pressed shirt. Focusing your attention in this way isn't only satisfying, but is another way to deepen your mindfulness.

- **Cook and eat with awareness:** Taking time to cook a meal is a wonderful discipline. Every time you chop a tomato, feel the knife slicing through it. Listen to the onion sizzling in the frying pan and smell the freshly cooked herbs. Cooking is a great way to develop your mindful awareness and improve your health because *you* decide how much (or little) sugar and fat goes into your cooking, not some restaurant chef. Use fresh, organic, local ingredients when you can and enjoy the taste of your meal. Eating slowly, tasting each morsel and being grateful to have food available is all part of mindful cooking and eating.

- **Be aware of your phone, TV and Internet usage:** If your work involves looking at screens all day, take a rest when you get home – take a screen break. Spend more time talking to your family and friends; set aside time for walking, reading or going to the theatre. Ensure that you have things to do in your diary that involve getting out and about.

To live mindfully is to live with greater wisdom and compassion. Wisdom is about the choices you make and your attitudes to life. Compassion is responding kindly to your own suffering and that of others. Mindful awareness helps you to wake up to your own life and make living and working with greater wisdom and compassion a reality. You're able to act with greater integrity and respond with increased empathy. You're in tune with your inner values and are sensitive to the needs and values of others.

Reflect on the following questions and jot down your thoughts in your journal:

- ✔ **Think about the wisest people you know.** What sort of work do they do? How do they behave when they're at work? What is their attitude to life? How mindful are they when they're at work, at home or with friends? How balanced is their lifestyle? Spend time with them and share what you think of them. Find out how they came to be so wise.

- ✔ **Think about the kindest, friendliest or happiest people you know.** How do they behave when they're with others? What sort of words do they use? How do they measure success? Try spending more time with them and find out what they do to develop these positive qualities.

Part II
Working with Mindfulness

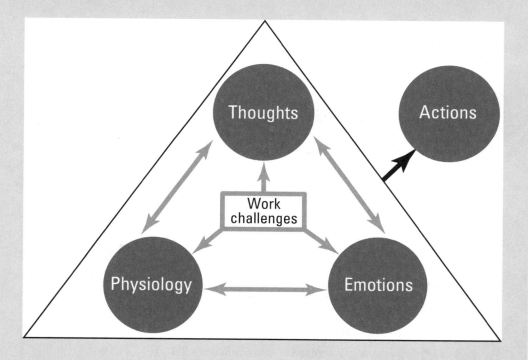

In this part . . .

- ✔ Understand how to make your whole working day mindful, from when you wake up in the morning to when you come home in the evening.

- ✔ Learn all about working with mindfulness. Whether working at your desk or walking to the water cooler, you can discover a range of ways for practising mindfulness.

- ✔ Work through the importance of developing mindful resilience in the workplace.

- ✔ Discover a brand new five-week training course that we've developed called 'Mindfulness At Work Training', which you can try out.

- ✔ Understand the importance of being kind to yourself.

- ✔ Explore ways to manage technology in a mindful way – yes, we hope to make you more mindful with an iPhone!

Chapter 4

Practising Mindfulness Day to Day

*I*n this chapter, you discover a whole host of different ways in which to be mindful. Best of all, many of the exercises we cover are short and easy to implement in the workplace. Here you find ways to just stop and be mindful as well as exercises that you can do *while* you're working. That way you don't use up too much time and yet still train your brain to work with greater focus, intelligence and creativity as your mindful awareness naturally grows.

Think of day-to-day mindfulness like interval training. In interval training, popular with fitness coaches, you do a burst of activity followed by a rest. These short bursts of exercise help to boost your cardiovascular health. In the same way, we encourage you to intersperse your working day with short mindful breaks. When you practise mindfulness regularly in this way, you start working and interacting with higher levels of awareness throughout the day.

Figure 4-1 compares the benefits of doing just one long mindfulness exercise a day to interval working with mindfulness in which you do mini-mindfulness exercises throughout the day. As you can see, the interval mindfulness helps to maintain your mindful awareness throughout the day, whereas doing just one mindful exercise in the morning is great, but can diminish as the day goes on.

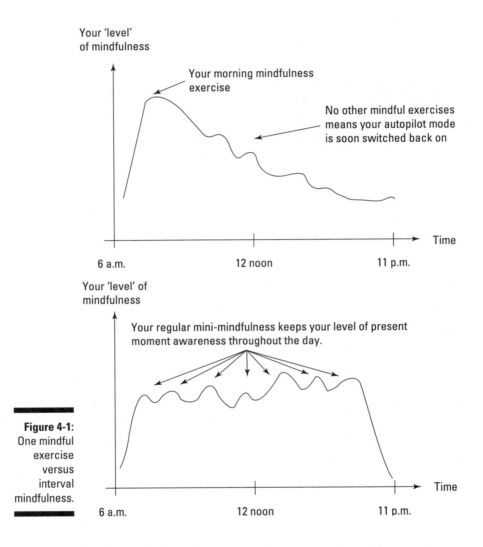

Your 'level' of mindfulness

Your morning mindfulness exercise

No other mindful exercises means your autopilot mode is soon switched back on

6 a.m.　　　12 noon　　　11 p.m.　　Time

Your 'level' of mindfulness

Your regular mini-mindfulness keeps your level of present moment awareness throughout the day.

6 a.m.　　　12 noon　　　11 p.m.　　Time

Figure 4-1:
One mindful exercise versus interval mindfulness.

As always, balance is the secret to success. Combining one longer period of mindfulness with short mindful exercises throughout the day makes you a mindfulness-at-work superstar!

Starting the Day Mindfully

The way you start your morning often sets the tone for the rest of your day. If you make a positive start with a short mindful exercise, you're off to a conscious, perhaps calmer start. You're then more likely to be able to maintain mindful awareness throughout the day.

Waking up too late every day, not stopping even for a moment to be in the present, makes your life more difficult. Rushing releases a burst of adrenaline into your bloodstream, narrowing your brain's attentional resources. You're much more likely to see others as annoying threats to your goal of getting to work on time – little mindfulness is evident in that state of mind. You're then probably running on automatic for most of the day, having used up a lot of your energy just getting to work and, before you know it, the day has ended and you're feeling shattered. If this scenario sounds familiar, don't worry. Discover a different way of starting your day in this section.

Making time for mindfulness

Consider setting aside a period every morning for 'quiet time'. This period can be your 'me time'. If you're a busy mum looking after your children all day or a stressed-out executive with lots of responsibilities, you may rarely make time for yourself. But having some quiet time just for you is a great boost to your energy, well-being, self-confidence and sanity. You can use this time to practise the mindfulness exercises in this book!

By choosing to make time for yourself to be mindful, you're sending a positive message to yourself. You're saying that you're just as deserving of rest and recuperation as anyone else. You see the importance of looking after yourself so that you can work effectively and give to others. If you think that you're too busy to set aside time for daily mindfulness, or even some other way to recharge, you're implying that you can give, give and give more without recharging yourself. Unfortunately, that's just not possible. Just as your body needs to sleep each night to function most effectively during the day, so your mind needs some form of rest to revitalise it. Mindfulness offers one way to do so.

I've (Shamash) been practising mindfulness pretty much every morning since I discovered the approach in 1998. I've lapsed for short periods over that time but then realised what I was missing. I'm grateful for those lapses because they made me realise just how easy it is to slip out of the habit.

I generally practise soon after I wake up. I choose from Mindfulness of Breath, Mindful Sitting, Mindful Self-compassion or Mindful Body Scan or I listen to a guided mindfulness practice. I don't like to be too rigid and I make up my mind up each morning regarding what practice I do.

Most people ask how long their daily mindfulness practice should last. I usually answer by asking: how much time are you willing to invest in mindfulness? Any length of time practising mindfulness is better than none at all. And most research suggests that the more time you can put in, the better. So, you decide. If you're willing to invest five minutes a day doing mindfulness, then five minute it is. If you're happy to practise 20 minutes of mindfulness every morning and evening, then go for that.

I met a friend last night who practises seven seconds of mindfulness every 20 minutes, and he loves it! An alarm goes off on his phone every 20 minutes and he stops to feel his body on the chair, look up and around the room rather than just his screen, takes one deep breath and then he's ready to get back to work. Experiment to see what works for you.

Consider saving up money for retirement. Some people save £50 a month and others save £1,000 a month. The amount you save is different depending on how much you want at the end, how much you can afford and how much money you think you need. Practising mindfulness is like putting money into the bank account of your own brain. The more time, enthusiasm and self-compassion that you put into your practice, the more you create a more mindful, happy, friendly, productive and creative brain. Start your mindfulness bank account today!

Here's a morning mindful exercise that includes many of the mindfulness techniques in one. Give it a try and, if you like it, begin your day with this exercise.

1. **Do whatever you need to do to ensure that you feel awake and ready to practise mindfulness.** Perhaps a stretch, a shower or a cup of tea.

2. **Sit or lie down wherever you feel comfortable.** You can use a chair, sofa, meditation cushion or your bed. Maybe you can sit outside if you're lucky enough to have a balcony or garden and some nice weather!

3. **Set your intention to practise mindfulness as best you can.** Remember why you're practising – to benefit yourself, others you spend time with or perhaps just for the sake of itself.

4. **Set your mindful attitudes: to practise with patience, acceptance and self-friendliness rather than self-criticism.** Bear in mind that your mind will wander; each time it does so, gently guide your attention back to whatever you're focusing on.

5. **Begin this exercise with deep, mindful breaths.** Feel your breathing each time you fill up your lungs, and breathe out slowly and smoothly. Notice what effects these deep breaths have on your body and feelings. The slower you can breathe out, the better. Slow outbreaths automatically balance your autonomic nervous system.

6. **Allow your breathing to find its natural rhythm.** Feel the sensation of your breathing wherever you can – around your nose, in your chest or your belly. Feel each in- and out-breath.

7. **Scan your body, starting with your head and moving down.** Feel the physical sensations in each body part non-judgementally: your neck, shoulders, arms and hands; your upper and lower torso; your hips, pelvis and buttocks; your upper and lower legs; and finally your feet.

8. **Open up your attention to notice the sensations in your body as a whole.**

9. **Open your attention further still, and take in any sounds that you can hear.** Listen to sounds without the need to label or identify the source – just notice volume and pitch, as if listening to music.

10. **Turn your attention inwards to your thoughts.** Watch and step back from your thoughts. Imagine placing each thought on a cloud and watching the thought clouds float by.

11. **Notice how you feel emotionally.** In particular, see whether you can feel an emotion in a particular part of your body. Imagine feeling that sensation together with your breathing.

12. **Finish with a compassion exercise.** Say the following words to yourself: 'May I be well, may I be happy, may I be healthy, may I be free of suffering.' Say them a few times, really appreciating their meaning and allowing the words to be felt in your heart area. Then send that compassion out to your family, friends, work colleagues and all others, including yourself: 'May we be well, may we be happy, may we be healthy, may we be free of suffering.'

13. **Acknowledge and congratulate yourself on your efforts to practise mindfulness this morning.** Your effort benefits not only yourself but also all those with whom you come into contact throughout the day.

Integrating mindfulness into your morning routine

Humans are creatures of habit. We love our routines. When I (Shamash) was training to be a schoolteacher, our tutor told us how much children love routines; they make them feel safe and secure. When I taught my science classes, I started with a mindful pause, took the register, went over homework, taught the pupils something new, did a fun exercise and finished with a mindful pause again. The children knew where they stood, and the process made my life easier too. If you follow a mindful morning routine, you too may feel safer and more energised and grounded.

As routines are so easy for humans to tune into, why not make mindfulness part of your daily morning routine? In this way, mindfulness becomes second nature. Just as you automatically brush your teeth, have a shower or prepare your coffee, you can also practise your mindfulness routine. Then, if you're not mindful when getting ready for the day, you feel that something's missing – a bit like not brushing your teeth.

Below is an example of a mindful morning routine. Feel free to adjust it depending on your lifestyle, responsibilities and preferences.

- ✔ **5:30 a.m. – You wake up naturally.** You used to need an alarm clock, but because you now go to bed at a reasonable time, you wake up on time too. You therefore wake up after a good night's sleep. You begin the day with a few mindful breaths and a smile as you prepare to get up.

- ✔ **5:31 a.m. – You have a short morning stretch, perhaps do a few mindful yoga exercises and then go downstairs to prepare yourself a cup of tea.** You listen to the sound of the kettle boiling and notice the steam rising. You begin reflecting on all the aspects of your life that you're grateful for. You enjoy the sound of water filling your mug of lemon and ginger tea.

- ✔ **5:45 a.m. – You sit down facing your garden and spend a few minutes looking out of the window and sipping your tea.** You then practise a mindfulness exercise for 10 minutes. You finish by describing your experience in your journal and noting three things you're grateful for in your life.

- ✔ **6:00 a.m. – You wake up the children to let them know it's time to get ready for school.** They're a bit groggy but you've more patience since you started practising mindfulness. They know the routine and before too long they're dressed and ready to go. Your partner helps to get them prepared for school. You remember how grateful you are to have such lovely children.

- ✔ **7:00 a.m. – You have breakfast together as a family.** Before eating, your youngest child says, 'Let's mindfully pause' and you all take three mindful breaths together. You eat and talk about the day to come and everyone shares how they're feeling and what's on their mind. As best you can, you eat with mindful awareness. You remind your children to look for the good things in the day, so you can share them that evening.

- ✔ **7:30 a.m. – You all leave the house together.** You've enough time to travel mindfully to work.

We know this scenario may sound hopelessly optimistic. The purpose of this description is to help you find one or two ideas that you can implement in your life. Begin with where you are at the moment. Try going to bed a little earlier and waking up a bit earlier. Spend a few moments deliberately thinking about what's going well in your life as a positive way to start the day.

Travelling Mindfully

A Gallup poll of over 170,000 people revealed that commuting to work is the least enjoyable of daily activities. Longer commutes are correlated with higher divorce rates, obesity, decreased exercise and higher consumption of fast foods. A third of those with journeys of over 90 minutes had chronic neck or back pain issues. But, if you've a long commute, don't despair!

The findings above suggest that identifying ways to make travel more mindful can have a significant effect on people's health, happiness, relationships, productivity and work success. Use this section to make travelling more tolerable, and perhaps even fun!

Driving with intent

Imagine waking up on a beautiful Sunday morning. You don't need to go to work. After getting ready, you decide to drive to your favourite park on the other side of town. You get into your car and, as you're in no hurry, take a few mindful breaths before setting off. On your way to the park, the driver in front of you is a learner. She's driving at the speed limit, which is fine. Eventually the learner turns off into a side street. You smile and remember how difficult you found learning to drive at first; you hope that the driver passes her test. You keep driving and see the traffic light in front of you change from green to amber. You gently bring your car to a stop, wind your window down and gaze at the sky. Further up, as you get close to the park, a ball flies in front of your car. You brake and a few seconds later a small child comes running after the ball. You think, 'Lucky I was alert and braked in time.' You're a bit flustered, but soon compose yourself. You park and enjoy your time walking in the park.

Now consider a really different scenario. You jump into your car, already late for work. You turn your radio up to help you wake up and speed your way down the street. A learner driver turns up in front of you. You think, 'That's typical. Hurry up!' You start beeping your horn because she's driving so slowly. The learner driver stalls her car because you've made her panic, and now you're delayed even further. You curse under your breath and breathe a sign of relief as the learner turns off into a side street. You spot an amber light and respond by accelerating. A speed camera flashes and you think, 'Great! Another ticket.' You decide to call work to let your boss know you're a bit late, and start fumbling with your phone as you speed down another street, past the park. A ball bounces in front of your car, which you don't notice . . . You can imagine how this scenario ends. Driving in this kind of rushed, unmindful way is both dangerous and illegal. But driving in this way is also common – the threat of being late for work makes people take far too many risks in relation to the small reward of arriving a few minutes earlier at work.

Here are a few tips for making your car journeys more mindful:

> ✔ **Start the journey with mindfulness.** By grounding yourself with a mindfulness practice, you set the tone for your journey. You can feel the sensations in your body for a minute, take three full deep mindful breaths or just set the intention to drive with full, mindful awareness, knowing that the vehicle you control isn't a toy but potentially life-threatening if handled without due care and attention.

✔ **Keep to the speed limit.** Even if the road is empty and you think that you can safely drive faster, don't. The discipline of sticking to the speed limit makes you more conscious of what you're doing. If you always drive over the speed limit, start changing your behaviour on your next journey. Driving a little slower than you're used to means that you're able to dedicate more of your brain's resources to driving with mindful awareness.

✔ **Undertake a mindful traffic light exercise.** When you notice the traffic light just about to turn red, stop don't accelerate. Use the time to look at the sky, practise mindfulness or think about how fortunate you are to own a car or to have a job. Being late for work is never an excuse for dangerous driving.

✔ **Expect delays.** If you expect to have a clear, straight run to work, and you don't, you're bound to feel frustrated. So, instead, expect delays, traffic, learner drivers and more traffic. Then, if you've a smooth journey to work, you can be pleasantly surprised rather than frustrated.

✔ **Switch off your phone.** Lots of research has demonstrated that using a phone while driving, even if the phone is hands-free, impairs driving ability to the same extent as drinking too much alcohol. Lots of accidents are caused by people who are texting rather than watching the road.

✔ **Be mindful of your surroundings.** Mindful driving is about maintaining an open awareness. Look both near and far to help you judge any dangers coming up. See driving as an opportunity to practise mindfulness.

✔ **Breathe.** Give full attention to the road ahead while simultaneously focusing on the feeling of your breathing. Doing so helps you to be completely alert and in the present moment.

✔ **End mindfully.** When you arrive at work, finish with another little mindful exercise, such as mindfulness of breath, mindfulness of sounds, or mindfulness of your body. Continue this process by walking with mindful awareness to your workplace rather than zoning out.

Listen to Track 1 of the audio downloads accompanying this book (go to www.dummies.com/go/mindfulnessatworkuk to download them). This track is designed to enhance your awareness and thus improve your driving. Try listening to the track once before using it in the car, though; if you find it distracting, don't use it. You may need to burn the track onto a CD to use in your car, unless you've got an MP3 player.

Thinking about trains, planes and mindfulness

If your journey to work or your working day itself involves travelling on trains or planes, you may find this section helpful.

Trains

Picture the rush hour in London. On the Underground, commuters race to get on the Tube, nudging each other out of the way, sighing in exasperation if the doors close before they get there and clenching their teeth in frustration as they constantly check the time. But a train comes every couple of minutes – is that really too long to wait? Obviously, if you live in a village and miss the one bus of the day, a sense of frustration is understandable, but you needn't feel uptight about train travel.

If you commute on the train every day, you can do so mindfully so that you arrive at work focused rather than frazzled.

Here are a few tips to help you be mindful on the train:

- ✔ **Practise a mindfulness exercise.** You can even pop on headphones and practise a guided mindfulness exercise during your journey. If you manage to get a seat on the train, doing so is even easier.

- ✔ **Expect delays.** Don't expect the service to be perfect. That way you'll be pleasantly surprised if it goes smoothly and not too frustrated if things go wrong.

- ✔ **Play the mindful station-to-station game.** See whether you can remain mindful from one station to the next. Focus on sounds, physical sensations or count the number of breaths you take. How many times does your mind wander from one station to the next? Have fun with this one.

- ✔ **Count the sounds.** Another game you can play on the train is to notice all the different types of sounds you can hear. You'll probably be surprised by all the different tones of sound that you normally ignore.

- ✔ **Pay attention.** Notice what's going on around you on the train. Watch the other passengers; observe the kinds of things they're doing and what they're wearing. Try to observe without judging. Most people focus their attention on a book, a newspaper or music. Try something different – open up and look with curiosity at the world around you. Trains are an amazing invention and certainly a lot quicker than walking, so you can remember to be grateful for that too. Notice how excited young children are when they're travelling by train and try to rustle up some of that enthusiasm yourself from time to time. You may end up having some fascinating conversations with strangers.

- ✔ **Wish them well.** From time to time, when you notice someone getting into your carriage, say in your mind, 'I wish you happiness'. This thought may be in sharp contrast to the kind of thoughts you normally have on the train but wishing others well engages your compassionate mind and reduces anxiety.

Planes

Several of my (Shamash's) clients regularly use mindfulness practices when they're on long-haul flights and swear that they no longer suffer from jet lag.

Sitting in a confined space for hours can be frustrating. If you can't sleep, what do you do? Practising mindfulness is a great idea in this situation.

You can listen to one of our guided mindfulness exercises through headphones. Or you can simply practise mindfulness of breath. The resultant state of mind is just as restful, if not more so, than sleep. For this reason, we highly recommend that you try these exercises on all flights.

Eating is another opportunity to practise mindfulness on flights. Unfortunately, unless you travel in first class, the meal may not be gourmet standard. But taking your time to choose whether or not you'll eat the meal, tasting the food, taking time to chew it and deciding when you're full all require the presence of mind that mindfulness offers. You probably digest the food more efficiently and feel much better afterwards.

Apparently, fear of flying is people's second-biggest fear after public speaking. If flying makes you anxious, consider these mindful tips to make you more confident in the air:

- ✔ **Identify your triggers.** For some people the trigger is the turbulence; for others, the take-off. Identify the aspect of the flight you're scared of.

- ✔ **Familiarise yourself with the noises.** You may begin to panic when the wings start flapping about or when you hear a strange noise underneath the plane 10 minutes before landing. If you know that the wings are designed to be flexible in the wind and that the noise you hear before landing is simply the landing gear locking into place, you won't feel so scared. Research the cause of your fears.

- ✔ **Sip herbal tea mindfully.** Instead of consuming lots of alcohol or caffeine, which makes you feel dehydrated and ultimately more anxious, drink water or herbal tea. Drinking in a mindful way, conscious of the taste and aroma, makes you feel more relaxed and in control. Your attention is on yours senses rather than on worrying.

- ✔ **Use drugs as a last resort.** If you've been given medication to manage your anxiety, see whether you can use other mindfulness techniques first. Most drugs have side effects – if you can control your feelings using other approaches, you will be much better off in the long run. (**Note:** Obviously, your doctor's advice should take precedence over whatever we suggest.)

- ✔ **Breathe through your anxiety.** If you feel anxious, mindful deep breathing is helpful. Begin by breathing out for as long as you can and then draw a slow, deep breath in. This slow mindful breathing helps to reduce hyperventilation. Focusing fully on the sensation of breathing helps to anchor you in the present so that you cannot ruminate on negative thoughts. The deep breaths make you more relaxed automatically, no matter what you're thinking.

Walking mindfully

'Walking is a man's best medicine.'

Hippocrates

Over 2,400 years ago, Hippocrates, considered the father of medicine, proposed the health benefits of walking. Not only is walking a great form of exercise, mindful walking is a superb way of developing mindful awareness. Whenever I (Shamash) run organisational workshops in mindfulness, I always make sure to explain how to do mindful walking. Many of my clients who find sitting still and being mindful impossible to achieve on a daily basis, love to practise mindful walking whenever they can.

Walking took you about a year to master. If you look down at your feet, they're pretty small compared to the rest of your body (I hope). The ability to balance on two feet isn't easy and is a skill that took lots of time and effort to master. Walking requires even more skills – passing the weight of your body seamlessly from one foot to another is no mean feat – pardon the pun!

Mindful walking is about being present as you're walking, rather than letting your mind just aimlessly drift to other thoughts or things you need to do.

You can practise mindful walking in lots of different ways. Here we describe one of the basic methods. It's Track 2 of the audio downloads you can find at www.dummies.com/go/mindfulnessatworkuk We suggest that you practise this technique slowly at home and then, when you've got the hang of it, you can mindfully walk at your normal pace when you're at work. Try this exercise for five to ten minutes to start with.

1. **Begin by setting your intention to walk with mindful awareness.** Take a few conscious deep breaths. Intend to be mindful of the sensations in your feet as you walk. If you're practising at home, you can take off your shoes or even practise barefoot in the garden.

2. **Stand with your feet hip-width apart.** Close your eyes for a few moments if you can balance. Feel the micro-movements in your legs and feet how these constantly keep you upright. Normally your balance is maintained unconsciously. Be aware of how this state of balance is a dynamic process, just as achieving balance in your own life requires constant subtle adjustments.

3. **Lean all of your weight onto your left foot.** Notice how this weight feels; identify the sensations in different parts of your foot. Now slowly lift your right foot and, being careful to balance, gazing at a fixed point in front of you if necessary, move your right foot forward and place it a few inches in front of you. Feel your right foot as your weight begins to shift onto that foot. Keep transferring your weight onto your right foot until you're ready to step forward with your left foot. Continue to move in this way, one foot after the other – lifting, moving and placing one foot after the other.

4. **Say to yourself 'lifting, moving, placing' as you walk.** Doing so will help you focus on the moment.

5. **Bring your attention back to your feet each time your mind drifts to other thoughts.** Be aware of any emotions that you're feeling too.

6. **Congratulate yourself at the end of the mindful walk, however it went.** What was important was your intention to be mindful rather than how mindful and focused you actually were.

If you want to expand your experience of mindful walking, you can also be mindful of the following:

- ✔ **Your muscles:** All the different muscles in your legs and body engaging with each step you take.

- ✔ **Your senses:** The sights you see, the sounds you hear, what you smell, the taste in your mouth, the feeling of your body.

- ✔ **Your thoughts:** Notice what thoughts pop into your mind rather than trying to push them out. As best you can, watch without getting involved with the thinking process.

- ✔ **Your emotions:** Be aware of how you're feeling, where you feel the emotion in your body and how the emotion changes with each breath and step you take.

Be creative in the way you practise mindful walking. Use strategies that work for you – that help you to be mindfully present no matter where you are and how fast or slowly you're walking. Mindfulness is essentially about awareness, that's all.

Taking Mindful Pauses

A mindful pause is simply a chance to stop and practise a short mindfulness exercise. People love the short mindful exercises that we offer when we're running a workshop or coaching session. The thought of a two-minute mindful exercise puts a smile on their faces.

We recommend that you do several short mindful exercises per day rather than one long mindfulness session. We suggest this approach because mindfulness is about being more present and awake in your everyday life – at work and home. If you practise regularly, this result is more likely to happen.

Pausing at your desk

A mindful pause is a great way to start your day at work. If you work at a desk, you can close your eyes and take a mindful pause using the audio files that you can download from www.dummies.com, or you can simply sit with your eyes half open and gaze at your desk. That's undercover mindfulness – no one needs to know that you practise mindfulness if you don't want to share it with others! Play Track 3 of the audio downloads available from www.dummies.com/go/mindfulnessatworkuk.

A mindful pause isn't a relaxation break. Relaxation can often be not only about letting go of muscular tension but also allowing the mind to drift freely. A mindful pause is about gently waking up – noticing thoughts, feelings and bodily sensations rather than tuning them out.

One of the challenges of mindfulness is remembering to practise. Use the following tips to remind you to do a mindful pause:

- ✓ **Pause between activities.** When you've finished one job and before starting another, take a mindful pause. For example, after answering lots of emails, take a pause before dealing with phone calls. After a meeting, take a few moments to pause before walking back to your office. After dealing with one customer on the phone, take a few mindful moments before you contact the next one.

- ✓ **Set a reminder on your phone.** You can set three alarms on your phone during the day. Then, each time the alarm goes off, you can do a short mindful pause.

- ✓ **Use a phone app.** Lots of mindfulness apps are available for all sorts of phones. You can set one to remind you to stop and take a breath or two.

- ✓ **Make an appointment with yourself.** If you use a diary, book in a few mindful pauses with yourself. That's one appointment worth turning up to.

- ✓ **Be creative.** One of our clients puts his mindfulness notes in among a pile of paperwork. When he comes upon the mindfulness notes, he stops to take a mindful minute and notes down his observations on the mindfulness exercise. Consider your work role and how you can creatively remind yourself to take a mindful break or three.

Chapter 7 takes you through the steps of the mindful minute.

Make a record in your journal or phone each time you take a mindful pause. Note down your thoughts, feelings and bodily sensations. Write down what you were doing just before the pause. You may notice interesting patterns emerging. If you find that the mindful pause has a positive effect on your mind state, you can keep using them!

Enjoying water cooler moments

The importance of taking regular breaks is a recurring theme in this chapter. In the past, smokers used to regularly leave the office to enjoy a cigarette. Fewer people smoke nowadays, and you may feel uneasy about taking too many breaks at work. But if you can, do take some time off – even a few minutes every now and then helps.

If your work involves sitting down all day, one nice way to take a mindful break is simply to walk to the water cooler and take a drink. Apart from the obvious benefits of rehydration, which has a surprisingly large effect on the functioning of the brain, spending a few minutes away from your work helps you to take a step back. Just as mindfulness involves stepping back and observing your thoughts and emotions, so taking a break literally means stepping back from all your tasks and duties. The break may remind you to do something important that you forgot, or you may think of a far easier way of dealing with a problem.

Talking to others and socialising helps recharge your brain too. Just a few minutes of chatting can help to dissolve any feelings that feel locked up inside you. A simple joke and smile always helps too.

Finally, a bit of walking every now and then is vital for your body. Recent research suggests that people who spend most of their time sitting have the highest risk of diabetes, heart disease and even premature death. Even if you do 30 minutes of exercise a day, you still need to think about sitting less for the remaining 23.5 hours.

Waking up and smelling the coffee

Another way to take a subtle mindful pause is when you go on your coffee break.

Most people let their minds have free reign and drift. But the problem with allowing this drift too often is that the mind goes to the same old worries and concerns. Tune in rather than out to fully recharge yourself.

Follow these steps:

1. **Set aside time for your break so that you can enjoy a mindful drink.**

2. **Be mindful as you prepare your drink.** Listen to the sound of the boiling water, watch the steam, smell the aroma and listen to the sound of water filling your cup.

3. **Sit down with your drink and switch off any potential distractions.** Choose a location where you're unlikely to be disturbed.

4. **Breathe mindfully.** Feel your breath, your body and the cup in your hands.

5. **Take a sip of your drink.** Feel the warmth of the liquid entering your mouth and going down your throat. Continue to hold the cup and watch the steam rising from it. Feel your breathing from time to time.

6. **Notice the tendency to rush or finish.** Take your time and let the temptation to rush arise and pass, like any other feeling.

7. **Express gratitude when you finish drinking.** Show appreciation for this opportunity to practise mindfulness.

If you work in a busy environment, taking this length of time over a drink may not be possible. Modify the exercise in accordance with your needs. Stopping for 60 seconds to really taste your drink can make a big difference to your mindset in that moment.

Ending Your Day Mindfully

Ending your working day with mindfulness helps to set boundaries. You signal to your brain that you've now stopped work – you can shift gear from the busy, doing mode to a more mindful being mode.

I (Shamash) had a client who is a head teacher at a school in London. He'd always been highly efficient and able to get through huge amounts of work quickly. Although he felt on top of things, he'd begun to suffer from anxiety. I coached him over the phone and discovered that his main problem was when he got home. He continued running around on doing mode. The strict timetable he followed at school continued at home. He'd think: 'First I'll have dinner, then I'll watch TV for an hour, then I'll go to the gym. I'll come home and iron a shirt for tomorrow, then I'll do X and then I'll do Y.' He gave himself no time to just be! I encouraged him to practise a mindfulness exercise at the end of each day so that he can mentally shift gear from doing mode to being mode. After a few weeks, he was better able to relax at home and his behaviour was less rigid. His anxiety began to dissolve.

Managing energy and sleep

I (Shamash) didn't used to be a productive person, though I worked hard. I worked late into the night, not getting nearly as much done as I could and woke up feeling tired the next day. It was only after I read a book on time management and actually wrote down how much work I did in each hour that I realised how much of my time was being wasted away. The exercise was a real eye-opener. Recording your use of time is an act of mindfulness and we highly recommend it. I'm more productive now, but still plenty to learn I'm sure!

Your productivity is linked to your energy level. Some people are morning people and are most energetic at that time. Others are afternoon or evening people. You may think that you know when your energy peaks in the day, but recording how you use each hour of the day is still a useful process and it takes little time to do.

Most people continue to work late into the evening, which can be a mistake. If you continue to work, your energy won't be effectively replenished for the next day. Working late actually reduces the amount of work you can achieve rather than increasing productivity. If you want to be successful in whatever work you do, you need to be operating close to peak performance. And peak performance is achievable only if you renew yourself for the optimal period of time.

Creating a boundary between your work and home life is key. Consider practising a mindfulness exercise as soon as you reach home. This signals to your brain that work time is over and you can shift mental gears and begin to relax and rejuvenate. Try to avoid checking your emails in the evening. To become more mindful, you need to set aside time to do something different and reset your brain so you're recharged for the next day. If you're checking your work emails at home and just can't help it, you may be addicted to doing so. This type of addiction is more common than you think. Check out Chapter 8 for more on technology addiction.

Sleep is important. A good night's sleep has a positive effect on energy level, willpower, general well-being, ability to communicate and focus. Studies suggest that you need 7.5 to 9 hours' sleep per night to operate at your optimum level. The exact figure varies from one person to the next. By keeping a record of your sleeping pattern, you can see on what days you're most energetic and how many hours you slept the night before. Mindfulness will probably help you to sleep better, too. And if you can't sleep, try a mindfulness exercise when you're in bed. Mindfulness is restful and should help you drift off.

Following a mindful evening routine

Your routine evening activities are a great opportunity to be extra mindful. Following a mindful exercise, you should be more focused as you cook, do the ironing, mow the lawn, vacuum and so on. These household chores are normally thought of as repetitive and boring – mindfulness allows you to see them in a different light.

By adopting a mindful approach to these activities, you're training your brain to be more focused and centred; even more importantly, you're better able to savour and enjoy the simple experiences in life. Then, when you arrive at work the next day, your mind continues to be present rather than frantically and excessively ruminating about future scenarios that are highly unlikely to happen and take up unnecessary time and drain energy.

Here's a list of a few typical evening activities and ways to make them more mindful after a busy day at work:

- **Watching television:** TV is a passive activity, so rather than watching one programme after another, record what you're really interested in watching, and watch that at a time that's right for you. Then you can get up and do something else. If you're stuck in the habit of watching several hours of television each night, try recording your TV habits – the act of writing them down can help you to shift the habit.

- **Cooking:** Cooking is a great opportunity to practise mindfulness. Connect with your senses as you cook. Prepare the meal with love and attention rather than just focusing on speed. You'll enjoy the process more.

- **Eating:** Really notice and appreciate every element of your meal. Use all of your senses to enhance the experience.

- **Talking with your partner:** Notice what you discuss. Is it always about work? Is it mostly negative or positive? Do you surf the net or watch television as you talk. Try looking at your partner in the eye a bit more than usual and see what happens! Be grateful for their positive qualities.

- **Doing sport or exercise:** These activities can be good for more than just your body. For example, run mindfully by noticing your breathing rate and the sensations in your legs as you run. Play tennis mindfully by maintaining some awareness of your bodily sensations in-between striking the ball. Attend a yoga class to practise mindfulness as you stretch and breathe.

- **Enjoying a hobby:** Hobbies are great for taking your mind off work. They also give you a chance to develop your mindful awareness by intentionally connecting your attention to your senses and refocusing each time your mind wanders. Any hobby or activity can be mindful.

Avoid looking at any form of screen in the last couple of hours before going to sleep. The light from screens sends a signal to your brain that it's still daytime and makes it harder for you to fall asleep because it lowers your levels of melatonin. This not only reduces sleep, but also can increase the chance of obesity, diabetes and other disorders according to a study published in Applied Ergonomics Journal.

Using mindful exercises

You can use mindfulness exercises to create a mindful end to your day. Do one at your desk or when you get home – or both, if you're keen! Remember, even one conscious, mindful breath counts as a mindful exercise.

Here's a mindful exercise that you can use to bring your working day to a close. You can take about five to ten minutes over this exercise.

1. **Sit up in a way that invites mindfulness.** You need to create a sense of wakefulness.

2. **Allow your eyes to close if you wish, and take three deep, full, mindful breaths.** Really feel each in-breath nourishing your being and each out-breath giving you a sense of letting go. Elongate your out- breaths as much as you can. Notice what effect these breaths have on your bodily tensions.

3. **Be mindful of your natural breathing as your breath finds its usual rhythm.**

4. **Notice your bodily sensations.** Let go of as much tension as you can and accept any that you can't release.

5. **Feel your feet on the floor.** Try to imagine that your feet are roots extending down through the earth.

6. **Reflect on how your day went.** Imagine all the events of the day, good and bad, just like leaves that blow away in the wind. Allow your thoughts to just emerge and fly away; don't resist or analyse them. Have a sense of letting go. Tomorrow is another day and you can resume your activities then. For now, let your concerns about work float away so that you can focus on your activities at home or engage with friends or hobbies that you enjoy.

7. **Come back to feeling your breathing, when you're ready.** Take three, full mindful breaths to signify the end of the exercise. Finish by acknowledging your efforts to practise mindfulness for both yourself and those close to you.

Appreciating the good

Humans have a tendency to focus on the negative as a result of our evolutionary roots (see Chapter 1 for more on this tendency). Make seeking out and reflecting on what's going well in your life a simple and important part of your evening mindfulness routine. In this way, you deliberately begin to create more positive thought patterns in your brain instead of worrying-type thoughts. These patterns can even be seen in brain scans and over time become positive habits. More realistic, honest and yet positive thoughts help to engage your parasympathetic nervous system, making your brain more calm, focused and reasonable. You can then access your high-level thinking brain, which is less activated when overloaded with what's going wrong in your life rather than what's going well.

Seeking out the good in this way is simply called practising gratitude. You can do it by leaving a notebook at the side of your bed and recording what went well that day, that week or what's going well in your life generally. You can take that journal with you when you travel, too. Each night, before drifting off to sleep, make writing down three aspects of your life that you're grateful for part of your routine.

When I (Shamash) was going through a really tough time at work, I intentionally tried to think of things to be grateful for about work. It was counter-intuitive, but really helped me to feel better. The tension created at work began to ease, and the feel of calm I felt gave me the space to think more clearly about how to deal with the situation more rationally.

See whether you can think of three different things to be grateful for each night. If that number is too challenging, begin with at least one that's different. Here are a few suggestions of things to be grateful for about work:

✔ You're receiving money to help to pay for your food/home/rent/travel/family/going out.

✔ You're working with one or more colleagues who you like.

✔ Your firm is contributing money to a pension or health insurance scheme on your behalf.

✔ You have access to a gym subsidised by your company.

✔ Work offers you a chance to interact with other people and socialise.

✔ Work gives you stability and income, which many people don't have.

✔ If you don't enjoy your work, at least you now know what you definitely don't like doing and so can start training in a different field or look out for new opportunities.

✔ If you don't like your work, at least you can now try to make your working day more enjoyable using the mindfulness strategies in this book.

✔ You may not enjoy your work, but your salary allows you to pursue your hobbies.

✔ Think about how your work benefits other people. You can be grateful that you're doing work that ultimately makes a difference.

You can also include aspects of your life that are nothing to do with work. You can be grateful for your health, your home, your family, your friends, the area you live in, your education, your ability to read and write, the food and drink that you can afford, the fact that you know about mindfulness, each of your senses. And most amazing of all, the fact that you're alive and a unique human being – there will never be another person with your exact set of talents and abilities ever again.

You can interpret how your life and work are going at the moment in hundreds of different ways. If things are going really badly at work, acknowledge mindfully that this situation is the case rather than resisting or fighting the emotions the situation creates. Then, when you're ready to do so, ask yourself what positive things you can discover from the situation. You may even be able to look back one day and be grateful for the opportunity to grow, which this experience gave you, or to use it to help others through similar difficulties.

Chapter 5

Boosting your Mental Resilience

. . . .

In This Chapter

▶ Managing multiple, conflicting demands more productively

▶ Developing effective strategies for working with difficult people

▶ Maintaining peak productivity while looking after your well-being

. . . .

*W*e all go to work to do a good job, and I'm sure that you're no exception. Unfortunately, the world of work can be challenging, which can make it difficult for you to perform at your best.

Change is the most common source of pressure at work. In the world of work, change is nothing new. In fact, you can argue that change is the only constant in life. What is different nowadays is that the pace of change is accelerating. Uncertainty and instability are the norm in today's work environment.

Other sources of pressure you may encounter in the workplace include relationships with colleagues and peers, lack of clarity about job roles, work demands, degree of control over work and support from colleagues and superiors.

This chapter explores how you can overcome work challenges by using mindfulness to boost your mental resilience. You find out how mindfulness can help you deal with work challenges more productively, leaving you with more energy and a sense of well-being. You discover strategies to help you flourish in times of change, managing multiple, conflicting demands more effectively. You develop a more mindful approach to encounters with difficult colleagues and bosses.

Recognising the Need for Resilience at Work

Resilience is all about your capacity to handle difficulties, demands and high pressure without becoming stressed. It's about not wasting energy on little things that really aren't important. It's about performing well under pressure. It's your ability to respond flexibly and adapt to changing circumstances (especially important in the present climate of constant change and uncertainty). Lastly, it's about your ability to bounce back from defeat and disaster.

The more resilient you are, the more quickly you will be able to recover from a setback, make the best of the new situation, and become a 'new and improved' version of yourself. From a business perspective, it's a no-brainer: A resilient workforce is a productive workforce. It's healthy, energetic, durable and enthusiastic – good news for both you and your company.

The modern day stress epidemic

Unfortunately most of the world is now facing a stress epidemic.

Take, for example, Bob, a busy account manager that I (Juliet) know who works for a multinational company. As Bob's workload increases he starts to think, 'There's so much to do and not enough time.' This anxiety leads to him making poor decisions. As a result of his poor decisions, he starts to worry about his professional reputation, and the possibility of losing his job. Bob really wanted to shine at work, so he decides to work harder, putting in long hours. He becomes stressed, and makes more mistakes, so he starts taking work home. He gets stuck in a vicious cycle of worrying, working too hard and feeling stressed.

The end result? The harder he works, the more he gets wrong and the more stressed he feels. Does this scenario sound familiar?

Everyone, at some point in their working lives, experiences stress. Work-related stress can be defined as 'an adverse reaction to excessive pressures or demands'. Workplace stress is common; indeed, in many countries workplace stress is the top cause of long-term workplace absence. It costs businesses billions. In the UK alone, in 2012 around 131 million days were lost to sickness absence.

More people than ever before say that they feel highly stressed. As many as 80 per cent of workers say they regularly experience stress at work, and up to 40 per cent say that their job is very or extremely stressful and is the number one stressor in their lives. Estimates suggest that around 50 per cent of staff say that they need help in finding out how to manage stress.

Research shows that workers with highly stressful jobs, but little real control over decision making, are 23 per cent more likely to have a heart attack than other employees. Prolonged periods of stress can lead to serious health problems, including cardiovascular illness and cancer.

Mindfulness has been scientifically proven to be highly effective in reducing stress, anxiety and depression. That's why many companies are now training staff in mindfulness to aid resilience and improve well-being, and productivity.

Understanding fight or flight

So, if change is the norm, and stress is reaching epidemic proportions, how can you become more resilient? How can you bring joy and happiness back to your day, not to mention improved productivity and personal effectiveness?

To answer these questions, you first have to understand a little bit about how the human brain has evolved. Scientists think that in ancient times, when our ancestors were faced with a threat (such as attack by a wild animal); their brain triggered the release of powerful hormones into the bloodstream. These hormones boosted their heart rate, muscle tension and breathing and helped humans to sprint away from danger – the *fight or flight* response. Other hormones worked as natural pain killers, repaired damaged cells and acted as clotting agents. Together, the effect of these hormones helped humans to escape mortal danger and live to hunt another day. After the immediate threat had passed, our ancestors' bodies probably returned to normal fairly quickly.

Your own brain's reaction to modern-day pressures (such as a critical boss, a failed pitch, a missed promotion or a missed mortgage payment) is exactly the same as that of your ancestors. When you feel threatened, your brain releases an excessive amount of hormones, which are designed to help you escape from mortal danger.

Under normal circumstances, when you're not under any great pressure, and you experience a threat, a temporary spike in your heart rate occurs as hormones are released. After the perceived 'danger' has passed, your body returns to normal. Unfortunately, many people now live their lives in a constant state of heightened arousal.

Each time you encounter a perceived threat, your heart rate peaks as hormones are released. Unlike our ancestors, however, many modern-day humans often remain under pressure for long periods, and their bodies never really return to normal. As a result of energy being diverted to fight or flight, the body doesn't have sufficient energy to undertake its routine body maintenance, including the brain. Under normal circumstances, you grow new brain cells to replace the ones you naturally lose. This process continues right into old age. When in fight or flight for long periods, these brain cells are not replaced, slowly diminishing your mental capabilities.

Remaining in this heightened state of arousal (stress) over long periods can lead to major health issues such as a lowering of the auto-immune system, cardiovascular illnesses, digestive complaints, respiratory problems, psychological illnesses, migraines, pre-menstrual tension (PMT), cancer and even premature death.

So, the human ability to recognise and quickly react to perceived threats has helped us become highly successful as a species, but is now a danger to our very survival. Mindfulness can help you develop resilience life's pressures, and new strategies for dealing with potential stressors in a more productive and less harmful manner, returning your body to a fit, healthy state.

Mindful Working to Enhance Resilience

Work is, and has always been, challenging. The digital age, constant change and the need for ever more efficient, cost effective ways of working has led to some unhealthy working practices.

Managing multiple, conflicting demands

Do you spend your working life juggling multiple tasks and conflicting demands? If so, you're not alone. As people take on more senior roles, they're increasingly expected to multi-task – work simultaneously on a range of different problems. For decades now, job descriptions have demanded the ability to multi-task.

The fact is that no one can really multi-task – the brain is not wired that way. The brain can only focus on one conscious task at a time. When you multi-task, in reality you're switching between tasks, doing one task, then switching to the next and the next and so on.

The brain is an energy-hungry organ. Each time you switch tasks, you use some of your limited energy supply. Research shows that multi-tasking reduces accuracy and performance, which explains why frequent multi-taskers are less productive. A limit exists to the number of things that you can hold in your brain at any one time. New ideas take up more working memory than things you're familiar with. Your memory starts to degrade each time you try to hold more than one idea or thought in your mind at a time, so you're better off to focus on just one thing.

The only way to do two or more mental tasks quickly and accurately is to consciously do one at a time. The only exception to this rule is routine tasks that you've done many times before. As a result, they've become embedded deep within the more primitive areas of your brain. In order to manage multiple, conflicting demands more productively, you need to plan your approach mindfully.

Managing tasks mindfully

Mindfulness can help you to become more aware of your mental processes, and choose the most appropriate strategy to deal with the work tasks you're facing.

Meet a client of mine (Juliet) – let's call her Jan. It's February and Jan has just been promoted to the post of chief editor for an alternative fashion magazine. Jan starts her day by working through her emails. She reads, replies to and deletes messages. A couple of the emails prompt her to do some work. Two hours later she still hasn't started work on the editorial for this month's magazine, and the deadline is the end of the day. Jan starts working on the editorial, but she finds it difficult to focus. After 30 minutes, she's interrupted by Frank who is working on a feature for next month's magazine. She helps Frank, and then refocuses her attention on her editorial. Because she feels pressed for time, she eats a sandwich at her desk for lunch while trying hard to finish her editorial. In the afternoon, she chairs an important meeting about a feature in the Christmas edition. She hasn't had time to prepare and feels uncomfortable throughout the meeting. The meeting overruns. The time is now four o'clock and she still hasn't completed her editorial. Jan tries to focus but just can't think straight . . .

Have you had days like this? I certainly have! So what could Jan have done differently? Let's rewind Jan's day and look at how she could have made her life easier:

Jan entered the office. She knew that she'd face multiple, conflicting demands, so she decided to start her day mindfully with 10 minutes of mindfulness practice in her office before people came in. She started her day by prioritising all the things she had to do.

She identified that her editorial was the most important thing that day. In order to complete this task she knew she needed to use her higher brain, (See Chapter 1) which is very powerful, but also very energy hungry. This prompted her to undertake this task early on in the day while still feeling fresh. Frank popped in to ask for help, and she agreed to talk to him in the late afternoon. She completed her editorial by 11 a.m. and then started working through her emails. She felt herself becoming distracted by a couple of emails that demanded her attention. Jan decided to go out for lunch. On her walk to the sandwich shop, she spent five minutes mindfully walking. She sat on a park bench to eat her sandwich, and spent a few moments mindfully savouring its taste and texture. She returned to the office feeling refreshed, with a clear head. She then spent 30 minutes, as planned at the start of the day, preparing for her meeting. The meeting was a great success, and finished early. She completed the work connected with the emails, helped Frank and left the office early.

Mindfulness helped Jan to acknowledge and park all the things that were going round in her head. It also helped her to regain her focus at lunch time. By prioritising, she got more done in less time.

Here's a quick mindfulness technique that you can use any time you want to regain your focus.

Using the three step focus break

This simple technique consists of doing three things for one minute each. Use Track 4 from the audio downloads available at www.dummies.com/go/mindfulnessatworkuk.

- ✔ Acknowledging your thoughts
- ✔ Focusing on the present moment sensation of breathing
- ✔ Acknowledging your bodily sensations

Step 1: Settle yourself into a comfortable, upright position with your feet firmly on the floor – avoid slouching if you can. Although you can do this exercise with your eyes open, most people find it easier with closed eyes. By closing your eyes, your brain has one less stimulus to deal with. Spend one minute recognising and acknowledging all the thoughts going round in your head. As thoughts arise, acknowledge them, and then let them go.

Step 2: Now narrow your attention to focus on the present moment sensation of breathing. Feeling the breath coming in and the breath going out. If you mind wanders, its fine – that's just what minds do. Just kindly, gently escort your attention back to where it needs to be. Remember there is no need to control your breathing or alter it in any way. Its fine as it is all you are doing is using it as a kind or anchor to direct your attention to.

Step 3: Spend one minute recognising and acknowledging how your body feels, right here and now. Become aware of the actual physical sensations in your body, including both the pleasant and unpleasant feelings. If you do encounter any unpleasant sensations try if you can to just accept that they are there without trying to make them go away and without judging them, bad, or irritating. Doing so will evoke an emotion which will increase your tension and make things worse. Accepting that the sensations as they are in the present moment adds no further fuel to the fire, and as a result the sensations may diminish or change.

This technique can be compressed or extended and can be used anywhere at any time. Creating a short break helps you return to the present moment. Returning to the present moment enables you to put things into perspective, see the bigger picture, and make wiser choices and decide how to get the most from the rest of the day.

You may find this exercise difficult at first, but with a little practice it should become easier. Practising this technique helps you to develop new neuro-pathways in your brain, or strengthen existing ones. The stronger the neuropathways are, the easier it is to recall and repeat the exercise in future. See Chapter 1 for more information on neuroplasticity.

Here are a few tips to help you master the three-minute focus break:

✔ Don't judge, rationalise or think about your thoughts, as doing so shifts you towards left-brain (logical) thinking. Just acknowledge that the thoughts are there and label them 'mental processes'. You may initially find this process difficult but it becomes easier with practice.

✔ Don't get cross if your mind wanders, as this wandering may start a rush of neurotransmitters signalling a response similar to 'fight or flight', which is not what you're aiming to do! If you do find yourself getting annoyed, be nice to yourself by acknowledging that 'it's okay . . . it's just what brains do'. This advice may sound trite, but recent neuroscientific research examining brain activity associated with self-kindness suggests that doing such things can reduce or neutralise the brain's reaction to threat.

✔ When checking in with your body you might wish to ask yourself 'How are my toes feeling now? Pause to observe then move up the body . . . How are my legs feeling now? . . . In some areas you may feel little or nothing; in others you may feel sensations such as tingling, stiffness, tension or heaviness. This part of the exercise is simply about checking in with the body in the here and now. It's about seeing things as they are in this moment – not changing them in any way.

✔ As thoughts come into your mind, recognise that you're having them, acknowledge them and then let them go. You may find it helpful to imagine the thoughts floating off on a cloud, drifting downriver, rolling away like the credits at the end of a film or being put in a box to deal with later. Experiment and discover which approach works for you.

Science provides explanations about how mindfulness exercises like the preceding one work within the brain.

- ✔ Paying attention to your breathing means that activity in the attention association area of the brain is increased. This means you are able to focus more attention on what's going on, helping you to see things more clearly.

  Sitting in an upright position means that you trigger positive neural circuitry, which makes you feel more positive.

- ✔ Focusing on the present-now experience means that brain activity starts to shift from habitual, automatic thinking to more creative, big picture thinking.

When you practise mindfulness sufficiently, your parasympathetic (relaxation) nervous system is activated, and later the sympathetic (arousal) nervous system is also activated, which can produce a mentally clear and alert state. As your amygdala (fear centre) activation decreases, you may feel your breathing rate, heart rate slowing down, and your blood pressure reduce.

Grouping tasks

Try to plan how you will tackle work tasks if you can at the start of the day. The tasks that you need to pay most attention to must be done when you're fresh and mentally alert, so do them first. If you're feeling tired or sluggish, take a five-minute walk if possible or get a quick breath of fresh air. If it's late in the afternoon and you're feeling tired, ask yourself whether getting certain tasks done today is critical. Maybe they can wait until tomorrow morning when you're fresher.

Try to group your tasks into blocks of time, according to the different ways you use your brain to work on them. Remember, routine tasks involving little thought use less energy than tasks that involve decision making or the creation of a new concept. Schedule time to do the latter when you're likely to be feeling fresh.

Starting the day by going through emails is a common mistake. Schedule emailing later on in the day in order to use your peak level of performance on the tasks that are most important.

Dealing with distractions

Avoiding everyday disruptions in the modern-day workplace can be challenging. Phones ring, emails and text messages ping and people unexpectedly appear at your desk.

Switching between tasks reduces your productivity and can increase the pressure you're working under. Although many of us would say that these distractions are outside our control, in reality we can generally take steps to minimise them.

Ask yourself:

✔ Can I divert my phone for a short while today while I tackle the tasks that need most concentration?

✔ Can I switch off or silence my mobile phone for a while?

✔ Can I log off for a while so that incoming emails won't distract me?

✔ Can I ask people not to disturb me for a while?

✔ Can I find somewhere quiet to work where I won't be disturbed?

✔ Is being contactable 24/7 organisational culture or am I just imposing this dictum on myself?

Simple actions like logging off from your email account or silencing your phone can help you complete your most important work tasks more quickly. You'll be surprised at the results.

Mindfully managing your emotions

When you've lots to do, the calmer and more focused you remain, the better. As emotions are regulated by the primitive brain, (see Chapter 1), remaining rational when in the grip of strong emotions is hard. Mindfulness can be used as a technique for working constructively with intense emotions such as fear and anger that often lead to misunderstandings and conflicts.

A simple mindfulness technique involves sitting with your eyes closed and focusing on your breathing. By concentrating on the rhythm of your breaths, you develop a sense of detachment, which stops your thoughts from spiralling further and further into depression or anxiety. In time you start to realise that thoughts come and go of their own accord, and that your conscious self is distinct from your thoughts. See Chapter 6 for tips on how to practise mindfulness of breath.

How your body affects your mind

When seeking to manage your emotions, you need to recognise that whenever you encounter a situation, your thoughts trigger a physiological reaction in your body. Bodily tensions and sensations have more of an impact on your thought and behaviour than you might think. The model below (see Figure 5-1) can help you understand what's going on and stop yourself spiralling into over-thinking, anxiety and distraction.

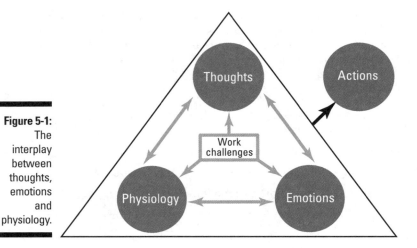

Figure 5-1:
The interplay between thoughts, emotions and physiology.

When you understand the link between thoughts, emotions and the body (physiology), you can start to develop more helpful strategies for recognising and managing your emotions.

Mindfulness can help you to better manage your emotions in three important ways:

- ✔ **Mindfulness helps you to train your brain to treat thoughts as 'mental processes' rather than reality.** This change can stop you responding on auto-pilot, triggering a physiological reaction in your body and sending you spiralling further and further into the unwanted emotion.

- ✔ **Mindfulness helps you to live your life in the present moment.** It reduces your tendency to try to anticipate the future ('This could damage my reputation') or link to past experiences ('At my last company people were fired for less!'). Focusing on the present helps you to notice, manage and process emotions.

- ✔ **Mindfulness helps you to accept emotions.** Accept the fact that you're human, and from time to time will be sad, anxious or angry – being so is natural and part of being human. You need to acknowledge the emotion, but not dwell on it, or add further fuel to the fire. Mindfulness encourages self-compassion and acceptance – being kind to oneself. By accepting things as they are, right here, right now, you don't perpetuate unhelpful emotional reactions to circumstances.

Trying the 'Managing emotions mindfully' exercise

This exercise helps you slow down your mental chatter and reconnect with your body. When practised regularly, you'll be quicker at detecting emotions as they arise and able to take steps to stop them escalating if they're unhelpful.

Go to a quiet place for between 5 and 30 minutes (depending on how emotional you are and how much time you have!). Sit in a comfortable upright position with your feet firmly on the floor. Now follow these steps:

1. **Focus on air entering your lungs on the in-breath, and leaving your lungs on the out-breath.** Observe how your chest feels and how your skin feels as you breathe.

2. **Observe any emotions you are experiencing.** For example, anger, fear or worry. Just observe – don't try to fix them or make them go away

3. **Acknowledge the noises that surround you.** Sounds in the room, sounds outside the room, and sounds elsewhere in the building or outside. Possibly even sounds in your body. Use these sounds as an anchor for your attention. Again no need to fix them or make them go away – just notice they are there.

4. **Check how your body feels at this moment in time by carrying out a body scan.** Start at your toes. Can you feel any sensations or stiffness? Continue the exercise by slowly moving up your body. If you do detect tension or discomfort, pause for a short while, and try releasing the tension progressively as you breathe out. Continue your body scan, exploring any bodily tensions or sensations until you've scanned from the tip of your toes to the crown of your head.

5. **Observe your emotions again.** Kindly and gently direct your attention to your emotions. Notice how they are in the present moment. Are they the same as before or different? If so, what has changed? When you're ready, open your eyes.

Your thoughts trigger both physiological and emotional responses to your experiences in life (see Figure 5-1 earlier in the chapter). These responses may be unhelpful, as you (often unconsciously) may draw the wrong conclusions and make things worse. The more tense your body is or the faster your heart is beating, the more likely you are to experience panic-induced defective negative thinking. Mindfulness practices like the one described above help you to stop this downward spiral, reducing mental churn and helping you see things more clearly. You discover that your present moment reality is often vastly different from your mental image of it. You train your brain to approach life with a kindly curiosity, rather than working in avoidance mode.

Dealing with difficult people

In your home and social life, you usually get to choose the people you wish to spend time with. In a work situation, that's often not the case. You encounter both clients and colleagues who you may find difficult to deal with. Working with difficult people can trigger strong emotional reactions, which can take up a lot of your mental energy, robbing you of the mental resources you need to deal with your workload.

Mindfulness can help you to respond to these situations in a more resilient manner.

Asking 'What's really going on?'

The first thing to explore is what's really going on. Why do you find this person so difficult or challenging? You need to recognise what responses have been triggered within you when you encounter this person. What are your thoughts . . . emotions . . . what has changed in your body . . . has your heart-rate or breathing increased? Are you feeling tension or even pain?

By recognising your own emotional state, and bodily tension you will be better equipped to deal with the situation. When approaching encounters with difficult people mindfully, you can reduce the pain and suffering for all concerned, and find ways to work together more productively.

You can't always control the things that happen in your work day, but you can choose how you respond to them.

Understanding whose problem it is

The next thing to ask is 'Whose problem is it?'

Consider Bob, the account manager described earlier in the chapter. Well, Bob's boss saw his potential and in his appraisal set him challenging goals in an effort to prepare him for a possible promotion. Bob did not know his boss was preparing him for promotion. He thought that his boss had set him up to fail and that his appraisal goals were an attempt to get rid of him. As a result, he started to hate his boss.

What can you learn from this scenario? Bob's failure to clarify why his boss had set him the goals made him jump to the wrong conclusions. His reaction to, and behaviour towards, his boss was making the situation worse.

When dealing with a person you find difficult, take a few moments to think about whose problem it is. Is it your problem? Or is it the other person who has a problem with you?

Thoughts are not necessarily facts! Drawing conclusions based on thoughts rather than facts is all too easy.

Bob's colleague encourages him to take a more mindful approach in future. In preparation for meeting his boss, Bob took a few minutes to practice some mindfulness. When Bob next met his boss, he started with a clean slate. He admitted that he's finding the goals he was set challenging. His boss laughed and said, 'They're supposed to be challenging. I set them to help you get ready for your next promotion!'

By practising mindfulness, Bob discovered that his thoughts are not all facts, and decided to start afresh with his boss. He knew he'd be tense upon entering the meeting, so he practised a little mindfulness to put himself in a more open frame of mind.

Bear these tips in mind:

- ✔ When preparing for a difficult encounter, practise mindfulness. Doing so stops your thoughts churning and releases any tension you're holding.

- ✔ Start the encounter with an open mind, as if you're meeting the person for the first time.

- ✔ If you feel your body tensing up during the meeting, or you start to become emotional, congratulate yourself on recognising that fact, and try to let go of the tension.

- ✔ After the meeting, spend a few moments reflecting on what, if anything was different about this encounter with the person.

The 'difficult' person may be creating the problem despite your best efforts to work productively with them. Treat this thought as a theory only; remember, this thought is not necessarily a fact! You cannot easily change the other person's behaviour and attitude towards you, but you can choose your response and behaviour.

If, despite your best efforts, your working relationship doesn't improve, just accept that you find this person difficult to work with and commit to making a conscious effort not to make things any worse. Use mindfulness to help you recognise and release any physical tension. Become conscious of your own emotional state. Recognise when thoughts start to spiral, and bring yourself back to the present moment. Mentally reward yourself for being more aware of what's going on, and taking steps to make the best of it.

No magic bullet or cure-all exists. You're not a machine; you're human and as such you will from time to time experience unhelpful emotions which impact on your relationships. Living your whole life in a relaxed, emotionless manner is unnatural. But living in a constantly heightened state of arousal is unhealthy and unproductive. Practising mindfulness gradually trains your brain to come back to the present moment and see things as they really are. Then you can break out of life on auto-pilot and respond to life's challenges (such as difficult people) wisely.

Mindful Ways to Maintain Peak Performance

Some people think that practising mindfulness will subdue you or make you less ambitious and driven. This is a myth. Some of the most productive people on this planet practise mindfulness because it helps them maintain peak performance for longer periods.

Some people joke that mindfulness is about doing nothing! MRI brain scans show that whilst practising mindfulness brain areas associated with attention become more active, rather than less.

Maintaining peak performance

Current thought on the psychology of performance suggests that in order to maintain peak performance you need to focus upon the factors that allow you to flourish and to achieve your aims. To do so, you need to practise mental skills to develop the power of your mind. Assuming that you're clear about your aims at work, you need to be mentally and physically fit to perform at your best. Don't worry; taking up marathon running or joining MENSA won't be necessary! You just need to work out what 'peak performance' looks and feels like for you. The Yerkes–Dodson curve is a really useful model for assessing this.

Introducing the Yerkes–Dodson curve

From a productivity perspective, you need some pressure (arousal) in order to perform. Put crudely, you need a reason for getting out of bed every morning. When you experience too much pressure that you become stressed, your worry increases and you may even start to panic. As a result, your performance drops off. This situation is illustrated by the Yerkes–Dodson curve (see Figure 5-2).

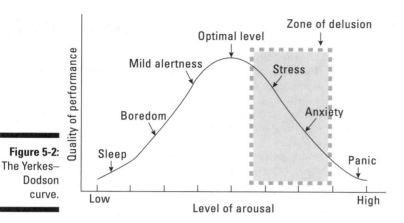

Figure 5-2:
The Yerkes–
Dodson
curve.

In order to maintain peak performance you need to recognise the point at which you slip down from Optimal and enter the 'Zone of delusion'. The more you try to push through stress and anxiety to get the job done, the more your performance drops off. In this deluded state you think you are getting things done, but actually you are achieving very little due to mistakes and your mind wandering. The more you try to push on, the further you slip down the curve, and the more your performance reduces.

Mindfulness helps you to recognise the critical point when your performance is dropping off. Recognising this fast means that it's possible to take a few quick actions to refresh yourself, and regain optimal performance. The further down the curve you descend, the more time and effort is required to regain your productivity. The earlier you notice, the less time it will take you to regain peak productivity.

Your personal Yerkes–Dodson curve

Spend a little time working out what your personal Yerkes–Dodson curve looks like. When you next find yourself 'in the flow', working and getting things done with ease, spend a few moments reflecting on how you got to this point. Did you reach peak performance quickly or was it a slow process? Use your mindful awareness to make a mental note of how your body feels. Repeat this exercise when you're feeling overwhelmed, stressed or downright panicked. How did you reach this point? What level of work are you capable of producing at this moment in time? How does your body feel – any aches or pains? How are your breathing and heart rate?

By establishing these reference points combined with simple mindfulness exercises, you can maintain peak performance for longer without sacrificing your health or mental well-being.

Using mindfulness to enhance productivity

Although it may seem counter-intuitive to stop and 'do nothing' when you're busy trying to meet a deadline, spending a few moments doing so can save you time and make you more productive. Regular mindfulness practice stops pressure and tension building up. Practice also helps you train your brain to deal with things that arise in a more productive manner – preventing them from unconsciously escalating or becoming something that they're not.

The simple 'Mindfulness for peak performance' exercise below takes only moments, but can save you hours of time wasted through working in a distracted, pressured manner. You could do this in a few minutes, or extend it if you have more time. To go with it, there's an audio track, Track 5, which you can download from www.dummies.com/go/mindfulnessatworkuk.

1. **Settle** yourself in a chair. Sitting in a comfortable upright, dignified position with your feet firmly on the floor and your arms resting comfortably. Focus on the physical sensations of taking a few breaths. Close your eyes or hold them in soft focus.

2. **Acknowledge what's going on in your mind (**your thoughts) in a detached manner, rather like watching the closing credits of a film.

3. **Observe how your body is feeling in this present moment.** Tune into any areas where you know you tend to hold tension. (For example your neck, shoulders, jaw or stomach). Approach them - exploring how they feel, like a scientist observing the subject of a research study. See whether you can release the tension and let it go. Don't beat yourself up if you can't.

4. **Ask yourself**, 'At this moment, what do I need to do to return to peak performance?' Listen for a response. Maybe you need to actively release the tension from your body, take a quick walk (even if just to the coffee machine) or work on something different for a while.

Use this technique to check in with yourself on a regular basis. When practised regularly, you'll quickly recognise the physical and mental signs telling you you've slipped from peak performance.

Being in the moment

Although you may think you are always in control, and fully aware of everything that goes on, in reality you are probably not. Your brain will decide what it thinks is important and focus on just that, missing the bigger picture. This is compounded by the fact that we spend very little time in the present.

Your mind wanders back to old memories and experiences in an effort to help you make sense of what's going on. It also spends a lot of time in the future, trying to anticipate what will happen next. As a result we are rarely in the present.

Mindfulness helps you to train your brain to be in the present moment. Stopping yourself from trying to anticipate the future and making decisions on auto-pilot makes your life easier and reduces self-induced tension.

An excellent way to improve your working life is to consciously make an effort to live more in the present moment. By being in the moment you make better decisions, see things more clearly and become more creative. You can enjoy precious everyday moments with your loved ones, and gain nourishment from the simplest of everyday things.

Being Kind to Yourself

The author Henry James said: 'Three things in human life are important. The first is to be kind. The second is to be kind. And the third is to be kind.'

Authentic leadership, resonant leadership and mindful leadership are new forms of leadership theory. They all emphasise the need to be kind to yourself, and with good reason. Research shows that people who make a conscious effort to be kind to themselves demonstrate greater well-being than those who judge themselves.

When something goes wrong, or you make a mistake, you may be far too quick pointing the finger of blame at yourself. As humans we tend to beat ourselves up for all failures, large or small, reducing our self-belief and self-esteem. You may unconsciously poison yourself with toxic self-criticism. In an attempt to anticipate the future, you may make up your own stories and then react to them as if they were reality. Doing so can lead you into a spiral of depression or anxiety.

By being kind to yourself, you can increase your personal resilience to the pressures of life by stopping your brain from jumping to conclusions and spiralling into stress and panic. In turn, you'll increase your happiness and productivity.

Kindness is on the syllabus

Until recently, there were few if any books on leadership, management and general workplace productivity that talked about the importance of kindness and self-compassion. In the 1920s and 1930s, *trait* theories asserted that leaders are born. In the 1940s to the 1960s, *behavioural* theories proclaimed that leadership is a set of behaviours that can be taught. In the 1980s, *contingency* theories proposed that leadership styles and actions are contingent on the situation. In parallel to contingency theory, in the 1980s and 1990s, *transformational* theories saw the leader as a change agent.

From 2001 onwards, *human potential* theories (incorporating authentic leadership, resonant leadership, mindful leadership and neuro-leadership) have shifted leadership development away from a focus on striving to live up to a set of leadership ideals to harnessing each leader's unique capabilities, encouraging them to be the best leader they can be while remaining true to their values and ideals.

Mindfulness has now moved from the margins to the mainstream. Mindfulness is a key element of all leadership theories based on human potential, and universities across the world are now incorporating mindfulness into their MBAs and leadership programmes. Despite this, many leaders still regard self-kindness as an alien concept within the workplace. Sound business reasons exist for why all employees should be encouraged to be kinder to themselves.

If you, like many other people, struggle with self-kindness, try the 'Cultivating kindness' exercise. There's an accompanying audio track, Track 6 at www. dummies.com/go/mindfulnessatworkuk. You may find it challenging at first, but it gets easier with practice. Follow these steps:

- ✔ **Settle yourself into a comfortable, upright, dignified position, and focus your attention on your breathing for a minute or so.**

- ✔ **Send yourself some kindness.** Imagine giving yourself a hug and accepting yourself exactly as you are – perfect in your human imperfection. Picture yourself surrounded by a warm glow of kindness.

- ✔ **Send some kindness to a dear friend.** Thank them for their friendship and support. Wish them well and imagine them surrounded by a warm glow of kindness.

- ✔ **Send some kindness to a neutral person – someone you've never met.** Wish them a happy life and send them kind thoughts. Imagine them surrounded by a warm glow of kindness.

- ✔ **Send some kindness to a hostile person – someone who you may have argued with or who makes you feel uncomfortable.** Wish them a happy life and send them kind thoughts. Imagine them surrounded by a warm glow of kindness.

Just imagining being kind releases oxytocin (a hormone associated with love) into your bloodstream. By thinking about being kind to people you find difficult, you can reduce the activation of your sympathetic nervous system (which responds to threat), and stop yourself responding on auto-pilot. You can then choose a better response to the situation.

Discovering the Neuroscience of Kindness and compassion

Fear can trigger a threat response in your brain. Your reaction is often disproportionate to the actual provocation. When in the grip of this strong emotion, your capacity for higher 'rational brain' thinking is diminished, and you're likely to revert to rote behaviours stored in the more primitive areas of your brain.

When you're kind to yourself, and accept yourself as human, prone to making mistakes from time to time, but doing your best, you're far less likely to trigger your threat system unnecessarily. Self-kindness can help you to enjoy life more, improve your relationships, increase your self-esteem and make you feel happier. All these things are likely to contribute to improved performance at work.

According to psychologist Kristin Neff, self-kindness 'means that we stop the constant self-judgement and disparaging internal commentary that most of us have come to see as normal'.

Try the 'Experiencing self-kindness' exercise. When you're upset, give yourself a hug, place your hand on your heart or gently rock your body. Your body responds to the physical warmth and care (just imagining a hug works in a similar way, too.) Hugging yourself has soothing benefits. Research indicates that physical touch releases oxytocin in your brain – the hormone associated with love and bonding. Oxytocin provides a sense of security soothes distressing emotions and calms cardiovascular stress.

Switching off your threat system

Kindness and compassion have an interesting impact on the brain.

Recent research utilised a MRI brain scanner to explore the areas of the brain that are activated when a person feels threatened. A volunteer was placed in the scanner and shown images that they found personally threatening. The brain scanner showed the brain circuits associated with threat lighting up exactly as predicted. Suddenly something unexpected happened. The areas of the volunteer's brain associated with threat reactivity stopped being activated. The disturbing images were still being shown, but were not having the expected impact on the volunteer's brain.

After the volunteer was removed from the scanner, researchers asked her what had happened. She explained that after a while the images became too disturbing for her, so she practised a self-kindness exercise that she'd been taught.

Until this point, it was thought that nothing completely shut off the human brain's threat system; that it was permanently on, scanning the horizon for threats and potential problems at all times. This research suggests that self-kindness can switch off the human threat system – a potentially useful discovery.

Rewiring your brain

The more you repeat a thought or activity, the more you strengthen the neural pathway associated with that specific thought or activity in your brain. The stronger the neural connection, the easier it is to repeat. Many thoughts and activities, when repeated often enough, become stored in the more primitive areas of your brain as 'habits' – things you do without thinking. Opinion is divided about how long it takes to form a habit. Estimates range from an average of 21 to 64 days.

By consciously making an effort to catch yourself when you're being overly self-critical, and accepting things as they are, over time you can rewire your brain to become more kind to yourself. Mindfulness exercises always include elements of self-kindness.

The cultivation of self-kindness is something that many people struggle with, finding it easier to be kind to someone else than themselves. Self-kindness and acceptance are important elements of mindfulness. By learning to accept yourself, faults and all, an enormous, self-imposed burden is lifted and life becomes easier. Practising self-kindness significantly increases your resilience at work.

Last, but by no means least . . .

It goes without saying that the healthier and happier you are the more resilient you will be. Be kind to yourself! Eat well, drink enough water and don't forget to get some exercise in.

Stop for lunch and spend a few moments in the present moment, fully appreciating the act of eating – the flavour, the texture, the taste – and how it feels to eat.

If you can, park a little further away to get a short walk each day. Take the stairs not the lift. At the very least get up and stretch at your desk every hour.

Your body will thank you for it, and your boss should appreciate the positive impact of your improved resilience.

Chapter 6

Discovering Mindfulness At Work Training

*T*o help you develop greater mindfulness in the workplace, we've developed a do-it-yourself version of our Mindfulness At Work Training (MAWT) course. This chapter and Chapter 7 take you through the basics of this five-week programme. You discover the core essentials of developing a more mindful approach to life's challenges and pressures in a way that's directly applicable to the workplace.

If you'd like us to deliver this programme in your workplace or offer to staff online, visit our website at `http://mawt.co.uk`

Introducing MAWT

MAWT is intended as a short introduction to mindful working practices that you can embed into your working day. MAWT has two parts: core training and work essentials.

As with all mindfulness training, MAWT is not something you can just read about and instantly you will become mindful – it takes time and repeated practice to develop. The time commitment is not great – with 15 minutes practice each day for five weeks you should notice some positive changes.

If you are experiencing acute mental distress, this course will probably not be right for you. See your doctor who will refer you to the best source of advice for you. If that doesn't help consider a course in MBCT or MBSR specifically for your condition.

Throughout the five week course you will be asked to actively participate. Each activity is clearly labelled with 'MAWT Activity'. Some activities involve thinking or reflection; others (such as practising mindfulness) are more experiential. Don't be tempted to skip these – they are important parts of the learning. You will need a notebook or journal to write in during the course. I (Juliet) treat myself to attractively bound tactile notebooks as I find them more pleasurable to write in – but any old note book, or even loose paper will do.

Getting ready

In this chapter you find the core training elements:

- ✔ **Week 1: Understanding mindfulness at work:** What mindfulness is and the science behind it. You start to recognise and step away from auto-pilot and begin embedding the core skills of mindful working.
- ✔ **Week 2: Working with the body in mind:** The interconnection between thoughts, emotions and physiology. You discover how the body controls the mind start to develop practices to improve your well-being and resilience.

In Chapter 7 you build on your core training to develop specific mindful working practices such as mindful communication, dealing with difficult people and strong emotions, and working in times of change. You also develop strategies to embed mindful working practices into your everyday working life that you can use for years to come.

MAWT is all about increasing your resilience to work's trials and pressures. Each week is designed to develop your resilience further, so resilience appears as a key element in each and every week's training.

Identifying the outcomes you desire

Before you start your MAWT studies, you need to ask yourself 'What am I seeking to achieve?' and 'What would I like to be different at the end of this course?'

If you're just looking for hints and tips on how to apply mindfulness to your working life, reading all or parts of the chapters in this book will suffice. The MAWT course set out in this chapter and Chapter 7 is written specifically to help people who are committed to developing new approaches to their work and to practising new skills that actively help them rewire certain areas of their brain.

Consider what you want to achieve. Maybe you want to reduce your levels of stress, keep calmer or stop thoughts whirring around your head so fast. You may want to improve your relations with colleagues or deal with a difficult person at work. Maybe you want to increase your concentration or develop a sense of well-being. Give this some thought.

Write down what you want to achieve in your journal. You can re-visit it later to review and keep your learning on track.

Considering alternatives to self-study

Before starting this course, remember that self-study based on a book isn't for everyone. Some people are happiest studying by themselves, while others benefit from having a group around them. Some people need to know the theory before giving practical things a try, while others like to dive straight in to trying out new ways of doing things.

Mindfulness can be a tricky subject to get your head round at first. Many things you're asked to do may be counter-intuitive or different to how you'd normally approach things. When you're new to mindfulness, you may find that you get things wrong and go off at a tangent. Discussion and exploration are a really important part of the learning process during the eight-week MBSR and MBCT courses. If you decide you want to embed mindfulness into your life at a deeper level, you may prefer to attend a taught course that gives you the opportunity to discuss and check your understanding, and get support if you're struggling with anything.

The lessons contained in these two chapters have been adapted to meet the needs of the modern-day workplace and solo student. They help you get started and experience a more mindful way of working. We suggest that you try to complete all the activities in this chapter and Chapter 7, as these form an important part of your study.

MAWT Part 1: Core Training

This section gives you the lowdown on what MAWT involves, how to prepare for it and what you can expect to achieve through it.

Preparing for MAWT

Before you start week 1 of the course, you need to do a few important things. First, you need to set a benchmark to measure your progress.

- **Spelling out what you hope to gain from the course:** List in your journal the three key things you hope to gain from the course.

- **Specifying what motivated you to pick up this book and commit to the course:** List in your journal what motivates you to commit to this course.

- **Identifying your current level of mindfulness:** Read the statements in Table 6-1 and rate each item as follows: 1 = almost always, 2 = very frequently, 3 = somewhat frequently, 4 = somewhat infrequently, 5 = very infrequently, 6 = almost never. Write your responses in your journal.

Table 6-1	Testing Your Current Level of Mindfulness with the Mindfulness Awareness Scale (Adapted from Brown and Ryan, 2003)	
1. At work I sometimes experience emotions that I am not aware of until later.	
2. At work I find it difficult to stay focused on what's happening in the present moment.	
3. When walking to or from work, around my workplace or out to lunch, I tend to walk quickly to where I'm going without paying attention to what I experience along the way.	
4. At work I often get so wrapped up in the goal I want to achieve that I lose touch with what's going on all around me and what I am doing right now.	
5. At work I tend not to notice feelings of physical tension or discomfort until they really grab my attention.	
6. At work I frequently run on 'auto-pilot' without much awareness of what I'm doing.	
7. At work I often rush through work activities without really paying them much attention.	
8. At work I often find myself listening to someone with one ear, while trying to do something else at the same time.	
9. At work I often find that my mind drifts off to consider things that may happen at work in the weeks or years to come or things that have happened at work in the past.	
10. At work I often find myself snacking on the job without being aware that I'm eating.	

Now add up your score. The lower the score, the less mindful you are.

- ✔ 10–20 = low
- ✔ 20–40 = moderate
- ✔ 40–50 = good
- ✔ 50–60 = excellent

If your score is low, that's fine – this MAWT course can help you improve this score. If your score is higher, there's always room for improvement. Try taking this test at the end of the course to see what's changed.

Assessing your current level of resilience

Next, you need to look at your resilience. Read the statements in Table 6-2 and rate each item as follows: 1 = strongly agree, 2 = agree, 3 = disagree, 4 = strongly disagree.

Table 6-2	Testing Your Current Level of Resilience
1. At work I'm a pessimist – I look out for hidden horrors lurking around each corner	
2. At work I struggle to make decisions or decide what to do next.	
3. At work I never ask my colleagues when I need help. What would they think of me?	
4. At work I struggle to put things into perspective and see the 'big picture'. I suffer from tunnel vision.	
5. When I have a big disappointment at work (such as being overlooked for promotion), I tend to feel bad and dwell on it for a long time.	
6. I work long hours, don't exercise and often find myself eating at my desk as I work through breaks.	
7. My life is dominated by my work. I rarely find time to do things that nourish me and make me feel good.	
8. I am fed up with constant change at work. Why can't things stay the way they are?	
9. At work I when things go wrong I avoid taking the blame – I may be considered incompetent if I admit to making a mistake	
10. At work little things grind me down.	

Now add up your score. The lower the score, the less resilient you are.

- 0–14 = low
- 15–26 = reasonable
- 27+ = good

If your score is low, don't worry. You'll steadily improve as you work through the MAWT activities.

Now you need to set aims for your study. In your journal, write three things you'd like to be different when you've completed the course; for example, 'I would like to be able to better focus on my work and to cut out distractions' or 'I would like to be able to cope better with all the changes going on around me at work'.

Week 1: Understanding mindfulness at work

Have you jumped straight to the 'Learning to be mindful at work' part of this book without reading any of the rest of it? Don't worry; you're not alone! If you have time, you will, however, benefit from reading Part I of the book, but if you're in a hurry, here' a summary of the basics.

Try to work through this course *one week at a time*. Avoid the temptation to jump ahead. Read and work through the teaching in each week, then experiment with and practise the techniques for a full week before moving on to the nest week

Debunking myths about mindfulness

- Mindfulness isn't a religion. You don't have to light incense, chant, become a monk or sit on top of a mountain (unless you want to!). You also don't need to sit in uncomfortable positions on the floor – a chair is fine.

- Mindfulness at work training isn't a therapy. If you want mindfulness-based therapy, consider an MBCT course or ACT, taught by a qualified psychotherapist as a therapeutic intervention.

- Mindfulness isn't all about relaxation. Mindfulness trains the brain to pay attention and can be hard work. Relaxation may or may not result and that's okay.

- Mindfulness isn't about suppressing your thoughts or blanking your mind. Mindfulness is about observing your thoughts, acknowledging them and choosing how you respond to them.

✔ Mindfulness isn't about thinking only positive thoughts. Part of mindfulness training is about teaching people to approach and re-examine things they find difficult.

✔ Mindfulness isn't about running away from reality. Mindfulness is about seeing clearly exactly what's going on in the present moment.

Mindfulness is all about training your brain to become more aware of what is happening as it is happening. It cultivates awareness of your thoughts, emotions and body, and the interplay between them, as shown in Figure 6-1. Mindfulness is experiencing the present moment openly and curiously without judging it as good or bad or trying to categorise it.

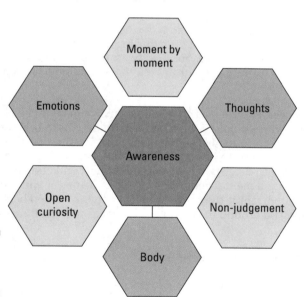

Figure 6-1:
What mind-
fulness is.

Mindfulness has been the subject of thousands of research papers. MRI brain scans have shown that as little as eight weeks of mindfulness training can improve the brain's wiring. It can lead to increased grey matter concentration in brain regions involved in learning and memory processes, emotion regulation, self-referential processing and perspective taking. Mindfulness also improves focus, concentration and decision making.

Recognising the benefits of mindfulness at work

In the modern-day workplace, change is the norm. Change of course is nothing new, but what is new is that the pace of change is increasing. Many workers are becoming stressed as a result of increasing demands, reduced time in which to get results and uncertainty about the future.

Work-related stress is a person's adverse reaction to excessive pressures or other types of demand placed on them at work. Stress is a good thing – in the right circumstances. Our ancient ancestors needed this stress reaction to escape from life-threatening situations such as being chased by a wild animal. When they encountered something dangerous, their threat system released powerful hormones designed to help them evade danger. After the danger had passed, their system returned to normal.

The problem is that nowadays most employees are not in danger of losing their lives, but their body reacts to workplace threats such as a critical boss or fear of looking stupid in front of work mates in exactly the same way. Remaining in this state of heightened arousal for long periods can have a huge impact on human bodies ranging from indigestion and sleep problems to cancer and death. In many countries, stress is now the most common cause of long-term absence from work. A high percentage of staff report that their jobs are highly stressful. Remaining in a stressed state not only hurts your well-being, it also has a huge impact on your work performance. In this emergency state, your brain devotes its energy to carrying out only essential tasks. Your body stops replacing brain cells and diverts energy away from higher- brain activity such as decision making, prioritising and strategy.

What employees need in order to thrive in this environment is the ability to detect stress and diffuse it before it becomes harmful to both their health and productivity. They need to recognise the point at which their performance is dropping off and take steps to bring themselves back to peak performance. They need to be able to deal effectively with multiple, conflicting demands. They need to develop a mental mind-set that can cope better with uncertainty. Lastly, but most importantly, they need to be able to take a step back from all the busyness going on around them and see things as they really are – in the present moment.

Mindfulness can assist with all these things.

Research concludes that mindfulness at work can:

- ✔ Help employees develop positive strategies for dealing with highly stressful environments and work pressures

- ✔ Enable employees to deal better with complexity

- ✔ Enhance employee self-regulation of thoughts, emotions and behaviours and make them more resilient when facing of challenges

- ✔ Improve task performance

John, a project manager working for a multinational company, decided to go on a mindfulness course I (Juliet) was teaching because he was struggling to meet work demands and was worried that his performance was suffering. In his workplace, change was the norm and things seemed to be changing all the time. During one eight-month project his line manager had changed twice and the division he worked for had been amalgamated with another. John said, 'Trying to deliver this project on time and on budget is hard enough without having to worry about whether I'll have a job next week or getting to grips with new managers. I've managed many projects over the years, often in difficult circumstances, but have never found it as hard as I'm finding it now. I always regarded myself as someone who was highly flexible and able to work with change and uncertainty, but now I'm starting to doubt myself and my capabilities.'

John isn't alone. Many things can make us feel stressed or under pressure at work. Pressure may be caused by change, difficult relationships, over- or under-stretching job roles, excessive demands, a lack of control over work and insufficient support and guidance from colleagues and superiors.

Some things in life you can change and others you can't. What you can change is the way you respond to them. Victor Frankl was an Austrian neurologist and psychiatrist who survived the Holocaust in the Second World War. In his book, *Man's Search for Reason*, he said, 'Everything can be taken from a man but one thing: the last of the human freedoms – to choose one's attitude in any given set of circumstances, to choose one's own way.'

While you can't argue with this statement, you may find it hard to put into action. To be able to choose your attitude and response to what life throws at you, you need to be aware of what's going on in your head and body. What you may not realise is that your thoughts and emotions have a tangible impact on your body. Your body also has an unconscious impact on your thoughts.

Mindfulness shows you how to progressively become more aware of your thoughts, emotions and body. By developing this skill, you can choose how you respond to challenges at work rather than responding on auto-pilot based on outdated mental programming and habits developed over the years. Now you need to put this into practice.

1.1: Mindful eating

Find a place where you have some privacy and can observe what's going on without being disturbed or concerned about people walking in on you mid-exercise.

Select something you like to eat or, if you want to make it more challenging, something you don't like eating! If the item is large, such as an apple, sandwich or chocolate bar, break off a small piece. If the item needs peeling before eating, do so now. If your food item has pips, make sure that the piece you break off has no pips. Now follow these steps:

1. **Hold the item.** Imagine that you've never held one before. ? Is it heavy or light? Spend a few moments considering its weight.

2. **Look at the item.** What do you see? What colours does it contain? Is it shiny or smooth? Try to spot details that you haven't noticed before.

3. **Touch the item.** Is it hard or soft? Is the surface textured? Does it feel any different if you touch it with your lips? Spend a few moments exploring how it feels, as if you've never touched one before.

4. **Smell the item.** How does it smell? Can you identify different smells or just one smell? Is it a strong smell or a weak smell? Does it have no smell at all?

5. **Put the item in your mouth.** Avoid the temptation to chew or swallow. How does it feel to have this piece of food sitting on your tongue? Are you aware of any sensations in your mouth?

6. **Chew the item.** Observe how the texture changes as you chew. Can you identify different flavours and sensations in your mouth? Spend a few moments longer than normal, just chewing.

7. **Swallow the item.** Feel the sensation of the food going down your throat towards your stomach. Be aware of any sensations that arise in your mouth and throat.

8. **Identify any remaining sensations.** Are you aware of any lingering flavours? Are your lips tingling? What are you thinking about?

Mindful eating reflection

Spend some time reflecting on this activity. Note down your reflections in your journal. Use these questions as a prompt.

- ✔ How did you feel while you were doing that activity?

- ✔ When was the last time you paid that amount of conscious attention to something you were doing?

- ✔ How was your eating experience changed by the simple action of focusing on it?

- ✔ Did you experience anything that surprised you?

- ✔ In what ways was this experience of eating this particular item different from experiences of eating similar items in the past?

- ✔ Can you make any other observations about this experience?

Mindful eating key learning points

The mindful eating exercise shows you that:

- A simple everyday experience like eating can be transformed by focusing on it.

- You spend a great deal of your life on auto-pilot.

- Your perception of what's going on may be very different from present moment reality

- You can start to train your brain to notice what's actually happening in the present moment.

When John did this exercise he said, 'I felt really silly at first. I used a segment of orange and ate it during my lunch-break. I was surprised that the orange tasted so sharp and sweet at the same time. It made my lips tingle and I started to salivate while I delayed swallowing it. It really shocked me to I realise how little I notice about what's going on in the present moment. It made me smile to think that some days I am so engrossed in my work that a gorilla could walk through the room and I wouldn't notice!'

Were your experiences of mindful eating similar or different to John's?

Working out whether you're conscious or unconscious at work

Most people think they are always fully conscious and in control of their actions. How much of your work day do you think you are you fully conscious of what you're doing? Scientists were asked a similar question in a recent TV documentary. None of the scientists came up with a definitive answer but they did all agree that what the brain is conscious of on a day-to-day basis is tiny in comparison to unconscious activity. Automatic processes are good in many respects. Think about how difficult life would be if you had to consciously remember to breathe, if you had to think hard every time you wanted your fingers to type on a computer keyboard or had to consciously tell your body how to digest food!

Routine tasks such as breathing, digestion and walking are stored in the more primitive areas of the brain. Skills we pick up such as using a computer keyboard or driving are also stored in the basal ganglia, our habit centre. Most activities stored in this area are carried out unconsciously.

The brain can only consciously focus on one thing at a time. If you try to juggle too many things simultaneously, some get stuck in the bottleneck of your short-term memory, called 'working memory'. You can extend the working memory by using auto-pilot habits – habits take less brain power and virtually no awareness.

While working on auto-pilot is wholly necessary for many things your body does, it can also cause problems. The human brain is pre-programmed to minimise threats and maximise rewards. In work terms, threats can be fear for your job, status or position. At work, your brain is constantly scanning for things you find threatening or think may be harmful to you. You're likely to respond to these threats on auto-pilot, unconsciously, based on past experiences and what you think may happen in the future.

Relying on auto-pilot can result in you blowing things out of proportion and getting stressed and tense about things that are only going on in your head; even though they haven't actually happened, they're just thoughts. Remaining in a heightened state of arousal (stress) is seriously bad for your health and over time reduces your ability to tap into higher-brain functions.

The more pressure you're under, the more negative you may feel. Negative thoughts and feelings amplify emotions and trigger more auto-pilot responses to things in life.

Mindfulness helps you close down some of these mental programmes that you've left open and running in the back of your mind. To develop mindfulness, you first need to be able to focus on one thing at a time.

Training your attention

One of the core skills of mindfulness is being able to direct your attention at will to where you want it to be. Sounds easy? Most people find this simple task really difficult at first.

The exercise below uses the breath as an anchor point on which to focus your attention. The reason we use breath is that breath is universal – everyone breathes! In this exercise, make sure that you do not try to *control* your breath - just *observe* it.

The exercise isn't about relaxing (although many people do find it so). Rather, the exercise is about 'falling awake' – becoming more aware of what's happening in your mind. Think of yourself as a kind scientist, inquisitively observing everything that's going on without judging or categorising it.

Find somewhere quiet where you won't be disturbed. You can try it on the train or bus home, in your lunch break (if you have your own office and can place a 'Do not disturb' sign on the door) or at home. If you can, listen to Track 7 of the audio downloads available at www.dummies.com/go/mindfulnessatworkuk, which guides you through the exercise. Alternatively, read the instructions below, set a timer for 10–15 minutes, and guide yourself through the exercise. If possible, select a gentle alarm tone so that you don't jump out of your seat at the end of the exercise.

1.2: Mindfulness of breath

1. **Settle yourself in a chair where you can sit in a comfortable upright position.** Both feet should be firmly planted on the floor, your shoulders relaxed and your head facing forward.

2. **Pay attention to the contact points between your body and the chair and floor.** Spend a few minutes exploring how your feet, legs, bottom and any other areas in contact with the chair and floor feel.

3. **Notice how feelings arise and disappear.** If you notice nothing, that's perfectly fine. The important thing is checking in with yourself and just observing what's there.

4. **Now focus your attention on your breathing.** Notice how your chest and abdomen feel as the breath enters, pauses and leaves your body. Observe how the air feels as it enters your nostrils, and leaves them.

   This exercise isn't about controlling your breath. No right or wrong way exists. Just observe what's happening right here, right now without judgement.

   If your mind wanders, that's fine – minds do wander! Give yourself a pat on the back for having recognised that your mind's wandered and bring your attention back to where you want it to be. It doesn't matter if your mind wanders 100 times; the act of recognising that your mind has wandered and bringing it back is what's important.

5. **Continue to use your breath as anchor within you for as long as you have time.** When your timer sounds, gently stretch your fingers and toes, and open your eyes, ready to start work again.

The science behind mindfulness of breath

Breathing calmly and gently activates the calming branch of your autonomic nervous system, the parasympathetic branch. The sympathetic nervous system modulates the bodies fight or flight response that arises when you feel threatened or agitated.

The simple act of your mind wandering, you recognising that it's wandered and then bringing your attention back to where you want it to be forms new neural connections in your brain. Every time you go through this process, you reinforce these neural pathways and make it easier to do the next time.

Practising exercises like mindfulness of breath for as little as eight weeks has been proven to thicken the parts of the brain's cerebral cortex responsible for decision making, attention and memory.

Mindful breathing reflection

Reflect on the following questions, and write your reflections in your journal:

- ✔ How hard did you find it to remain focused on your body or your breath?
- ✔ How many times did you need to bring your attention back?
- ✔ Did you find yourself at any time making judgements about your experiences or being self-critical?
- ✔ Can you make any other observations about this experience?

Mindfulness of breath key learning points

Practising mindfulness of breath regularly is important. The exercise helps you to cultivate the ability to disengage from auto-pilot. It trains your brain to focus attention at will. Over time, you develop the ability to treat thoughts as mental processes rather than facts, giving you time and space to decide on the right course of action rather than responding on auto-pilot.

When you try the mindful breathing exercise remember these three important things. Firstly, your mind is designed to wander – accepting this fact helps you in your mindful practice. Repetition is key to success – you don't have to like this exercise or find it relaxing, you just have to do it. Getting angry or frustrated won't help you master this skill – these emotions just make it harder, so be kind to yourself if you're struggling.

Consider the project manager, John. He didn't find this exercise easy at first, and started to get frustrated. 'I thought that sitting doing nothing for 10 minutes would be easy. How wrong I was. My mind kept wandering and I kept thinking about the project I was working on. As instructed, when I noticed my mind had wandered, I brought my attention back to my breath. Two breaths later my mind wandered off, thinking about the latest reorganisation. Again I bought my focus back to my breath. After 10 minutes of fighting with my thoughts, it was a relief when it was time to end.'

Despite the difficulty, John persisted. A few days later he said, 'I started to become really interested in my thought patterns. It really drove home to me just how much of my energy I was spending thinking about work, worrying about the reorganisation and trying not to drop any of the balls that I was trying to keep in the air simultaneously. I started to give myself a pat on the back each time I noticed my mind was wandering. A few days later another strange thing started to happen – I started to look forward to my 10 minutes of peace each day. It still wasn't easy, but I started to feel more relaxed and clear-headed.'

Your experiences may be different from or similar to John's. Some people find the mindful breathing exercise easy; others find it hard. Even people who've been regularly practising it for 20 years or more still have minds that wander.

You don't have to like the MAWT exercises; you just have to do them. Rather like going to the gym and training a muscle, you can train your attention to focus where you want it. Every time you do the mindfulness of breath exercise, you'll be rewarded. With each repetition, you're strengthening the links in your brain connected with focusing your attention. Over time, focusing your mind becomes easier and a normal part of your working day.

By discovering that thoughts are only mental processes, you create a gap between a stimulus (such as a thought) and your response (often unconscious and on auto-pilot). You can then use this gap to consciously choose what to do next. You can decide to try a new approach or choose to use a tried and trusted approach – the important thing is that you have a choice. When living your life on auto-pilot, you have no choice because you're often unconscious of what's going on. Cultivating mindfulness at work allows you to respond more wisely to the day-to-day challenges that you face there.

Committing to being more mindful at work

Now is the time to make a commitment to becoming more mindful at work. Becoming mindful isn't a quick fix – it takes time, practice and commitment – but the rewards are immense.

Many people moan that they've too little time in their day to devote 10–20 minutes to developing their mindfulness skills. Step back and think about it. If you cannot spare 10 minutes of the 1,440 minutes you have to play with each day, maybe you need to examine how you're living your life.

If you look for time to fit mindfulness training into your life, you'll find it. Most people find time each day to brush their teeth or to eat breakfast. Instead of thinking of mindfulness as 'another thing to fit into my busy day' regard it as 'a short practice each day that really makes a big difference to my life and work, saves me time and helps me manage my work more efficiently'.

Make a commitment to your practice. Make sure that you want to practice not because the authors of this book say you should, but because you want to experience the benefits of mindfulness in your life. Make an appointment with yourself and write it in your diary. Find the time of day that's right for you; experiment and see what works. Find a space to practise in where you won't be disturbed and the lighting and heating levels are right for you. Remember, your brain loves to store things as habits, and habits feel safe and secure. Aim to make mindfulness a habit in your life by establishing (if possible) a regular time of day and place to practise.

Week 1 reflection

Reflect on the progress you've made as follows:

- ✔ Write in your journal one key thing you've discovered from this week's study.

- ✔ List three ways in which mindfulness can help you at work

- ✔ List three ways in which you'll start applying what you've discovered to your work

Learning check

Check what you've learned in Week 1 by answering the following questions:

1. **In your own words, what is mindfulness?**

2. **Name one or more thing that changes in the brain when you practise mindfulness.**

3. **Why is the brain's tendency to work on auto-pilot simultaneously a good and bad thing?**

4. **How can 'being in the present moment more' benefit your work?**

Week 1 home practice

Carry out the following mindfulness practice at home:

- ✔ Practise the mindfulness of breath exercise (Track 7) at least six times during the week.

- ✔ Find something you do at work on auto-pilot (such as always sitting in the same chair in meetings or at lunchtime, or always parking in the same area) and try something different.

- ✔ Eat one thing mindfully each day – use all of your senses to experience it.

With Mindfulness, practice is key. Practice mindfulness at home to begin with. Once you have got to grips with it you can start to practice more at work. If things don't go to plan one day, don't worry. You're human and lapsing is okay! Remember, learning mindfulness isn't like being on a diet. If you lapse one day, it doesn't mean you've failed and don't have to bother for the rest of the week. Tomorrow is another day – just start afresh. Practice each day for a week before moving onto week 2.

Week 2: Working with the body in mind

In week 1 you discovered what mindfulness at work was all about, the benefits it can bring you, and the benefits and problems associated with working on auto-pilot. You started training your attention by focusing on your breath – using your breath as the anchor for your attention.

You also discovered, by eating food mindfully, what a rich experience everyday activities can be if you just focus on them. Maybe you also realised just how many things you do unconsciously, and how much you may be missing out on.

A Finance Director for an international magazine (let's call her Linda), signed up for one of my (Juliet's) mindfulness course. At the start of week 2 she pulled me to one side and burst into tears. She explained that one evening a month ago her four-year-old son had asked her to play with building bricks with him. She agreed to do so, but spent the whole time on her smart phone catching up with emails – she lay only three bricks in an hour.

A couple of weeks ago her son had asked her to go out for a walk with him. It was a beautiful sunny Sunday morning, and her brother and family (who were visiting) came too. A work issue had been playing on her mind. As she walked, she mulled over the issue. She concluded that her colleague Jan was not on-board with the project, and could not be trusted. Maybe her boss was in on it. Maybe this whole project was a plot to make her fail so that Jan could look after number one. Her colleague Tom had been a bit withdrawn recently – maybe he could see the writing on the wall, and was protecting his job by keeping his head down. She remembered her boss's words at her last appraisal: 'Your ability to manage finance isn't in question, but I do feel that your people skills could do with improving.'

Linda felt the sun on her face, and looked down at her son. She noticed that his clothes were covered in grass stains, as were those of her niece and nephew. All the children had big grins on their faces. Seeing the confusion on her face, her brother said, 'James won!' She stared at him, feeling even more perplexed. Her brother added, 'The rolling down the hill race. James won!'

Linda told me that she was distraught about the degree to which work was forcing her to give up on the important things in life. She realised just how much of her son's growing up she was missing.

I suggested that this realisation was cause for celebration, not tears. Linda was confused, and a little irritated. I explained that recognising how much time you're spending on auto-pilot is the first step to breaking out of life in that mode. After all, you cannot change something if you're not aware of it.

I also encouraged Linda not to beat herself up about what had happened in the past. I told her: 'The past is history, tomorrow is a mystery, but today is a gift, which is why it's called the present.' I explained that feeling bad about things never helps – it just makes things even worse.

I suggested, 'You may decide to devote some time to being with your son mindfully in the present moment, or you may decide that at this moment work has to take priority. The point is that now you know that you have a choice.'

Mindfulness encourages you to be kind to yourself, befriend yourself and to forgive yourself. Mindfulness gives you choices – you can choose to do things differently. You always have a choice in life, even when you think that you have no choice.

Reflection on week 1

How did you get on with the mindful eating exercise? Write your reflections in your journal

✔ How many times did you manage to sit down and focus on your breath? Describe your experiences.

✔ What auto-pilot habit did you try to do differently last week? Describe your experiences.

✔ In your opinion, how much of your life is currently spent on auto-pilot? Describe below a few things you think you're currently missing out on?

✔ Do you find it easy to forgive yourself or do you judge yourself harshly for each and every mistake?

✔ What were the main things you found useful from week 1's exercises?

Key learning recap from week 1

In week 1 you explored the human tendency to work on auto-pilot. You discovered that life was full of amazing experiences – many of which you miss. You also discovered that for much of the time you respond to life events based on habits stored in the primitive areas of your brain, and these responses are often based on outdated information and may, as a result, be inappropriate. You discovered that mindfulness creates a gap between a thought and your response to it. This mindful gap gives you choices – respond as you've always done, try something different or do nothing.

Week 2 builds on this knowledge.

2.1: The body scan

The body scan is all about getting back in touch with your body. Your body has more of an impact on your mind than you may expect. Mindfulness of your body sensations encourages you to shift into approach mode rather than work in avoidance mode (see Chapter 5 for more about the interaction of thoughts, emotions and physiology).

A guided version of this exercise is available as an audio download (Track 8 at www.dummies.com/go/mindfulnessatworkuk). Alternatively, read the guidance below, and set a timer to stop you worrying about drifting off. Select a quiet place where you won't be disturbed and then follow these steps:

1. **Sit on a comfortable chair, with your feet firmly on the floor.** Ensure that your back is upright and comfortable and your head is looking forward. Your arms can rest on the arms of the chair or your lap. Remain aware of your posture throughout the exercise if you can, and correct yourself if you notice that you're slouching.

2. **Focus your attention on your breath.** Feel the sensations of your breath coming in and your breath going out. Do so for approximately ten in and ten out breaths.

3. **Focus your attention on the toes of your right foot.** Identify whether you can feel any sensations, such as hot, cold or tingling. See whether you can feel your toes in contact with your socks or shoes. Spend a few moments exploring your toes, then repeat the process with your left foot. If you can't feel any sensation at all, just notice the lack of sensation – that's absolutely fine.

4. **Compare your right and left toes.** Do they feel any different?

5. **Focus your attention on the soles of your feet.** Start with your right sole, identify what you feel. Repeat the process with your left sole and then compare the sensations you experienced with your right and left soles.

If at any point during the exercise you feel any discomfort, treat it as an opportunity to explore what's going on. Approach the discomfort with kindness and curiosity. What does it feel like; what sensations arise? What thoughts enter your mind? What emotions are you experiencing? Then try letting go of the discomfort as you breathe out.

6. **Focus on your lower leg.** Spend time exploring the right lower leg, then the left and then compare the two.

7. **Focus on your knees.** Examine the sensations in your right knee, then your left knee and then compare the two.

8. **Focus on your thighs and bottom.** Explore how they feel when in contact with the chair.

9. **Try to explore the sensations in your internal organs.** Focus on your liver, kidneys, stomach, lungs and heart. You may not notice any sensation at all – and that's okay.

10. **Focus on your spine.** Move up your spine slowly, focusing briefly on one vertebra at a time.

11. **Focus on your right arm.** Identify the sensations in your right arm, then your left arm and then compare the two.

12. **Focus on your neck and shoulders.** If you experience any tension or discomfort, try Letting it go as you breath out.

13. **Focus on your jaw and facial muscles.** Identify all the feelings and sensations.

14. **Focus on your scalp.** Finish with your head. You've now worked your way from the bottom to the top of your body.

When in avoidance mode (for example, when trying to avoid pain), your sympathetic nervous system (SNS) is more highly activated – you're in fight or flight mode. When in approach mode, your parasympathetic nervous system (PNS) is more highly activated, resulting in a greater sense of relaxation and mindful awareness. Exercises like the body scan cultivate an approach mode of mind, activating your PNS, relaxing you and reducing your SNS-induced state of heightened arousal.

Simply put, mindfulness exercises like the body scan help you shift from a nervous system that's on danger alert, to a nervous system that's more relaxed, open, creative and intelligent.

Body scan reflection

- ✔ How did you find this exercise?

- ✔ Did you manage to keep your attention focused throughout, or did your mind wander?

- ✔ Did you find this exercise harder or easier than the mindful breathing exercise?

- ✔ Did you notice any marked differences between sensations in different parts of your body or on different sides of your body?

- ✔ Did you encounter any discomfort in your body? If you did, what was the impact of approaching the discomfort, examining it with openness and kindness and breathing the discomfort out?

- ✔ Can you make any other observations about this experience?

Body scan key learning points

This activity helps you to reconnect with your body. It's another opportunity to practise focussing your attention on one thing at a time. It helps you to develop an approach mode of mind.

2.2: Three-step body check

This version of the body scan can be done anywhere, as long as you've a chair, about three minutes to spare and are unlikely to be disturbed. It's quick and easy to use at your desk.

Figure 6-2 shows the three areas of your body on which to focus attention during this exercise.

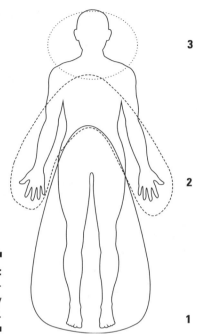

Figure 6-2:
The three-step body check.

You can do this exercise with your eyes open in soft focus (just slightly opened and looking downwards) or closed. Sit in a comfortable, upright position with your feet firmly on the floor and follow the instructions in the audio download available on www.dummies.com/go/mindfulnessatworkuk (Track 9) or follow the steps below:

Step 1: Feet, legs and lower body

Centre yourself by focusing on the sensation of taking three slow breaths.

Notice the sensations you experience, such as heat, cold or tingling, when you focus your full attention on your feet. Pause to observe then repeat with your legs, followed by your bottom.

Step 2: Chest and arms

Repeat as in Step 1 above, focusing on your chest and internal organs, followed by your arms.

Step 3: Shoulders and head

Repeat as above focusing on your neck and shoulders. Follow this with your jaw, nose, facial skin and scalp.

Finish by centring yourself by focusing on the sensation of taking three slow breaths.

Three step body check reflection

Please reflect on the following questions and note your responses in your journal

- ✔ How hard or easy did you find this exercise?
- ✔ What parts of the body were tense or tight?
- ✔ If you were feeling thirsty, where did you feel the sensation?
- ✔ How hungry or full up did you feel? How did you notice that exactly?

Three-step body check key learning points

Many people carry stress and tension in their body. This exercise helps you locate and release the tension. The exercise provides an opportunity to experience how your body feels in a direct, experiential manner (something you may rarely do). Mindfulness helps you to reconnect with your body. Doing so can act as an early warning system, help you maintain your well-being and boost your resilience at work.

Exploring the mind–body connection

Thoughts have more impact on the body (and vice versa) than most people realise. In the modern world, you can easily become detached from the body you live in and take it for granted. Your behaviour is frequently driven by your fears and emotions. These fears and emotions become locked in your body in the same way as thoughts and feelings become locked in your brain.

What you may not realise is that your body is acutely sensitive to the smallest emotions that flit across your brain. Your brain can detect your thoughts before you've consciously registered them yourself and your body reacts to thoughts as if they were real. A great deal of research backs up this finding.

In one experiment a volunteer was asked to hold out an arm and repeatedly state, 'I am weak, I am weak.' Another volunteer was asked to push down the first volunteer's arm to see how much force it took. Next, the first volunteer was again asked to hold out their arm but this time repeatedly stating, 'I am strong, I am strong'. This time their arm proved harder to push down. Just saying 'I am strong' made the person stronger.

Another example involved students who thought they were testing out headphones. They were told that they needed to test the headphones while jogging. The students were divided into two groups and both were asked to listen to a radio show including an editorial advocating student ID cards.

The students in one group were asked to shake their heads from side to side as they listened; those in the other group were asked to move their heads up and down. As they left the headphone test room both groups were asked their opinion on student ID cards. The group who moved their heads up and down (nodding their head) supported the argument for student ID cards much more enthusiastically than the group moving their head from side to side (shaking their head).

You may spend so much time in your head that you forget you have a body at all. You may feel disconnected from your body. This situation can undermine both your physical and mental well-being. The sense of disconnection from your body is often reinforced if, like many people, you don't like your body much. This dislike can lead you to ignore or mistreat your body, treating it like the enemy, berating it when it does not do exactly what you want it to do. Many people treat their body like a stranger, rather than a friend that houses them, transports them and serves them without fail 24 hours a day, 365 days a year.

Mindfulness helps you reconnect with and befriend this long-lost friend. In return, your friend, the body, repays you by acting as an early warning system, alerting you when things need attending to and keeping your performance at peak level.

2.3: Appreciate the good

There may be things at work that you don't like. Equally, however, there are likely to be a number of things that you do like but fail to notice or fully appreciate.

Happiness is a state of mind. It involves looking at the same thing with different eyes. Life is happening right here, right now – so why not make the most of it? Consider the simple action of smiling. Smiling tells the body that everything is okay. As a result the body stops pumping adrenaline into the body, immediately. Your blood pressure lowers quickly, and your immune system is also boosted rapidly. Scientists say that smiling has the same positive effect on your happiness as eating 2,000 chocolate bars – and fewer calories!

Part of mindfulness is learning to pay attention to, appreciate and really benefit from the good things in life. Each day can be full of small pleasures – if you notice them. Huge benefits can be gained from spending more time celebrating the good in life, each little win and each time you achieve something.

Huge benefits can be gained from spending more time celebrating the good in life, each little win and each time you achieve something.

When you really appreciate something, your brain releases endorphins. Endorphins are neurotransmitters that make you feel really good. They're your in-built reward system, and have addictive characteristics.

Serotonin can induce comfort and contentment while reducing stress and increasing optimism. Research also shows that serotonin improves brain function. Dopamine can act as a motivator, keeping you focused on goals, and creating a sensation of pleasure when you achieve something. It also helps you to maintain attention.

The more things you appreciate and enjoy, the more feel-good hormones your brain releases and the better you feel and the more resilient and productive you become.

Reflection on appreciating the good

Reflect on the following questions and note your responses in your journal.

- ✔ Write down the names of three people in your life who make you feel good.
- ✔ List five or more activities or things that make you happy.
- ✔ How can you give these people, activities or things some additional appreciative attention?
- ✔ What do you think would occur if you paused for a moment to fully appreciate it when pleasant things happen to you?
- ✔ Pick one thing to focus on really noticing and appreciating for the next seven days.

How you feel about things (good or bad) has a real, tangible impact on your body as well as on your mind. If your body feels good, it has a positive impact on your thoughts.

Week 2 home practice

Your week 2 home practice should be as follows.

- ✔ Practise the body scan (Track 8 of the audio download tracks available at) at least six times during the week.
- ✔ Think of two things you're grateful for or appreciate each day, then observe their impact on your body.
- ✔ Think of one thing you really enjoy, and make time to appreciate it and benefit from it more fully.

Remember, these mindfulness activities are there to help you not to add another pressure to your day. You may encounter days when it feels difficult to squeeze in a few minutes to do the body scan, but these are probably the very days you need it most, so make an extra effort.

Week 2 Reflection

Note in your journal one key thing you've found out from the week 2 exercises, and three ways that you will start applying what you've learned to your work.

Learning check

1. Is this statement true or false: 'My body can detect thoughts before I have consciously registered them myself.'

2. In your own words, describe what 'approach mode' means.

3. In your own words, describe what 'avoidance mode' means.

4. Is this statement true or false? 'If I am finding the mindfulness practice boring or frustrating, I'm not benefiting from it.'

5. Is this statement true or false? 'When you practise body scans, if you cannot feel sensations in each part of your body you're not trying hard enough.'

Check out the answers in the Appendix.

Chapter 7

Applying Mindfulness
At Work Training

*I*n Chapter 6 you discovered some of the basics of mindfulness and started training your brain to be more mindful. This chapter builds on these foundations by exploring key things that you do at work, and some alternative mindful strategies that pay dividends. You continue your Mindfulness At Work Training by applying mindfulness to communication, difficult people, strong emotions and work related change.

Continuing Your Mindfulness at Work Training (MAWT)

This section takes you through what you need to know about mindful communication in the workplace, how to deal with people who challenge you, the expression of strong emotions in the workplace, and the difficulties arising from change.

Week 3: Mindful communication at work

If you've been participating in this course, in week 2 you discovered how the mind and body are more connected than you think. You practised the body scan to help you reconnect with your body. You discovered the benefit of appreciating the good things in life.

Week 2 Reflection: Jot your responses in your journal

- ✔ How did you get on with the body scan exercise in week 2? Did it have on impact on your mood or work in any way?

- ✔ Did you find some areas of the body more difficult than others?

- ✔ Did you try the three-step body check? Did you find it beneficial?

- ✔ Did you manage to spend more time appreciating something that you enjoyed or found good at work? Did this impact on your mood or work in any way?

Week 3 is all about communication at work. You explore mindful communication strategies, mindful meetings and how to present more mindfully. You start by looking at mindful communication.

Mindful communication

Mindful communication is all about cultivating the skill of listening more closely to colleagues and developing greater clarity about how to respond. In the busy world of the modern-day workplace much of our communication is conducted without listening enough, and jumping to solutions before we've even identified what the real issue or problem is. When trying to juggle multiple, conflicting demands we're often distracted and only pick out of conversations what we want to hear without hearing the whole story. Ideally we need to be as fully present as we can when communicating. Being fully present allows us to get to the nub of the issue more quickly, and saves time and frustration for all concerned.

Mindful communication involves four steps. When communicating mindfully at work, you need to:

1. **Connect. See things through another person's eyes. Listen to them mindfully in the present moment and ask for clarification if necessary.**

2. **Agree. Identify areas that you agree on.**

3. **Collaborate. Work with the other person as an equal to find a way to resolve the situation.**

4. **Achieve. Work together to find a mutually agreeable solution or compromise, or simply agree to disagree.**

I (Juliet) have a friend who works as a factory line supervisor – lets call
her Gill. Gill worked for a well-known frozen food producer. Her boss asked
her to increase the line's production by 10 per cent. The production line
was already working at full capacity, and Gill knew this directive would be
unpopular with the staff. She also knew from experience that when she tried
to get the line to go faster more mistakes were made and production actually
decreased. Also, some product lines were being moved to another plant and
she was anxious her production line might be moved, and her team face
redundancy. Gill had recently moved to a new house and started to worry
about what would happen if she lost her job. She was also worried about Paul
the packer, who was reaching retirement age but had little else in his life but
work. How would he cope if he lost his job; would he become reclusive and
depressed? And what would happen to Marie? Her son had special needs and
she was paying for additional tuition out of her low wage. Gill started to feel
overwhelmed and that she was a failure

Consider Gill's predicament. Re-read the four-step mindful communication
model above. Apply the model to the case study. What could Gill have done
to address this issue with her manager and her team? Jot your ideas in your
journal.

3.1: A mindful minute

When practising mindful communication for the first time, you may benefit
from this short exercise, which helps you prepare to communicate. Although
the exercise is called the mindful minute, you can extend it if time permits.
This exercise is designed to be done anywhere, anytime, seated or standing.
You can also find an audio track (Track 10) to accompany it online at
www.dummies.com/go/mindfulnessatworkuk Follow these steps:

1. **Centre yourself (about 20 seconds).**

   Feel your feet feel in contact with the ground. Imagine that your feet are
   rooted to the ground and that your legs are like tree trunks, firmly supporting you in place. Use your feet as an anchor for your attention.

2. **Acknowledge what's going on (about 20 seconds).**

   Now focus your attention on everything that's going on – the thoughts
   entering your mind, sounds, smells and bodily sensations. Acknowledge
   your experiences and let them go without judging or getting involved,
   just noticing the present moment.

3. **Take a mindful pause (about 20 seconds).**

   Now focus your attention on nothing but your breath. Feel the breath
   coming in, and the breath going out. If thoughts arise, kindly acknowledge them and let them go.

Using this exercise before mindful communications isn't essential, but many people find that it helps by creating a short space between the busyness of their working mind and the present moment state that's ideal for mindful communications.

Try using the mindful minute technique during your work day, in preparation for a mindful conversation with someone. When you've practiced this three or more times, complete the reflection below.

Reflection on 'a mindful minute'

Note your responses in your journal.

- ✔ When and why did you use the mindful minute technique?
- ✔ How easy or difficult did you find it?
- ✔ Did you feel different before and after the exercise?
- ✔ How did it impact on your communication with colleagues?

Another essential ingredient for successful communication is working in *approach mode*: approaching the topic of conversation with open curiosity and interest and avoiding the temptation to jump to conclusions or make decisions without the full facts.

3.2: The approach technique

In order to move from an avoidance to an approach state of mind, you need to be aware of the motivations behind your thoughts and emotions. Discovering these may take time, effort and practice.

The next time you've a decision to make, large or small, try applying this simple technique:

1. **Use the 'mindful minute' or 'three-step break' technique to centre yourself.** Observe your mental chatter and bring yourself back to the present moment.

2. **Define the decision that needs to be made.** Write it down on a piece of paper if it helps.

3. **Identify two or more other possible courses of action.** Undertake this task with a 'beginner's mind' just like a child might when approaching a task for the first time, with gentleness and curiosity. Don't spend too much time thinking about them, just make sure that you explore all possibilities and don't dismiss the absurd or seemingly impossible.

4. **Identify your default response, that is, how you'd normally respond.** Write it down if doing so is helpful.

5. **Identify which of the courses of action are 'avoidant'.** Spot which possible decisions are based on avoiding something undesirable and which are more 'approach' focused.

6. **Make your decision.** If your chosen course of action involves a new way of responding, ensure that you give it a chance and try not let any inbuilt negativity creep in. If you decide that your 'default' reaction is the correct response, that's fine too. The important thing is to create a small gap between the stimulus (a call to action or need to make a decision) and your response (how you behave and think), so that you can decide on the best way forward.

Try this activity three or four times during the week and then complete the following reflection.

Reflection on the approach technique

Reflect on the questions below and note your responses in your journal

- ✔ When did you use the approach technique?
- ✔ How did you feel?
- ✔ Did you feel different before and after the exercise?

Applying the approach technique to every decision isn't practical, but using it regularly helps you develop a greater awareness of what is motivating your decisions and actions. This knowledge can help you break out of behaviour and thought patterns that no longer serve you well.

Mindful meetings

Many studies show that meetings are unproductive and costly. A mindful approach to meetings can help them become more productive from both the leader's and the participants' perspective. Chapter 9 covers mindful meetings in depth.

So how can mindfulness help you to have more productive meetings? You need to start by approaching and re-examining what you're trying to achieve. Read the section on mindful meetings in Chapter 9 and try out the exercises for yourself. The next time you lead or attend a meeting, spend a few moments afterwards reflecting on your experiences.

To best prepare you for leading or participating in a meeting, try listening to the accompanying audio track (Track 11) which prepares you to be mindful before and during the meeting itself. You can download it from www.dummies.com/go/mindfulnessatworkuk

THE SCIENCE BEHIND IT

Presentation symptoms and science

Being nervous of presenting is a form of social phobia. The thoughts that arise out of this phobia can trigger physiological reactions in your body, that impact on your emotions and impact on your thoughts. Physical symptoms can include palms sweating; stomach churning and feeling weak at the knees. Mindfulness can help you manage or reduce these difficult feelings and therefore probably improve your presentation skills.'

MAWT ACTIVITY

Reflection on mindful meetings

Reflect on the questions below and note your responses in your journal

- Did you mindfully prepare for the meeting? (If so how?)
- What, if anything was different about the meeting?
- Did you manage to remain 'present' in the meeting?
- Did any emotions arise during the meeting? How did you handle them?
- What was the most useful thing you gained from adopting a more mindful approach to attending or leading meetings?

Mindful presentations

Research suggests that many people fear public speaking more than death. Giving a presentation is unlikely to kill or mortally wound us, and yet your threat system may well be activated in the same way as if we face a life or death situation.

PLAY THIS!

Listen to the audio track 'Mindful presentation' (Track 12 at www.dummies. com/go/mindfulnessatworkuk), which helps prepare you mentally before giving a presentation. If you found the guidance helpful, make sure you spend a few minutes listening to the track before you next deliver a presentation.

As you have discovered earlier in the book, practising mindfulness can help you to stop the fight or flight reaction, or notice when it occurs and take steps to stop it escalating further.

Here are some tips to help you present in a mindful way.

- **Allow plenty of time to prepare**. The human brain hates uncertainty, and attempts to create certainty by trying to anticipate what might happen next. By creating a structure and content, uncertainty is reduced and the brain is free to focus on other things

✓ **Before you present, try to set aside some time to be mindful too.** The simple action of focusing on the breathing and recognising moment by moment sensations will bring your mind and body back to equilibrium. This can be done with eyes in soft focus if you are in a public place just before you present – no one will notice. As mindfulness is about 'falling awake' you will remain fully aware of what's happening around you as you ground yourself in the present moment.

✓ **Stretch your body mindfully.** The way your body is feeling can heavily influence your emotions and thoughts, often at an unconscious level. Before presenting, if possible physically release tension by stretching, wiggling your hands and feet and rotating your shoulders. Feel the sensations in your body as you stretch. You can also mentally release tension by detecting tension in the body, and releasing it with the out breath.

✓ **Let go of ideas of 'success' or 'failure'.** When you start your presentation, it's time to relax as all you can do is present to your audience now, in the present moment, and it will be as it will be. By recognising the brain's tendency to be on the lookout for problems, you can make a conscious effort to balance, and not allowing your thoughts and emotions to spiral out of control.

✓ **Don't forget to breathe!** It's amazing how many times even professional presenters can forget this. Sometimes the act of becoming tense can lead you to hold your breath. Your mind goes blank and the brain focusses its attention on keeping you alive by prompting you to breathe again.

✓ **Speak slowly, with pauses.** Speaking slowly signifies to your audience that you are in control rather than panicking. The slower pace also gives you time to think and reflect on what you want to say. The pauses also offer a moment for you to connect with the audience, to check how they are responding to your talk. Most people speak too quickly when presenting, so watch out for this one. Be mindful of the way you use your voice - if your throat aches, you are probably pushing it too hard. Be kind to yourself – try to work in harmony with your body, treating it as a friend rather than an enemy. Speak from your belly and sips water from time to time.

✓ **Manage the situation if you get flustered or feel your tension rising.** Create a few moments of mindfulness for yourself by trying one of the following:

 • Asking the audience to 'take a moment to consider' something you have just presented. Leave 30 seconds to a minute for them to do so, while you have a mindful pause to re-centre yourself

 • Asking the audience to discuss something amongst themselves. While they are doing this you can grab a few moments of mindfulness before asking them to feed back

 • Asking the audience to 'Think of a time when you . . .' and while they are thinking, grab a few mindful moments for yourself.

✔ **Remember, you are in control of the room.** Irrespective of your job role or status, when presenting, you are the leader in the room, you are in control. Use this powerful thought to take and hold control throughout your presentation. You can get the audience to stand, sit down, listen, or discuss. Remember that in most presentation situations, you are the only one who knows exactly how the presentation should go, so if you deviate, miss a bit out, take less or more time on one part – only you know. This realisation can be truly liberating!

✔ **Try turning fear into focus.** The feeling of butterflies, in your stomach the wobbly knees, or a cold sweat is simply a natural surge of adrenaline, preparing you for action. You get this same chemical reaction when we are really looking forward to something, but experience it as excitement or a buzz. By approaching and embracing this, you can use it to help you focus and give the performance of a lifetime!

You might also like to get your audience to try out some mindfulness as you start your presentation. I often use start meetings and presentation with a quick three step break. I explain that mindfulness is a form of brain training that helps people to focus their attention, then suggest that if they are happy to give this technique a try, to settle into their chairs with their eyes closed or in soft focus. I leave them around 30 seconds focusing on observing thoughts, 30 seconds on observing breathing, and the last 30 getting a sense of how their body feels. Most people are happy to join in, and those who aren't, are happy to sit quietly for a minute.

Hold your breath right now (for as long as you can) and at the same time try to think about something.

How did you get on? Was it more difficult than expected? This shows the importance of speaking slowly and taking breaths when you present. Try to slow your breathing down if you are getting tense, remembering that a better oxygen supply to the brain will improve your quality of thought and ability to get your message across.

Reflection on mindful presentations

Think about a presentation you gave in the past that did not go to plan. Read and reflect on the questions, and jot your answers in your journal.

1. **What thoughts were in your head as things went wrong or you found yourself off track?**

2. **What emotions did you experience?**

3. **What sensations did you feel in your body? Where specifically did you feel them?**

   Now think about a presentation you're planning. If your work does not require you to present, imagine that you're giving a presentation to your manager and the top team on how productivity can be increased in your department.

4. **What are the key things you will do to prepare for the presentation?**

5. **How will you use mindfulness before and during the presentation?**

6. **If you begin to feel fearful or anxious, what steps will you take to counter the negative effects of these emotions?**

7. **What three main things will you take away from the activity on mindful presentations?**

Week 3 reflection

Read and reflect on the questions, and jot your answers in your journal.

✔ What are the three main things that you will take away from this week's activities?

✔ How will you apply what you've learned to help you communicate better in future?

✔ What mindfulness practices do you feel would best help you improve your communications at work?

Week 3 home practice

Your home practice for week 3 should focus on the following:

✔ Practice Mindfulness or breath or body scan each day

✔ Try to apply mindful communication techniques into three work activities during the next 7 days

Week 4: Mindfully working with difficult people and strong emotions

In week 3 you discovered how to apply the mindfulness lessons you discovered in weeks 1 and 2 to improve the way that you communicate at work. You also applied mindfulness to day-to-day work communications, meetings and presentations.

Reflection on week 3

Read and reflect on the questions, and jot your answers in your journal.

✔ How are you getting on with practicing mindfulness of breath and body scan?

✔ Describe occasions in the previous week when you applied mindfulness to your communications at work.

✔ What happened as a result that was different?

✔ What (if anything) was difficult?

✔ What aspects of mindful communication do you need to work on?

Week 4 is all about working with strong emotions – both in yourself and in others. You start to train your brain to be more aware of your emotions as they arise, and use this awareness to restore your sense of equilibrium quicker. You also explore powerful techniques to help you when confronted with strong emotions from difficult colleagues. You discover how to better manage your responses to difficult situations at work, thus maintaining your equilibrium and sense of well-being. You can start by looking at how mindfulness can help you to manage your own emotions.

Managing your emotions mindfully

In order to find out how to manage your emotions better, you need to understand a little about what emotions are and how you generate them. Advances in neuroscience in recent years have helped us to understand how the brain generates emotions.

Emotions such as love, hate or joy are specific responses to a particular stimulus, and are usually of fairly short duration. In comparison, mood is a more general feeling, such as happiness or sadness, which lasts for a longer time. Emotions are complex and have both physical and mental elements. Emotions consist of subjective thoughts, physiological (body) responses and expressive behaviour.

When one of my (Juliet's) clients – lets call him Charlie, a junior account manager, received a call from a particular client, his heart sank. He knew that this client was usually highly demanding, and in the past had complained about him to his manager.

He told me that in the split second before lifting the receiver, he thought, 'Best be on my guard; whatever I do he'll never be happy.' His body became tense, his heart beat a little faster and he felt nervous. He felt his confidence ebbing away.

So what was going on? The work situation (a client he perceived to be difficult) triggered thoughts (be on guard; I can never make this person happy). The thoughts triggered physiological changes (tension and heartbeat) and generated emotions (anxiety, fear and negativity).

This short example illustrates how a situation triggers thoughts and, in turn, these thoughts (or judgements) trigger changes in the body and emotions. If you're like most people, you're unaware of this process happening because it does so unconsciously. Sometime later you may (or may not!) notice that you're tense and angry, but probably won't connect the physiological change or the emotion to the thoughts that triggered them.

Introducing the basal ganglia and amygdala

Many conventional patterns of thinking are held in neuro-circuits in the primitive parts of the brain, in particular the basal ganglia and amygdala.

The basal ganglia acts as the brain's 'habit centre', managing semi-automatic activities such as walking or driving. The amygdala is the source of strong emotions such as fear and anger. Information processing in the basal ganglia and amygdala is often not brought to conscious attention.

A potential threat can trigger fear, anger or the urge to flee (sometimes called an 'amygdala hijack'). The reaction is often disproportionate to the actual provocation. When in the grip of these emotions, your capacity for higher 'rational brain' thinking is diminished, and you're likely to revert to rote behaviours stored in the basal ganglia.

Thoughts are powerful things. Each time you generate a thought, you develop a new neural pathway in your brain. The more you think something, the stronger the connection becomes in your brain – so you are, literally, what you think! Your thoughts are often the culprits that are responsible for triggering emotions. Emotions are the result of the release of hormones into your bloodstream by the parasympathetic nervous system or the sympathetic nervous system (for more on these, see Chapter 5).

Emotions can be challenging to manage for three reasons:

✔ **You're often unconscious of the chain of events that has caused the emotion.** This makes it difficult to stop the emotion from happening.

✔ **When in the grip of strong emotions such as fear, your brain may divert energy away from rational, higher-brain thinking to the muscles in your legs and your heart rate in order to help you escape from the perceived threat.**

✔ **You're often driven by fears and emotions locked in your body as much as by thoughts and feelings locked in your brain.** The body is acutely sensitive to even the tiniest emotions that move across your mind. The body can detect thoughts before you've consciously registered them yourself – often reacting as if they were real rather than just thoughts. The body's response to these thoughts can then further enhance your fears and worries.

Mindfulness has proven to be highly effective in teaching people to manage their emotions better. Here's how it works. It all starts with awareness. Practising mindfulness helps you observe thoughts as they arise. Treating thoughts as 'mental processes' rather than facts, stops you responding on auto-pilot and regarding them as real, and your brain triggering a physiological and emotional response.

4.1: Using mindfulness to explore difficult emotions

This activity helps you to observe your emotional responses dispassionately. You'll find an accompanying audio track, Track 13, at www.dummies.com/go/ mindfulnessatworkuk. Follow these steps:

1. **Find a comfortable place where you won't be disturbed for 10 minutes or so.** Ensure that you've a comfortable chair to sit on.

2. **Focus your attention on nothing but your breathing for a few minutes.** Feel the breath coming in and the breath going out. Experience how your lungs feel when they inflate and deflate as you breathe. Don't try to judge or categorise what's going on, just observe your breathing with kindly curiosity.

3. **Shift your attention to a difficult or challenging situation at work.** Try not to pick anything too challenging or raw, as at this stage you're just starting to find out how to use mindfulness to deal with emotions.

4. **Picture the difficulty or work challenge in your mind's eye.** Picture it as vividly as you can; really put yourself in the situation as if it were happening right here, right now.

5. **Observe what's going on.** Try to look at the situation as though you were a scientist looking in. What thoughts are drifting into your mind? How does your body feel? Can you feel tension in any specific area? Are you experiencing any emotions and, if so, what are they? Be careful to remain detached; don't get involved, don't look for a solution, don't make judgements – just observe.

   If you find you're becoming too uncomfortable, just let the situation you're visualising go and return your focus to your breathing. Likewise, if you notice that your mind has shifted from being mode (observing what's going on) to doing mode (trying to solve the issue or thinking about it), just return to observing with kindly curiosity.

6. **Refocus on your breathing.** When you've observed the thoughts, bodily responses and emotions generated by the situation you've visualised, return to a focus on your breathing for a few minutes before finishing the activity.

Reflection on exploring difficult emotions

Read and reflect on the questions, and jot your answers in your journal.

1. What was the situation or difficulty you focused on during this activity?

2. What thoughts did you observe?

3. Did you observe any responses in your body (for example, tension, changed heart rate or other sensations)?

4. Did you detect any emotions emerging?

5. Did you observe anything that surprised you or you did not expect?

Practising activities such as using mindfulness to explore difficulties, the body scan and mindful breathing makes you become more aware of emotions as they arise. You become more aware of your mind–body connection, that is, how thoughts, physiology and emotions trigger and change one another. This knowledge helps you detect emotional responses early on before they escalate into something more difficult to manage.

Four key mindfulness exercises to help you manage your emotions better are:

✔ The body scan, which helps you detect changes in your body so that you can use your body as an early warning system.

✔ Mindfulness of breath, which helps you to notice thoughts as they arise, helping you to create a gap between a situation and your response to it and thus buying you time in which to decide on a wise course of action.

✔ Mindfulness to explore difficult emotions, which helps you explore the impact of specific work challenges on your thoughts, body and emotions. This knowledge helps you stop things escalating.

✔ A mindful minute, which creates a gap and allows you to detach from the situation for just long enough to put things into perspective and avoid responding on emotional auto-pilot.

Mindfully dealing with difficult people and strong emotions in others

So, back to Charlie, the junior account manager, and the call from his 'difficult' client. Charlie had just lifted up the receiver. Sure enough his client was being demanding and, what's more, he sounded really angry. He wanted some reports from Charlie that were not scheduled to be sent over until next week, and thus were only half written. He wanted a further discount on a venue that he'd already been offered a substantial discount on and he was moaning about a venue he'd used the previous week. Ultimately, he threatened to take his business to a competitor. As he was a major client, Charlie was desperate not to lose his business. He'd been assigned to this particular client in the first place because his company had always had an easy working relationship with him in the past. His company thought that the client was such a sure bet that Charlie, a junior with little experience but plenty of drive and determination, would be able to manage him.

Charlie was not in a good place to take the call. His mind was racing, his heart was pounding and he was starting to panic.

I used mindfulness to help Charlie work through what had occured. We identified together the facts:

> ✔ **Facts about Charlie:** Charlie recognised that he was young and inexperienced as an account manager. He did not understand why this 'easy' client had suddenly become 'hard'. He was keen to prove himself and progress within the company. He had determination and drive. He wanted to do a great job for all his clients.

> ✔ **Facts about the client:** He had recently been promoted to a new role managing the sourcing of corporate venues. His predecessor was regarded by colleagues as being too lax and poor at bargaining with suppliers. He wanted to prove that he was able to drive down costs and get a better service from suppliers.

I explained the need to create a few moments to centre himself, observe his emotions and see things more objectively. I suggested that a good way of doing this was to summarise what he thought the client wanted from him, and agree to take action and call him back at some later point.

Mindfulness training had taught Charlie that thoughts are only 'mental processes', so he decided to acknowledge and let go of his doom-laden thoughts and start his next call in the present moment with no past baggage.

His next call to the client went much better. As no one was in the office just before he called, he practised mindfulness for three minutes before picking up the phone. Charlie's calmness and understanding of the client's needs had a positive impact on the latter. The call ended on a positive note, for both Charlie and his client.

Reflection on managing emotions case study

Reflect on the case study and the questions which follow. Note your responses in your journal.

> ✔ If Charlie had continued his call when the client first phoned, what do you think may have happened? Why?

> ✔ How did Charlie's mindfulness practice help him prepare for his next interaction with his client?

> ✔ Can you make any other observations?

What Charlie's story illustrates is the need to recognise how your thoughts impact on your emotions and physiology. Only by recognising what's going on in your own mind and body can you manage yourself and be in a fit state to identify what's going on in others. From this position you can then recognise that, in most cases, you are not causing others to become angry or exhibit other strong emotions, their own issues are responsible, many of which you're completely unaware of.

When you've practised mindfulness for a little while, you'll develop the ability to step out of auto-pilot, where your life is spent trying to anticipate the future based on what's happened in the past. You'll develop the capability to observe your thoughts, and how they impact on your body and emotions. By having a greater awareness of what's going on, you can nip things in the bud when you start to spiral down into despair, panic and 'catastrophising'.

4.2: Using mindfulness to help you work with difficult colleagues or clients

Encountering difficult people at work is probably a universal experience. Try the following activity to prepare you for your next challenging encounter.

1. **Spend a few moments thinking about an encounter with a difficult colleague, client or customer. Briefly summarise it on a sheet of paper**

2. **Sit comfortably in a chair, with your feet on the ground, in a comfortable upright dignified position.** Focus your attention on your breathing. Feeling the breath coming in and the breath going out. Count six breaths (one inhalation and one exhalation equal one breath).

   If your mind wanders, don't worry. Just congratulate yourself on recognising that your mind has wandered and begin counting again at 1.

3. **Now bring to mind the difficult encounter. Approach it with openness. Focus on it fully.** Observe your thoughts, emotions, and any sensations in your body

4. **Approach and explore this difficult encounter with kindness and curiosity.** Stay in being mode – being with the memory of the difficult encounter. If you find yourself trying to find solutions to problems or alternative ways to behave, you've slipped into doing mode. Kindly escort yourself back to the present-moment experience of observing what's going on. If things feel too difficult, remember that you can let it go, and return back to your breathing at any time.

5. **Shift your attention to focus on observing how the 'difficult person' is behaving.** How are they behaving? Can you notice anything about their body (for example, is it stiff or relaxed?).

6. **Wish the person you've been thinking of well in his or her life and career.** Wish them happiness and good health. If you're uncomfortable doing so, that's fine; this step of the exercise can be challenging. Don't get annoyed, just acknowledge that at this moment in time you find it hard, and skip to the final step of the exercise.

Let the memory of the difficult encounter go and focus on your breathing again until you reach a count of six in- and out-breaths. Open your eyes and return to your day.

Reflection on approaching difficulty

Please reflect on the following questions and note your answers in your journal.

1. Were there any patterns or themes that emerged in your thoughts about the difficult person?

2. How did the memory of the difficult encounter impact on your body and emotions?

3. What did you notice when observing the other person's words, emotions and bodily response?

4. Did you feel able to wish the other person well? How was this experience for you?

5. How do you feel now about the other person?

6. Are there any things you can do to help you manage your own emotions better in future encounters with this person and other difficult people?

When you try this exercise for the first time, you may be surprised at just how strong your bodily and emotional response is to something that is, after all, only a thought – just a mental process. Thoughts can be powerful. When you're not aware of your thoughts, your actions are driven by old memories and assumptions about the future. As you've seen from this exercise, just thinking about a difficult encounter can produce strong emotions and have a profound impact on your body. Imagine how different your encounters with others may be if you were able to approach them in the present moment, observing what's going on right now, without bringing past baggage, concerns and expectations about the future into the equation?

When you next feel yourself becoming emotional, or you encounter others displaying strong emotions, try adopting out a quick mindful approach. Follow these steps:

1. Stop and observe the thoughts going round in your head. Acknowledge them and let them go.

2. Check to see how your body feels, right here, right now. Are you holding any tension? Is your heart beating faster? Observe and acknowledge

3. Check your emotional state. Observe and acknowledge

This exercise need take no longer than three minutes, and many people complete it in one minute. When you've completed it, you'll have a better understanding of the impact the encounter is having on you and can decide what to do next, based on present-moment, up-to-date data rather than on autopilot based on old data.

The exercises outlined in this chapter can be challenging at first, so don't forget to be kind to yourself as you practise them. Remember, you're not a machine – you're a person!

Week 4 reflection

Reflect on your experiences in week 4.

- ✔ **Reflect on your learning in week four of the course.** Note your responses to the questions below in your journal.

- ✔ **What are the three main things that you want to take away from this week's activities?**

- ✔ **How will you apply what you've discovered to help you deal with emotions in yourself and others better in future?**

- ✔ **What mindfulness practices do you feel would best help you manage your emotions in the future?**

Week 4 home practice

Your home practice in week 4 should be:

- ✔ **Continue to practice Mindfulness of breath or Body scan each day.** If you find it boring, remember that you don't have to like it, you just have to do it.

- ✔ **Try identifying one or more people you find difficult to work with.** In a quiet time when you will not be disturbed, practice using mindfulness to approach them (one at a time!) with an open mind and observing the impact that the situation has on you, as outlined earlier in this chapter.

Week 5: Mindful working in times of change

In week 4 you explored how mindfulness can help you manage your emotions better. You began to notice at an earlier stage when your emotions started to emerge and your thoughts started to spiral you away from the present moment. You also learned to observe your emotional response to others and observe their responses to you.

Reflection on week 4

Please reflect on the following questions. Note your responses in your journal.

- ✔ How are you getting on with practicing Mindfulness of Breath and Body scan?

- ✔ Did you have any 'difficult encounters' with colleagues or customers this week?

✔ Which mindfulness techniques did you try using?

✔ What impact did using these techniques have?

✔ Can you make any other observations?

In week 5, you discover why humans can find it so hard to change. You explore more mindful strategies for both leading change and coping with imposed change at work.

Exploring why humans can find change so difficult

Change is nothing new; it's the only constant in life. What is new is that the pace of change is accelerating. In the past, management theories on change assumed that change in a work context had a distinct start, a period of adaptation and a return to business as usual. Nowadays, one change follows another in rapid succession, with little or no business as usual.

So, if change has always been a factor in human lives, why do so many of us find it so difficult? In order to understand why this is so, you need to understand several factors: the human threat system, the human negativity bias and habit formation.

As you read in Chapter 5, humans have a highly evolved threat system. We are always scanning the horizon looking for potential threats and problems. In an effort to minimise threat and maximise reward, we devote more brain activity to looking for potential problems than looking for potential opportunities and new ways of doing things.

Your brain is an energy-hungry organ. To conserve energy, behaviours that you repeat frequently become stored in the more primitive, energy efficient area of your brain. The benefit of this is that it allows you to function more efficiently and apply your precious brain power to new things. The downside is that when things become habits you do them on auto-pilot, and they may not always be the most effective or the most appropriate thing to do.

Charlie, the junior account manager you encountered in week 4, had certain ways of doing things that worked well for him. When his company was faced with the need to reduce costs, it cut some posts in the administration and finance teams. This meant that Charlie was given additional responsibilities for these aspects of his work. Charlie was not too happy with the changes but understood their logic and was glad to have kept his job. Over the next few weeks Charlie tried hard to adapt, but struggled to change. At his appraisal, his manager raised concerns about his performance and future prospects.

So why was it that Charlie, an intelligent man, determined to get on, who understood the need for change at work, found the situation so challenging? Many of Charlie's working methods had become habits, hard-wired into his brain. He'd reinforced these habits over time by being rewarded (via praise from colleagues and success in securing contracts) for the results they pro-duced. His brain's attempt to maximise reward (continuing to be praised and receiving bonuses for performance at work) and minimise threat (not meet-ing targets, disappointing or alienating colleagues and clients) was driving him to continue working as he had in the past. No matter how hard he con-sciously tried to change, and understood the logic and need for the change, he resented his new administration and finance responsibilities, and uncon-sciously avoided doing them, prioritising other tasks instead.

The problem with changing habits is that they are, by their very nature, uncon-scious. Only by becoming conscious of what is going on can you change them. The problem is compounded by the fact that habits are stored in the more primitive areas of the brain. Messages from this area travel faster through the brain than messages from the higher brain. This means that habits are likely to kick into action long before you're consciously aware of them.

Mindfulness can help you to change habits over time by making you more aware of your thoughts and actions in the present moment, creating a gap between a stimulus (such as the need to do a task at work) and your response to it.

5.1: Habit releasers

Unhelpful habits can be replaced with more productive ones – with a bit of practice. Use the following activity to try something different and observe what happens:

1. **Think of a different work-related habit each day this week.** For exam-ple, maybe you always tackle your emails first thing in the morning, always sit in the same place in meetings or always arrange your desk in a certain way.

2. **Do something different and observe your reaction.** Reflect in your journal

   • Your response to the change (thoughts, emotions and physiology)

   • What impact (if any) this had on other people?

3. **Use your journal to make a note of the impact your habit releasers have each day.** Include in your notes:

   • The day of the week and what you changed.

   • The impact of the change on your thoughts, emotions and physiology

   • The impact of the change on others?

Mindfully leading change

Most leaders nowadays spend much of their time implementing and managing change. Many older models that you may have learned connected with managing people through change, such as the change curve, assume that change has a start, period of adaptation and end where the new way of working becomes the norm. These old models of change management are proving ineffective in the modern-day climate of 'bumpy change', where one change is rapidly followed by another and then another.

In order to be effective in leading change today, you need to focus on two things. First, you need to manage your own thoughts, habits and emotions, and generally take care of yourself so you're fit to lead others. Chapter 14 covers how mindfulness can help you manage yourself. Second, you need to understand the reasons why people resist change and take steps to help them embed change in their brain and replace old work habits with new ones.

5.2: Understanding how to lead change mindfully

Try this new mindful approach to leading change the next time that you're called upon to do so. Follow these steps:

1. **Understand why humans resist change.**

    Research shows that at a conscious level, most employees accept the need for change. However, this doesn't mean that they like it! As a leader, you need to understand that many of the behaviours that you want your staff to change may have unconscious drivers, which take time to alter. You need to acknowledge that, although many of your staff may say they want to change, at an unconscious level their brains are screaming, 'Danger! Danger! Go back to your tried and tested ways of working! You know they work!'

    As a change leader, you need to apply knowledge of the human negativity bias and habit formation to your change leadership strategy. You need to make an eight-week or longer plan that actively helps employees to change their mental mind-set. You need to plan activities that help people explore and become rewarded for new desired

2. **Clearly define between four to six key things that you need to be different after the change.** Note them in your journal.

    Most people cannot retain more than seven things in their working memory at the same time, so in this case less is more. Detailed change plans may be great for you, but are not the best way to get employees to remember and memorise the desired outcomes.

3. Help your team understand change from a brain perspective.

- Explain why the negativity bias (see Chapter 1) exists, and how our threat system, intended to help us escape from life-and-death situations, is often triggered by things that aren't life-threatening at all, and when in a state of fight or flight our capacity for rational thinking is diminished.

- Explain that many things that we do at work over time become habits. These habits are good because they're energy efficient and allow us to do more things, but as they are mainly unconcious they can be difficult to change.

- Explain that current theory suggests that it takes around five to eight weeks to form a new habit, and that if the team is to change it will take a conscious effort from all concerned to do things differently and practise what they preach.

- Explain how brain training techniques such as mindfulness can help them through the change process.

4. Engage your team in creating the solution.

Invite your team to a change planning session. If you're comfortable doing so, lead your team through a quick mindfulness exercise to get them centred and ready to work through the change task with an open mind. The three-step focus break (see Chapter 5) or a mindful minute (described earlier in this chapter) are good exercises to try. When introducing mindfulness exercises to your team for the first time, consider your language. You may want to call the mindfulness activities 'attention training' or 'focus breaks' or 'a purposeful pause'. Choose language that suits the culture of your organisation. Explain to the team why the change is needed and describe the four to six outcomes that must be achieved to make the change a success.

Mindfully monitor yourself (thoughts, emotions, physiology) from time to time to ensure that you're in a good place to lead the session. Also monitor your team members' emotions and physiology. Negativity breeds negativity, so try to nip it in the bud by moving on to a different subject or actively engaging with a more positive team member. Some tension in the room is natural – change is an emotive subject, but if you detect too much emotion or tension, try taking a break or working on another area where success is more easily achievable.

5. Apply the action plan that your team helped you produce.

If the action plan involves redundancies, it will probably be difficult to engage staff in new ways of working until the uncertainty surrounding which members of staff are leaving is over, and any staff due to leave have left.

If you're comfortable doing so, encourage staff to discover about mindfulness at work via a book, online course or taught course so that they're better equipped to deal with the change.

After this period has passed, hold regular meetings, and regularly interact with your staff, actively making opportunities for them to practise working, thinking and acting in different ways. Make sure that you recognise and reward staff when they display new, desired ways of thinking and acting.

In your interactions with staff try to always be fully present, working in approach mode. Let go (as far as you can) of expectations about how meetings should go, and the extent to which the changes have been embraced at this stage of the process. Although at times change can be a brutal process, try to encourage self-kindness among your staff. As a result of practising self-kindness, your staff are less likely to activate their fight-or flight response, (which can lead to negative thinking), and more likely to activate their parasympathetic nervous system, helping them to feel calmer about the changes. Use your mindfulness skills to gain a greater appreciation of the dynamics at play in the room, observing events as they unfold, and choosing the best way to respond for long-term individual and organisational benefit.

Ensure that your new plan of action is adhered to over an eight-week or even longer period.

Many scientists believe that while people can never erase a habit from their brains, they can replace it with another one. Until recently it was thought that forming a robust habit takes 21 days. In 2010, researchers working at University College London concluded that habit formation takes approximately 66 days, with some people taking as little as 18 days and others over 84 days.

6. **Continue to recognise and reward staff for displaying new desired work behaviours.**

   To ensure that new working habits become embedded fully, and are more dominant in the brain than old ones, as a change leader you need to continue to reinforce new behaviours in your staff. Consider awards for innovation or ways to reward individual staff who have contributed to greater efficiency.

Reflection on mindful change

When you've had the opportunity to try out this activity for yourself, complete the following reflection, recording your thoughts in your journal.

- ✔ How did this method of leading change differ from your previous methods?
- ✔ How did staff react to your use of mindfulness in meetings?

> ✔ How easy or difficult did you find it to confine your desired change outcomes to between four and six?
>
> ✔ Did you notice any old habits coming back into play in yourself or your staff? If so, what actions did you take?
>
> ✔ What was the outcome of your change efforts?

5.3 Mindful strategies for coping with imposed change

Think of an occasion on which a change was imposed on you at work. Then answer these questions – recording your response in your journal:

> ✔ What was your initial reaction?
>
> ✔ How did the reactions of others shape your reactions and thoughts?
>
> ✔ Did you jump to any conclusions that were later proven to be wrong?
>
> ✔ Did you experience any stress or excess tension during the process? If so, what steps did you take to help yourself?
>
> ✔ After the change had taken place, were things better or worse than you expected them to be?

Change can be a positive thing, for example moving to a new house, getting a new job or marrying someone you love. At work, if you're not in a supervisory, management or leadership role, chances are that at some point you'll be subjected to an imposed change at work.

Imposed changes are different to changes that you choose for yourself. Some people may immediately embrace the imposed change, while others may express denial, anger or extremely reluctant acceptance.

When unexpected, unwanted or imposed changes are announced, try applying this simple model. Follow these steps:

1. **Give yourself a mindful minute when the change is announced.** Doing so brings you firmly back to the present moment and allow you to observe things in a calmer, more rational manner

2. **Notice the announcement's impact on you in the present moment.** Observe your thoughts and changes in your physiology – Is your breathing or heart rate faster? Can you feel any tension or other sensations in your body?). Pay attention also to your emotions.

   Make sure that you explore what's going on for you with openness, kindness and curiosity. Avoid flipping into doing mode – trying to solve the problem or anticipate the consequences of the change. Simply observe.

3. **Take steps to notice and release any tension in your body.** If possible, give yourself a three step body check (see Chapter 6) and, if you encounter any tension, try releasing it as you breathe out.

4. **Check your understanding of the change.** Make sure that you've a firm grasp of why the change is needed and what the next steps are going to be. Don't base your opinion on rumour, or the opinions of others. If you are unsure about anything, ask your manager for clarification.

5. **Focus your efforts on the things you can change or influence.** Arguing about an aspect of the change that has been set in stone saps your energy and impact on your mood. Accept what you cannot change, and focus your energy on things that you can change.

6. **Practise mindfulness on a regular basis.** Doing so helps you reduce tension and see things more clearly.

Week 5 reflection

Reflect on the following questions and note your responses in your journal.

- ✔ Which three main things will you take away from this week's activities?
- ✔ How will you apply what you've discovered to help you better cope with change in the future?
- ✔ What mindfulness practices do you feel would help you most during times of change?

Week 5 Home practice

For your week 5 Home practice:

- ✔ Continue practising mindfulness of breath or Body scan each day. If you have time, try practising one after another to stretch yourself further.
- ✔ Try applying some mindfulness to changes you are facing, and observe the results

Post-Course Summary

You've now reached the end of the Mindfulness At Work Training.

In weeks 1 and 2 you discovered the bare essentials of mindfulness and started to establish mindfulness practices of your own. In weeks 3, 4 and 5, you applied mindfulness to everyday work challenges including communication, dealing with emotions felt by yourself and others, and coping with change. You also continued to embed a regular mindfulness practice into your life.

The more you practise mindfulness, the easier it becomes to switch it on and off as you need it. Shamash and I recommend that you try to practise some form of mindfulness for at least 10 minutes each day. Doing so is time well spent and an investment in your career and sense of well-being. Check out the activities on the audio downloads and practise those that work best for you.

When you understand why each activity is structured as it is, and the importance of the language used, feel free to create your own mindfulness practices to help you in specific situations.

✔ Mindfulness is about being in the present moment, not about visualising yourself in a beautiful place far away from the here and now!

✔ MAWT is about cultivating awareness of how work situations impact on your thoughts, physiology and emotions, and the interaction between these three responses to any given situation.

✔ Practising mindfulness can be hard, especially when your mind is restless. Focusing and refocusing your attention on your breath or other chosen anchor is what you aim to do. Relaxation may or may not be a by-product of the process.

✔ When practising mindfulness, be kind to yourself to avoid triggering an unwanted threat response.

Although taking time out to practise mindfulness when you're really busy seems counter-intuitive, doing so always pays dividends. Just a few minutes of mindfulness is sometimes all it takes to return you to peak performance.

We were only able to fit a basic version of the MAWT course in this book. If you or members of your organisation would like to attend a full version of MAWT taught in-person or via an online course, visit www.mawt.co.uk for further details and free downloadable resources. We'd love you to pay a visit!

Chapter 8

Practising Mindfulness in the Digital Age

*T*his chapter helps you to manage one of the most beneficial but also most challenging aspects of living in the information age – digital technology. Mindfulness offers you the presence of mind to be able to choose when to use technology, to identify what sort of technology you need and to recognise when a more real-world approach is called for. When you do use technology, you discover how mindfulness offers a way of working with it that involves a greater degree of presence, wisdom and compassion.

Choosing When to Use Technology

Technology includes any application of scientific knowledge for practical purposes. In the industrial age, technology was dominated by mechanical machinery driven by the steam engine. But in the 21st century, your daily life is probably dominated by digital technology. This recent explosion in the use of digital technology is impacting every single organisation in some way.

The evolution of the human brain didn't take modern technology into account. So these changes are creating a big challenge, even for the powerhouse that resides in your skull. The pervasive use of technology often means that you may not even question your use of email or texting to communicate – mindfulness offers a chance to momentarily reflect before you immerse yourself in sending another deluge of messages out into the World Wide Web.

Recognising the pros and cons of technology

Digital technology certainly has many benefits in the workplace. Communication via texts and instant messaging is almost immediate. Video conferencing means that time isn't wasted on travelling to meetings. Work can be completed on the move. With laptops and smart phones, you can stay connected and keep working in planes, trains and automobiles. And with the processing power of computers, technology is used to manage huge amounts of data from customers to help you decide how best to serve their needs.

Are there any drawbacks to the use of technology? We think so, especially if you use it unskilfully. Here are a few disadvantages that are often overlooked:

- **Compulsive use of digital communication:** Email can change from a tool to an addiction. Constant checking of email, even when other tasks are more pressing, wastes both time and energy and ultimately reduces the company's productivity. See the sidebar 'Checking messages can be addictive'.

- **Reduced ability to focus:** Too much use of technology can make you distracted, as you jump from one task to the next. A lack of extended time working on just one task reduces your brain's ability to focus.

- **Less face-to-face time:** The more time you spend using technology, the less time is available for face-to-face meetings. This reduction in human contact can make working relationships a little shallower and result in lower levels of trust and understanding between people.

- **Inefficiency resulting from multi-tasking:** With technology comes the temptation to multi-task. Multi-tasking leads to reduced productivity and a lack of satisfaction. Chapter 18 explains why the ability to multi-task is actually a fallacy.

Mindfulness can help you to notice your new relationship with technology so that you're more in control rather than being a slave to your digital devices.

Rebalancing your use of technology

Using technology too much is a problem. If you're used to checking your phone every minute of the day for messages, you may struggle to concentrate when in a meeting or listening to your boss. Inefficient habits when online may mean that you end up surfing from one website to another instead of completing your tasks. And deciding to always communicate via technology rather than meeting face to face can lead to loss of opportunities to discuss new ideas and create a deeper and more trusting relationship with colleagues or customers.

Checking messages can be addictive

Do you find yourself constantly checking your emails throughout the day and evening? Can you resist reading that text message on your phone so you can get on with your work? If not, the culprit is probably dopamine – a chemical released in your brain.

The latest research shows that dopamine causes 'seeking behaviour' – that is, it makes you seek out things to address your basic needs, such as food, sex and warmth. But dopamine also makes you seek out facts, making you curious about new ideas. Dopamine activates your goal-directed behaviour.

This seeking behaviour is rewarded by a separate but complimentary system called the opioid system. So, as an example, say that dopamine makes you seek chocolate. When you get the chocolate, your brain rewards you with opioids.

Texts, emails, Twitter and Google all offer you instant gratification for whatever you're seeking. If you feel a bit lonely, you start seeking companionship. The ping of a new email makes you feel wanted, and a bit of your pleasure chemical is instantly released. You feel momentarily satisfied, but your desire to check email again returns immediately. Suddenly you can't stop texting, emailing or surfing online.

What makes technology particularly addictive? Three elements:

✔ **A cue triggers dopamine:** The sound of the text or ping of the email activates a cue – an important requirement for dopamine release. Your seeking behaviour begins!

✔ **Unpredictability is a key element in dopamine activation:** The sound of a text being delivered means you have a message from someone, but you don't know who and you don't know what it contains. The desire to check that message right now, no matter what you're doing, is fuelled by dopamine.

✔ **Short messages boost dopamine:** Because the information doesn't reveal all the information you desire, just an alluring snapshot, texts, Whatsapp messages and tweets make the experience short and super addictive. You text back or click the link to find out more – and the seeking continues.

All this stimulation and seeking behaviour is both draining and depletes your attention. Constantly checking your digital devices affects your productivity because you can't focus. So, what can you do about it?

Turning off the cues is the easiest way to remove the temptation. Without hearing the arrival of emails, texts and tweets, you're less likely to keep checking. Also, consider leaving your phone behind from time to time or blocking your Internet access occasionally.

Having described the downside to over-use of digital devices in the preceding section, you need to recognise that an aversion to technology can be an issue too. If you're the CEO of the organisation and decide not to make best use of technology, your competitors may surpass you. Using outdated technology may frustrate your staff and mean that you struggle to attract the talent you need to succeed.

A balanced approach is the answer. Most companies have embraced the use of technology, and that's probably a good thing. But you may not know how to use technology in a more mindful way so that you're not in a constant state of distraction or miscommunicating with others as you respond on a purely emotional level. We think that a set of strategies is urgently required in the workplace to help individuals make more conscious choices in their use of technology.

One of the most effective ways of managing your technology is having downtime – time when you switch off from technology. Computers are different from humans. Computers work best if they're never switched off. They can go on and on working without rest. However, if you stay connected and switched on without time to recharge, you burn out. Your attentional resources deplete rapidly, as do your energy levels, enthusiasm and intelligence. So having a few minutes, a few hours, a few days and sometimes a few weeks away from technology is key to your success. See the sidebar 'Dealing with information overload'.

Here are a few ways to create digital downtime, based on how much time you have available:

- ✔ **A few minutes:** Take a few minutes break every half hour or so if you work on a computer all day. Taking a step back, concentrating on a few deep, conscious breaths and walking around are good for your body and mind.

- ✔ **A few hours:** When the work day is over, take a break from the screen. It's very common for people to work on a screen all day, and relax at home by watching another screen. Refresh yourself by socialising, doing a spot of mindfulness practice, taking up a hobby or participating in sport.

- ✔ **A few days:** Take time off from technology every week. Aim for at least one day off per week if possible. Saturday is a good day for many people. See whether you can leave your phone behind, avoid checking email or social media and do something more natural and energising for you.

- ✔ **A few weeks:** If you can, take a few weeks holiday at least once a year. On holiday, see if you can have an extended period of time away from phones, computers and so on. This is probably when you'll have your creative juices flowing as your mind comes up with unique solutions for challenges you've been facing in the workplace or home life. I've had some of my greatest business ideas whilst on a mindfulness retreat which involving mainly sitting, walking, stretching and had no access to phones, TVs or iPads. If you're connected digitally every day, you'll be amazed at how clear your mind becomes following a break from all that for a week or so.

Dealing with information overload

The term 'information overload' was coined by Alvin Toffler in 1970. He predicted that access to large amounts of information would cause people problems – and he wasn't wrong!

Information overload is an ever-worsening problem in the workplace. It occurs when you take in more information than you're able to process, which then results in you delaying decisions or just making incorrect decisions.

Referring to this period in time as the information age isn't accurate. Information has been available since the invention of the printing press hundreds of years ago. The difference now is the massive amount of information available to pretty much everyone. Computers continue to store and are able to share more and more information, but the human mind can only manage so much. The human brain has evolved over millions of years to manage our everyday environment, but the technology that allows us to view the written word and visual images on screen has only been around for a few years – the brain hasn't had time to properly evolve in relation to these environmental changes.

The problem of information overload can easily spread in the workplace. For example, if one person has too much information in their email inbox, he may share it or pass it to others without processing that information effectively. Then more and more people are overloaded with too many emails to deal with and too little time.

Consuming up to 100,000 words a day, via email, websites, social media and other digital sources isn't unusual. Accessing this amount of information can take up to 12 hours and works out as roughly three-quarters of the day. The need to managing this relentless onslaught on the brain is one reason why mindfulness is gaining popularity in the West.

Managing information overload isn't easy. Here are a few solutions for mindfully dealing with information overload in the workplace:

✔ **Spend time disconnected:** That way no new information can come in and you can start and complete one task at a time. Use mindful breaths between and during tasks to keep you in the present moment.

✔ **Ask people specific, clear questions so that you receive clear-cut answers:** Listen with mindful awareness so you know exactly what they said.

✔ **Keep communication short:** Rather than writing long emails and having extended conversations on the phone, limit your time on these tasks and get to the point! If you don't, you end up finishing work late and limiting your free time. Quality counts, not quantity. Be conscious of your use of time.

✔ **Schedule face-to-face time every day:** Meeting up with someone and having a more relaxed chat gives you a break from text and allows you to recharge your brain.

✔ **Read information that you need to know rather than what you want to know:** Save fun reading for your spare time and focus on completing your essential tasks first. Doing so prevents you taking in too much information, feeling unfocused and being unmindful as a result.

Mindfulness gives you choices. Without mindfulness, you can spend hours flitting from website to website and email to email while your high-priority work gets left behind. Mindfulness exercises help you to wake up. Mindfulness gives you the presence of mind to switch off and be more creative, constructive and conscious in your working life.

Communicating Mindfully

Communication lies at the heart of being human. In the workplace, you're bound to be communicating often with others. And when you're not communicating with others, you're communicating with yourself, being aware of your thoughts, emotions and even sensations in your body.

Mindful communication is about bringing a greater level of conscious aware- ness and reflection to how you communicate. With greater awareness, you're better able to understand what others wish to express to you, as well as able to choose when and how to communicate your own thoughts.

Communication has been transformed by technology. Whereas in the past face-to-face conversations were the only way to communicate, you can now share your thoughts in lots of different ways. With the advent of the telephone, a person on the other side of the world was only a few button pushes away. And with the creation of the Internet came not only email but also live video chat via platforms such as Skype and Google Hangout – and free to boot! Finally, and most recently, communication has taken another step change with the creation of social media, dominated by Facebook, Twitter and LinkedIn.

For example, just today I've been on social media to share a blog post, exchanged several emails about a meeting tomorrow, had two phone calls from colleagues about work on my website and exchanged three text messages and some 'whatsapp' messages. And this is a very typical day, where I kept my phone off for large chunks of the day whilst working on this book! If I didn't know about that discipline of switching off technology, I would be getting disturbed all day.

Face-to-face conversations are now just one option and are often the option less chosen because of the investment of time required. Are face-to-face meetings worth the effort? Regular face-to-face interactions build up social networks in the brain through subtle visual cues and signals. If you spend thousands of hours online, you miss out on this training. Young people growing up in the modern age may have a reduced ability to socialise resulting from lack of face time.

Face-to-face communication has many inherent benefits that aren't so easy to access online or over the phone. These benefits include:

- ✔ **The personal touch:** When you've met a colleague, customer or supplier in person, the relationship changes. You're more likely to keep in touch and you have a clear image associated with that name. The in-person meeting can lead to conversations, ideas and insights that would never be discussed in other ways.

✔ **Non-verbal communication:** Spending time face-to-face means that you pick up all sorts of clues from a person's body language that you won't get via other forms of communication. This point is key. A pause when you mention the new deal may tell you that the other person is somewhat reluctant to commit to it. If you manage a salesperson via email alone, you never pick up that she speaks too loudly and quickly. You don't understand the pressure your designer is under until you see his face. With this extra information, you can make better decisions.

✔ **Teams work better when together:** Research described in the *Journal of Computer-Mediated Communication* found that teams working face-to-face made fewer errors and reported improved teamwork and performance.

✔ **Dealing with tricky situations:** When a situation is slightly emotionally charged, a face-to-face conversation can work best. Positive non-verbal communication can help to diffuse unnecessary tension. Online communication may cause the difficulties to spiral into bigger problems if not nipped in the bud.

According to management guru Peter Drucker: 'The most important thing in communication is to hear what isn't being said.'

A mindful communicator choses what is the most effective form of communication and then gives that communication their full attention. Mindful communication also keeps in mind the limits of the medium of communication.

Below are seven forms of communication, rated hierarchically according to the level of feedback they provide – least to most:

1. **Instant messaging:** Expect instant replies. Little or no emotion. Fast.

2. **Text:** Very short; great for catching attention but too short for any meaningful communication. No emotional communication to couch the words spoken. The same message can potentially be read as positive or negative.

3. **Email:** Lacks any emotional feedback. Neutral emails can be read as negative or rude.

4. **Social media:** Some forms also include emotional feedback, but the stream of messages often scatter the attention thinly. Not often used in business environment, but this trend is changing.

5. **Telephone:** Tone of voice can provide much more feedback than previous methods. Needs to be used more, not less.

6. **Video chat:** Probably the best form of technology-based communication. Facial expression enhances the information exchanged. Some of the social network parts of your brain are receiving feedback and engaging.

7. **Face-to-face meeting:** The ultimate form of communication. Tone of voice, body posture, speed of speech and a wide range of facial expressions are clearly observable. No risk of technology breakdown. A handshake or friendly hug, together with eye contact, increase trust and improve well-being. Slow.

Emailing mindfully

Email is both incredibly convenient and incredibly stressful. As the existence of over 3 billion email accounts demonstrates, however, it is certainly popular.

Here are some facts about email:

- Over 100 trillion emails are sent every year
- The average office worker spends over a quarter of her day on dealing with emails
- The average employee sends and receives 40 emails a day, and 1 in 12 receives more than 100 emails a day

Hey you, focus here!

I (Shamash) recently interviewed Daniel Goleman, a world expert on emotional intelligence in the workplace. Daniel has just published a new book, *Focus: The Hidden Driver of Excellence*. In our interview, he explained that two main types of attention exist: top-down and bottom-up. Top-down attention is intentional, conscious focus. Bottom-up attention is living on auto-pilot, being distracted by every ping of an email and ding of a text. Technological devices are designed to capture your attention; as a result, becoming more mindful is increasingly important as a means of keeping your brain on task, enabling you to do the work that you find interesting and meaningful. Daniel recommends that each time you notice you're scrolling through Facebook, checking emails or texting unnecessarily, simply guide your attention back to your work. Each time you guide your attention in this way, you strengthen the networks in your brain that allow you to focus in the moment. Directing your attention back to work is just like practising mindfulness of breath, in which you notice when your mind has wandered off into thoughts and then gently guide your attention back to the present moment.

Email is a tool for your own use. When you check email when you need to, and respond efficiently, all may be well. But you may be in the habit of checking email too often, hoping for that next interesting message to come flying through.

Mindful emailing is using email with greater awareness and wisdom. The purpose of using email is to communicate for the benefit of both you and your recipient.

Try these tips to help you use email more mindfully and productively:

- **Make a brief emailing plan:** Use a notebook to jot down who you plan to send emails to and a few brief points that you want to make each day. Then, write those emails first. You can check new emails later. Making a plan may only take a couple of minutes but can save you hours of time reading and replying to emails that aren't important.

- **Watch out for email addiction:** Decide in advance how many times a day you're going to check your emails. For some people, once is enough; for others, once an hour is necessary. Unless your primary role is dealing with emails, you need to ensure that you're not in the habit of constantly checking your inbox. If you find that even sticking to a nominal number of checks a day isn't working, write down the actual times of day that you're going to open your inbox. Imposing discipline on yourself in this way helps you retrain your mind so that you focus on what's in front of you rather than being constantly distracted by often unnecessary messages.

- **Breathe before sending:** Before you send an email, take three mindful breaths. Doing so helps you to become more mindful, gives you an opportunity to reflect on what you've written and helps you to stay focused. Give it a try!

- **See your email from the other person's perspective:** After you've taken your mindful breaths (see preceding point), imagine how the other person is going to feel when they read your email. You may decide that it needs editing before you send it. You may even give them a call instead!

 Chade-Meng Tan, the man behind mindfulness programmes at Google, recalls one staff member who tried this technique. Apparently, when this person said they'd tried something different and made a phone call, everyone in the room gasped! At Google, technology obviously rules.

- **Send at least one positive email every day:** Focusing on the good helps to rebalance your brain's natural negativity bias and makes both you and your recipient feel better. Praise an employee for settling into the team so quickly, thank your boss for her help with the report yesterday or congratulate Michelle on her sales presentation. A positive email is a great way to start the day.

Control your emails; don't let them control you. Choose who you want to respond to instead of reacting to every new email that lands in your inbox. Cultivate good email habits, such as limiting the time you spend on them and focusing only on those that are essential. Above all, be mindful and present as you deal with emails. Use your favourite mindful exercises before and after emailing to help you achieve greater focus.

Turn off your message notifications, so that you aren't alerted each time a new one arrives. Doing so is your first step towards reducing the amount of time you waste in this way.

Phoning mindfully

One day one of our clients wanted to do something different. When he received a routine email from accounts, he decided to phone the sender rather than simply email his response. The phone seemed to ring for quite some time before a tentative voice said, 'Hello?' Our client told the woman that he was the Mark she'd been emailing for years but had never actually spoken to. They went on to have a pleasant conversation and Sarah in accounts said the call made her feel less like a machine and more like someone who actually works with other people. That encounter was certainly a wake-up call for our client!

Mindful phoning means bringing a greater degree of awareness to the process of being on the phone. With mindful phoning, you need to be aware of several things:

- ✔ What the other person is saying
- ✔ Their tone of voice
- ✔ What you want to say
- ✔ Your state of mind
- ✔ What you want to achieve from the conversation
- ✔ How you can be of help to the other person

Try this exercise next time you make a phone call:

1. **Take a few moments to be mindful:** Practise a short mindful pause by feeling your breathing, your bodily sensations or connecting with one of your senses.

2. **Write down the aims of the conversation you're about to have:** This only takes a few seconds.

3. **Stand up:** If you usually sit down all day facing a computer, making a phone call provides a great opportunity to get to your feet and move your body around a bit.

4. **Listen more than you speak:** Make sure that you listen to the other person's tone of voice as well as their actual words.

5. **Be aware of your emotions.** If the conversation makes you feel anxious or angry, notice the feeling in your body. Feel the emotion with your breathing and then speak from your wise mind rather than reacting automatically to your feelings, saying things you may later regret. Try to tap into greater levels of mindfulness as the conversation progresses. Breathing mindfully can help!

6. **End the conversation when you need to, rather than dragging it out unnecessarily.**

The key to mindful phoning is to do a short mindful exercise before phoning. Then you'll be more focused and present during the call itself.

Using a smart phone mindfully

Smart phones are pretty smart. They can check emails, update social media, surf the web, take photos and make videos, edit videos, upload to YouTube, write a blog post, access loads of apps, work with documents, enable video chat, manage your calendar, help you find a restaurant, use global maps with GPS, tell you the time anywhere on the planet, let you read and listen to books, buy products and even learn mindfulness! Oh, I almost forgot: You can make phone calls too.

Smart phones are particularly addictive and can drain your mental focus and creativity when used excessively. A study of 1,600 managers conducted at Harvard University revealed that:

- ✔ 70 per cent check their phone within an hour of waking up.
- ✔ 56 per cent check their phone in the hour before they go to sleep.
- ✔ 51 per cent check their phone continually when they're on holiday.

Prime minister bans smart phones

Prime Minister David Cameron doesn't allow use of mobile phones and Blackberries during meetings. He wants his ministers to be totally focused when they're talking with him. He's not alone. More and more senior executives ban phones from meetings. One executive even fines his staff five pounds for using their phones and donates the money to charity. He actually asks his secretary to call everyone's phone during meetings to try to catch people out!

Compulsively checking your smart phone becomes a problem when it starts interfering with your everyday life. Reading your emails instead of listening to someone speaking in a meeting is one example. But what about scanning through your Facebook updates when you're listening to a customer on the phone – such behaviour may cost you and your company lost revenue.

If you think that you need an injection of mindfulness to bring your smart phone habits under control, try these tips:

✔ **Be conscious:** When you feel the desire to check your emails or suddenly find yourself gazing at your beloved iPhone, ask yourself what emotion you're feeling. What emotion are you trying to avoid? Anxiety, boredom, loneliness perhaps?

✔ **Be disciplined:** Turn off your device in certain situations, such as when you're driving, attending meetings, playing with your children and eating supper with your partner – all the key moments in your day when focus is called for.

✔ **Ride the wave:** When you feel an urge to check your phone, take mindful breaths and be with the feeling rather than acting on it. Your compulsion should gradually weaken.

✔ **Don't give up:** If you relapse into your 24/7 phone-checking habit, don't feel defeated. Try again. You don't need to beat yourself up about it. Your smart phone really is addictive, so be friendly to yourself and have another go.

If you can afford to do so, use one phone for work and another for your personal life. That way you can literally switch off from work at the end of the day.

Here are a few strategies to help you manage your smart phone with mindfulness:

✔ Don't check your messages in the morning or evening.

✔ Switch off notifications on your phone except those for text messages.

✔ Set your phone on flight mode whenever you're focusing on a piece of work.

✔ Turn off your phone when attending meetings, going for a walk or enjoying time with friends.

Engaging with social media mindfully

Social media, such as Facebook, Twitter and LinkedIn, has changed the way many businesses operate. Entire companies have emerged to help organisation manage their social media – the way they connect with their customers and suppliers. And traditional advertising is finding itself working less effectively as social media is far more interactive, engaging and fun for consumers.

Here are some key principles to consider when using social media in a way that means personal and business use overlap, as often happens in small to medium-sized organisations:

✔ **See business social media as part of your working day:** So, when you're with family, keep it off. Just as it would be rude to start checking your emails when your partner is talking to you, so too is using social media for business purposes.

✔ **Update at set times:** Update social media using apps such as Buffer or HootSuite so that you reduce the time you spend turning on and off all the separate social media channels.

✔ **Be friendly:** You can easily end up seeing people as just another number. They're not – behind each connection is a human being. If they have a comment or question, do respond. If you've too many messages to respond to individually, acknowledge their comments in a group response.

✔ **Seek to make genuine connections rather than superficial contacts:** Customers will feel better for it, and so will you. And those connections may lead to more business.

✔ **Give more than you receive:** Seek to help others. Seek to help others. If someone has a question which isn't directly related to your business, you can still help out. Just as you wouldn't ignore someone in person who asked you a question, don't ignore them when online either.

Writing mindfully

Pretty much every modern business in the world has a presence on the Internet. And websites need content. Although such content is increasingly in the form of video and audio, the Internet is still awash with the written word. To be successful online, you need to be able to write well or hire someone with that skill.

Writing effectively is also important for communication. Emails, text messages, reports and even presentations involve writing. So, how can you write in a way that engages your readers? And what does mindfulness have to contribute to the art of writing?

Having written five books, I (Shamash) have spent a lot of time in the last few years just writing. And here's what I've learnt about writing in a mindful way:

- ✔ **You need to look after yourself:** Writing well requires that your brain is working at its optimal level. You can't achieve this state for long if you're feeling tired, hungry, cold or stressed out. Ensure that you go to bed on time and get enough sleep. Eat something every few hours, and make sure that meals contain plenty of fruit and vegetables. Keep a bottle of water to hand – the brain works much better when properly hydrated. Make sure that the room is at a comfortable temperature; you feel more relaxed as a result. Finally, if you're under a lot of pressure take regular breaks and find time to socialise and exercise. Even if you're facing a big deadline, try to prioritise breaks and make time for mindfulness practice. Doing so will make you more efficient.

- ✔ **Timing is everything:** Keep a time journal to identify at what time of day you're most efficient. Then do your writing at that time. You need to make that time sacred – avoid phone calls, meetings, emails and any other distractions.

- ✔ **Mindfulness exercises keep you focused:** Practise mindfulness exercises as often as you can. Use the mindful body scan or do some informal mindfulness when you're walking or eating. Try to connect with your senses whenever mindfulness comes to mind.

- ✔ **Outside distractions need to be removed:** To be able to write well, you need to focus. Block out as many distractions as you can. Silence your phone; don't tell other people where you're working; close all other programs on your computer.

- ✔ **You need to manage your inner critic:** You need to take that inner voice who judges everything you do in hand. For some reason, the process of writing really wakes it up! Fortunately, you can use mindfulness to manage your inner critic. First, you notice those negative thoughts and then you say to yourself 'inner critic' and have a little smile. Smiling sends a signal to your brain (neurons connect the brain to the muscles that are used to smile) that you're not scared of that voice. Fighting or frantically running away from your inner critic can exacerbate its judgemental voice. Each time you address your inner critic in this way, you weaken its power until eventually, if you're lucky, it dies altogether.

- ✔ **Writing non-judgementally is a powerful tool:** Mindfulness means moment-to-moment non-judgemental awareness. So, try a period of time just writing down whatever comes into your head, without judging it. Don't correct sentences, delete words or fix spellings. Just go with the flow and write. Doing so is a true mindfulness process – being in the moment and allowing whatever arises to be as it is. Later on, you can go back and correct your mistakes.

If you write on a computer, lots of software is available to help you stay focused. I like to simply put Microsoft Word into 'Focus' mode. Then you just see the document you're writing and all other windows disappear – ideal for you budding mindful writers out there! Another option is Ommwriter – available for Mac, PC and iPad.

Using Technology Mindfully

Can technology be used mindfully? We think that anything done with awareness, wisdom and compassion is a form of mindfulness. Although mindfulness has traditionally been associated with more natural surroundings, there's no reason why mindfulness can't be applied between uses and whilst using technology.

Technology can help to make you *more* mindful. Various phone apps, computer programs and online courses encourage greater mindfulness. Even a few computer games show you how to be more mindful or remind you to tune into your breathing.

Focusing on one task

Multi-tasking is actually impossible. When you multi-task, you actually switch from one task to another, creating the illusion of doing several tasks at once. Multi-tasking is often an inefficient way of working. Chapter 18 discusses multi-tasking in detail.

Are you a so-called multi-tasker? If so, you're not alone – nowadays most people try and use multi-tasking to finish more work in less time. Multi-tasking can become particularly prevalent when using technology. But, alas, the strategy often backfires. The process can also lead to you feeling unfocused, making mistakes and getting wound up.

Here are some common examples of multi-tasking when using technology that lead to less efficiency rather than more:

✔ **Having lots of windows open on your computer:** Having too many windows open not only slows down your computer, making your work take longer to do, but also makes you more likely to move between one task and another, rather than finishing one task and then starting the next.

✔ **Emailing while working:** Most people leave their email program open all day and reply to messages as they arrive. Doing so distracts you from your work and can leave you feeling frazzled by the end of the day. Try turning your email notification off for a day to see what happens.

✔ **Sending texts while crossing the road:** Typing a text message needs your full attention. You're breaking the law if you use your mobile phone while driving, for good reason – you can't concentrate fully on two things at once. The same applies to crossing the road.

✔ **Using your phone or computer while eating lunch:** Make time for a break at lunch. Applying a mere 15 minutes of mindfulness helps you make better choices about what you eat and aid your digestion. If that's too hard for you, try just a few minutes of eating without distractions. Your whole afternoon may go more smoothly if your lunchtime is a bit more mindful. One of our clients decided to have a relaxing lunch in the local park every day, no matter how busy she was. In the end, several colleagues joined her. Because staff burnout was a big problem in their company, they were making a wise choice to rest at lunchtime.

✔ **Using digital technology while driving:** It can be tempting to check emails, send texts and see who's up to what on Facebook while behind the wheel. If you lack mindful awareness, you may easily develop this dangerous habit. See Chapter 4 for more on mindful driving.

If you're a multi-tasker and are convinced that doing several tasks works for you, then so be it. But if you feel life is too frantic and would like to explore a different way of working, give single-tasking a try, even for short blocks of time. Do one thing at a time, with your full attention and see what happens. Start with 10 minutes or half an hour – whatever you can manage.

Try keeping just one browser window open at a time on your computer. Doing so makes you feel more focused and efficient. Complete the task you need to do with that window and then close it.

Discovering technology that enhances focus

As well as all the methods of discovering mindfulness that are available online, programs to enhance your focus also exist. They block Internet access or analyse how you've used your time while on the computer. We describe a few of them below.

SelfControl (`http://selfcontrolapp.com`)

SelfControl for Mac is a free program that can be used to block whatever websites you find yourself wasting time on. So, for example, you can block access to your

Facebook and Twitter accounts as well as your email, for a time period of your choice. I (Shamash) like using this for several hours during the day when I need to focus on writing or just need a break.

Freedom (www.macfreedom.com)

The whole Internet itself can seem like a distraction sometimes. This program works on Mac, Windows and Android and blocks complete access to the Internet for whatever period of time you choose.

RescueTime (www.rescuetime.com/)

If you use your computer a lot, RescueTime may be a good program for you. It runs in the background and keeps a record of how long you spend using different programs during the day. It then uses the data to calculate how productive you are. The program presents graphs to show you at which parts of the day you were most productive, and which periods of time you spent surfing the Internet, reading blogs and so on. The amount of detailed feedback this program provides is fascinating. The basic version of the program is free too.

For more information on technology to enhance your mindfulness, see the resources section in Chapter 20.

Gathering of minds at Wisdom 2.0

Every February for the last few years I (Shamash) have attend the Wisdom 2.0 Conference in San Francisco. This conference started as a small gathering in 2009. The event focuses on living with greater presence, compassion and wisdom in the digital age. It addresses the great challenge of our age: to live connected to one another through technology in ways that are beneficial to our own well-being, effective in our work and useful to the world. The conference brings together leaders from the field of technology with teachers from the wisdom communities, such as mindfulness or yoga practitioners. Wisdom 2.0 has flourished and in 2013 almost 2,000 people attended. Speakers have included the CEOs of the Ford Motor Company and LinkedIn, the founders of Twitter, PayPal, eBay and Facebook and mindful teachers Eckhart Tolle, Jon Kabat-Zinn and Jack Kornfield. If you can't attend, you can find videos of many of the excellent talks online at www.wisdom2summit.com or on www.youtube.com

Part III
Mindfulness for Organisations

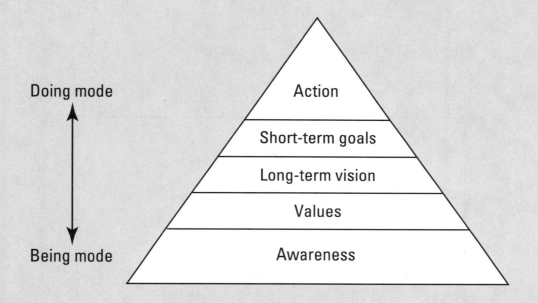

In this part . . .

- ✔ Use mindfulness to improve team dynamics and performance.

- ✔ Enhance internal and external business relationships.

- ✔ Apply mindfulness to a range of specific business functions.

- ✔ Understand the importance of mindfulness coaching – and whether it's for you.

- ✔ Commission and implement mindfulness training in your workplace.

Chapter 9

Improving Team Performance with Mindfulness

*T*he old adage 'many minds are better than one' is true. Working as part of a great team is usually better than struggling alone in isolation. Team working can increase creativity as members share knowledge and build on each other's ideas. It can provide a great opportunity for members to develop and acquire new skills. It can get things done more quickly and, when it works well, increase employee satisfaction. But as any leader knows, teamwork can also be one of the most challenging aspects of the job. In this chapter you discover how mindfulness can help you make teams work together more effectively. Let's get started by exploring team dynamics.

Identifying and Harnessing Team Dynamics

As a leader, you already know the impact that team dynamics can have on your team. As a team member, you'll have observed its impact also. You can see team or group dynamics at play in a variety of situations: the family gathering for Christmas or a wedding, friends socialising in the pub or a group of people meeting for the first time.

Although you may have seen many complex theories on team dynamics in management textbooks and academic journals, understanding team dynamics is really quite straightforward.

Understanding team dynamics

Few humans exist in isolation. As a human, in common with many other animals, your behaviour is likely to be based largely on habit, adapted and influenced by your social networks. These social networks include family, friends and work colleagues. Your behaviour is also likely to be influenced by social and cultural norms.

The modern workplace is rarely set up to accommodate the human need to connect, understand and work with each other. Neuroscience research into areas such as how the brain enables you to undertake tasks such as decision making and prioritising (cognitive neuroscience), the way the brain processes social interactions (social neuroscience) and how the brain deals with emotions (affective neuroscience) is beginning to identify the drivers of human social behaviour.

Chapter 5 describes the evolutionary principle, which means that your brain seeks to minimise danger and maximise reward. This fact often motivates humans to spend more energy avoiding things they think may be risky or non-beneficial than approaching and exploring new possibilities. Many aspects of work can be seen as threatening or rewarding, including:

- ✔ **Job role or position within the organisation.** Your position in the organisational hierarchy is likely to shape your social relationships at work; that is, those with whom you feel relaxed or those with whom you have much or little in common.

- ✔ **Extent to which you can control your working environment.** In a senior or specialist role you may have a high degree of control over your work, but in administration or manual labouring role you may have little. Research suggests that staff with low job control are more prone to stress and four times more likely to die of a heart attack than those with high job control.

- ✔ **Sense of equality.** Lots of research demonstrates that humans are drawn to fairness and dislike unfairness. If you feel unfairly treated, or see others unfairly treated, you're likely to experience a strong threat response.

So what's all the above got to do with mindfulness? Mindfulness can help both leaders and employees to become more aware of these social dynamics as they arise and change in the present moment. This awareness is key if you're to be successful in identifying team dynamics at play and harnessing them for the good of all concerned.

Before we look at specific ways that mindfulness can be used to assist with team dynamics at work, we need to look how social dynamics work.

I (Juliet) used to work with Peter. Peter (not his real name) worked for a major rail maintenance operator in the UK and managed large teams that are responsible for repair and maintenance of the railway tracks and buildings. Peter approached me as he knew that in a few weeks time he would be managing a major renewal project that involved coordinating a team of signal engineers (who maintain the signals) and Pway Engineers (who maintain the track). The team of signal engineers had a different working culture to that of the Pway engineers. Although all are dedicated to keeping the trains running safely, communication problems are evident between the teams and all sorts of other frictions existed.

I helped Peter to identify some of the social dynamics at play in his work. The signal engineers regarded their *job role* as being more skilled and of higher status than the Pway engineers, whom they described as 'monkeys'. As highly trained and qualified engineers, the team had considerable *control* to decide on the right course of action, and how the job would best be carried out. They felt a strong sense of social cohesion with other signal engineers, and those on the railway who had similar technical jobs. They had little in common with the Pway staff, who mainly did routine, manual, heavy work.

The Pway staff regarded the signal engineers as 'geeks'. They argued that, without the tracks themselves, electric masts, points, bridges and other railway infrastructure, no need for signals would exist. Their work was thus, in their eyes, of equal importance. They felt that their *job role* as Pway workers should be equal to that of the signal engineers, and resented the *inequality* evident in the signal engineers being treated with more respect by those in charge. On top of these issues, they had less control over their work, which was often dictated by factors beyond their *control*. If new track was late being delivered, they could not lay it. If the signal engineers were at work on one area, they had to work somewhere else. They regarded the signal engineers with mistrust, as several years ago a signal engineer had reported a (now redundant) Pway engineer for larking about on the job. They saw *inequality* in the situation whereby signal engineers always seemed to spend the last hour of work 'doing nothing' while they bust a gut to get the job finished in time.

Peter recognised that the Pways staff worked in a much more uncertain environment, and had much less control, both factors that humans can find highly threatening. He also recognised that the roles of the two teams were different so they were unlikely to feel part of the same social group as they had little in common. Peter saw that the Pway staff were feeling threatened by the apparent preferential treatment they felt the signal staff received. Peter started to understand how these factors may be making the Pway staff feel unconsciously threatened, and that this situation explained why they sometimes appeared to be arguing over trivial points or being difficult. It was just their brains trying to look out for them, trying to keep them safe and well.

Although Peter could see the problems, and why the friction was occurring, he was not sure how to deal with it. This situation where mindfulness (Had I known about it then) would have come in.

Managing team dynamics mindfully

If you look at Peter's dilemma from a mindful perspective. you discover that:

- ✔ Consciously or unconsciously the Pway staff were feeling threated by the working methods and attitudes of the signal staff. This threat was likely to release powerful hormones into their bodies, and to some extent diminish their capacity for rational behaviour.

- ✔ Over time, both the signal and Pway staff had created their own mental record or story of what was going on. It was highly likely that they then treated this story as reality – a solid fact – and based their behaviour to each other on this story rather than what was actually happening. Believing their story to be reality, it was likely that their brains were actively seeking evidence to reinforce this picture of what was going on.

- ✔ Peter needed to find a way to get his teams to start work with a clean slate, working together in the present moment rather than defaulting to auto-pilot reactions.

Peter's task was to:

- ✔ Try to get staff to work from a present-moment perspective, working on present-moment facts and setting aside past working relationships

- ✔ Try to get both groups to feel that they were equally valued on this job (similar status)

- ✔ Help increase certainty as far as practical for the Pway staff

- ✔ Provide some more autonomy if possible for the Pway staff

- ✔ Try to engender a feeling of 'all working together to make this project happen on time and to maintain line safety' (a feeling of all being related or belonging to the same group)

- ✔ Offer a reward for all staff if the project was completed on time to the required standard (fairness and valuing all).

So how could Pater have applied this knowledge to his work challenge? It might have gone something like this . . .

At the planning meeting Peter gathered together team leaders from the Pway and signal teams. He ran through the tasks, describing what needed to be done and when, and outlined the fines that would be incurred if they overran and trains were stopped or delayed as a result.

Peter explained his findings, and asked for ideas about how they could start this job with a clean slate. He encouraged the staff to look at what was happening in the here and now. Together, they made plans to address the six points that Peter had identified. It was agreed that some Pway staff and signal staff should swap places so that they could gain a greater appreciation of each other's roles, and also increase certainty and relatedness for both groups. They agreed on the joint reward of a free breakfast for all if things went according to plan.

Peter started the project by bringing the staff together and emphasising that everyone was responsible for getting the job completed, to the required standard, on time. He explained that the company would get fined for lateness and delays caused, and that would impact on each and every one of them. He emphasised the importance of all the workers playing their part, with no job being any more or less important than another.

The team leaders worked hard to nip things in the bud when staff reverted to old thought patterns and behaviours. They brought team members back to the present moment if they started to spiral into anger or frustration in anticipation of what would happen next, based on past experiences. They reinforced Peter's messages and changed the subject if anyone started to moan about other teams working on the project.

Peter's project finished early, leaving time for an additional quality check at the end, resolving some last minute issues. Breakfast was enjoyed by all, and Peter gained a sense that this shared experience was the start of better working relationships within his teams.

Here are some tips for mindfully creating better team dynamics:

- ✔ Use up-to-date models to identify things that may detract from good working relationships within your team.

- ✔ Lead your team with fresh eyes every day. Focus on what's happening in the here and now, rather than what you think is happening based on past experiences.

- ✔ Remember that, although your team members are there to do a job of work, they're human beings, not human doings!

- ✔ Be constantly aware of the huge impact that emotions and physiology have on thoughts. If your team members are worried, angry or uncertain, their work suffers. Help your team to create as much certainty as possible and stay focused on the present moment.

- ✔ Give your team a break – literally and emotionally:

- ✔ Encourage staff to take a few moments to refocus their efforts by taking a three-step focus break (see Chapter 6).

- ✔ Encourage team members to celebrate success and achievement, ticking off each little job as another task done.

- ✔ Encourage self-kindness. As a leader you probably want all your team members to strive to be the best they can, but working harder and harder and later and later results in less performance. Encourage staff to take some time out and come back to the task with fresh eyes and renewed attention.

Walk the talk! Demonstrate a mindful approach to your work and the way you lead. Doing so encourages your team members to adopt new, healthier, more productive working habits.

Remind your team members that the problem isn't the problem! Your interpretation and response is what can cause the problem. You may not be able to make the problem go away, but you can alter the way you think about it and respond.

Improving Team Performance

As a leader, your primary role is to motivate and lead team(s) to achieve desired organisational outcomes. A key aspect of this leadership role is identifying team dynamics at play, and encouraging good working relationships and understanding between different teams and team members.

When trying to improve team performance, leaders often lose sight of what's really important. Mindfulness is a great way to bring yourself back to the present moment, see what's really important and refocus your efforts.

As more neuroscience research into mindfulness emerges, leaders are adopting more mindfulness techniques to assist them lead effectively in times of constant change, pressure and uncertainty. Wise leaders are introducing mindfulness within their teams, helping their staff to get more from their job role and to find a new way to relate to their work.

Lastly, as a leader, keeping your eye on the goal is vital. What is it that your team are supposed to be doing for your organisation? What is the greatest contribution you can make? We need to look at each of these in turn.

Recognising what's important

Why do you do the job that you do? Why do you work for the organisation you work for?

You may have chosen to work for your company based on a mental picture of it formed from your perceptions of its products, services, mission and vision or what you have read. You may have been lucky enough to have insider knowledge gained from friends and family. When you started to work for your company, you may have found that your perception of what it was like to work for it was different to the reality – for better or worse!

THE SCIENCE BEHIND IT

How we make sense of the world

Schema theory is an attempt to make sense of how humans organise knowledge and form pictures of the world. The theory states that all knowledge is organised into units. These units are called 'schemata'. Schemata represent knowledge about concepts: objects and the relationship they have with other things.

As a simple example if you think about a cat, you'll have knowledge of cats in general (four legs, long tail, ears, teeth, whiskers). You're likely to have knowledge of a specific cat (black, long whiskers, loud meow, loves food, called Bramble). You may also think about cats in the wider context (pet, living being, furry, hunter). Your knowledge may include that they're warm-blooded mammals. Depending on your personal experience, you may add in 'bite, scratch and hiss' if you've had a negative experience of cats. If you're very concerned about hygiene, you may add 'shed hair everywhere, dirty paws,

carry fleas'. If you're a cat lover, you may add 'purr, rub against my legs, sit with me and keep me company'.

All of this information combined creates your picture of the world. This picture remains in place until you encounter new information; you then decide if you should alter your picture of the world to accommodate the new information or dismiss it and keep your picture of the world exactly the same.

The above explains why different people can have a different picture of the same thing – and thus react to the same thing differently. Practicing mindfulness helps you to see the bigger picture. By recognising that your mind 'edits out' things it thinks are irrelevant, you can train your brain to consciously observe more details when you need them to gain a more balanced view.

In much the same way, when you applied for the job role you now hold you formed a mental picture of what the job role was all about, the difference you could make, and probably things you could improve or introduce. Again, you may have found the reality somewhat different to your perception of how it would be. Why is this?

Humans tend to dislike uncertainty. Thus, when you don't know what the future holds; your brain tries to anticipate what will happen in the future based on past experience. Your brain then treats this mental picture of the future as a fact until something happens to make you alter or replace this representation of reality.

Being conned into thinking that how you see the world is the same as how others see it is all too easy. The same applies to what you think is important. In order to be effective as a leader, you need to take a step back now and again to see what's really important for yourself, your team and the organisation as a whole.

Mindfully seeing what's important

Here's a 15 minute exercise to help you identify important issues at work. Follow these steps:

1. **Settle yourself into a dignified upright position in a chair or on the floor.** Make sure that you're in a place where you feel comfortable and where you won't be disturbed for a short while. Put a pen and notepad nearby.

2. **Spend around three minutes focusing on the sensation of breathing.** Feel the breath coming in and the breath going out. Experience your breathing in the present moment, as it is right here, right now. You've nothing else to do in this moment except experience breathing. Nothing else matters.

   If your attention wanders, congratulate yourself on recognising that it has done so and then gently escort your attention back to your breath.

3. **Spend around three minutes focusing on how your body feels at this moment in time.** Start at your feet and work up to your head:

   • Look for sensations such as stiffness or tingling. In some areas, you will feel sensations and in others nothing.

   • Let go of any expectations regarding how your body should feel; just see what's there at this moment in time.

   • Gently escort your attention back to your body if your attention wanders.

4. **Spend two minutes focusing on what you currently do for your organisation.**

   See what arises. Observe your thoughts impartially, with kindness and curiosity. Avoid the temptation to think about what's arising and to get involved or judge it – just observe.

5. **Spend two minutes focusing on what your team could do to add most value to your organisation**

   See what arises. Again, just observe and avoid the temptation to think about it.

6. **Spend two minutes focusing on how you could be leading your team in this present moment**

   See what arises. Again, just observe and avoid the temptation to think about it.

7. **Return your attention to your breath.** Focus on your breathing for the remaining two minutes.

8. **Open your eyes and spend a moment gathering yourself together.**

9. **Write on the pad the thoughts that emerged in steps 4, 5 and 6.**
Consider whether:

   - Any disparities exist between your job role to date and what you should be doing in the future

   - Your team's efforts are focused in the right direction

   - Anything needs to be done differently in the future

Five minutes to refocus your work efforts

If you've been practising mindfulness for some time, you may wish to try a shortened 5 minute version of the 'Mindfully seeing what's important' exercise. Follow these steps:

1. **Settle yourself into a dignified upright position in a chair or on the floor.**
Make sure that you're in a place where you feel comfortable and where you won't be disturbed for a short while. Put a pen and notepad nearby.

2. **Spend two minutes focusing on the sensation of breathing.**

3. **Bring your focus to your job role and spend two minutes asking yourself:**

   - 'What do I currently do for my organisation'?

   - 'How should I be leading my team in this present moment?

   See what thoughts emerge.

4. **Bring your attention back to your breath.** Focus your attention on your breath for the remaining minute.

5. **Open your eyes and spend a moment gathering yourself together.**

6. **Write on the pad the thoughts that emerged in step 2.** Consider whether;

   - Any disparities exist between your job role to date and what you should be doing in the future

   - Your team's efforts are focused in the right direction

   - Anything needs to be done differently in the future

Introducing Mindfulness to Your Team

Mindfulness is increasingly being offered to employees as a development option. More research into the impact of mindfulness in the workplace is needed, but data suggests that it can help you:

- ✔ Function better when under pressure

- ✔ Focus your attention better on the task in hand

- ✔ Improve the way you manage strong feelings and emotions

- ✓ Respond differently to challenges and difficulties at work
- ✓ Improve relationships with colleagues
- ✓ Look after yourself better at work

If doing more of the same isn't producing the results you desire, why not try a different approach? Why not offer staff mindfulness lessons in work time? See Chapter 12 for more information on introducing mindfulness to your organisation. Mindfulness equips staff with the tools and techniques that can help them work with their brain rather than against it, and gain new perspectives and ways of working.

Keeping your eye on the goal

As a leader, keeping your eye on the goal is crucial. From time to time, you need to check and, if necessary, redefine your team's purpose and goals. Peter (who we met earlier in the chapter) redefined his team's purpose using the 'Mindfully seeing what's important' exercise.

Peter identified the following:

- ✓ His job title is 'senior infrastructure project manager'.
- ✓ His role is to ensure that projects are delivered on time, to budget and matching specifications.
- ✓ He currently spends 60 per cent of his time documenting, agreeing, monitoring and refining project plans; 20 per cent on reporting to stakeholders and documenting items; 10 per cent directly supervising work teams to ensure project delivery to the required standards; and 10 per cent on routine administration and attending organisational planning and strategy meetings.
- ✓ He is finding it more difficult to deliver projects on time and to budget despite being confident that his skills as a project manager are still effective and have improved over time.
- ✓ He is spending an increasing amount of time managing team dynamics and adverse reactions to organisational change.
- ✓ Peter concluded that, at the present moment and for the foreseeable future, the important things he needs to do are:
- ✓ Manage projects on time and to budget
- ✓ Provide more support to his direct reports to help them cope with the organisational changes and uncertainty they are facing

Peter rescheduled his diary to allow more time to lead and support his team, which led to improved team working and projects being completed faster and to a higher standard. He identified those aspects of his project management role that required the most skill and those that were more administrative. He started developing a member of his team as a project management assistant, supporting her to take on some of the more routine aspects of his work. He made more of an effort to identify the impact that planned changes were likely to have on his direct and indirect teams, and actively involved them in deciding the way forward.

As you can see, by taking time out to clear his mind using mindfulness, Peter was able to identify what was important in the present moment and to take steps to restructure his work and the work of his team to ensure that organisational goals continued to be met.

Staying focused using mindfulness

To mindfully keep your eye on the end goal, bear these tips in mind:

✔ Set aside regular time to practise mindfulness. Doing so reduces your tendency to work on auto-pilot and help you see things more clearly.

✔ Every three months or at the end of your mindfulness practice, ask yourself, 'What's important in my work at this present moment?' Restructure your work if necessary.

✔ Every six months or so, test your understanding of where the organisation is heading. Try to:

  • Arrange to meet with a few carefully selected senior managers to identify the organisation's key priorities at this moment in time and how your team can best contribute.

  • Prepare for each meeting by practising mindfulness for five to ten minutes, ideally just before walking into the meeting.

  • In the meeting really focus on what's being said, avoiding the temptation to jump to conclusions.

  • After the meeting identify four or five key things you've discovered, and decide whether any of your work goals need to change.

Enhancing Internal and External Business Relationships

Whatever your role within an organisation, actively cultivating good businesses relationships with colleagues and external contacts and clients is important.

Most relationships at work develop and are maintained with little effort. Some, however, require a lot of input. In the busy world of work, you need to make time to be really present when you're involved in one to one or group interactions with others. Many people say, 'Of course I'm fully present when I meet with people; I'm in the same room at the same time.' Although you can't argue with this statement, many people are rarely present. Their body may be there but their brain is juggling multiple things, retrieving related past experiences and trying to anticipate what will happen next. Mindfulness can help you quieten the mind, reduce your 'mental noise' and return to the present moment. In the present moment, you can see more clearly what is going on in full Technicolor glory – body language, facial expressions, tone and intonation, all of which add to the message but are often unnoticed.

The next sections show you how to be 'ready for anything' in meetings and get the most from your face-to-face interactions.

Becoming mindfully ready for anything

Managers and staff spend a huge amount of time in meetings. Research suggests that many managers regard much of this time as unproductive. With a little mindful preparation, this need not be the case. Most meetings are arranged with one or more goals in mind; indeed, many start with a set agenda. 'Without a reason to meet, why meet?' I hear you ask! While establishing the issues to be discussed is a good idea, retaining some flexibility to deal with equally or even more important things that arise unexpectedly in the moment is useful.

Are you one of those people who are too busy to prepare for meetings, arriving just in time and 'winging it'? You're not alone! However, taking a little time out to prepare leads to better meetings in which you get more done.

When preparing for meetings, use a three-minute focus break (see Chapter 5) to calm your brain chatter and return to the present moment.

Consider:

- ✔ Why the meeting has been arranged
- ✔ The organisational benefits that may be achieved
- ✔ What you can contribute to the meeting and gain from it
- ✔ Who will be there and why

Bear in mind that all the above points may or may not be true and accurate; they may just be mental constructs you've put in place to make sense of the world. Your thoughts here are only a starting point – be open to the meeting taking a new direction if beneficial.

Being in the meeting

When you enter the meeting room, try to ensure that you're fully present. The same applies if you're holding a one-to-one meeting in your office. Make an effort to be aware of any preconceived ideas you bring into the room with you, and try to set them aside as they may be inaccurate or unhelpful. If you've been practising mindfulness for a little while, you should find it easier to quieten your brain chatter and accurately identify these ideas, realising that they're only mental constructs and that they should be treated as such.

If, as the meeting starts, you find that lots of thoughts are going around in your head, try grounding yourself in the present moment.

Grounding yourself in the present moment

You can use this simple MAWT (see Chapters 6 and 7) technique when you enter a meeting as a participant or as the chair. If you're chairing the meeting, you may wish to start with a mindful minute (see Chapter 7) for everyone to centre themselves in preparation for the meeting. State the following:

- ✔ Observe your thoughts as mental processes that come and go. No need to fix them or do anything with them, simply focus on observing them.

- ✔ Experience how:
    - • Your feet feel in contact with the floor
    - • Your bottom feels in contact with the chair
    - • Your neck, shoulders and jaw feel in this moment in time

- ✔ Observe any sounds in the room or outside the room. Observe which are constant, which change, and notice any impact the sounds have on you.

- ✔ Return your focus to the meeting.

- ✔ Check every now and again that you're still in the meeting in the present moment and that your thoughts have not hijacked you and taken you elsewhere.

As the meeting continues, try really focusing on each agenda item, seeing it with fresh eyes and contributing to the discussion when appropriate. When you're more present in meetings, you may notice a host of other things going on that others may miss as their minds take them in different directions.

You may notice positive or negative body language, weariness or subjects that keep arising that aren't on the agenda, are dismissed and then pop up again. These subjects may need to be discussed and resolved in order to make the remainder of the meeting more productive. If appropriate, try to get these hidden issues on to the table and discussed. If doing so is wholly inappropriate, publically acknowledge that you've noticed them, and propose another time to discuss and resolve them. While this approach may seem counter-intuitive because you're adding more items to an already packed agenda, if people are distracted by a burning issue the meeting is likely to be unproductive or take longer. Surfacing, acknowledging and setting aside time to discuss important hidden issues saves you time in the long run.

Always ensure that meetings end with a thank you – so few meetings do! If you're the chair, propose a mindful minute to end the meeting. Next, sincerely thank attendees for their time and attention, and acknowledge what's been achieved. This simple act pays dividends. If done correctly, it has the power to activate people's parasympathetic nervous system (associated with rest and relaxation), resulting in them leaving the meeting feeling good. In addition, it recognises and rewards the efforts people have made to make the meeting a success and engenders a sense of completion and accomplishment.

Following up mindfully

Always make sure that you follow up promptly on the promises you made in the meeting. These problems may include minuted actions and more informal promises such as getting data for someone or even a favour that someone asked of you in a coffee break.

Always make a note of these promises before you leave the meeting room. Your mind may easily be hijacked when you leave the meeting room, and as your working memory becomes overwhelmed, it may drop these promises and you may forget them. Noting the promises down means that you can delete them from your working memory, which frees it up to do other things.

Deliver on your promises as promptly as you can – especially the informal ones. Sometimes the more you think about doing something, the more of a story you create in your mind about it. This self-created story (based on your past experience and anticipation of the future) is treated by your brain as reality. It may procrastinate or try to avoid doing the task. Diving in and getting a task done without over-thinking it probably leads to its faster completion and stops you wasting time and distracting yourself from other tasks by over-analysing it.

Boosting Team Morale

Mindfulness can benefit individuals and teams in many ways, but isn't a magic solution or cure all. Being more mindful as you carry out your work can help you improve relationships with those you work with, and become more aware of what's happening, both of which are important when trying to boost team morale.

Morale is all about the team's capacity to consistently pull together in pursuit of a common purpose. Organisations with high morale tend to experience higher productivity and staff engagement. They have lower employee turnover and absenteeism, and a happier workforce.

Team morale may suffer as a result of change and restructuring, poor communication or a lack of control over work. Often managers are so busy with their inner story that they fail to realise what's happening right before their eyes. Increased complaints about work or team members, greater workplace conflict, more absenteeism and higher staff turnover are all indications that morale may be low.

The leader's morale can also have a profound impact on the morale of the team. Maybe you've been lucky enough to have worked for an energised, enthusiastic, positive boss. You may also have worked with a negative or disenchanted manager and noticed that this experience is a very different one. Team morale often starts with the leader, so leaders need to be good role models.

Improving morale with mindfulness

Here are a few tips for boosting morale:

✔ **Set a good example.** Whether you're the boss or the most junior member of staff, you can still set a good example at work. Mindfulness shows you that you may not be able to control everything that life throws at you, but you can choose your response. Your behaviour has an impact on how others think and behave, so make sure that you set a good example.

✔ **Look for signs of poor morale and nip them in the bud.** The sooner you notice that morale is taking a turn for the worse, the easier it is to do something about it. Always be mindful of the signs of low morale, such as increased absenteeism, work conflict and complaints. Look for the causes, and take steps to bring things back on track. If you're a leader, try to discuss the issue with the team in an open and honest way and really listen, without judgement, to people's responses.

✔ **Bring in the good.** When you become particularly busy, you may find it yourself stopping doing the things that nourish you (such as meeting friends for coffee or playing a musical instrument) and to focus more on the things you think are important, such as work deadlines and projects. This focusing more on work is a mistake. When you're busy you need more of the things that nourish you, not less! Make sure that you pencil into your diary time to do the little things in your life that feel really good. If you're a leader, try to encourage your team members to make time to do what they enjoy too. Discourage routine late working, and encourage staff to have a more appropriate life/work balance.

✔ **Celebrate success and gain a sense of completion.** Do you find yourself complaining that you've got nothing done today? In reality, you've probably got lots done, but you just haven't acknowledged it. When you're busy you may find that one job tends to merge into another and another, giving you little sense of completion. Mindfulness shows you the need for a sense of completion; the need to be kind to yourself and acknowledge that you have completed one task, before you start the next. Each time you complete a task, congratulate yourself on a job well done – however small –'another email responded to – yes!', 'another meeting concluded – yes!', 'another customer order completed – yes!'. Congratulating yourself helps you recognise just how much you've achieved and allow you to end the day with a sense of achievement.

✔ **Create certainty and avoid threat.** Mindfulness shows you how your brain craves certainty and tries to avoid things that may be threatening. If little certainty exists at work, most people try to create some by anticipating what will happen next. This self-created story may be accurate or inaccurate, and yet you're likely to respond to it as if it is real and really happening. If things are uncertain at work, try to find out as many facts as you can, and be aware of when your mind is trying to fill in the gaps. Try to respond only to present- moment facts rather than worrying about things that haven't happened, and may never happen. As a leader, be mindful of the negative impact of uncertainty on team morale. Try to create as much certainty as possible. Be open and honest and take steps to actively involve staff in what's going on. Doing so gives staff a greater sense of control and certainty, reducing stress and improving morale.

✔ **Encourage staff to get in the happy habit.** Happiness is a state of mind. Try to encourage happiness in the workplace. The Action for Happiness (www.actionforhappiness.org) website offers lots of free resources including posters for the workplace.

Focusing team effort with mindfulness

Mindfully refocus your team's efforts on what was important in this moment in time – just like Peter did earlier in this chapter.

Mindfulness is all about being able to switch your attention to the present moment, seeing things as they really are rather than how you perceive them to be. Even if your team has little knowledge of mindfulness, you can still use mindful techniques to focus on what's important in the here and now.

Try to make time to prioritise prioritising. Individually or as part of a team, make time to regularly reassess what's important. Try to do this reassessment early on in the workday, when your mind is fresh. If possible, use the mindfulness technique described earlier in this chapter, 'Mindfully seeing what's important'.

THE SCIENCE BEHIND IT

Habit releasers

Habit releasers are a tool introduced in Mark Williams and Danny Penman's book, *Mindfulness: A Guide to Finding Peace in a Frantic World*. Habit releasers can be a great way of exploring the power of habits and breaking away from acting on auto-pilot. By mindfully doing something different, and observing the impact of doing so, you can start to change deeply embedded habits. Try these two steps:

1. Select one simple thing which you normally do on auto-pilot to do differently. It may be sitting in a different chair, parking in a different area of the supermarket car park or using a different hand to do something like brush your teeth.

2. Observe the impact this small action has on your thoughts, emotions and physiology.

You may be surprised at what you discover!

Recognise the power of habits. The more often you perform a task in a certain way, the more likely you are to do it in the same way in future. Each time you repeat a behaviour or set of actions, you strengthen the connections in your brain associated with those activities. Routine tasks you do regularly become habits and get stored in a primitive part of your brain as a 'habit'. Research suggests that you cannot erase a habit when it has been formed, but you can, over time, replace it with another set of behaviours and thoughts. Use this knowledge to help yourself and others change habits so that they can do things differently at work.

Improving team relationships with mindfulness

TRY THIS

Sometimes conflict may occur between members of your team. Maybe an actual incident has created problems or possibly team members simply don't get on. Whatever the cause, your team is less effective if it doesn't pull together. As the leader, you need to resolve such situations. Follow this three-step guide:

1. **Diagnose problems.** At the first signs of poor relationships within your team, using the diagnostic methods used by Peter (detailed earlier in this chapter), or another method of your choice, to bring the issues to the surface.

2. **Bring the problems into the open.** While problems remain beneath the surface and not discussed, there's little you can do about them. Bringing them to the table in a supportive non-judgemental environment allows them to be explored and resolved. To ensure that the meeting is as productive as possible:

   - Prepare yourself for it by practising mindfulness for a short while to centre yourself and help you approach the meeting in a supportive, non-judgemental, less reactive manner.

   - Create a calm space for the discussion to take place.

   - Explain to the people involved that you think there may be some tension and you'd like to help all of them discuss it, air their views and collectively agree a way forward. Avoid telling them what you think is going on – let things unfold in the moment.

   - Allow all sides equal time to state their case, without interruption. Be mindful to ensure that everyone sticks to present-moment facts rather than judgements and 'their own story' of what's going on.

   - Allow the team members to decide a way forward for themselves. Only intervene or mediate if absolutely essential.

3. **Observe the unfolding situation and support all concerned as they make the changes needed.** Reward and encourage improved behaviour.

   Be mindful that, however hard you try, some people are never going to get on. In this case, encourage people to 'sit with the difficulty' (see Chapter 7) and find a way to acknowledge the discomfort and accept the impact that the person has on them without causing themselves any more unnecessary pain.

Chapter 10

Using Mindfulness to Assist Different Business Functions

Cultivating mindfulness is a valuable skill for staff working at all levels of the organisation, in all business functions, in all industries. Mindfulness won't diminish your drive for excellence and attention to what's important. It won't make you weak or ineffective, or brainwash you into donating all your worldly goods to a worthwhile cause in a far-flung corner of the world. Also, despite media portrayal of mindfulness, you do not have to sit cross-legged on a cushion, light incense or become religious!

To get the most from mindfulness, you really need to attend a course, and practise mindfulness each day, but these hints and tips should prove valuable to specific business functions. Many of the tips and techniques provided are equally applicable to multiple job roles. We make a start by looking at human resources.

Mindfulness for Human Resources

What's in a name? 'HR' (human resources), 'personnel' or even 'human capital management' are all names for the business function responsible for recruitment and selection of staff, defining job roles and setting pay structures. HR teams may also develop policies on how staff should behave and be treated, including equal opportunities and employee assistance programmes. Where the learning and development function sits under HR, the department is also responsible for developing staff at all levels. Although some aspects of HR such as telling someone they've got the job or have been promoted are satisfying, other parts can be highly stressful. Potentially stressful parts of the job include dealing with grievances and dismissals. This sometimes earns the HR function the nickname of 'the personnel police' or 'policy pushers'. In this section are suggestions on how mindfulness can help you to mindfully manage three key functions of most HR departments.

Managing downsizing and redundancies mindfully

The economic downturn has led to cost-cutting initiatives in both the public and private sectors. In many organisations, these initiatives have led to downsizing and redundancies year on year.

While you may not be able to halt the tide of redundancies, you can undertake the process in a manner that's kinder to yourself and those people at risk of redundancy. We start by focusing on the impact that managing redundancies has on you.

Although managing redundancies and dismissals is likely to be a key element of your work that you've probably studied and practised over the years, this doesn't necessarily make it any easier. Even the most cold hearted of HR professionals are likely to experience form of negative response to the task. As Chapter 5 explains, everything that you do or think has an impact on your thoughts, emotions and physiology, but in most cases you're unaware of the impact. This lack of awareness can be a good thing because it frees up your brain to work on other things. It can also be bad news if you start to unwittingly activate your sympathetic nervous system, flooding your body with powerful hormones that can be damaging. You may also unwittingly carry around tension in your body, which can have a profound impact on your decision making. So although you may think that you're giving your best at all times, your actions and responses may be being governed by a host of things you're completely unaware of.

This is where mindfulness comes in. Mindfulness training progressively trains you to direct your full attention to where you want it to be. It allows you to passively observe the interplay between your thoughts, emotions and physiology, and make conscious choices about how to best respond, rather than being governed by your unconscious mental programming.

Mirror neurons

According to researchers, a mirror neuron is a neuron that fires in the brain both when you act and when you observe the same action performed by someone else. So, in effect, mirror neurons 'mirror' the behaviour of others. In humans, mirror neuron activity has been found in the premotor cortex, the supplementary motor area, the primary somatosensory cortex and the inferior parietal cortex.

The exact function of the mirror system is still subject to speculation, but scientists believe that mirror neurons help us to understand the intentions of others, their mental state, and to pick up new skills by imitation.

Neuroscientist Marco Lacoboni argues that mirror neurons are the neural basis of the human capacity for emotions such as empathy. He believes that, when observing the physical or mental experiences of others, our mirror neurons make us experience similar feelings or sensations. This may explain why, if we're surrounded by angry people, we become angry, or if we observe people eating, we start to feel hungry.

Mirror neuron theory has important implications for the world of work. It impacts on the leader–follower relationship and for those, such as HR staff, who routinely have to manage highly charged emotional situations.

Another factor to consider is the potential impact of mirror neurons. Mirror neurons may cause you to experience the emotions of the people surrounding you, which may impact on your decisions and behaviour. Mindfulness helps you to focus attention on the present-moment experience, allowing you to notice when your emotions are being influenced by mirror neurons, and decide on a wise course of action.

While you cannot necessarily 'manage' the emotions of others, you can take steps to avoid any negative emotions you are harbouring from spiralling out of control. By being fully present in meetings with others, you can observe as and when emotions start to spiral and take steps to avoid things escalating.

Here are a few mindful ways in which you can keep your meetings on track when strong emotions arise in others:

✔ **Take a few moments out.** Change the course of the conversation or just pause for a few moments to avoid adding more fuel to the fire.

✔ **Acknowledge the emotions, and try to help the person identify the thoughts driving them.** You can ask them, for example, 'I can see you're really upset. Would you like to share with me what's going through your mind?'

✔ **Demonstrate empathy.** Although you've a job to do, the world may be falling apart for the employee in front of you. Be as kind and compassionate as you can be while still ensuring that you deliver the organisational messages you need to.

✔ **Cultivate empathy.** If you find yourself suffering from compassion fatigue (common in the caring professions) and becoming immune to the suffering of others, make it a personal priority to cultivate empathy. Mindfulness can help you do so. You need to care about the people you are dealing with professionally while at the same time ensuring that you do the right thing for your organisation.

You may also wish to try out some of the mindfulness exercises described below.

Dealing with discipline and grievances mindfully

As with redundancies, dealing with discipline and grievances involves both care and doing the right thing (legally and ethically) for your organisation.

Preparing well for these sorts of meeting is crucial. Most HR people are fully aware of the need to check the facts from all concerned, company policy and the law. What you may fail to do is check that you're mentally prepared for the meeting. In other words, you need to ensure that you enter the meeting in the present moment rather than your body being there but your attention continually being hijacked by thoughts about other jobs you have to do or what you'll be doing when you get home. You also need to try to ensure that your thinking isn't overly influenced by past experiences or by what people *may* be saying or how they *may* be behaving.

Only through practising mindfulness regularly do you gain an appreciation of the elaborate stories that your brain creates when trying to anticipate the future. The problem with these stories is that your brain can treat them as reality, and you can start to experience emotions in response. For example, if when entering a grievance session you think that the manager concerned will become angry and the employee tearful, you may unconsciously interact with the manager in an assertive or even aggressive manner and treat the employee with patience and concern.

By being in the present moment and following an appropriate meeting structure, allowing each part to unfold moment by moment and responding to present moment facts, your meeting is likely to run more smoothly for all concerned.

Increasing employee engagement

Several research studies suggest that training staff in mindfulness can increase employee engagement. In addition, mindfulness has been shown to improve interpersonal relations, help employees improve the quality of relationships, increase resilience and improve task performance and decision making. Mindfulness training can improve your ability to cope effectively with your own and other's daily stresses, thus improving the quality of your relationships.

Applying some techniques

The following techniques have been developed for HR staff, but may be equally applicable and useful for other business functions.

Dropping into the present moment

When dealing with difficult issues, maintaining your balance and well-being by dropping into the present moment every now and then is important. Doing so helps you to:

- ✔ Observe what's grabbing your attention and regain control when your thoughts are spiralling.

- ✔ Release any tension you're experiencing and reduce the risk of your physiological responses impacting on your decisions.

- ✔ Shift yourself from avoidance mode to approach state of mind (see Chapter 1), which helps you to become more productive.

This exercise can take as little as three minutes or be extended to take up to ten minutes.

Sit yourself in a comfortable upright position. Close your eyes or hold them in soft focus. Regain your equilibrium using the **NOW** technique:

1. **Notice (but don't judge or start to interact with):**

   - The sounds in the room and nearby

   - How your body is feeling – any tensions or sensations

   - Any emotions you may be feeling

2. **Observe the impact (if any) that the points under 'Notice' above are having on one another.** For example, does a certain sound make your body tense? Are your emotions having any impact on your thoughts? Is a trend or theme emerging as you observe your thoughts? Again, you don't need to do anything or solve anything; just observe what's happening in the present moment.

3. **Wait.** Resist the temptation to jump into action based on what you've noticed and observed. Just let everything go and give your brain a break by focusing on nothing but your breath for a short while. Fully experience the present sensation as the breath enters your body and leaves your body; do so playfully, as if for the first time.

Open your eyes and make a decision on what's the best use of your time **NOW**, in this moment.

Mindfully managing difficult meetings

When planning difficult meetings such as discussing job losses or giving notice of redundancies, being in the present moment is important so that you can judge the situation as it unfolds based on present-moment facts rather than mental projections about what may happen in the future or did happen in the past. Doing so can make the meetings less stressful for all concerned. Follow these steps:

1. **Ensure that you've all the relevant documents ready and are fully acquainted with all the facts and people involved.** Be as well prepared as you possibly can be.

2. **Practise mindfulness for a short period.** Try Mindful Breathing, or the Body Scan or Mindfulness of Sounds and Thoughts, which can all be found in the audio downloads. If you've less time, try the three-minute focus break (see Chapter 5) or a mindful minute (see Chapter 7).

3. **Start the meeting by stating its purpose and what you are going to cover and specify when people will have the opportunity for questions.** This last point may sound obvious, but it's amazing how often this detail is missed when emotions are running high.

4. **Check in with yourself regularly to check that you are operating in approach mode in the present moment.** Periodically observe your thoughts or tune in to how a specific area of your body feels.

5. **Try to see things through the eyes of your audience.** They're likely to be feeling threatened, which will influence their thoughts and behaviour. When in the grip of the strong emotions, they're unlikely to be fully aware of their words and actions. This situation is natural; try not to take people's responses personally. Try to remain kind and considerate, bearing in mind the situation these people find themselves in. Remember, while managing meetings like this may be a regular occurrence for you, being threatened with redundancy may be new to them.

6. **Be kind to yourself!** Meetings about redundancies or grievances, for example, can be unpleasant and emotions can run high. You are a human being and not a machine, and as such you're entitled to feel emotional (angry, sad or even anxious). The important thing to remember is that the emotion is transient – it will come and go – it won't last forever.

Mindfully supporting staff

In your role you're likely to have many one-to-one informal and formal meetings with staff who may be worried about a variety of work-related issues. Your role isn't only to provide them with sources of information and support, but also to tap into how you can best help them in this specific moment in time. Unfortunately, if you've been involved in many meetings with staff over the years, acting on auto-pilot is all too easy. You need to remember that each meeting is unique and should be approached with a beginner's mind – as if you're experiencing it for the first time. Although approaching meetings this way may require a little more effort, the outcomes make it worthwhile. Follow theses steps:

- ✔ **Jump into the present moment by setting aside thoughts of what you were doing before the person walked in or what you need to do later on.** If you've time before the person arrives, practise a short mindfulness technique.

- ✔ **Closely observe what's unfolding in the present moment.** Rather than responding in a routine manner to what you think the person's needs are at this stage of the process, really listen to what is being said and how it's being said.

- ✔ **Respond based on what's being asked for in the present moment rather than on what you think you should be hearing.** Be honest, open and authentic.

- ✔ **Recap and summarise at key points in the meeting to clarify understanding and reassure the other person that you've heard and understood what they're saying.** A quick overview gives the other person the chance to correct your understanding if necessary.

- ✔ **Provide a quick summary at the end of the meeting and agree on what should happen next.**

- ✔ **Check in with yourself.** After the other person has left, let go of any tension or negative emotions you may be harbouring so that you're ready to tackle the next part of your day. A three step body check (See Chapter 6) or three minute focus break (see Chapter 5) should help you do this.

Mindfulness for Occupational Health

A great deal of research has concluded that mindfulness is great for well-being. Hundreds of research studies over the last 40 years have demonstrated the effectiveness of mindfulness in reducing anxiety, stress and depression. Mindfulness has also been proven to help people with chronic pain, such as back pain, and even to boost immunity. Several workplace studies have demonstrated its effectiveness in reducing sickness absence.

Improving staff well-being with mindfulness

Taking proactive steps to improve staff well-being is now more important than ever. Ongoing restructures and redundancies are taking their toll on those who are 'lucky enough' to still have a job. Research conducted in 1997 identified that, not only do survivors of redundancy frequently feel guilty, but continued uncertainty can have a huge impact on people's health and increase long-term sickness absence. A constant sense of uncertainty can cause excessive stress; which can also lead to increased occupational accidents and serious illness such as heart disease, high blood pressure or diabetes.

The Chartered Management Institute recently estimated that illness at work costs UK employers £12.2 billion a year, as a result of sick days taken. According to the Integrated Benefits Institute, which represents major US employers and business coalitions, poor health costs the US economy $576 billion a year.

Organisations can work to improve the well-being of their staff in many ways. Offering mindfulness courses to staff is a good way to improve not only well-being but also productivity and interpersonal skills. Some organisations offer staff mindfulness courses in work time and some outside working hours; some make attendance on mindfulness courses compulsory for certain staff, while others prefer it to be optional. While some organisations prefer to stick to the most widely researched method of teaching mindfulness (an eight-week MBSR or MBCT course – (see Chapter 12), others integrate aspects of mindfulness training with other well-being initiatives. See Chapter 12 for more information on introducing mindfulness to your organisation.

Tackling stress with mindfulness

It should come as no surprise that stress has become one of the greatest causes of long-term sickness absence from work. Mindfulness has been used to treat stress since the 1970s. MBSR was developed specifically to deal with mental distress such as stress, and thousands of research studies demonstrate its effectiveness in doing so.

As with all mindfulness at work interventions, evaluating staff both before and after taking part in a mindfulness course using well-recognised measures is important. If you wish to reduce stress specifically, you first need to meaure individuals current levels of stress. Consider getting staff to complete the DASS 21 (a shortened version of the DASS (Depression Anxiety Stress

Scales), developed by the University of New South Wales in Australia. The DASS 21 measures the severity of a range of symptoms common to depression, anxiety and stress. This measure can then be used as a benchmark pre-and post mindfulness training.

A word of caution – mindfulness isn't a sliver bullet. Simply attending a mindfulness course will not reduce stress. Reducing stress takes effort and commitment on the part of the stressed participant, who needs to practise what they're taught for a short time every day for the entire duration of the eight-week course. Research suggests a direct correlation exists between time spent practising mindfulness and the benefits experienced. In general, the more time spent practising, the more benefit is derived. Note also that, if a staff member is *very severely* stressed, a mindfulness course may prove unsuitable as the staff member may not be in a fit state of mind to work with the techniques they're taught. In this instance, seeking clinical help would be wise.

Reducing sickness absence with mindfulness

Well people who are well managed result in a well organisation. Well-being at work isn't the sole responsibility of the occupational health team but the responsibility of the whole organisation. Policies and working practices can have a huge impact on staff well-being, and are worth reviewing if staff absence and sickness are on the increase.

Mindfulness can equip staff with the tools to deal with life's challenges more effectively, which can reduce stress and anxiety. Mindfulness can also help people to stop small things escalating out of control and causing unnecessary stress. Mindfulness can help people live with long-term health conditions, including back problems and even cancer, by giving them new ways of dealing with their mental and physical pain.

Offer staff a place they can go to practise mindfulness in work time when the need arises. Just knowing that there's somewhere quiet that they're allowed to go to centre themselves and regain a more positive frame of mind can make a massive difference. Organisations offering this facility to staff report that the facility is rarely abused and is highly valued. Allowing staff to leave their desk for 10 minutes every now and then can save hours of unproductive time in the office and weeks off sick.

Mindfulness for Learning and Organisational Development

In order to serve your organisation well as a member of the learning and development team or organisational development team, you need to be able to see the bigger picture and think creatively. You may also at times have to focus your attention on statistics and diverse organisational performance data. A major part of mindfulness is all about training your brain to focus your attention where you want it to be. You won't be surprised to discover that research demonstrates that mindfulness does indeed improve your ability to focus on the task in hand. Evidence also exists that mindfulness training can increase your creativity and ability to step back and see the bigger picture.

Improving learning with mindfulness

Mindfulness can help improve learning within your organisation in two key ways:

First, practising mindfulness can improve your capacity to learn. It does so in several ways. Research studies have shown that mindfulness can improve your working memory. (Working memory gives you the ability to hold and use a limited amount of information in your brain for a short time; you couldn't perform mental arithmetic or follow a set of directions without it.) Working memory is essential for learning and development. Research has shown that practising mindfulness can result in positive changes in the brain areas associated with learning and memory processes, among other things.

Second, elements of mindfulness can be incorporated into many development programmes to make them more effective. A few are described below:

Using mindful minutes at various points during a training day

How? You can use them at the start, after lunch or as a break between two different topics.

Why? Mindful minutes help participants to quieten their mental chatter, and put them in a more receptive frame of mind for learning. It helps them release any tension and make it easier to absorb what is being taught. (See Chapter 7).

Explaining that 'thoughts are not facts', they're simply a mental process that you have created

How? Use this knowledge to help people to be more open when exploring new ideas or when challenging old, ineffective ways of working.

Why? Many people have a tendency to react to thoughts as if they were facts, especially when busy or under pressure. As an example, say that your boss likes you and is impressed by your work, but you think that your boss dislikes you. You start building up a story in your head about your working relationship. You may worry about being treated unfairly, overlooked for promotion or picked on. Your brain is then likely to treat these thoughts as facts, which in turn have a negative impact on your interactions with your boss.

Making mental constructs of the world as we see it is normal and helpful. However, if these mental constructs are different to present-moment reality they're not helpful.

Explaining the difference between approach and avoidance modes of mind

How? Explain the motivations underpinning both modes of mind and how cultivating an approach mode of mind is more productive. Staff can use this knowledge when trying to generate new ideas or new ways of thinking about things. Understanding the modes of mind is also useful for exploring things that underpin resistance to change. See Chapter 1 for background information.

Why? Many people live their lives in avoidance mode of mind, their actions and thoughts motivated by the desire to avoid something happening. Living in this way closes your mind to new ways of doing things and new opportunities.

Explaining the human threat response

How? Explaining the human threat response can help people understand why people find it difficult to focus or think straight at certain times. This understanding can also help them recognise when they're feeling under excess pressure, thus allowing them to take steps to return to peak productivity and put them back in control. See Chapter 1 for background information.

Why? Modern-day stressors can lead us to a high state of arousal, triggering a surge of strong hormones through our body that are intended to keep us safe from moral danger. In this state our brain is focusing on keeping us alive, so our capacity for higher-brain functions (which are unnecessary for survival) are diminished. These higher-brain functions include decision making, strategic planning and big picture thinking.

Improving strategic thinking with mindfulness

In order to offer maximum value to an organisation, learning and development initiatives need to be linked to organisational strategy. Organisational development teams work to improve organisational performance, and need a good grasp of strategy and the bigger picture.

Many mindfulness techniques help you develop the capability to think out of the box. Research demonstrates that practising mindfulness helps you to see the bigger picture. Other research studies suggest that practising mindfulness can help you to let go of your personal agenda. It can also help to increase creativity.

When undertaking complex planning and strategy work, you can easily get bogged down in the detail. Juggling stakeholder wants and needs with financial targets is never easy. When you can't see the wood for the trees, try this mindfulness technique. It helps you to step back and view things with a fresh mind, and encourage creativity. This exercise takes about 25 minutes, which may seem like a long time, especially when you're really busy. However, you can easily waste 25 minutes getting nowhere if you just continue working as you are. The act of focusing on your breath and body brings you back to the present moment (even if your mind does keep wandering!) and encourage an approach mode rather than an avoidance mode of mind.

Mindfully seeing what's important

1. **Find a room where you won't be disturbed for the next 25 minutes.**

2. **Write down the questions you're struggling to resolve.** Identify a maximum of three key questions and write each on one sheet of A4 paper.

3. **Settle yourself into your chair, sitting in a comfortable, upright position.** Close your eyes or hold them in soft focus.

4. **Focus your attention on the present-moment experience of breathing.** If thoughts arise, that's fine; just part of the process. Just acknowledge them, let them go and refocus on your breath.

5. **Spend five minutes seeing how your body feels in this present moment.** Start at the feet and work slowly upwards to your head. Notice any sensations, and how they differ. If you notice any pain or discomfort, try breathing into it on the in-breath, and letting it go on the out-breath.

6. **Open your eyes and concentrate your attention on the questions.** Restrict yourself to a maximum of two minutes to answer each question. Write down whatever pops into your head, however random, without judging or trying to make sense of it.

7. **Close your eyes or hold them in soft focus.** Spend around five minutes focusing your full attention on your breath.

8. **Look at what you've written on your A4 pad.** Identifying any key themes or things that leap out at you.

If you're really pushed for time, follow only steps 1 to 6, or better still, just focus on one key question.

Introducing mindful practices into the workplace

Unlike many other development techniques, mindfulness isn't a concept that you can grasp intellectually and then instantly benefit from. Most benefit is derived from practice. Practising mindfulness helps you, over time, to change the way you think and behave. This means that in order to introduce mindfulness into your organisation, you need to find an external mindfulness teacher (unless you're lucky enough to have a qualified one working for you already!). As a long-term goal, developing internal capacity to deliver mindfulness programmes is desirable, but this is likely to take a minimum of 24 months from start to qualified teacher status. This time can be reduced if you develop a member of staff who has already been practising mindfulness for some time.

You can also cultivate and encourage mindfulness in the workplace by starting meetings with a mindful minute or using the three-minute focus break technique when things are going round in circles or getting stuck. You may also wish to provide a quiet room where staff can go to spend a few quiet moments practising mindfulness to recharge their batteries and regain clarity of mind. No special equipment is needed – just comfortable, upright chairs and maybe a few large cushions for people who like to sit on the floor. Decorate the room with calming colours and install a blind at the window that staff can adjust to their liking. Lastly, a CD player with an MP3 socket would be useful, as staff may wish to follow guided practice on a CD or on their MP3.

For more information on commissioning mindfulness training, see Chapter 12.

Mindfulness for Service Delivery and Customer Service

Customer service and customer-facing staff are among the most important personnel in the organisation nowadays. They're the face of the company, interacting with customers on a day-to-day basis. Top companies appreciate the need for excellence in customer service, and the importance of achieving customer loyalty.

In order to be fully effective in these roles, you need to be fully in the present moment and avoid auto-pilot responses. This can be easier said than done, especially when you're dealing with customers face to face or on the phone all day long, many with similar questions and issues that need addressing. This section provides some mindful strategies for maintaining customer focus, communicating with clients and dealing with customer feedback.

Maintaining customer focus

Maybe you think that you know what your customers want and need, but are you sure? When was the last time you really listened and fully focused your attention on the customer? Many companies focus intensively on customer needs and desires when they're bringing a new product to market, but fail to keep their finger on the customer's pulse as soon as sales targets are being met. Wise companies dig beneath online reviews and recommendations, regularly making opportunities to hear what the customer has to say and act on it to ensure that their products and services continue to meet or exceed customer needs. When interacting with customers (one to one as a customer service representative or when running a focus group), mindfulness can be highly beneficial.

Take a few moments before talking to customers to observe your mental chatter, acknowledging whatever arises, and letting it go kindly without judgement or any further action.

1. **Centre yourself for a few moments by focusing on your breath.**

2. **Focus your attention for the duration of your meeting or phone call entirely on the present-moment experience of assisting, advising or listening to your customer.**

3. **Start with initial questions, but if unexpected things arise, go with them, really listen and reflect on what's said.** This approach is particularly useful if you're running a focus group.

4. **Make sure that the customer feels heard and that their input is valued.** Reflect back and summarise to confirm understanding, especially if the conversation is lengthy or complex.

5. **Check in with yourself regularly to check that you're 100 per cent focused on what's unfolding in the present moment, and that your mind has not wandered to the past or the future.** If your mind has strayed, be kind to yourself – you're only human! Kindly and gently escort your attention back to the present-moment discussion or conversation.

6. **Summarise after the call or meeting what you've gained from your interaction with the customer, and ensure that trends and new ideas are reported back to other areas of the business.** Identify whether you felt any strong emotions during the discussion. Take a moment to explore the impact these had on your thoughts and body.

Dealing with customer feedback mindfully

While most companies have some form of procedure for dealing with complaints, few have a process for dealing with positive feedback!

Dealing with criticism and hostility can be particularly challenging. When people are critical or hostile, feeling threatened is natural, even when you know that it isn't personal, and the customer is far away at the end of the phone line. Most customer service staff have been trained to deal with situations like this in a manner that's professional, polite and that, hopefully, leads to a happy customer. Unfortunately, dealing with difficult customers can take a toll on the staff member, as customer service training rarely shows you how to manage your mind and the importance of self-kindness.

Mindfully working with customer feedback

The next time you have to work with a customer who is distressed or angry, try this:

✔ **Be as 'fully present' as you can during the conversation.** Remember that, while your product or service may have been the catalyst for their anger or distress, there may be hidden factors driving the intensity of their reaction that may have nothing to do with you, your company or products.

✔ **Be compassionate towards them – think of them as a human in distress.** Adopting this attitude does two things. First, it can help diffuse a volatile situation. Second, it reduces your threat response, reducing the pressure you put on yourself. By reducing your threat response, your hormones return to normal and you can think more clearly and act more calmly.

✔ **Give yourself a few moments to check in with yourself after the call or meeting to make sure that you're in the right mental and physical shape to deal with the next customer.** Sitting at your desk, starting with your toes and working towards your head, see whether you're holding any tension anywhere. If you find any tension or discomfort, breath into it on the in-breath, and release it on the out-breath. This small act of self-kindness does two things. First, it allows you to fully release any tension you may still be unconsciously holding (remember that bodily tension can have a major impact on thoughts and mood). Second, it puts you into a more receptive, open, present moment state for dealing with your next customer interaction, free from the baggage of your last meeting.

If you work in a call centre or in an environment in which you don't have full control of your time, try to use your breaks to recharge your batteries and check in with yourself using step 3 above. Taking a few minutes out a few times a day is good for you and good for business. When in a state of (often unconscious) stress, your ability to provide an excellent service to customers is reduced, and you are much more likely to pick up bugs and viruses as your auto-immune system is diminished. Maintain your peak performance with these mini mindfulness exercises.

Communicating mindfully with customers

Chapter 7 shows you how powerful mindfulness can be when communicating with others. The same principles apply to your communications with customers, whether face to face or via the phone, email or letter.

Mindful communication spot check

When you've just written a letter or email, pause and take a few full breaths before you send it. As you do so, try forgetting the email and everything else and just focusing on your breathing. Then read the letter or email from your customer's perspective. According to Mirabai Bush, who taught mindfulness to staff at Google, doing so helps to clear up potential misinterpretations.

Mindfulness for Marketing and PR

In 2013 the job-finding website CareerCast listed public relations manager as the fifth most stressful job in the USA. Stress can be helpful, motivating you to strive and achieve more. But it can also cloud your judgement, have a negative impact on your mood, reduce your ability to make good decisions and cause serious illnesses.

In some organisational cultures, stress can be worn as a badge of honour; if you're not seen to be openly stressed, you're judged to be not working hard enough. Similarly, some organisations may encourage a culture of working long hours. Both stress and a poor life/work balance are bad for business. The statistics and research backing this up are hard to ignore.

When you're really busy, stopping and 'doing nothing' – even for five minutes – may seem counter-intuitive. Spending five minutes practising mindfulness can sometimes feel like doing nothing, but in fact you are working hard to develop the neural pathways in your brain associated with directing your attention to where you want it to be, and switching yourself into a more helpful mode of mind. You may want to direct your full attention to communication, consumer trends, culture or your own working methods, for example.

Communicating powerfully

The foundation that underpins powerful communication is a deep understanding of yourself: your beliefs, perceptions, judgement and intentions.

Humans are strongly motivated by their beliefs. These beliefs are often unconscious, but can override or impede what you consciously intend to do or say. Remaining fully present is impossible unless you understand what's motivating your feelings and behaviour in the moment. Practising mindfulness can help you develop a conscious understanding of your beliefs. This conscious understanding allows you to decide the extent to which your beliefs shape and influence your work.

As Chapter 14 shows, although you may think that you see the whole picture, your brain just picks out what it feels is most relevant at any given time and you make up the rest based on past experience and knowledge. If you accept that your perceptions of any given situation are likely to be limited, you can use mindfulness to help train yourself to see more and guess less.

Your judgement also plays a role in how you communicate. Again, this may be unconscious and can be highly damaging, both to yourself and others. When you feel judged harshly by others, your threat system motivates you to take defensive action. Practising mindfulness helps you recognise this response and minimise its harmful impact.

Lastly, but most importantly, you need to ensure that outcomes you desire from your communication are linked to your intentions. Make sure that you are fully aware of your intentions before you start to communicate, as these intentions gently steer you through your meeting or presentation. Try to remain open to what others are trying to communicate, and what a positive outcome looks like from their perspective.

You need to create a supportive atmosphere where powerful communication can thrive. For more information on mindful communication, see Chapter 7.

Keeping in tune with consumer and cultural trends

However much time you spend reading trade journals and industry reports, try to accept that you'll never be 100 per cent in tune with consumer and cultural trends. A better starting point is accepting a 50–70 per cent level of understanding, and using your eyes and ears to fill in the gaps when working with consumers or conducting market research. Don't forget that, while you only have one mouth, you have two ears and two eyes – use them wisely to see what's unfolding in front of you in the present moment.

When analysing consumer research and sales data, quickly note down your top three observations immediately after reading. Take a mindful minute. This mindful pause can take the form of focusing your attention on taking 10 full breaths, or mindfully drinking a hot drink, focusing on nothing but the present moment sensations, smells and tastes. What you do doesn't matter; the important thing is to quieten your mind, jump fully into the present moment and reduce your state of arousal so that you can view things with a clear, open mind.

Following the mindful minute, revisit the documents and look for any alternative trends or key facts you may have missed. Bear in mind that the researchers or authors of the documents will have interpreted the facts they were presented with according to their own judgement. They may have missed or discarded something that you think is important. Looking at the documents with a beginner's eyes can yield surprising results and eureka moments.

Improving responsiveness

When you practise mindfulness, you discover that a distinct difference exists between 'reacting' and 'responding'. Reacting is seen as defensive, often based on auto-pilot reactions stored in the fast to react primitive areas of your brain. Reactions are often fuelled by emotions, rather than rational, higher-brain thoughts. Responding is altogether more thoughtful. By pausing before acting, you allow yourself time to apply your more powerful higher brain. Responses contain reasoning, and are guided less by emotion and more by logic.

Although responding may seem more passive, a response is more active and can change the direction of an interaction. Practising mindfulness helps you to become more centred and aware of others. By embracing mindful prevention of reacting, you can focus on more beneficial responses that improve your interaction with clients and colleagues alike.

Chapter 11

Integrating Mindfulness with Coaching

Most medium- to large-sized organisations now offer coaching for their staff. The reason is simple – coaching is one of the most effective ways of achieving staff development. Even Eric Schmidt, the executive chairman of Google, has a coach; as he says, all great performers and athletes have a coach – and the same should go for executives looking to improve their performance.

Business and executive coaches are increasingly integrating mindfulness into their approach. The early adopters practised mindfulness for many years before the emergence of supporting research gave them the confidence to openly introduce the techniques to their clients. Nowadays, as mindfulness goes mainstream, we find that business coaches are approaching us to help them incorporate the techniques in their own work. Offering ways to help clients fulfil their potential is what coaches are all about, so their own mastery of the techniques creates a win–win situation!

Discovering Mindful Coaching

Mindful coaching is the process of sharing mindfulness-based values and exercises to help individuals or teams to develop both professionally and/or personally. The development occurs as a result of an increased awareness of someone's internal patterns of thoughts and emotions, and their awareness of outer opportunities and challenges.

Traditional coaching was often based on the GROW model developed by Sir John Whitmore:

G – Goals

R – Reality

O – Options

W – What next?

The goals element involves helping the client to discover what he wants to achieve. The client is then asked to reflect on the reality of his current situation. What's actually happening for him right now? Next, he comes up with various options for achieving his goals. In this stage he's asked to let go of self-limiting beliefs by considering questions such as, 'If money was not an issue, what would you do?' Finally, in the 'what's next?' stage, the coach asks the client to commit to one or several specific actions that he will take over the next few weeks or months, until the next coaching session.

Several traditional coaching values are shared with mindfulness:

✔ Empathy and compassion

✔ Curiosity and openness

✔ Listening in the present moment

✔ Awareness of one's thoughts and emotions

✔ Trust and respect

✔ Clarity and focus

✔ Wisdom and reflection

However, several values are seemingly in conflict with traditional coaching approaches, as shown in Table 11-1.

Table 11-1	Mindfulness vs Coaching
Mindfulness	*Coaching*
Emphasises acceptance, but gives you the tools to change	Emphasises change
Shift toward being – non-striving	Shift towards doing and action – striving towards goals
The core of your being is whole, complete and well	Emphasis on changing outer circumstances and inner attitudes to reach a sense of well-being
Present-moment focus	Future focus
Holistic – sees the big picture; considers the effects of one's actions on others	Self-focused; emphasises personal achievement

The traditional coaching model is very much goal-orientated. The basic premise is to find out what you really want to achieve at work, set realistic yet challenging goals and then work at meeting those goals.

Mindfulness goes beyond goals and goal-setting. Rushing too quickly to set goals without reflecting on where you are now, what you notice within and around you and, most importantly, whether such goals are appropriate is a wasteful use of energy. Mindfulness offers the awareness and insight from which goals and their outcomes can emerge. Figure 11-1 shows how mindful coaching combines the best of mindfulness and traditional coaching.

	Mindfulness	**Mindful coaching**	**Traditional coaching**
Figure 11-1: Mindful coaching combines the principles of mindfulness and coaching.	• Emphasises 'non-doing'	• Values reflection and action	• Action focus
	• Present focus	• Present and future focus	• Future orientation
	• Values acceptance	• Values acceptance and change	• No emphasis on acceptance

Seeing mindfulness as a coaching toolbox

We hesitate to recommend mindfulness as a 'tool' because present-moment awareness is so fundamental that it underlies all other tools and techniques. For this reason, although you may be considering using mindfulness as a tool with your clients, we suggest that you see mindfulness as a tool box – without mindfulness, you don't have a base from which to use all your other tools.

Mindfulness is useful in coaching because it offers clarity of insight.

Remember, the essence of mindfulness is non-judgemental awareness. If you can look at your problems, challenges and difficulties without judgement, you're much better able to see them for what they are. You can then make a decision and take action – which is what coaching is all about.

Figure 11-2 illustrates how mindfulness can underlie the coaching process.

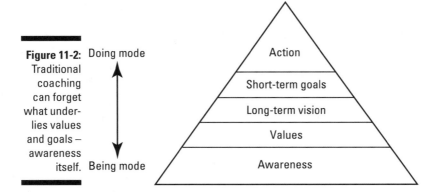

Figure 11-2: Traditional coaching can forget what underlies values and goals – awareness itself.

So, the paradox between mindfulness as associated with non-doing or being, and coaching as to do with doing/action isn't so much a paradox after all. They work together well.

Let's say you're being coached at work. Consider what it would be like to undertake coaching without a deep and full awareness of yourself. You'd set goals that aren't right for you. You'd keep missing opportunities to achieve your goals. And your approach would be mechanical, automatic and unfulfilling as you wouldn't be truly present.

And imagine if, when being coached, you practised mindfulness and non-doing but never set any goals or reflected on your actions. You'd live in the present moment but your achievements in the workplace would be limited. You wouldn't be stretching yourself at all and would probably be bored or unfulfilled – not an ideal state of mind if you're coaching clients.

We think that combining both approaches is best – spending time practising and cultivating mindfulness and time-setting and achieving realistic goals in line with your own values. That's coaching with mindfulness and a great way to work with clients.

Personal practice is crucial if you want to be an effective mindfulness coach. You can't hope to be able to coach others in mindfulness if you're not mindful yourself. When you're mindful yourself, you not only explicitly teach the principles of mindfulness, you also embody mindfulness. And when you embody mindfulness, you send unconscious signals to others about the benefits of mindfulness.

Take a few minutes to listen to a talk by one of the great mindfulness teachers: Jon Kabat-Zinn, Thich Nhat Hanh, the Dalai Lama, Jack Kornfield or Matthieu Ricard. What effect does their tone of voice and ideas have on you? Do they make you feel more calm and present? Does their talk increase your own level of mindfulness?

Mindfulness is always much more than a tool, technique or exercise. Mindfulness is a way of living and being.

Applying mindfulness in coaching

You can integrate mindfulness into coaching in lots of different ways. No one way is better than another. You need to identify the needs of your client and use that knowledge to decide how to coach them most effectively with mindfulness.

Different levels of mindfulness can be applied to coaching, as described below:

✔ **Level 1 – Being mindful as a coach:** This level is the least effective way of offering mindfulness coaching. The coach practises mindfulness exercises regularly in his own life and intends to be fully present with clients when he works with them. He sees the coaching session as an opportunity to be mindful. He doesn't teach any mindfulness in the session as he lacks the training and experience. Hopefully, all good coaches take this approach.

✔ **Level 2 – Bringing in mindful attitudes:** The coach not only practises mindfulness himself but also shares some key attitudes of mindfulness in the coaching session. Mindfulness attitudes include curiosity, self-compassion, compassion for others, acceptance of what can't be changed, recognition of the impermanence of people, events and situations, understanding that people are connected not separate, and valuing your own personal, self-centred goals but also considering their impact on others.

✔ **Level 3 – Introducing short mindful practices:** The coach actually begins using the word 'mindfulness' and recommends that the clients try some mindfulness exercises. He doesn't actually guide mindfulness in the session but does offer a book or guided audio to work through. The coach recommends working through a selection of exercises each week.

✔ **Level 4 – Guiding mindful exercises in the session:** If the coach is trained in mindfulness, he guides some mindful exercises in the session. Training is particularly important at this stage so that the coach doesn't guide the exercise ineffectively or offer mindfulness to clients when actually they may need some other form of support or guidance.

✔ **Level 5 – Using most of the session to teach mindfulness:** Most of the session is spent explaining the principles of mindfulness and showing clients ways to implement mindfulness into their work and everyday life. The coach starts and ends the session with guided mindfulness exercises and uses the middle of the session to explore how mindfulness can be applied to the challenges the client is dealing with at work or home.

I (Shamash) train mindfulness coaches, and ensure they are able to offer up to level 5 mindful coaching. That way, they have the choice to use approaches that are most relevant for their clients. If you're looking to train as a mindful coach, ensure you're trained to offer a range of mindfulness exercises to your clients depending on their needs.

No matter what kind of coach or consultant you are, never underestimate the power of simply listening mindfully. Ask open, simple questions such as 'Can you tell me more about that?' or 'Anything else you'd like to say?' and then listen with mindfulness. Leading your clients in this way helps them to be more mindful and can lead to a deep level of transformative insight.

One level is no better than another in this model. If you're a coach, use the right level for you and your client. If you're inexperienced with mindfulness, start with level 1. If you've been practising mindfulness for years, consider further training in mindful coaching and begin work at levels 4 or 5, if that's what your client needs.

Introducing Practical Ways to Integrate Mindfulness into Coaching

People seek out coaching to meet a particular need – whether fixing something that's gone wrong or desiring to improve their performance.

Your clients may have a range of problems. They may be overwhelmed with pressure at work. Maybe they're unable to clarify their goals. Perhaps they're lacking in self-confidence and are hope that coaching will give them a boost. Or maybe they want to improve their ability to communicate with colleagues at work.

Some clients seek out mindful coaching because they want to improve their performance. I (Shamash) have developed a mind fitness course designed to improved such clients' focus, intelligence and creativity. Mind fitness coaching combines mindfulness with other exercises from positive psychology and guided imagery to help people train their minds just like an athlete trains his body.

This section describes two key benefits of mindful coaching – increased clarity and reduced self-doubt. Obviously many other benefits exist but working on these two here introduce you to a few creative ways to use mindful coaching with your clients.

Brain surgeon seeks mindful coaching

I (Shamash) have a client who is a brain surgeon. He'd attempted to incorporate mindfulness into his life by working through guided exercises and reading up on the subject but, after several months of practice, found he was still suffering from low mood, frustration and lack of fulfilment. In our first session, he described the exercises he used and what he hoped to gain from one-to-one mindful coaching. As he talked, it became clear to me that what he needed was more self-compassion. His work involved seeing other people suffering, day in, day out. That's not an easy situation for anyone. People in the caring professions sometimes disengage from their sense of compassion because they fear that they'll suffer from 'compassion fatigue'. In fact, what they suffer from is 'empathy fatigue'. Empathy is feeling the suffering of another person – and sharing the suffering. Compassion is feeling the suffering of another person *and* having a positive desire for the suffering to end. Compassion has a positivity that sooths the suffering, whereas empathy doesn't. My sessions with the surgeon now focus on practising and developing not only mindfulness but also self-compassion and compassion for others. Research on compassion has discovered that it is the most powerful emotion for improving an individual's sense of well-being and, as a result, their resilience.

As you can see, mindful coaching isn't simply teaching mindfulness. Mindful coaching is about really listening and then helping your client, based on your own intuition. For this reason, continuous personal and professional development in mindfulness and related topics is crucial if you want to meet your clients' needs most effectively. You also need to find the most experienced practitioner you can when looking for coaching yourself.

Increasing insight and clarity

Picture a snow globe. You shake it and it fills with imitation snow. When the snow flakes settle, a pretty little village or Christmas scene is revealed.

That snow globe provides a good metaphor for the clarity that can be revealed through mindfulness. Mindfulness gives your clients an opportunity for their frantic thoughts and emotions to settle down. With time, as your clients find out how to step back from their thoughts, they see their own situation with greater clarity and can identify what they need to do to improve it.

Have you had that experience? Been so busy with your work and personal life that you couldn't see what you needed to do next? And then, after practising mindfulness exercises or having a nice holiday, free from distractions, have you been better able to see your situation clearly and known how to change things? We think that mindfulness is *the* best approach for increasing a client's clarity and insight.

Mindfulness can lead to clarity and insight in the following ways:

- Mindfulness exercises give you time to become more aware of your thoughts about various situations at work.

- Mindfulness makes you become more aware of your feelings about various situations at work.

- Mindfulness puts you in touch with your bodily sensations, which can lead to 'gut feelings' that are surprisingly accurate.

- Mindfulness can help your mind calm down. Within that calm, you're better able to see situations for what they are rather than your idea of them.

- Mindfulness helps you become more accepting and less judgemental, which means that you don't colour work situations and projects with your own issues. Instead, you have the clarity of insight.

Here's another analogy that may work for you. Picture mindfulness as the process of cleaning a window. Mindfulness is the act of cleaning, the dirt on the window represents recurring thoughts about the past and future, and the scene through the window represents the world around you. Each time you work through a mindfulness exercise, the windows of your perception are cleansed and you're better able to see what's in front of you. Without mindfulness practice and mindful values, the window can easily become a little dirty again and prevent you from seeing what's going on.

Below are a few practical exercises to try with your clients to help them gain greater clarity and insight.

You can try these exercises on yourself or your clients:

- **One minute of silent reflection:** Ask your clients to close their eyes and relax for a few moments. Then tell them to ask themselves, 'How can I best take care of myself?' Tell them to observe any ideas, feelings or emotions that emerge. Then tell them to ask again, 'How can I best take care of myself?' Give your client a minute of silence to reflect on the question.

    You can change the question so that it seems right for your client or yourself.

- **Mindful movement:** No reason exists why you can't do some mindful movements with your client if you're working one to one. Ask the client's permission and, if willing, guide some short mindful movement exercises. You can use Tai Chi or Qigong, if you're familiar with those disciplines. If not, simply ask clients to stand up and close their eyes. Then, as they feel their breathing, ask them to sweep their arms up and down in front of them for a couple of minutes. Many of our clients enjoy mindful movement more than the sedentary exercises such as mindfulness of breath and mindful minutes (see Chapters 6 and 7 for more on these).

✔ **Switching chairs, switching perspective:** Mindfulness is about stepping back and seeing things from different perspectives. So, if your client is in conflict with a colleague, place an empty chair in the room. Ask the client to imagine a colleague in the chair and to notice his feelings and share his thoughts about the person and situation. Then, ask him to sit in the other chair, imagining that he is his colleague, speaking to himself. Again, ask him to notice his feelings and share his thoughts. This exercise can help clients to step back from their own view of a situation and see things from the other person's perspective.

✔ **A touch of frost:** This exercise teaches the power of acceptance versus avoidance. Ask clients to hold a piece of ice in their hands and to try to avoid what they're feeling as much as possible. Suggest that they think about something else other than the discomfort. After a minute, ask your clients to rate how painful they found the experience. Then ask them to practise one minute of mindful breathing and then to hold another piece of ice. This time, they need to accept the sensation. Ask them to feel the sensation together with their breathing. Tell them to allow the sensation to be there, and to almost relax into it. Again, ask them to rate their pain and share their observations and insights. Ask your clients how this experience relates to the challenges they're facing in the workplace. This exercise demonstrates the power of mindful acceptance and often leads to many insights.

Overcoming self-doubt

Self-doubt is a sense of fear or uncertainly about yourself and your ability to achieve something. When I (Shamash) was at university, I was quite shy. I could deal with small groups of people but giving presentations to a roomful of other students made me feel anxious. Around that time, I began to study and practise mindfulness and other ancient Eastern philosophies. As a result, I discovered the danger of believing one's own self-limiting beliefs and discovered how to see them as thoughts rather than facts.

Consider the following question: if you were absolutely guaranteed to succeed, what would you do with your life? Would you continue to work for the same company or would you apply for a different job? Would you try to gain promotion? Would you quit your job and go travelling around New Zealand? Asking your clients this question can often lead to interesting answers.

The following exercise helps you to clarify your client's true desires and goals in both career and personal life, and offers a way to let go of limiting beliefs. Try it yourself first.

From self-limits to self-empowerment exercise

1. **Bring yourself into the present moment by focusing your attention on your breath and bodily sensations.**

2. **Ask yourself: 'If I could be successful in anything I chose to do, what would I do?'**

3. **Notice the thoughts, feelings, images and ideas that emerge.** Do you feel excited or nervous? Are you full of ideas or drawing a blank? Whatever emerges is fine – and interesting! Notice how your mind is reacting to the question.

4. **Refocus your attention on the present moment. Feel a few breaths.**

5. **Ask yourself again: 'If I could be successful in anything I chose to do, what would I do?'**

6. **Notice what happens in your mind. Be fully aware of what emerges in your consciousness.**

7. **Step back from the limiting thoughts and beliefs that make you think you wouldn't succeed; dispense with all the various reasons why your ideal scenario wouldn't work. Be the observer of those doubts rather than being stuck within them.**

8. **Place the thoughts on clouds or into bubbles, or whatever other technique you prefer, to create some distance between you and your thoughts.** Picture doubts as trains that approach a platform and then whizz away.

9. **Refocus your attention each time your mind wanders. This wandering is fine and perfectly normal.** Just kindly bring your attention back when you notice.

10. **Finish the mindfulness reflection with a few mindful breaths.**

Now consider what you discovered. Did you identify your heart's desire? Try to identify the self-doubts or limiting beliefs that are holding you back. Did you enjoy watching them fly away into the distance or did that approach not work for you? Did this exercise make you feel frustrated or curious? If you felt uncomfortable, in what part of your body did such feelings manifest themselves?

Your answers to these questions lead to further insights about yourself and are a step towards experiencing greater self-confidence and less self-doubt.

Hopefully you can see the value of this mindful exercise for your clients. Figure 11-3 below shows how such a process can help your clients to step back from their self-limiting beliefs and perhaps achieve goals they previously thought were impossible.

There's no right or wrong response to this exercise. Just notice what happens.

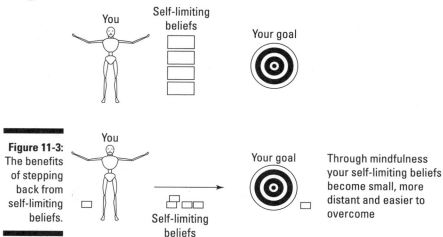

Figure 11-3: The benefits of stepping back from self-limiting beliefs.

Coaching Team Members in Being Mindful

Effective teams drive performance forward. When members of a team work well together, their organisation can thrive. When teams don't get on so well, the company can subsequently suffer; productivity goes down, innovation is stifled and profits can fall.

If you're a manager, and you see hostility within your team, a lack of focus or excessive negativity and frustration, you need to take action. Deciding on the best form of change to improve team performance is vital for its success as well as yours.

Team coaching is often seen as a way forward. Although not always as effective as one-to-one coaching, team coaching efficiently helps the group as a whole clarify its mission and accelerate its progress. Even if your team is performing well, team coaching can still help to identify ways to increase its productivity.

Offering mindfulness to teams is an ideal way of introducing mindfulness to an organisation. As mindfulness is often taught in groups, integrating mindfulness exercises into group coaching is a great way to familiarise people with the concept.

Integrating mindfulness into your team coaching

How do you decide whether mindfulness is the right intervention for your team? If you want to help your staff develop the following attributes, mindfulness is probably a good choice:

- ✔ Greater resilience, resulting in an improved ability to cope with the pressures of the job
- ✔ Improved ability to communicate through the development of emotional intelligence
- ✔ Better ability to regulate emotions
- ✔ Improved ability to focus, resulting in increased productivity
- ✔ Greater ability to produce creative ideas and solutions as a result of more headspace

Consider the needs of your team before you decide on the best developmental approaches for its members.

Mindfulness isn't a panacea for all your problems. Ask your team members what they suggest too. If a particular technical skill is identified as lacking, that may be more of a priority to begin with.

If you're considering introducing mindfulness to a team within an organisation, bear these tips in mind:

- ✔ **Share the science:** Lots of research has studied the effects of mindfulness. Some of these are workplace-focused. Make sure that you share these findings to help convince your audience that mindfulness isn't some airy-fairy technique but a systematic way of cultivating self-management through shifts that take place in the brain.
- ✔ **Keep it secular:** Mindfulness is now part of mainstream psychology courses and not just seen as an Eastern philosophy. Stress that, although these insights were often gained in ancient, Eastern disciplines, modern-day business schools now introduce mindfulness as a useful business tool.

✔ **Make mindfulness optional:** Allow staff to decide whether or not they want to find out about mindfulness. To force someone to practise mindfulness when they're not really interested in it makes things difficult right from the start.

✔ **Offer shorter mindfulness exercises:** In a workplace setting, offering the longer mindfulness exercises, such as the 45-minute body scan, may not be realistic for busy people. Instead, offer shorter exercises that are easier to integrate into the working day or in the morning before work.

✔ **Use the right language for your organisation:** For some organisations, using the word 'mindfulness' is fine. For others, you may prefer to use 'awareness training', 'attention training' or 'focus training'. Alternatively, integrate mindfulness into resilience training.

✔ **Use trained mindfulness teachers:** Mindfulness can involve lots of subtleties and nuances. If you want to offer mindfulness to your organisation and you're not a qualified instructor yourself, make sure that you bring in an experienced mindfulness teacher.

✔ **Offer on-going mindfulness classes:** For staff who found a mindfulness course useful, consider offering a short daily or weekly class. Also try to set up a separate, designated room where staff can go to practise and cultivate mindfulness. The ability to practise mindfulness in a quiet space at work can boost staff morale, enhance their focus and improve productivity. Staff also feel more valued and cared for. You can that this situation is win–win for your organisation and its employees.

Overcoming barriers to mindfulness

You may face a few barriers when you try to introduce mindfulness to teams within an organisation. Although they don't present major challenges, an awareness of the usual pitfalls may help you to prepare for them if they do arise. Below is a list of the barriers you're most likely to face and possible solutions for dealing with them:

✔ **Barrier – Participants' lack of interest:** Some of the trainers or staff at the organisation may not know what mindfulness is and therefore won't understand how it can benefit the organisation.

✔ **Solution – Introductory talk:** Inviting a well-qualified and experienced mindfulness coach to speak to the trainers at the company can help. If the trainers then express an interest in the concept, organise a six-to-eight-week mindfulness course for them. Some of these people may begin regular mindfulness practice. Finally, over the longer term, perhaps after a year or so, some of the in-house trainers may go on to train to become mindfulness coaches themselves and then offer it to staff.

✔ **Barrier – The idea that mindfulness doesn't fit company culture:** Some people may think that mindfulness is airy-fairy, weak or linked to a form of esoteric practice. As a result, they may feel that it doesn't link to their organisational culture.

✔ **Solution – Initial meeting and explanation:** Meetings with the key decision-makers explaining the scientific and psychological basis of mindfulness can help. Let them know that they don't need to light incense or do anything much out of the ordinary in the mindfulness sessions. Describing the mindfulness curriculum may help too.

You can also ensure that a mindfulness intervention fits in with the culture of the company. For example, if you've become aware in advance that the staff are rather conservative, consider omitting mindful movement or mindful eating from the sessions. You can adapt the course so that it involves more theory and is based on shorter mindful exercises that are carried out seated. You can also offer audio exercises that staff can then try out in the privacy of their own homes. If the word 'mindfulness' clashes with company culture, use a different word that feels right for that organisation.

✔ **Barrier – Doubts about the return on investment:** Managers may be unclear about the organisational gains that may result from their investment in mindfulness; they may expect to see a financial gain.

✔ **Solution – Build a case study:** Try to work out anticipated reductions in absenteeism or increases in productivity (see Chapter 15 for an example of these benefits and how to calculate them) and to calculate how much money those developments would save the company. Juliet's website www.mindfulnet.org has lots of advice on building case studies.

Rolling Out Mindfulness through Coaching

If you're sold on the idea of mindfulness and want to offer it throughout your organisation, you can do so in several ways. This section covers how you can use coaching to achieve this aim.

Dealing with individuals

Coaching mindfulness one to one is probably the most effective way to introduce mindfulness into an organisation. If those responsible for staff development in your organisation are fully trained mindfulness coaches, you're obviously laughing. However, this situation is rarely the case and so you have to commission a mindfulness coach.

Mindful coaching, though relatively new, works best for senior executives wanting to discover mindfulness because:

- ✔ **They're busy and need to make the most of the limited time they have available:** Through individual coaching, the time can be adjusted to meet their needs.

- ✔ **Their decisions can affect thousands of employees:** With such an important job, you want to ensure that their training is highly effective. The best mindfulness coaches can help achieve that.

- ✔ **They have private questions:** As they say, it's lonely at the top. Senior executives have fewer people available to them to act as a sounding board. A mindfulness coach can both teach the programme and act as a mindful listener.

- ✔ **They're used to a coaching format:** Most executives have probably been getting some form of coaching for years. Integrating mindfulness into this process is a smooth way in.

- ✔ **They can learn via the phone:** Senior leaders sometimes need rapid access to a mindfulness teacher. Coaching can take place over the phone and, although not ideal, can be much more effective than you think.

One of the key benefits of starting with the senior executives when you're trying to introducing mindfulness into an organisation is that you can more easily achieve management buy-in. When the senior leaders experience just how powerful mindfulness can be, they're more likely to invest in the process for those lower down in the organisation.

Bill Ford gets mindful

Bill Ford is the great grandson of Henry Ford. Bill is executive chairman and former CEO of Ford Motor Company, and is coached in mindfulness by Jack Kornfield, a renowned mindfulness teacher. When the economy crashed in 2008, Bill was faced with the prospect of the whole company collapsing. He used mindfulness to maintain his resilience, make the right decisions and manage the difficult times. The wrong decisions may have led to the demise of a historic business and the loss of many jobs. Who knows, perhaps mindfulness kept Ford in business! Bill Ford invested in more green technology, against the wishes of many of the senior leaders – a compassionate choice. Going against the wishes of highly resistant and conservative staff, previously focused on profits rather than the environment, wasn't easy but mindfulness helped him remain focused and calm until the situation was resolved. Ford now continues to thrive and is investing £1.5 billion in green technology in the UK alone.

Working with teams

If you're an experienced mindfulness coach and are leading a team, begin with a short introduction to mindfulness, from the scientific perspective, and then guide a brief exercise at the beginning of a team meeting. Try something simple, such as a few minutes of mindful breathing or a body scan.

If you're not a mindfulness coach, hire one. Lots of mindfulness coaches are out there looking for work. Follow these steps to ensure that you pick the right coach, define what the coaching is meant to address and check outcomes:

1. **Find a mindfulness coach with relevant training and experience.** Ideally look for someone with extensive experience in practising and teaching mindfulness together with a coaching qualification. See Chapter 12 for more information.

2. **Conduct a short meeting with the coach to discuss what you want the coaching to achieve.** Get to know the coach better and ask about the kind of activities he'll do with the group.

3. **Determine what outcomes he'll measure, if you want to monitor progress.** Maybe you want to address staff well-being and resilience, or improve team productivity.

4. **Measure outcomes after the course.** Conduct a follow-up meeting with the coach to assess what worked and what may be in the process of changing.

5. **Share your findings.** Tell other managers about the results of the mindfulness course and ask team members to share their experiences with colleagues. Hopefully, other teams will be interested in exploring mindfulness.

By starting with teams, you can integrate mindfulness into your organisation from the bottom up.

Involving the whole organisation

If you want to spread the mindfulness approach across the entire company, you need to get the CEO or senior leaders on board. They may initially be sceptical so you can begin by coaching a few teams and then presenting the results. Ultimately, the person who's chief in command needs to embrace the principles of mindfulness before it can be applied at all levels of the organisation.

To ensure that mindfulness filters down most effectively, mindful leadership is key. Chapters 13-15 cover mindful leadership in all its guises.

Below are a few ideas on how you can introduce mindfulness into an organisation, whether you're a coach or an executive.

If you're a mindfulness coach:

✔ Use your contacts to set up a meeting with senior executives in an organisation that you feel may benefit from mindful coaching.

✔ Describe the evidence base for mindfulness and ask senior executives how you can meet their needs.

✔ Prepare a proposal outlining how mindfulness can address staff retention issues, lack of focus in meetings, reduced productivity and so on.

If you're a senior executive or HR manager:

✔ Invite a mindfulness coach to a meeting.

✔ Check out his credentials and ask him to describe relevant experience of introducing mindfulness into the workplace.

✔ Suggest various ways in which mindfulness coaching can be introduced into the organisation, such as on a one-to-one basis, in groups or tailored to individual teams, and ask the coach whether he can devise a suitable programme.

Chapter 12

Commissioning Mindfulness Training in the Workplace

· ·

In This Chapter

▶ Introducing mindfulness training to your organisation

▶ Getting to grips with the different approaches

▶ Making sure that you pick the right mindfulness teacher or coach

· ·

*I*ntroducing mindfulness to an organisation can be a daunting experience, but it needn't be. This chapter provides all the information and key things to consider when piloting mindfulness within your organisation. If you follow the steps detailed in this chapter you should create a win–win–win scenario. Your staff benefit, the organisation benefits and you look good for having the idea and following it through. We make a start by looking at the basics.

Bringing Mindfulness Training to Work

There are a number of ways that you could introduce mindfulness to your organisation. This section will help you establish what you hope to achieve, which in turn will help you select the best approach.

Starting with the end in mind

As with all effective personal and professional development initiatives, you should always start with the end in mind. The first question to ask yourself is what outcomes you're hoping to achieve. To put it another way, you need to identify what you hope will be different (in organisational and individual terms) immediately after and in the months following the programme.

Choosing from the menu of possibilities

Mindfulness can help your organisation and your staff in many ways, some of which are easier to evaluate than others. Here's a menu (based on research outcomes) of the possible benefits that mindfulness can bring to your organisation:

✔ Improved relationships with colleagues and customers

✔ Improved empathy, self-kindness and kindness to others

✔ Increased focus and concentration

✔ Improved productivity

  • The ability to gain fresh perspectives

  • Improved strategic thinking

  • Improved decision making

  • Improved communication

  • The ability to deal better with complexity

  • Increased creativity

  • Improved ability to learn

✔ Improved resilience and well-being

  • Better management of emotions (including anger and upset)

  • Reduced stress, anxiety and depression

  • Prevention of burnout

  • Better self-regulation

  • Improved quality of life

✔ Improved staff engagement

  • Reduced staff sickness and absence

  • Improved employee engagement

  • Development of a more positive outlook

✔ Positive changes to brain structure

The above list of potential benefits from mindfulness training was taken from *Making the Business Case for Mindfulness*. This publication includes research references, mindfulness at work case studies and lots of material too long to include in this chapter. The publication is available on a donation basis from my (Juliet's) website www.mindfulnet.org

When you've decided on the most desirable outcomes you're seeking to achieve, you need to state them as learning and development (L&D) outcomes. These desired outcomes can form the basis of discussion with mindfulness trainers, and ensure that those leading the project have a clear idea of what 'success' looks like to you.

Outcomes should always be demonstrable, so must always be written in behavioural terms. Outcomes are different to aims and objectives. Aims and objectives are usually shared with participants before or at the start of the course. Outcomes, on the other hand, are there to help the organisation shape the structure, order and evaluation of the course and aren't normally shared with participants. Think carefully before sharing outcome statements with participants as doing so may positively or negatively impact on the evaluation data. When presented at the outset with the outcomes the organisation wishes to achieve, some participants report overly positive outcomes as they wish to promote mindfulness within the organisation. Others may play down the outcomes for a variety of personal reasons.

Here are a few example outcomes for a taster session and full pilot, respectively:

Example of outcomes for a mindfulness at work taster session

Your outcome statement may read as follows: By the end of the session, participants will:

- ✔ Be able to explain in simple terms what mindfulness is
- ✔ Be able to explain in simple terms how mindfulness works
- ✔ Have experienced some simple mindfulness practices
- ✔ Have developed strategies to transfer what they've learned into the workplace
- ✔ Be keen to find out more about mindfulness, and possibly attend further training

Example outcomes for a mindfulness at work pilot

Your outcome statement may read as follows:

By the end of the eight-week course, participants will:

- ✔ Be able to explain what mindfulness is
- ✔ Be able to explain how mindfulness works both from a practical and basic neurological perspective
- ✔ Have practised using a wide range of mindfulness tools and techniques
- ✔ Have applied what they've learned to their work

✔ Have improved their productivity (based on self-reporting evaluation measures)

✔ Have improved their resilience (based on self-reporting evaluation measures)

✔ Demonstrate a more positive outlook (Based on staff survey outcomes before and after)

Building in evaluation

When considering introducing mindfulness (which for some members of staff may be regarded as radical), you need to be able to justify your decision to do so in business terms. Gathering robust evaluation data relating to measures that matter to your organisation is essential.

Many people make the mistake of trying to bolt on evaluation measures at the end. To really be effective, they should be 'designed in' at the outset. When you've agreed on your outcomes, the mindfulness specialist you're working with should be able to design evaluation measures for your individual mindfulness programme. You can then use these evaluation measures pre- and post-training. You can use an online or corporate survey tool to reduce the work involved. Many free online survey tools do basic analysis of results for you, saving on inputting time and time to complete calculations and statistics. You may find it prudent to make it a condition of attending the course that participants agree to complete both pre- and post-training evaluation questionnaires in a timely manner. Also make sure that participants are happy to have their collective data shared with others in an anonymous format.

Your pre-mindfulness evaluation measures may include:

✔ A measure of mindfulness, such as the Mindfulness Attention Awareness Scale (MAAS)

✔ Organisational measures such as 'My organisation is a great place to work' or 'I look forward to coming to work'

✔ A measure of depression, anxiety and stress using a measure such as the DASS 21 (Depression Anxiety Stress Scales; see Chapter 10 for more)

✔ A measure of self-kindness, such as the Neff self-compassion tool

The post-course evaluation should include the same measures, but you may also wish to include a question such as:

I feel that mindfulness has helped me . . .

1. Function better when under pressure

2. Focus my attention on the task in hand

3. Improve the way I manage strong feelings and emotions

4. Respond differently to challenges and difficulties at work

5. Improve relationships with colleagues

6. Look after myself better at work

7. Be a more effective employee

(Answer choices = No change, To a small extent, To some extent, To a great extent, Significantly)

Discuss early on who will be conducting the evaluation. Participants may be more willing to share data with an independent person outside the organisation (such as the mindfulness specialist). This external person can then render the data anonymous before it is presented to the organisation. If the participants know in advance that the answers they provide will be anonymous, they're more likely to be open and honest. Conversely, you, or your Learning and Development team, may wish to conduct the evaluations yourselves.

One final thing to consider is the most appropriate method for delivering the course. For a taster or introductory session, a trainer led approach is generally best. Taster sessions can usually be run by one mindfulness specialist for large numbers of people. However, for mindfulness training purposes, smaller groups are better to allow for discussion and reflection on experiences. Mindfulness can be taught to larger groups with the support of additional trainers. If your group includes senior managers, they may possibly feel that exploring their reactions and experiences in relation to mindfulness practices is inappropriate in a group setting. In addition, senior managers may not find it easy to attend all sessions and mindfulness training isn't something you can dip in to and out of. Senior staff often find one-to-one mindfulness coaching a better learning option.

Considering options for introductions and pilots

You can introduce mindfulness into an organisation in many ways. The correct approach varies from organisation to organisation. Experienced mindfulness specialists should be able to adapt their approach to meet your specific organisational culture and needs, giving your project a greater chance of success. Here are two options to consider.

A brown bag lunch session

This kind of session can be a good option for companies where mindfulness training may be met with resistance or where time off for 'personal development' is frowned upon. If staff are allowed a 15-minute break in the morning, 30 minutes for lunch and a 15-minute break in the afternoon, these breaks can be combined to create a one-hour slot at lunchtime. Participants can bring their own packed lunch (or you can provide a simple buffet) and eat while listening to an introduction to mindfulness. The introduction may include mindful eating and another quick technique such as the three-minute focus break or mindfulness of breath. At the end of the session, participants should complete a brief paper-based questionnaire including questions such as:

✔ I would be interested in attending a mindfulness course. (Strongly disagree, Disagree, Agree, Strongly agree)

✔ I think that mindfulness can help me in my work. (Strongly disagree, Disagree, Agree, Strongly agree)

A half-day session

A half-day session can provide a much more in-depth experience of mindfulness and can form the first part of a longer programme. The half-day session may include:

✔ Underpinning theory:

- What mindfulness is

- The research behind mindfulness

- Applications of mindfulness

- The fight-or-flight response

- Living on auto-pilot

- The mind–body connection

✔ Mindfulness practices

- The raisin exercise

- Mindfulness of breath

- Body scan

- The three-minute focus break

✔ Experiential learning

- The opportunity to experience mindfulness practices

- The opportunity to discuss experiences with another participant or the group as a whole, if desired

Administer a short questionnaire at the end of session to gauge interest and find out whether participants think that mindfulness training is something worth offering more widely or as a full course.

Taking care of the practicalities

A number of practical considerations must be borne in mind when organising a mindfulness taster or full course. First is the *availability of a suitable room*. Ideally, the room should be reasonably private (not one with glass walls that people can stare through, for example). The room should also be reasonably quiet and not too hot or cold. Most mindfulness at work specialists require a fairly standard training room with comfortable chairs, tables and possibly a digital projector, screen and flip chart. Some (but not all) mindfulness trainers require a room with yoga mats, with space for the participants to lie down for some of the mindfulness practices in week 3 (if teaching the full eight-week MBSR or MBCT courses). Some mindful movement exercises use basic yoga techniques. Alternatively, mindful movement can be taught sitting on chairs. Ideally, the mindfulness trainer should have the opportunity to view the training room before they start delivering.

For an introductory session for a large number of people, a theatre or cabaret room layout is ideal. When teaching mindfulness to a group of 12–15 people, the room is best set up as a classic 'U', with the trainer at the top. Alternatively, you can use a circle or cabaret-style set up if space permits. A classroom-style layout, with one small desk per person and everyone sitting apart, is likely to be unsuitable for mindfulness training as it restricts group interaction.

In many organisations members of the learning and development team are responsible for training rooms. Thus a member of this team will probably ensure that the room is set up in advance of the mindfulness trainer arriving. Sometimes the rooms are communal. If so, you need to ensure that the trainer knows how to get the equipment set up, and who to call if they need help.

The next practical consideration is how you *market and publicise the development opportunity to staff.* Is the mindfulness taster or full course 'a personal development opportunity' or 'a professional development opportunity', or both? Is it about staff well-being or productivity? Is it about resilience or creativity? You need to be clear about the purpose of the course in the message you send. Also consider the medium of communication: posters, flyers, emails, postings on the intranet, announcements in staff newsletters and presentations during team briefings are all possibilities. Lastly, consider who's best placed to do what. Mindfulness specialists may be happy to help you develop your promotional materials or even produce a first draft of flyers and intranet content. Don't be afraid to ask for help – being the in-house champion of the project doesn't automatically mean that you're a mindfulness expert!

The final practical consideration is *selection of participants.* If you're running a large-scale mindfulness taster or introduction, selection isn't an issue. However, if you're running a full mindfulness course, you may need to vet participants to ensure that they're suitable. Mindfulness is effective in treating anxiety, depression and stress, but if people are suffering from particularly high levels of any of these problems, they may struggle with the course and possibly spoil the learning experience for others. One solution is to ask potential participants to complete an assessment tool such as the DASS 21 (see Chapter 10). This tool is freely available on the Internet. Potential participants whose scores indicate severe or extremely severe depression, anxiety and stress may need to seek a therapeutic version of the course outside of work. When running a full mindfulness course, also consider the mix of people attending to ensure an even balance of job roles and departments. You may also wish to avoid line managers and their direct reports attending the same course.

Give careful consideration to whether *attendance is to be voluntary or compulsory*. Participants will be more engaged in learning if they're doing so voluntarily. Willing participants are more likely to practise the skills at home than those who are coerced into attending. Notable examples exist of mindfulness being taught as part of compulsory programmes, such as for staff with poor attendance records or as part of leadership development. In these cases, many people who would not have attended a course voluntarily have discovered the benefits of mindfulness; indeed, some of them have gone on to become mindfulness champions in their organisations.

Generally, especially if this event is your first attempt at introducing mindfulness into your organisation, starting with volunteers is best.

Working in partnership and managing expectations

Being the mindfulness project leader in your organisation doesn't automatically mean that you have to be an expert on all things mindful. You may need more support from your training provider than you'd normally expect from a consultant or training provider.

Start conversations with potential providers with this fact in mind, and see how much support they're willing to offer and whether they'll partner you in the project. Although mindfulness has come of age, mindfulness in the workplace context is still in its adolescent stage. As pioneers of mindfulness in the workplace, you need to consider whether you can work together to write up and share your data outside the organisation, if all goes well. Your experience adds to the research base and helps other organisations considering mindfulness training. This approach to working should benefit both of you. Make sure that you clearly define who is responsible for what and when, so that you can manage each other's expectations. Remember that you are both in this together and, unlike some box-ticking staff development activities, the outcomes really matter.

Identifying follow-up strategies

Following on from the (hopefully successful) mindfulness introduction, you need to agree what is to happen next. If others need to be involved in making the decision, make a date in their diaries in advance to ensure that you don't lose momentum. Try to get everything in place for the follow-up before you begin the introductory session.

So now you've a good idea of how to introduce mindfulness into your organisation. Let's move on by considering the different approaches to teaching mindfulness.

Making Sense of the Different Approaches to Teaching Workplace Mindfulness

No 'standard' approaches to mindfulness training in the workplace exist, which can make choosing the approach that best suits your organisation's needs rather tricky. The syllabuses of different mindfulness courses can be adapted for use in the workplace. These adaptations may include:

✔ Ensuring a 100 per cent secular approach to teaching

✔ Using corporate language

✔ Using learning techniques that adult participants may be more familiar with

✔ Balancing didactic theory input with time for experiential learning and personal reflection

✔ Using workplace examples and analogies

This section provides an outline of four different approaches to teaching mindfulness. Two are workplace specific (Search Inside Yourself and Mindfulness Based Work Training), the other two generic but well researched and easy to adapt for the workplace. The syllabuses for all four are readily available in books or on the Internet.

Mindfulness Based Stress Reduction (MBSR)

MBSR was developed in the USA in the 1970s and has been the subject of much research. MBSR and MBCT are similar and share around 80 per cent of their content. The main difference is that MBSR focuses on treating mental distress (such as stress) in general. MBCT focuses more on *how* a person thinks.

Until fairly recently, MBSR has been mainly used in a clinical setting, helping patients with diverse conditions ranging from stress to chronic pain, tinnitus to substance abuse. In order to teach MBSR, instructors need to have completed lengthy training. MBSR training is delivered using a well-researched eight-week syllabus developed by Jon Kabat-Zinn.

In order to advertise that they're running an 'MBSR' course, trainers must follow this eight-week syllabus. If training is advertised as 'based on MBSR', it is likely to use key aspects of the established syllabus but may deviate from it or have additions created by the trainer. Adaptations to suit individual client needs will make the latter the case for most workplace courses.

A good example of an adapted syllabus is that set out by Michael Chaskalson in his book, *The Mindful Workplace: Developing Resilient Individuals and Resonant Organisations with MBSR* (Wiley-Blackwell, 2011). His syllabus includes some elements of MBCT, and is based on the two hours per week, eight-week model. It presumes 45 minutes of home practice each day but session duration and home practice can be adapted to meet client needs. For example, the course can be run for four half days, with two weeks in between each half day and each half day covering two of the eight sessions. Chaskalson's course is structured as follows:

- ✔ Week 1: Automatic pilot
- ✔ Week 2: Dealing with barriers
- ✔ Week 3: Mindfulness of breath, body and movement
- ✔ Week 4: Staying present
- ✔ Week 5: Acceptance: allowing and letting be
- ✔ Week 6: Thoughts are not facts
- ✔ Week 7: How can I best take care of myself?
- ✔ Week 8: Acceptance and change

Chaskalson has worked with many top organisations and executives using this approach, and evaluation data suggests that he is getting positive results. For more information on this approach to teaching mindfulness in the workplace, visit www.mindfulness-works.com or invest in a copy of Chaskalson's book.

Mindfulness Based Cognitive Therapy (MBCT)

MBCT was developed in the UK in the1990s by Zindal Segal, Mark Williams and John Teasdale. As with MBSR, MBCT was first developed to help people with depression in a clinical setting. The National Institute for Health and Care Excellence (NICE) is an independent organisation, and was set up by the UK government in 1999 to decide which drugs and treatments are available on the National Health Service (NHS) in England and Wales. MBCT is approved in the UK by NICE as a 'treatment of choice' for recurrent depression. MBCT is similar to MBSR. MBCT blends mindfulness with aspects of cognitive behavioural therapy and is more focused on helping people find out how to manage their mind than MBSR.

In 2011 Mark Williams (co-creator of MBCT) co-authored with the journalist Danny Penman, *Mindfulness: A Practical Guide to Finding Peace in a Frantic World.* This book contains details of an eight-week MBCT course, adapted for a non-clinical population. It includes a CD of the mindfulness exercises covered on the course for the readers to practise at home. The exercises each take between 8 and 12 minutes, which is less time than traditionally taught on MBCT and MBSR courses. The course also includes practical exercises (such as 'habit releasers'), which aren't part of the core MBCT syllabus. The Williams and Penman course is structured as follows:

- Week 1: Waking up to the autopilot

- Week 2: Keeping the body in mind

- Week 3: The mouse in the maze

- Week 4: Moving beyond the rumour mill

- Week 5: Turning towards difficulties

- Week 6: Trapped in the past or living in the present

- Week 7: When did you stop dancing?

- Week 8: Your wild and precious life

For further information on this approach, visit the book's website at `http://franticworld.com`.

'The Mindfulness Exchange' and my (Juliet's) organisation 'A Head for Work', are both major providers of mindfulness in the workplace training, are leading the way in developing William and Penman's approach. Both base their workplace mindfulness training on the eight-week course described in the book. Evaluation data from courses using this approach suggest that this method of teaching mindfulness is highly effective in the workplace. For information on these two providers, visit `http://mindfulness-exchange.com/` or `www.aheadforwork.co.uk`.

If you're looking for an online eight-week mindfulness course try `www.livemindfulonline.com`, recently developed by Shamash. It includes lots of videos, downloadable audios, mindful exercises, weekly emails and an online community, combining both MBSR and MBCT.

Mindfulness At Work Training (MAWT)

MAWT is a five-week mindfulness course developed by the authors of this book based on MBCT, with the addition of specific applications of mindfulness in the workplace.

Weeks 1–2 cover the key aspects of mindfulness usually taught on weeks 1–4 of an MBCT course. Weeks 3–5 apply mindfulness to key work challenges, and include some aspects taught on weeks 5–8 of an MBCT course. As with MBCT and MBSR, home practice is an essential component, with short exercises (around 10 minutes each) included. A MAWT course is structured as follows:

- ✔ Week 1: Understanding mindfulness at work
- ✔ Week 2: Working with the body in mind
- ✔ Week 3: Mindful communication at work
- ✔ Week 4: Mindfully working with difficult people and strong emotions
- ✔ Week 5: Mindful working in times of change

The MAWT course is described in full in Chapters 6 and 7 of this book and core exercises are provided on the accompanying MP3. A core component of all mindfulness training programmes is the 'enquiry' process. This process allows participants to explore the impact of the exercises for them, and how they relate to their lives. In workplace courses the enquiry process is normally done in pairs, and no one is pressured to share anything with other participants if they don't wish to do so. In the self-study version of this course (included in this book), personal reflection replaces the enquiry process. MAWT can also be run as a taught course delivered in-house. Visit www.mawt.co.uk for more information.

Search Inside Yourself (SIY)

Search Inside Yourself was developed by Chade-Meng Tan (known as Meng), one of the first engineers to be hired at Google. When Google allowed engineers to spend 20 per cent of their time pursuing their own passions, Meng decided that he wanted to help his workmates nurture emotional intelligence through the practice of mindfulness. Meng worked with a range of people including emotional intelligence expert Dan Goleman, mindfulness trainers, psychologists and a CEO. He ultimately created a seven-week personal growth programme. SIY was launched in 2007, and since then more than 1,000 employees have participated in SIY courses with excellent results. Participants rate the programme at 4.7 on a five-point scale.

In 2012 Meng decided to make the principles and components of SIY available to companies everywhere and published them in his book, *Search Inside Yourself: The Unexpected Path to Achieving Success, Happiness (and World Peace)*. His programme focuses on the five key domains of emotional intelligence – self-awareness, self-regulation, motivation, empathy and social skills – and integrates mindfulness practice, science and leadership applications at all levels. The course can be taught in many ways. In the example below, SIY is taught via three modules:

- ✔ SIY 101: Introduction to emotional intelligence (2 hours)
- ✔ SIY 102: Day of mindfulness (7 hours, prerequisite: SIY 101)
- ✔ SIY 103: Developing the five domains of emotional intelligence (10 hours, prerequisite: SIY 101)

Each module contains elements of mindfulness. To find out more about this approach to teaching mindfulness coupled with emotional intelligence, invest in a copy of Meng's book or visit www.siyli.org.

Listen to Shamash's interview with Meng for free on www.shamashalidina.com

Hiring an Experienced Mindfulness Practitioner

Unlike many development courses routinely offered to staff by organisations, mindfulness isn't an abstract concept that can be quickly learned from a book and translated into a course delivered by a member of the learning and development team. Even attending an eight-week course does not equip you to teach mindfulness to others.

A large amount of what is taught by mindfulness trainers is directly in response to individual participant needs. This aspect of teaching mindfulness cannot be covered by any book or by attending one course. It relies on a deep understanding of mindfulness gained over years of practising it, not to mention regular supervision from an even more experienced trainer. This section gives you the information you need to choose the mindfulness trainer best suited to your organisation.

Checking out credentials

At present no mandatory requirements exist for mindfulness trainers to comply with teacher training standards. So, from a corporate 'buyer's' perspective, remember 'buyer beware!' In the UK, the 'Good Practice

Guidance for Teaching Mindfulness Based Courses' was developed by the network of Mindfulness-Based Trainers in 2010. The network includes representatives from the major UK universities that offer mindfulness teacher training. Compliance with the standards is optional. The guide outlines acceptable:

✔ Prior training and background relative to the people being taught

✔ Foundation training

✔ Mindfulness-based teacher training

✔ Ongoing good practice requirements

Further information can be found on Mindfulnet's teacher training information page at www.mindfulnet.org/page30.htm or on the UK Network for Mindfulness-Based Teacher Training Organisations website at http://mindfulnessteachersuk.org.uk.

In the USA, no similar network exists so, on the whole, best practice is set by the Center for Mindfulness, which is part of the University of Massachusetts (UMass) Medical Schools. UMass teacher training is based on MBSR. Further information can be found at www.umassmed.edu/cfm/certification/index.aspx.

No specific standards currently exist for trainers who teach mindfulness in the workplace. Good practice suggests that, as a minimum, trainers teaching mindfulness in the workplace should:

✔ Have good knowledge of the type of organisation that the training will be delivered in or, better still, work experience in the sector

✔ Have good knowledge of and skills in teaching adults in the workplace

✔ Have in-depth knowledge of the mindfulness content and underpinning theory gained though attending courses, self-directed learning and attending seminars in related subject areas

✔ Have followed well-established, regular mindfulness practice for at least 12 months prior to attending teacher training

✔ Have attended a recognised teacher training course (based on MBSR or MBCT or similar), with a minimum duration of 12 months; this course can include both face-to-face teaching and web-based learning or tuition

✔ Be engaged in regular supervision sessions with suitably experienced mindfulness trainers to encourage personal reflection and further development

Shamash and I were talking and agreed that when we were at school, some of our teachers were excellent at their job and others were terrible! They were all qualified and had done the necessary training. You may find the same with mindfulness teachers. Read their CVs and other credentials with a pinch of salt rather than as an ultimate guide to their competency. We have both met many mindfulness teachers that wouldn't meet the above credentials but are excellent teachers, seem to have a natural ability to be mindful and have years of experience. We have also met highly trained mindfulness teachers who need more training and experience, and quite a number who cannot translate mindfulness for a corporate audience. Take time to meet the teacher, get to know them, and discuss your needs at length before hiring them.

Clarifying organisational experience

At present mindfulness teacher training is generic and not tailored to workplace delivery. Many fine mindfulness trainers with years of experience may struggle to adapt their mindfulness training to the needs and constraints of individual organisations. Some of the methods currently taught routinely in mindfulness teacher training may not sit well in an organisational setting. For this reason, checking out potential trainers' understanding of the business sector that you operate in is important. Make sure that your chosen mindfulness trainer uses language, analogies and methods that sit well with your audience.

Judging compatibility

When selecting a mindfulness trainer for your organisation, try to select one who is happy to adopt a partnership-working approach. Being open and honest is important so that you can establish a collaborative means of working built on trust.

Your chosen trainer should feel comfortable wearing several hats. She may need to help you write flyers and publicity material. Maybe she can assist you in designing, administering or even managing the evaluation process. The trainer must be equally at home training employees and presenting outcomes with you in the boardroom. If she'll be required to send emails directly to participants (for example, welcoming them to the course, confirming home practice or chasing evaluation completion), you need to be sure that she uses appropriate corporate language. Think carefully about what you require from your mindfulness trainer at the outset to manage expectations all round.

Agreeing on what's possible

When you enter into discussion with a mindfulness trainer for the first time, do so with an open mind. Let the trainer discuss what mindfulness can do for you and your organisation – possibilities may exist that you haven't yet considered. Make sure that the trainer is fully aware of what's important for you. Doing so early on in the process helps you both identify whether any of the outcomes you desire are unachievable. Discovering this at the outset is much better than later in the process. Also agree early on how success will be measured, both in training terms and in relation to organisational outcomes.

In summary, when selecting a mindfulness trainer, look for one who ideally has sector experience and thus understands how your staff work and the pressures they may be under. Make sure that the trainer has attended recognised mindfulness teacher training, and by the time she reaches you has had a minimum of two years' personal experience of practising mindfulness. Make sure that she's flexible in her approach, and willing and able to wear several hats to help you during the critical phase of piloting mindfulness within your organisation.

Mindfulness trainers' details can be found on the Mindfulnet teacher's page at www.mindfulnet.org/page5.htm and on the Be Mindful website at http://bemindful.co.uk/learn/find-a-course.

Hiring a Mindfulness Coach

Learning mindfulness as part of a group has many advantages. Hearing about the experiences of others, which may be different from or similar to yours, is a significant part of the learning process. A strong argument can also be put forward for learning mindfulness one to one, however, and here's where a mindfulness coach comes in.

Identifying the benefits of mindfulness coaching

Mindfulness coaching is a more costly option, but is often more appropriate for senior staff who may not wish to discuss certain aspects of their behaviour, thoughts and habits with their peers. It can also be effective for people needing more tailored development who want to discover mindfulness in conjunction with addressing a specific work-related issue.

Choosing the right coach

Choosing a coach to teach you mindfulness involves many of the same rules as apply to choosing a mindfulness trainer. The coach needs to have both a deep understanding of mindfulness, gained from their own, long-established personal mindfulness practice, and knowledge of how and why mindfulness is taught in the way that it is. Many good coaches are jumping on the mindfulness bandwagon who lack sufficient knowledge and experience of mindfulness. Such coaches may be able to teach you some useful mindfulness tools and tips, but you won't gain the benefits that result from a mindfulness course.

Ideally, your mindfulness coach should:

✔ Have attended a recognised mindfulness teacher training course

✔ Have gained a recognised coaching qualification

✔ Have a minimum of two years' personal mindfulness practice

✔ Be a member of a recognised coaching organisation

✔ Attend regular professional development sessions and supervision in both mindfulness and coaching

Mindfulness Pilot Checklist

Hopefully you now have all the information you need to successfully pilot mindfulness in your organisation. Use the checklist below to ensure that you deal with each step.

Action	Completed?
Stage 1: Start with the end in mind	
Identify organisational outcomes.	
Select a mindfulness at work trainer with whom to work in partnership	
Select the most appropriate training approach (MBSR, MBCT, MAWT, SIY, other).	
Agree on the best way in which to introduce mindfulness to your organisation, in partnership with the mindfulness trainer (for example, offering a taster session then a course for those interested, or starting with a full pilot course).	

(continued)

(continued)

Action	Completed?
Agree a marketing strategy and web/email/newsletter/flyer content.	
Ensure that evaluation measures are integrated into the training.	
Stage 2: Run an introductory session (if applicable)	
Publicise the opportunity using various electronic and physical media, with endorsement from a senior member of staff (if possible).	
Arrange a suitable room. Book equipment such as digital projector (if applicable).	
Evaluate the outcomes.	
Share the evaluation data with other key decision makers to decide on 'next steps'. Involve the mindfulness trainer in any presentation of outcomes, if possible.	
Stage 3: Running a mindfulness course pilot	
Publicise opportunity using various electronic and physical media, with endorsement from a senior member of staff (if possible).	
Arrange a suitable room for the duration of the course. Book equipment such as digital projector (if applicable).	
Agree on criteria for selecting participants.	
Select course participants.	
Inform successful candidates.	
Brief line managers so that they are supportive.	
Complete pre-course evaluation.	
Invite participants to attend day 1 of the course, and provide ongoing communication via the learning and development team and/or the mindfulness trainer.	
Stage 4: Evaluate	
Ask all participants to complete a post-course questionnaire.	
Evaluate the pre- and post-course data to determine whether the outcomes have been achieved and benefits gained, both in individual and organisational terms.	
Share the evaluation data with other key decision makers to decide on 'next steps'. Involve the mindfulness trainer in any presentation of outcomes, if possible.	

Part IV
Leading with Mindfulness

Market

Define:
- Market
- Customers
- Competitors
- Targets

External

Customers

Define:
- Who?
- Why they buy
- Ideal clients
- Other factors

Business vision:
Targets:
- Financial
- Business
- Unique features / value adds

Operations

Define:
- Targets
- Systems
- Quality
- Efficiency
- Resources

Internal

Staff

Define:
- Structure
- Skills and Capability
- Morale
- Flexibility

For Dummies can help you get started with a huge range of subjects. Visit www.dummies.com to learn more and do more with *For Dummies*.

In this part . . .

- ✔ Learn how to thrive on the challenges of leadership.

- ✔ Discover how you can manage even the most complex situations with the simplicity of mindfulness.

- ✔ Enhance your team's creativity by thinking without boundaries.

- ✔ Apply mindful leadership in times of change.

- ✔ Clear your mind to let you focus on what's important.

- ✔ Create strategies to allow your organisation to flourish wisely.

Chapter 13

Thriving on the Challenges of Leadership

*M*ost people spend a huge amount of their time at work. It stands to reason, therefore, that work should make you feel good about yourself, give you a sense of personal mastery and be fun. Unfortunately, many find work to be stressful, demotivating and frustrating. Great leaders identify what motivates people and match their skills to those needed by the organisation, thus creating a win–win situation. In order to create this situation, leaders need to be in a fit state to lead others.

Ideas about what makes a good leader have changed dramatically over time. In the 1920s and 1930s, trait theories argued that leaders were born. From the 1940s to the 1960s behavioural theories argued that you can be taught leadership – it is just a matter of adopting the right behaviours when attempting to lead. You can be autocratic ('I am the boss, do it this way') or democratic ('Let's decide how we should do this').

In more recent times, contingency theories (such as situational leadership) argue that no one leadership style is correct and that as a leader you need to adopt the correct leadership style for the situation. Transformational theories view leaders as agents of change. As a transformational leader you can 'transform' the workplace via team work or team development, or by acting as an agent of change or a strategic visionary.

Mindful Entrepreneurs

Shamash and I (Juliet) really enjoy coaching top entrepreneurs in mindfulness. We enjoy helping take them and their business to higher levels of success. As Jim Rohn said 'work harder on yourself than you do on your job'. In our own experience, the more mindful you are, the better you get at seeing the bigger picture. This has helped us both to expand our organisation and help more people. Creative solutions arise more easily. Limiting beliefs fall away. Life becomes easier and more enjoyable. Some of the entrepreneurs that we have coached have gone on to at least double their income, and more importantly, found more time to be with their friends, family and follow their passion. If you're leading your own organization, remember Jim Rohn's quote, try getting some suitable coaching and notice what happens to your business as you become a more mindful leader.

Human potential theories are the latest development and are concerned with the performance of the leader from a human perspective. These theories incorporate authentic leadership, resonant leadership, mindful leadership and neuro-leadership. Human potential theories are concerned with maximising your potential as a leader by being true to your values, and finding out how to work in harmony with yourself rather than trying to be something you're not. Mindfulness is a core element of human potential theories of leadership.

If you look at leadership theories over the last 70 years or so, you can easily see how each leadership theory has built on the last theory. You can also see why human potential theories are gaining in popularity. We live in a VUCA world – **v**olatile, **u**ncertain, **c**omplex and **a**mbiguous. This new world may go part of the way to explaining why some leadership theories are no longer effective. Yet many leaders, and you may be one of them, continue to base their leadership behaviours on outdated models. Why? Because like everyone else you probably do a fair amount of your work on auto-pilot. Over the years you've probably developed habits, which have been rewarding, and you repeat these patterns of behaviour with little or no conscious thought.

Adopting new, human potential theories of leadership can be scary, as you discard the security blanket of your old methods of leadership and take a leap into the unknown of being yourself, and maximising your potential as a leader. In this brave new world, you need self-knowledge and the courage to be true to yourself. In return, you can shed the heavy burden of trying to be someone who you are not in favour of being the best you can be.

Thriving Rather Than Surviving

Being a leader is a challenging role, especially in times of recession and economic crisis. Being a senior leader can also be a lonely and isolating experience. At times when you feel under pressure and uncertain about the future, you'll find keeping your team motivated and engaged tough. As a leader, you may also feel less inclined to seek support and guidance from your peers. Catastrophising as thoughts spiral round and round in your head is all too easy.

Imagine missing a report deadline at work. In reality this situation is hardly life or death, is it? But your mind is likely to make up its own story about what's going on, blowing the matter out of all proportion. As you discovered in Chapter 5, your cavemen threat response can have a serious impact on your performance, health and happiness. By practising mindfulness and learning to observe thoughts as mental processes, you can change things.

Take the example of Dave and Ken, two middle managers from the same organisation that I (Juliet) have coached (names changed). Both applied for the same senior leadership role. An external candidate was appointed, so neither got the job. How they dealt with the situation was very different.

Dave's thoughts started to spiral down as he catastrophised about the situation. He tried to get on with work, but his mind kept on wandering to what went wrong at the interview, and how this might threaten his career.

Ken, however applied mindfulness to his feelings of failure and rejection. He noticed himself starting to spiral down and his body becoming tense. He practised mindfulness for a short while, calmly observing his thoughts without reacting or thinking about them further, recognising the impact of his thoughts on his emotions and then noticing how his body feels. He released the tension he felt and then focused his attention on the present-moment sensation of breathing. Ken returned to his work. He acknowledged feeling sad and a little angry about missing the promotion, but did not let these thoughts and emotions have a negative impact on his work and well-being.

This example graphically illustrates how mindfulness can help you, as a leader, pick yourself up after a fall, avoiding falling into a downward spiral of despair. Mindfulness also teaches you that the problem is never the real problem! Your perception and response to life's challenges is what can throw you out of the frying pan and into the fire!

While many things are beyond your control at work, you always have a choice about how you respond. Choosing how you respond is empowering – it hands control back to you.

Three ways to lead and thrive

Leadership can be challenging, and its easy to forget to look after yourself. Here are three simple exercises that can help you balance work demands with the need to care for your well-being.

Soaking in the good

Think about the little things that make you feel good in life. Examples may include stroking a pet, hugging a loved one, someone appreciating something you've done or seeing the first flowers of spring.

Ask yourself if you can give these small pleasures a little extra attention. As you experience them, try pausing for a moment to really soak in the good they provide. Allow your body time to release feel-good hormones so that you can derive maximum benefit from these pleasurable experiences.

Soaking in the good is free and takes little time. It can also reduce your threat response, activating your parasympathetic nervous system, flooding your system with feel-good hormones. You may be amazed at the impact it has on your life.

Smiling

When you smile, you're telling your body that everything is fine. This simple action turns off your threat system. Your body immediately stops pumping adrenaline around your body, your blood pressure drops and feel-good hormones such as serotonin is released.

Being kind to yourself

Do you find it easier to demonstrate empathy and kindness to others rather than yourself? Maybe you dismiss the idea of self-kindness as selfishness?

Sometimes you need to be selfish for your own preservation! Try to avoid beating yourself up for mistakes you make, things you get wrong or things you should have done. Being kind to yourself can help reduce or eliminate the detrimental effects of fear, guilt and shame.

Taking time out to consciously accept yourself and make friends with the person you really are helps you increase your happiness and creativity. This time out is especially important if you're a leader. Self-acceptance also helps to train your brain to work in approach mode rather than avoidance mode. A befriending exercise such as 'Cultivating Kindness' in Chapter 5 helps you to deactivate your threat system, making it easier to concentrate and gain a fresh perspective. Befriending yourself can be really hard when you first practise it, but does get easier over time and is definitely worth working on.

For leaders, the ability to identify and overcome outdated mental programming without triggering the threat system is vital. If you're really serious about being a better leader, and thriving rather than surviving, you need to prioritise time to learn mindfulness and embed practice into every day you spend at work.

Being a More Mindful Leader

Human potential models of leadership all centre around the concept of being the best you can be, maximising your innate leadership qualities while being true to yourself and your values. All human potential theories incorporate mindfulness in some shape or form.

This section briefly explores models and ideas around becoming a more mindful leader.

Authentic leadership

Authentic leaders are leaders who demonstrate the genuine desire to understand their own leadership behaviour in order to serve the needs of the organisation and its staff most effectively. Their behaviour and decisions are based on strongly held values and beliefs. By upholding these values and beliefs, they increase their personal credibility and win the respect and trust of their team, colleagues and peers.

Authentic leaders actively encourage collaboration and the sharing of diverse viewpoints, leading in a way that others perceive and describe as 'authentic'. Authentic leadership is all about leaders as individual people. It can be likened to a self-awareness approach to leadership and leadership development.

According to Bill George, former CEO of Medtronic and author of *Authentic Leadership* (Jossey Bass, 2004), authentic leaders are motivated by their mission, not your money. They tap into your values, not your ego. They connect with others through their heart, not their (sometimes artificial) persona. Authentic leaders should live their lives in such a way that they would be proud to read about their behaviour on the front page of their local newspaper.

George defines authentic leadership as having five dimensions. Authentic leaders:

- Understand their purpose
- Practise solid values

> ✔ Lead with the heart
>
> ✔ Establish connected relationships
>
> ✔ Demonstrate self-discipline

He believes that acquiring these five dimensions isn't a sequential process, but happens throughout a leader's life, often over a long time period.

Mindfulness is a key element of authentic leadership. It underpins all five dimensions described above. It helps leaders increase their self-awareness and self-regulation. It helps them to be kinder to themselves and to protect their values.

Working out whether you're an authentic leader

This activity will give you an indication of how 'authentic' your leadership style is.

Score the questions below as follows: 0 = not at all like me, 1 = a little like me, 2 = mostly like me, 3 = an accurate description of me.

1. **I actively seek feedback to improve the way I communicate and work with others.**
2. **I always say exactly what I mean.**
3. **My actions are always fully consistent with my beliefs.**
4. **I always listen very carefully to others' views and opinions before reaching a conclusion.**
5. **If asked to do so, I can quickly and easily give a true description of how others view my strengths and weaknesses as a leader.**
6. **I never play games – what you see is what you get.**
7. **As a leader, I feel that I need to model behaviours that are consistent with my beliefs.**
8. **I recognise that others may not share my views on life and leadership, and am open to others' ideas.**
9. **I understand what motivates me, and the values that underpin my work as a leader and my life in general.**
10. **If I make a mistake I always admit to it and am ready to take full responsibility.**
11. **My values and beliefs have a huge impact on the decisions I make.**
12. **I actively seek out others' views to challenge the way I think about things.**

Enter your scores in the table below:

Authentic Leadership Traits							Score for Trait
Self-awareness	1		2		3		
Transparency and openness	4		5		6		
Embodiment of values	7		8		9		
Seeking a balanced perspective	10		11		12		
					Total overall score		

Interpret your trait score as follows:

0 = a trait you do not display or do not value

1–3 = a trait you can work to improve

4–6 = a trait you display

7+ = a trait you truly embody

To work out your overall score, add up the figures in the right-hand column. The authenticity of your leadership style is shown below:

0–13 = a low level of authentic leadership behaviours displayed

14–26 = a moderate level of authentic leadership behaviours displayed

27–36 = someone who leads with authenticity

If possible, repeat the exercise with one or more colleagues, peers or members of your team. Don't forget to emphasise the need to be honest! Do your team members see you in the same way that you see yourself?

Resonant leadership

Resonant leaders are individuals who manage their own and others' emotions in ways that drive success.

The idea behind resonant leadership is that, rather than constantly sacrificing themselves to workplace demands, leaders should find out how to manage these challenges using specific techniques to combat stress, avoid burnout and renew themselves physically, mentally and emotionally. Many of these techniques are derived from mindfulness practices.

Resonant leaders:

- ✔ Are highly self-aware
- ✔ Demonstrate a high level of self-management
- ✔ Are highly socially aware
- ✔ Are emotionally intelligent
- ✔ Actively work to manage their relationships

Mindful leadership

The latest thinking on effective leadership suggests that leaders need self-awareness (a clear idea of what makes you tick, your strengths, weaknesses, beliefs and motivations) and must be well-grounded and centred.

In addition, leaders need to be able to manage how their mind deals with multiple demands and constant connectivity so that they can maintain peak performance and well-being.

Mindfulness helps you to manage how their mind by regulating and focusing your attention, making you more aware of your thoughts and emotions. Dan Siegel, clinical professor of psychiatry at UCLA School of Medicine and co-director of the Mindful Awareness Research Center, refers to mindfulness practice as 'good brain hygiene', which is as important to your health as brushing your teeth.

If you want to explore this subject further, two key authors in the field of mindful leadership are Michael Carroll (*The Mindful Leader,* 2007) and Michael Chaskalson (*The Mindful Workplace,* 2011).

Practising Mindful Leadership

As you process the continuous stream of information coming in from the world around you, your brain selects the things it deems most relevant and often dismisses the remainder. Academics and researchers argue that business performance is strongly influenced by this continuous stream of individual and organisational 'meaning-making'.

Mindfulness encourages a state of active awareness, openness to new information and willingness to view situations from multiple perspectives. Adopting a mindful attitude allows you to suspend judgement until you have all the facts. Doing so refines your 'meaning-making processes', giving you a more balanced view of the world around you.

This state of active awareness cannot be achieved by simply grasping the idea of mindfulness as an intellectual concept. To fully benefit from mindfulness, you need to regularly apply it to your workday practices. When you gain sufficient knowledge and confidence, you can help others around you by introducing a few simple mindfulness practices into their working lives. We now look at practical ways to incorporate mindfulness into your work as a leader.

Making mindful decisions

If you've been in a leadership or management role for any period of time, you're probably well versed in various models of decision making. What you may not be familiar with is looking at your mindset and unconscious mental programming when making decisions. As discussed throughout this book, your thoughts have a huge impact on how your body feels (for example, tension) and emotions (for example, happiness and fear). Similarly, holding tension or anger in your body has an impact on your thoughts. This impact is often unconscious, but can have a profound impact on the decisions you make.

A number of researchers have concluded that, when making decisions, emotions and negative information have a huge impact. Surprisingly, numeric information, analytic and logical arguments often have less impact. See Chapter 2 for more on the benefits of mindful decision making.

By practising mindfulness you become more aware of the different factors at play when making a decision, including the impact of your own meaning-making process, which leads to less subjectivity in decision making.

Four steps to making mindful decisions

Try this activity to improve your approach to making decisions. Follow these steps:

1. **Spend a few moments centring yourself in the present moment.** Focus on the sensation of breathing to make you relax and exist in the present moment.

2. **Clearly define the decision that you need to make.** Close your eyes, or hold them in soft focus (eyes looking down and three-quarters closed). Just sit with this question, using it as an anchor for your attention. Avoid the temptation to start making the decision or to think about it in any way; just keep on repeating the question in your mind.

3. **Imagine the question to be answered placed on a workbench in front of you for closer examination and study.** Spend a few moments exploring it, with kindness, and curiosity. Consider:

   • Any negative information you may have associated with the decision – observing how this negative information impacts on your thoughts or emotions

- Your emotional state in the present moment

- Any key numerical or statistical information that you may have

4. **Open your eyes, evaluate all the information you have to hand and make your decision.** You can now make a decision taking into account all the factors involved and being fully aware of any bias you may have initially felt.

Communicating ideas and expectations

Chapter 7 has lots of information about mindful communication. The key thing to remember is that you're likely to spend a great deal of time on auto-pilot. You may be physically in the same room as the person you're communicating with, but at some point your mind is likely to wander elsewhere. As a leader, you need to make a real effort to be 100 per cent present when communicating. You need to train your brain to notice when your mind wanders to the past or future or to matters unrelated, and gently bring it back to the present moment. In this state of present-moment awareness, you're better able to pick up verbal and non-verbal cues from your audience. You're better able to identify emerging areas of support and build on them. Similarly, you can pick up on areas of dissent and take time to explore or address them. Most importantly, people feel that you're really listening to them and that you value their time and input.

Mindfully encouraging others to speak up and contribute

A key part of being a leader is encouraging people to voice their thoughts and contribute to discussions and meetings. When you're in a mindful, present state of mind, you're better able to encourage people to share their ideas and support them in working collaboratively.

To improve the quality of your meetings, follow these steps:

1. **Remove anything that causes a distraction.** At the start of a meeting or collaborative working session, ask people to switch off their phones and so on.

2. **Set the tone for the meeting or working session.** You need to set the scene:

    - State clearly and concisely what you're trying to achieve.

    - Gain consensus from everyone present.

    - Reassure people that you're open to hearing their opinions and ideas (there's no such thing as a stupid question or suggestion). Back up this statement by making sure that you acknowledge and capture in writing every idea put forward.

    - Do not openly criticise someone's input (whatever you secretly think of it). Value that person by acknowledging their contribution.

3. **Create opportunities for everyone to share ideas and thoughts.** Don't expose people or put them on the spot. If they're initially too shy to contribute, be gentle and supportive.

4. **Recap what has been discussed and decided on so far to maintain direction and momentum.** At regular intervals, pause and give a brief overview.

5. **Make the final decision.** Remember that you're the leader and that the final decision rests with you. If this decision is different to group consensus, always ensure that you thank everyone for their contribution, and let them know that you've really heard and considered their input.

Solving problems mindfully

Defaulting to old ways of thinking and behaving is all too easy when you're trying to solve problems – after all, they've served you well in the past. Mindful problem solving takes a more holistic approach.

Mindful problem solving

1. **Take steps to ensure that you're fully in the present moment.** Spend a few minutes doing a short mindfulness exercise of your choice, with your eyes closed or in soft focus.

2. **Place the problem you wish to solve on your 'workbench' of the mind.** Try to picture the scene if you can. Observe how it makes your body feel and any emotions it invokes. Try your best not to judge these feelings and emotions as good or bad – just sit with them.

3. **Ask yourself the following questions.** After asking each question, observe the challenge sitting on your workbench and wait for an answer. Acknowledge each answer as it arrives.

   • How/why has the challenge arisen?

   • What factors are involved?

   • What are the possible solutions?

4. **Observe your answers with kindness and curiosity.** Avoid the temptation to drift away from the present moment by focusing on your answers. Observe any strong reactions that are elicited by any part of your exploration. Are you experiencing an emotion, for example excitement or fear? Is your body responding, for example, with a clenched jaw or fluttering in your stomach?

5. **Open your eyes and make a decision on the best way to solve the problem.** You can now make an informed and dispassionate decision, having considered all the facts.

6. **See the problem as a challenge.** Research suggests by reframing problems as positive challenges to learn and overcome, you're more likely to take a proactive approach and find effective solutions

After practising mindfulness regularly for eight weeks or longer you should be able to use techniques like this one much more rapidly, as you develop the ability to quickly tune into the present moment and observe things more objectively.

Creating a positive and inspiring workplace culture

As a leader, you're the one who sets the tone in the workplace. Being true to yourself and your values is important; that is, you need to be authentic.

If you truly value people's creativity and innovation, make sure that working practices reflect and celebrate these aptitudes. For example, your company could set up a system that identifies and rewards staff who are innovative. Google staff are allocated time each week to work on their pet projects or ideas that interest them. This freedom has led to the development of many of Google's most profitable products.

If you value mindfulness, and want to cultivate a more mindful workplace, consider:

- ✔ Offering staff mindfulness training in work time.

- ✔ Setting aside space for people to get away from their desks or work areas to clear their minds and grab a few moments of mindfulness. Leading organisations are creating these spaces, and this privilege is highly valued and rarely abused.

- ✔ Cultivating a culture in which staff feel comfortable leaving their work area for a short time to practise mindfulness somewhere quiet.

- ✔ Offering mindfulness drop-in sessions, possibly at lunch time, which people can join as and when they want to.

As Mahatma Gandhi famously said, 'be the change you want to see'. If you want to encourage openness and honesty, be open and honest yourself. Many leaders paint a vivid vision of what an organisation is like to work for, but fail to follow this vision through by making sure that the fundamentals are in place to make the vision a reality.

Mindfully take a long hard look at your organisation, and what it looks like from an employee's perspective. Does it really match up to the vision painted of it? Ask yourself what you can do to change things for the better, embodying your beliefs and values.

Coping with Stress and Pressure by Building Resilience

Did you know that a lack of control over your work can be a major source of stress? The Whitehall II Study found that leaders experience the lowest level of stress in organisations. This low level may be in part because they have a high level of control over their work. While leaders do have a higher degree of control over their work than many other employees, the high pressure, fast-changing environment that most leaders work in can be a major source of stress. Stress is now reported to be the number one cause of workplace sickness and absence. A huge volume of research carried out over the last 40 years demonstrates the effectiveness of mindfulness to reduce stress.

Mindfulness can build your resilience in the following ways:

- **It improves well-being.** It helps you gain more benefit from the pleasures in life and creates a greater capacity to deal with challenging events.

- **It improves physical health.** Scientists have discovered many ways in which mindfulness can improve physical health. These ways include lowering blood pressure, reducing chronic pain and improving sleep.

- **It improves mental health.** Hundreds of research studies have concluded that mindfulness is effective in reducing stress, anxiety and depression. It can also help with eating disorders, couples' conflict and even obsessive-compulsive disorder.

- **It helps you manage you mind better.** Make sure that you remember that you should be in control of your mind – your mind should not be controlling you! Creating a small gap between a stressful or difficult event and your thoughts puts you back in control

- **It helps you to cope better with the difficulties in your life.** Mindfulness works, in part, by helping people to accept their experiences – including painful emotions – rather than reacting to them with sense of aversion and then avoidance. By approaching and exploring things you find difficult, their grip and impact on your life usually diminishes.

While you cannot always control the challenges and stressors that arise at work, you do ultimately have 100 per cent control over how you respond to them. However, gaining this control can take practice!

Reading a book about mindfulness is all very well, but is no substitute for actually practising it and hardwiring it into your brain. The best way to cope well under stress and pressure is to develop regular mindfulness practice. After discovering and practising the basics for eight weeks, as little as ten minutes formal practice each day can help you take control of your responses to life's challenges. Here are a few hints and tips to help you build your resilience.

Maintaining peak performance

The trick to maintaining peak performance is recognising when your performance starts to drop off and taking steps to restore it. The Yerkes–Dobson curve, described in detail in Chapter 5, illustrates this scenario.

To maintain peak performance, try this exercise:

1. **Practise the body scan (see Chapter 6) to identify the key areas of your body in which you hold tension.** These areas vary from person to person. Detecting tension in these areas can act as an early warning system, alerting you of the need to take mindful action. (At work you can do a three step body check at your desk – Chapter 6 tells you how.)

2. **Deal with any tension you detect in these key areas.** Try:

   - Breathing into them and then letting the tension go on the out breath

   - Giving yourself a few minutes break away from what you were doing by walking outside or from one area of the building to another or by leaving the office premises altogether

   - Eating or drinking something mindfully. Spend a few minutes really experiencing the taste, smell, and sensations as you swallow the drink or eat the food

   - Stretching at your desk – really experience the sense of stretching and moving your muscles

   - Spending a few minutes focusing on sounds, with your eyes closed or in soft focus – just observe them as they arise and vanish without out categorising them or having to do anything

3. **Return to your work.** Your improved performance more than compensates for the few minutes that you've spent practising mindfulness.

Implementing mindful strategies for rejuvenation

Mindfulness teaches you how to manage your own mind. It shows you that you've a choice in how you respond to life. Just because you've always done things in a certain way doesn't mean that you have to continue to do so. Mindfulness is also about creating a balance in your life between things that nourish you and things that deplete you.

You may find that, when you get particularly busy, you drop things that seem unimportant such as playing a musical instrument, playing a sport, spending time with friends or little pockets of time to yourself. The more you spiral away from being mode into doing mode, the busier you're likely to become. Here are a few mindful strategies you can try to rejuvenate your life:

- ✔ **Do a quick audit of the activities you do each day.** Note which ones nourish you (make you feel good or give you a sense of mastery or achievement) and which deplete you (sap your energy or make you feel bad).

- ✔ **Note whether your day includes at least a few things that nourish you.** Time spent on these things is an investment in your well-being and should be an important part of your day.

- ✔ **Recognise that some activities can both nourish or deplete you.** Decide what you can change (in your mindset or actions) to make certain activities more nourishing than depleting.

- ✔ **Spend a little time each day practising mindfulness.** Set a time in your diary and don't let your busy workload rob you of this important investment in your productivity and well-being.

- ✔ **Do one thing a day mindfully.** Take a mindful shower, be mindful of your bodily sensations as you work out at the gym, eat or walk mindfully.

- ✔ **Take a few minutes to pause and gain maximum benefit from something that you enjoy.** Savour every mouthful of that chocolate bar. See all the colours of that beautiful sunrise or sunset. Relish a hug from your children or loved one. Pausing to really experience things you enjoy in the present moment makes your body release feel-good hormones, which reduce stress and increase immunity and general well-being.

Stop surviving and start thriving by experimenting with different aspects of mindfulness. Your investment in time and effort will pay handsome dividends.

Chapter 14

Leading without Boundaries

Mindful leadership is all about being fully in the present moment, experiencing life, warts and all, including moments of success and failure. Mindfulness is all about being the best you can be, ensuring that your leadership style is in harmony and alignment with your values. This style of leadership involves being reflective; having the ability to stop, be silent and learn. Mindful leadership is about knowing yourself, your thinking patterns, how you feel and behave. It encourages you to engage more fully with the world around you, adopting an open and flexible approach. It encourages empathy, understanding, and kindness to yourself.

In this chapter you find out how you can apply these attitudes and approaches to your own leadership style. The first section starts by clearing the decks and creating the space to lead.

Creating the Space to Lead

When leading in times of complexity and change, you can easily become engulfed in day-to-day work challenges. Sometimes it can feel like you don't even have a moment to draw breath. Taking time out to stand back and observe the bigger picture is always important and even more so when you're really busy. The busier you are, the more you need to really know yourself, be kind to yourself and make the most of the limited time and personal energy at your disposal. Unfortunately, when busy, you may start to focus too much time and energy on what you think is important at that moment in time, failing to see the bigger picture. Project deadlines and important meetings may become disproportionately important in comparison to taking time out to be kind to yourself. A weekly massage, exercise, going to the theatre or meeting with friends can become distant dreams. In times of high pressure, ensuring that you've a sense of balance in your life is vital.

Seeing the bigger picture

When you're really busy, believing that you don't have a second to pause is all too easy. You start to think that every second counts and that you mustn't waste time on things like eating lunch, pausing to enjoy something beautiful or even allowing yourself a few seconds to pat yourself on the back for a job well done. Time away from desk or office equals lost productivity (or so you think!). When working in this mindset, you may feel as though you're being a bad employee or setting a bad example by 'doing nothing'. The reverse is true.

When the going gets tough, the tough get mindful! Recent research showed that mindfulness can widen your attentional breadth, making you aware of more things simultaneously; and lots of research demonstrates that mindfulness helps people see situations from a broader perspective.

Mindfulness helps you to notice patterns of behaviour and thoughts in yourself and others. Most importantly, creating a gap to think before responding allows you to put things into perspective and helps you to focus on what's really important and the best use of your precious time and energy.

Mindfully seeing the bigger picture

Try this activity to gain a sense of perspective. Follow these steps:

1. **Find somewhere where you will not be disturbed for 15 minutes.** If this is impossible at work, try doing the activity at home, or arrive early, park at the far end of the car park and sit in the car.

2. **Close your eyes or cast your eyes downwards.** Spend a little time steadying your mind and stepping back from your brain chatter. Start by counting your breaths. Count 1 on the in-breath, 2 on the out-breath. Continue until you reach a count of 20. If your mind wanders, smile and gently escort your attention back to focusing on breathing, and restart your counting at 1.

3. **Focus your attention on what your organisation does.** What services does it offer or what products does it make? Try to visualise these services or products and place them on the workbench of your mind. Spend a couple of minutes exploring them with playful curiosity.

4. **Focus your attention on how your work contributes to the organisation's success.** Place your role on the workbench of your mind and explore it.

5. **Explore all your work tasks, looking at them impartially without starting to think about and deal with them.** If helpful, picture these tasks as boxes, each sealed with a label, on the workbench of your mind. Consider:

    • Which of the boxes are really important from an organisational perspective?

    • Are there any boxes that invoke strong emotions?

    • Are any of the boxes taking up more space on the workbench than they need to?

6. **Return your attention to** your **breath.** Focus on the breath coming in (count 1) and the breath going out (count 2) for a count of 10.

7. **Open your eyes and spend the last few minutes reflecting.** Consider:

    • Which work tasks are really the best use of your time?

    • Are there any tasks that you're focusing on more than you should because you like them or avoiding because you don't like them?

    • Is the time you're allocating to each task appropriate when you consider how great or little impact it has on your department and the company as a whole?

Try to do this activity fairly regularly, at least once a month, to help you stand back and look more strategically at how you spend your working time.

From time to time you can easily become overwhelmed with things to do, all of which seem both important and urgent. At times like this, try using the a variation of the three-minute focus break (see Chapter 5), as described below.

✔ **Close your eyes or hold them in soft focus.** Spend a minute observing your thoughts as mental processes and then letting them go.

✔ **Focus your attention on how your heart feels, pumping blood and oxygen round your body.** If you cannot detect this, focus your attention on the air entering and leaving your body through your nostrils.

✔ **Expand your attention to the sounds around you, in your body, in the room and outside.** Observe how your whole body feels, sitting in this room in this moment.

✔ **Ask yourself, 'What is the very best use of my time in this present moment?'** Open your eyes, and reprioritise your work for the rest of the day.

Making time to be yourself

When was the last time you took time out to be yourself? Maybe you're already an authentic leader and are really comfortable in your own skin. Maybe the essence of who you are and what you stand for is the same both at work and home. If this is true, congratulations! You probably have mutually supportive and trusting relationships with your colleagues. Because of this your actions and ideas are favourably received, leading to better outcomes and results.

Possibly your authenticity has led to you having a higher profile in the organisation. By being authentic and true to your values, your life is probably easier and you're happier as a result.

If this doesn't sound like you, don't worry. Despite numerous articles being published on the subject, relatively few truly authentic leaders exist out there in the real world. Trying to be something you're not, day in, day out, can be hard work, but being truly 'authentic' as a leader can have its downside too. If the real you is a jerk, 'being authentic' becomes simply an excuse for bad behaviour!

Assuming that the real you is quite a sound, intelligent person, how can you spend more time being you? Indeed, are you really aware of who the real 'you' is after so many years of wearing the costume of 'the leader you think you should be'?

A good place to start is looking at what happiness and success mean to you personally (as opposed to how society, your friends or family view them) and what really makes you 'happy'. Doing so takes courage, honesty and a true desire to be free of the opinions of others.

Do you measure your own personal success in terms of money, status or possessions? Or do you measure it in terms of relationships with others, family, happiness, personal growth and development, or the difference you're making in the world? No right or wrong answers exist here; everyone is unique. We've all had different childhoods and different experiences along the way that have helped to shape who we are and what we value. Decide what's right for you.

Finding the real you: step 1

Practise some mindfulness and, after 10 minutes or so (when hopefully you've activated your rest and relaxation parasympathetic nervous system, and have shifted brain mode from avoidance to approach), ask yourself these questions:

- ✔ What really makes me feel happy in life?
- ✔ What does success really mean to me?

With each question, allow time for the answer to emerge. You might wish to imagine the questions dropping like a pebble into a lake, and the ripples circling out. Try to observe the answers without thinking about them too much. Don't worry, you won't forget them, and you'll have time to think about them more later on.

After finishing this mindfulness practice, jot down what the answers that emerged. Write the happiness themes on one piece of paper and the success themes on another. As you reflect on them, you may wish to add more thoughts to the page or turn the page into a mind map.

You may need to repeat this exercise several times over a week or more before you're happy that you've got the genuine answers that really resonate for you.

Finding the real you: step 2

When you've a clear idea of what makes you happy and what personal success looks like for you, you can repeat the exercise, focusing this time specifically on your work.

What makes you happy at work? It may be gaining promotion or increasing your status. It may also be about developing and supporting others to take on new roles or get promoted or even eventually take on your job when you leave. At a simple level, happiness at work may depend on gaining a sense of personal mastery of your work, knowing that your unique input into a task was what made the real difference.

Similarly, what does success look like for you? It may be much the same as your idea of success in your personal life or as simple as meeting most of your work deadlines. It may be about increasing profits, turning round a failing part of the business, growing your customer base, increasing customer satisfaction or improving employee satisfaction.

Every day authenticity

Try to have a mindful, authentic moment every day. It may be:

- ✔ Saying no when you would normally say yes as a result of peer pressure.

- ✔ Taking a few moments out of your busy schedule to be yourself – eating that ice-cream, practising mindfulness to bring things back into balance or taking time to enjoy a coffee with a true friend.

- ✔ Making a little time each day to focus on making a difference in the workplace – putting in place things that align with your personal values, slowly over time changing the organisation's culture.

Take a stand each day and you'll be happier, healthier . . . and attracting the life that you really want.

Being good to yourself

At school or as you grew up, you were probably taught to be kind to others. Do you treat yourself as well as you treat your friends and members of your family? Research into 'self-compassion' shows that most people find it much easier to be kind to others than to be kind to themselves. This is true for a variety of reasons. Self-compassion may be viewed as self- indulgence or as a weakness. People may fear that, by being kinder to themselves, they'll become weak or lose control. Some people regard self-compassion as being selfish.

You may work in an organisational culture that celebrates long hours and the need to be 'seen' to be busy at all times. You may feel, especially when busy, the need to push yourself harder to get things done. In the current economic climate businesses need to provide better services or products using fewer resources, which compounds this type of organisational culture.

In this environment, cultivating self-care and befriending ourselves can be difficult. Befriending yourself may seem a pink fluffy thing to do. However, sound scientific reasons exist for cultivating self-care, including:

- ✔ Many people are unconsciously in a constant state of threat, which over time can lead to long-term serious illness. Recent neuroscience research into self-compassion and kindness suggests that self- compassion can reduce or neutralise the brain's reaction to threat.

- ✔ Practising self-compassion can reduce shame and self-criticism.

- ✔ People who score high on tests of self-compassion tend to be happier and more optimistic.

- ✔ Research conducted in 2012 demonstrated that cultivating compassion increases activity in the right amygdala, which helps decrease depression and anxiety.

Learning to be kinder to yourself can be hard at first; after all, you're asking yourself to unlearn the habits of a lifetime. Chapter 5 describes a mindfulness activity to help cultivate self-compassion.

Managing your time and energy

Over the years you'll have found ways of managing your time that work for you and get results. However, these patterns of time management may become entrenched and stored in the brain as habits. Because they're habits, you find yourself repeating them without even being aware that you're doing so. To adopt a more mindful approach to leadership, you may need to throw away your old rule book.

Table 14-1 compares some old approaches to leadership with more mindful workplace practices.

Table 14-1	Comparing old leadership habits to new mindful approaches
Old Rules	*Mindful Ways*
As a leader, you need to be constantly in touch. Phone and email communications should be responded to instantly.	Research shows that constant interruptions from the phone and email messages reduces productivity and can lead to burnout. ✔ Remember that you do have a choice. You don't have to answer the phone if you're in the middle of something. You can always call people back later. ✔ Emails don't have to be responded to instantly. Log off for a while. You'll be able to focus on your work and get more done if you only check them at set times, for example in the morning, at noon and at the end of the day.
Being a good leader means making the most of your time. Cram as much as possible into your day. Save time by scheduling meetings back to back.	Many meetings are highly unproductive. Back-to-back meetings are even less effective. ✔ Meetings often overrun, which has a cumulative effect. This is both unprofessional and can lead to stress. ✔ Back-to-back meetings give you insufficient time to prepare yourself between meetings, leading to wasted time. ✔ Knowing that you have multiple meetings can make it less easy to focus on the present moment as your mind strays to mentally prepare you for the next meeting.
As a leader, you need to be organised. Timetable similar amounts of time to do similar tasks. Tight timescales make you work faster and harder.	Planning your day can be a good thing, but be honest – most tasks take a lot longer to complete than you initially think. ✔ Tasks that you're doing for the first time are likely to take more time. ✔ Be realistic when allocating time for tasks. Doing so helps you manage the expectations of others and reduce the pressure you put on yourself.

(continued)

Table 14-1 *(continued)*

Old Rules	Mindful Ways
To be a good leader, the ability to multi-task is essential.	Research shows that regular multi-taskers get less done. In reality, your brain finds it impossible to multi-task; it just switches attention from one task to the next. Information about the previous task is stored in your working memory. Unfortunately, working memory space is limited, leading to you failing to recall information and having to repeat work.
As a leader, you need to be on top of your game at all times. You should monitor emails at home, even if you don't respond to them.	Numerous research studies show that being constantly connected at all times is bad for you. Failure to unplug from your work and electronic devices may lead to reduced productivity and burnout. Make sure that you set clear boundaries between your work and your personal life.

Proactively manage your energy levels throughout the day so that you've the physical stamina to deal with everything you need to do.

Did you know that:

- ✔ Complex tasks such as prioritising and decision making use the newest parts of your brain, which require significantly more energy to run than the more primitive areas of your brain.

- ✔ Your brain consumes energy at 10 times the rate of the rest of your body per gram of tissue.

- ✔ Glucose is the main energy source for your brain. As the size and complexity of your brain increases, energy requirements increase.

- ✔ If the energy supply to your brain is cut off for 10 minutes, it causes permanent brain damage. No other organ in the human body is as sensitive to changes in its energy supply.

- ✔ Researchers asked runners on a treadmill to exert as much force as they could on a bar in front of them. They measured the force, then gave them simple sums to do. The amount of force they were able to exert reduced significantly as their brains processed the sums.

The above examples graphically illustrate the need to actively manage your energy levels. Practising mindfulness helps you to get to know yourself better. Specific mindfulness practices such as the body scan (see Chapter 6) put you in touch with the signals that your body is sending you. As a result, you become more aware of its needs – for hydration, for food to top up energy supplies, or for movement to ease physical tension.

Time taken to be kind to yourself and manage your energy will be more than repaid by increased productivity, reduced duplication and a more positive mindset.

Enhancing Leadership Creativity

Never has there been more of a drive for leaders to be creative. Few would argue that businesses are experiencing change at an unprecedented level. Products have shorter and shorter life cycles; some high-tech products need fundamental redesign every 6 to 12 months. Work life has become more unpredictable and less stable. Most people will change jobs 11 times before they hit their mid-forties. The demand for creativity at work is increasing. Many education experts and leaders from top companies now argue that creativity and innovation have become crucial 21st-century skills.

As you practise and develop your own mindfulness exercises, your ability to be creative also grows. Research shows that mindfulness can enhance flexible and critical reasoning skills, reduce cognitive rigidity, improve insight and refine problem- solving skillsFind out how in this section.

Thinking without boundaries

Remember when you were a child and invented stories about fairies, spacemen and super heroes? You generally think of children as being more creative than adults. Worryingly, research carried out in 2010 based on 300,000 creativity tests going back to the 1970s concluded that creativity has decreased among children in recent years. Since 1990, children have become less able to produce unique and unusual ideas. They're also less humorous, less imaginative and less able to elaborate on ideas. Researchers blame the current focus on testing in schools, and the idea that there is only one right answer to a question, leaving little room for unexpected, novel, or divergent thought.

Many neuro-scientists believe that creativity is innate – it can never really be lost but it does need to be nurtured. As adults, notions of right and wrong can cause creativity to decline. So how, as an adult, can you increase your creativity and discover how to think again without boundaries?

Learning from your own experience is critical to help you adapt and survive. Consciously or unconsciously, you improve your performance based on previous experiences. But experiences can also hinder your performance if you get stuck in the past and your thinking becomes rigid. This is where mindfulness comes in. By practising mindfulness, you can reduce your mental rigidity. Mindfulness encourages you to let go of habits and find alternatives when appropriate. By observing thoughts as mental processes and letting them go without further mental processing, you create a pause. This pause allows you to decide on the most appropriate response rather than defaulting to old ways of thinking and behaving. The act of noticing habits and using habit releasers (see Chapter 7) can be powerful. By consciously observing what happens when you do things differently, you start to break down cognitive rigidity and increase cognitive flexibility.

Feeling a little uncomfortable when doing new things or trying to do things differently is natural. Your inner voice may be screaming at you 'this isn't the way to do it!' Two key reasons for this response exist. First, the old way of doing things feel safer. Your brain has evolved to maximise reward while minimising threat. From your brain's perspective, defaulting to old, tried and tested ways of doing things feels safer and more rewarding. Second, if you've done something a certain way for three months or more, the process has probably become hard-wired into the primitive areas of your brain. This means that you can repeat the behaviours without any conscious thought, and little energy is needed to run this mental programming. Doing something new involves use of the newer areas of the brain, which take much more energy to run.

Over the next few days, try to notice some of your habits at work. These habits may include:

✔ Always tackling your emails in a set order

✔ Using a speaker phone in an open plan office or talking too loudly

✔ Using electronic devices during meetings

✔ Being late for meetings and appointments

✔ Always listening to the same radio station or CD on the way home

Select one of these habits and try doing things differently. Observe:

✔ The impact of your action. What thoughts, emotions or bodily sensations develop?

✔ The impact of this action on others around you.

Doing things differently isn't usually the real challenge - your mental resistance to it is. Simple exercises like this help you to make your thinking and behaviour patterns less rigid, opening up a world of creative possibilities.

Tapping into your intuition

An increasing number of senior leaders are now questioning why business decision making should always be strictly analytical. They argue that sometimes it should be intuitive; in other words, they suggest going with their 'gut instinct'. Not long ago this type of thinking would have been dismissed as nonsense but that's no longer the case. Conventional decision making has many limitations, which is why leaders faced with unprecedented challenges are now open to trying a new approach. The business environment is often ambiguous and there isn't enough information on which to base a rational decision.

Until recent years, intuition was confined to the realm of philosophy. In recent years, psychology and neuroscience research have discovered more about the way in which we make decisions, so intuition has become an area of academic study.

According to cognitive experiential self theory, we routinely process information in parallel; we use rational processes such as logic and analysis on the conscious level, while relying on instinctual and emotional cues on the non-conscious level. This means that you're probably already using reason and intuition simultaneously, but are unaware of it.

Mindfulness is a way of directing your attention on to something you choose such as the breath, your body, sounds or thoughts. By focusing your attention in this way, understanding or insight (although not the aim) is often the result. Insight and intuition have much in common. Insight is a sudden knowing of something, or understanding of some aspect of your life. Intuition can be described as knowing something immediately at a gut level without conscious reasoning.

For example, when I (Shamash) was practising a mindful exercise whilst travelling on a holiday in New Zealand last year, I had a strong feeling I should contact an old business partner. So, on my return, I did so. From that contact, we developed a completely new business model that went on to be extremely successful. Without mindfulness, that insight may not have had the space to arise. Can you think of an example when a flash of insight arose when relaxing in a bath, watching a sunset or going for a calm stroll?

Managing Complexity with Simplicity

Few would argue that the ability to 'manage complexity' is now an essential quality for leaders and managers alike. You can manage complexity in two ways – you can work in harmony with your brain or battle against it, trying to bend it to your will. In this final part of the chapter, we look at ways that mindfulness can help you manage complexity with simplicity.

THE SCIENCE BEHIND IT

Why we are unaware of 95 per cent of what we do

A number of neuro-scientists have conducted studies which suggest that only 5 per cent of your cognitive activities (decisions, emotions, actions, behaviour) are conscious. The vast majority of the things you do and the decisions you make are conducted unconsciously. Why is this so?

To use a computer analogy, this lack of consciousness of so much that you do can be partly explained by the different 'operating systems' that different parts of your brain use. The oldest parts of the brain use a simpler operating system that is fast and requires little energy to run. You're often unaware when this operating system is running. The newest parts of your brain are capable of performance that exceed your wildest dreams, but the new operating system is still in development and a little slow. You also need a lot of energy to run this circuitry, but are aware when it's happening. As a result the brain processes as much as possible using the faster operating system of your more primitive brain areas, retaining energy to run your newest, most powerful neural circuitry only when needed.

Recognising that the past is history and tomorrow is a mystery

In the words of Alice Morse Earle, 'Yesterday is history. Tomorrow is a mystery. Today is a gift. That's why it is called the present.' If today is a gift, why is it that so few of us spend time appreciating it? When seeking to manage complexity, you need to keep things as simple as possible. You need to try to confine your precious energy to focusing on present-moment facts rather than reliving the past or trying to crystal gaze into the future.

Most people think that they're fully in control of everything they do and fully aware of everything that's happening as it happens. This is a common misconception – most cognitive tasks are done unconsciously. Research by scientists at the Max Planck Institute for Human Cognitive and Brain Sciences, using fMRI brain scanning technology, demonstrated that your decisions are made seconds before you become aware of them.

Numerous research studies also demonstrate that, even when we think that we're fully in control of our actions and behaviours, our brains may have other ideas. In one experiment volunteers were asked to catch a remote control helicopter flying round a room. Each developed their own mental strategy to do so – each one different from the next person. However, when their movements were tracked on computer, they were all using similar movements to catch it – despite thinking they were doing completely different things. In effect their brains had worked out the most efficient way of doing the task, without the volunteers' awareness.

Working memory

Working memory can be thought of as a mental jotting pad. You use it for remembering phone numbers, pin codes, verbal directions or anything else where no external written or electronic record exists. Working memory is important because it provides a mental workspace to hold information while mentally engaged in other activities. Your ability to do this is vital if you wish to continue to learn new things and develop as a leader.

If you were asked to write a report that included statistics, your brain would probably process the task like this. First, you may need to hold numbers in your working memory. Second, you would retrieve information from your long-term memory about how to calculate averages. Third, you would add the numbers together and then divide them by another number stored in your working memory. This would produce the average number, which you would probably then type into your report.

Working memory is limited in many ways. Most people can only hold between three and four things in working memory at any one time. Distractions such as the phone ringing, trying to hold too much information in your working memory or trying to tackle a mentally demanding task can lead to a loss of information. When information is lost, it's gone for good.

You cannot stop this unconscious mental processing from happening, but you can be aware of it. Most of the time your neural circuitry serves you well, even though you're not always fully aware of what's going on. But at times your brain can make bad decisions based on old programming. By practising mindfulness you can develop the capability to jump into the present moment when you need to and see what's happening, moment by moment, and consciously decide what happens next. This is a useful capability to cultivate if you wish to stay ahead of your game.

Working mindfully with your brain

A senior executive I (Juliet) worked with, let's call her Kate, was struggling to cope with an increased workload. She was managing multiple teams based in six different countries. She was expanding into new markets in the East, while trying to diversify products sold in the West. Scheduling conference calls at a convenient time for all often involved working early or late, not to mention frequent flights to offices abroad. Trying to manage multiple teams simultaneously, coupled with long working hours and constant connectivity, was making her increasingly stressed. Her colleagues were beginning to find her behaviour erratic, and becoming concerned.

Kate heard about mindfulness from a friend, and her company was happy to pay for mindfulness coaching to unpick the causes of her stress and give her the tools she needed to manage her mind better. Here's what Kate discovered:

- ✔ Working memory capacity is limited, so you need to consciously manage this precious resource.

- ✔ When your mind wanders, you may lose critical information from your working memory.

- ✔ Multi-tasking is a myth and a waste of energy – constant multi-taskers are less productive due to re-working and duplicated effort.

- ✔ Tasks that take most mental energy need to be done at the start of the day, ideally one at a time – this way you get more done more quickly.

- ✔ Constant connectivity can exact a huge mental toll. It often leads to a high state of arousal for long periods, which can lead to a significant drop in performance and serious illness.

Kate recognised just how little of her time she was spending in the present moment and how much her mind was wandering. She also noticed the tension she was carrying in her body. Kate started to practise mindfulness for 10 minutes when she got up in the morning, and 10 minutes when she got home as a mental segway between work and home life. This practice helped Kate reduce her stress levels and focus better when at work.

Kate also restructured the way she worked. She scheduled in time to do the most mentally taxing tasks at the start of the day. She grouped similar tasks together. In-between different tasks or before some meetings she used the three step focus break (see Chapter 5). A combination of these changes helped Kate to focus and remain productive for longer.

Kate timetabled in certain times when she was not contactable, informing her colleagues and teams in advance in order to manage their expectations. Kate also put a stop to some of her really early and late conference calls. Giving herself a break from constantly thinking about work allowed her time to stop, relax and recharge, further reducing her stress levels.

Over the next few months Kate discovered to her surprise that most of her work could be fitted into an 8:00 a.m. to 6:00 p.m. timeframe. On the few occasions when it was essential to hold meetings outside of office hours, she reclaimed the time on another day. With more spare time at her disposal, she was able to engage with her rest and relaxation more frequently, which led to her feeling better in herself. She was able to catch up with friends she'd been neglecting and put some fun back into her life.

As you can see, the volume and complexity of Kate's work did not decrease; rather, how she managed it and her attitude towards it are what changed. By finding out how to work wisely with her brain, and developing awareness of her thoughts, emotions and physiology she was able to thrive on the challenges of leadership, while taking better care of her own well-being.

- ✔ Get to work on your most mentally challenging tasks when your brain has most energy at its disposal. Also try to group similar tasks together – you'll get more done in less time.

- ✔ Practise the three-minute focus break at work in-between different types of tasks or before important meetings. Put on your headphones and pretend to listen to your iPod if you feel self-conscious.

- ✔ When you're in a meeting, be in the meeting! Monitor yourself to make sure that you remain fully present – you'll get more done and make better decisions.

- ✔ Schedule in 'only contact me in an emergency' times and let everyone know about them. Switch off the phone, computer and other electronic means of communication. Although it may initially feel like going 'cold turkey', switching off in this way encourages your body to switch off its fight-or-flight response and help you regenerate.

Maintaining clarity and focus

The more complex and challenging the world becomes, the more you need to work on consciously maintaining clarity and focus. This chapter touches on a number of ways in which you can work with your mind and use mindfulness to help you maintain this clarity and focus.

Here are a few mindful tips to help you remain calm and focused in the increasingly frantic world in which we live:

- ✔ If you really need to focus and you really can't, try closing your eyes or holding them in soft focus. Doing so blocks out visual stimulation, giving your brain one less thing to process and thus making it easier to focus.

- ✔ Pick a sensory experience (for instance, focusing on an object or playing with a stress toy or focusing in on the sensations in your body). Focus all your attention on it – dismissing any incoming thoughts as 'mental processes' and kindly letting them go. Focusing in on a present-moment experience like this helps to slow your brain chatter and bring you to a clear, alert state of mind.

✔ Use mindfulness to help you recognise when your mind starts to spiral into elaborated thoughts that are coupled with emotions. 'If I miss the deadline, my boss will think I'm useless and I'll be next for redundancy' is an example. These elaborated thoughts can have a powerful negative impact on your life. Acknowledge them as simply 'mental constructs', works of fiction created by your mind, and not facts. Kindly acknowledge them, congratulate yourself for recognising them and let them go.

✔ Remember that your phone and computer have both on and off buttons. Don't let the off buttons start feeling neglected! Use them more frequently. Technology is supposed to be there to assist your performance, not hinder it. Having times when everyone knows you're non-contactable helps you focus better on the present-moment task you need to complete, and get more done in less time.

Hopefully this chapter has given you a few ideas on how to remove your self-imposed boundaries and become the best you can be. To paraphrase Charles Darwin, it isn't the strongest species that survives, nor the most intelligent, but the most adaptive to change. Mindfulness cultivates your awareness - this awareness is the key to changing the way you think and behave as a leader while simultaneously taking care of your well-being as a human being.

Chapter 15

Leading People, Change and Strategy

- -

In This Chapter

▶ Leading in the midst of constant change

▶ Helping your organisation to flourish

▶ Developing a mindful organisation

- -

*L*eading people and change are arguably the two most demanding aspects of a leader's work. This chapter explores how mindfulness can transform the leadership of people and change, and how the organisation can become more mindful while still keeping a keen eye on the bottom line.

Leading Mindfully when Change is the Norm

In the recent past, change projects at work were managed on the assumption that they had a distinct beginning, middle and end. Arguably the most widely known model argues that after the initial shock and denial stage comes a feeling of loss, and in the final stage people start to experiment with the idea of doing something in a new way, eventually embrace it, and the new way of working becomes 'business as usual'. This model is great to bear in mind when major change happens occasionally, and there's time to embed changes and return to a state of business as usual.

Another commonly used model proposes that in the initial stages of change an organisation prepares for change by breaking down old structures and ways of working, which causes uncertainty. In the middle stage, employees work to resolve the uncertainty and look for new ways to do things, and start to support and embrace the desired change. In the final stage (when people have embraced the change) comes further work to embed the new way of doing things into everyday business.

The problem with both models is that the pace of change for many organisations is now so rapid that there's rarely time to complete stage three (embedding and business as usual) before the next change is necessary. So just as the sense of loss and uncertainty starts to recede and people start to explore new ways of doing things, they're plunged straight back into shock, denial and breaking down what they've only just built up.

It's no wonder that most change programmes fail, and that change fatigue is costing the UK and US economies billions each year.

Meeting modern-day challenges with mindful solutions

With little 'business as usual', one change follows another and another, and little if any time exists to consolidate and embed each change.

Constant, 'bumpy change' requires a new approach to leading change initiatives, centred on human processes of habit formation.

While many change management projects focus on the steps necessary for organisational change, the Prosci® ADKAR® model focuses on five actions and outcomes necessary for successful individual change, and therefore successful organisational change. In order for change to be effective, individuals need:

- ✔ Awareness of the need for change
- ✔ Desire to participate and support the change
- ✔ Knowledge on how to change
- ✔ Ability to implement required skills and behaviours
- ✔ Reinforcement to sustain the change

Knowledge and practice of mindfulness, together with some basic knowledge of how the brain works, on the part of both the leader and employees makes this model even more effective. In the words of Jon Kabat-Zinn, father of mindfulness-based stress reduction (MBSR), 'You can't stop the waves, but you can learn to surf.'

Developing new change strategies

A UK head of operations that I (Juliet) worked with, lets call him Dan, was faced with the necessity of cutting costs by 10 per cent. He'd had to make similar cuts in the three previous years. Staff numbers had already been reduced, and working methods had changed and changed again. As a result, many staff were feeling disengaged from the company.

Approach or avoidance?

Depression often occurs after a period of prolonged stress. High levels of cortisol are released into the bloodstream and the right side of the brain becomes more active. Research by Davidson and Kabat-Zinn in 2003 concluded that, after practising mindfulness for eight weeks, stressed workers showed a significant increase in left-brain activation (specifically the left pre-frontal cortex part of the brain).

A tendency towards right-brain activation can lead to an avoidance mode of mind; in contrast, left-brain activation is likely to promote an approach mode of mind. These modes of mind manifest themselves in the following ways:

Approach mode of mind (Promotion)	Avoidance mode of mind (Prevention)
Increased activation in the left prefrontal cortex	Increased activation in the right prefrontal cortex
Motivated by attainment of positive ends	Motivated by the avoidance of negative ends
Global processing	Local processing
Cognitive flexibility	Cognitive rigidity
Attentional flexibility	May lack ability to focus for prolonged periods
Flexible mindset	Rigid mindset

We'd identified together that humans crave certainty, and certainty was in short supply. We speculated that many of the team were exhausted with the constant change, and probably felt threatened by the possibility of future changes that may reduce their status or security. We speculated further that many of his team were working in avoidance mode.

Embedding change individually and organisationally

Dan was concerned that the employees' experience of the last few years may make his next change initiatives even more difficult to implement. Dan knew that mindfulness training could help his staff become more resilient, increase their sense of positivity and make them more likely to adopt an 'approach' mode of mind in relation to the changes ahead.

Dan offered staff the option to attend mindfulness training in work time. The courses were publicised to staff as a personal development opportunity that could increase well-being and resilience in times of change. At the same time, Dan started to run focus groups on the challenges ahead to gain ideas about the best way forward. He was honest and open about the challenges that the organisation, and specifically the operations department, was facing. He encouraged staff to take the lead in problem solving and solution finding throughout. All focus groups and problem-solving forums started with a three-step focus break (see Chapter 5 for more on this), which served two purposes: it centred staff and focused attention on the task in hand, and it also helped him 'model' mindfulness to his team.

Dan knew that habits, once formed, are stored in the primitive areas of the brain and are therefore repeated unconsciously, making them difficult to change. He knew that, in order to change habits, people need to be aware of them. At the start of the working groups he used light-hearted, fun activities to help staff become more aware of their habits and mental mindsets. This approach helped his team become more aware of their mental programming and defaults, and the fact that they could change them. Those who were attending mindfulness courses often chipped in with things they had been discovering about themselves, and their experience of doing things differently.

Once the way forward had been agreed and accepted by most members of staff, Dan made efforts to reinforce new ways of thinking and working, celebrating success and small wins along the way. Doing so helped to reinforce the new ways of working, which over time became 'the way we do things round here'. Within a few months the old ways of working and thinking were used less, and as a result they became less dominant, and most of his team seemed to replace them with the new habits.

Try these tips to make dealing with change less challenging:

- ✔ Use mindfulness to help you to identify your unconscious habits and thinking patterns. Decide whether they're serving you well and, if not, consciously work to find new ways of acting and thinking. Repeat these over a two- to three-month period to form new dominant ways of thinking and acting that are more productive.

- ✔ Use the ADKAR® model next time you start to plan for an organisational change. Visit www.change-management.com for more information.

- ✔ Habits take time to form, so organisational changes may be slow to be adopted. Help employees form new habits by providing opportunities to discuss, experiment with and practise new ways of thinking, behaving and working over a 8–12 week period. The more new habits are practised, the stronger the neural pathways in people's brains become and the easier repeating the 'habit' is.

> ✔ Staff facing redundancy need just as much support as staff making the transition to the new way of working. Mindfulness training can help those being made redundant deal with the challenges that they're facing, giving them back a sense of control.

Creating Strategies that Allow the Organisation to Flourish

In order to keep pace with change, you need to adapt your strategies. If you want to get ahead of change, a more strategic approach is needed. You have to anticipate trends and proactively define new and innovative ways forward. In order to do so, you must be agile and authentic.

Agility is now an essential leadership skill. The increasing speed of change demands that organisations need to become more nimble and flexible. Your ability to spot change on the horizon, anticipate what may happen next and develop strategies in advance is vital.

Authenticity is another essential skill in times of volatile, unpredictable change. Your ability to create clarity by describing your vision and painting a picture of the future is more important than ever. You need to be able to lead with confidence and have the courage to take a stand. You need to build trust and confidence within your teams and be genuine in your communications. Change tends to cause anxiety and confusion. Your role as a leader is to bring a level of certainty about the direction of travel and evoke a sense of purpose for your staff.

Identifying organisational culture

If you really want to make radical changes to the way your organisation operates, you need to gain a good understanding of its culture.

Whats your culture?

There are many tools and models are available to help you identify the characteristics of your organisations culture.

You might wish to use Cultural 'dimensions', a framework for cross-cultural communication pioneered by Hofstede and discussed practically in 'Riding the waves of Culture' by Fons Trompenaars. Alternatively you might wish to consider The 'Cultural Web' a tool to help align your organisation's culture with strategy developed by Gerry Johnson and Kevan Scholes in 1992.

An alternative way to work on cultural change is to identify sub-cultures that may exist within an organisation and investigate why they may find it difficult to inter-relate. Rapid and constant change has a huge impact on organisational culture and can result in a 'non-culture' – a kind of vacuum left where a cohesive culture used to exist. This vacuum needs to be filled with a new collective coherence.

Mindfulness, as you know, helps you to step into the present moment and see what's really going on. This ability is useful when seeking to identify sub-cultures. You need to map the sub-cultures that exist and how these relate to each other. For example, manufacturing may have a completely different sub-culture to finance. Once identified, take time to celebrate the sub-cultures and encourage them to flourish. The idea behind this move is that you bring them out into the open and thus have a better chance of understanding of what you're dealing with. Trying to make a sub-culture comply with a corporate ideal often pushes it further underground, which makes it impossible to change. Giving people a unique sub-culture that they can be proud of often encourages that sub-culture to move closer to corporate intent.

Where a weak and dysfunctional sub-culture exists, try to give it a helping hand. Weak sub-cultures can seriously undermine organisational cohesion. Identify why confidence has been lost and help the business area add value to the organisation once more.

The final stage of the process involves weaving together the diverse sub-cultures. By getting members of staff from different cultures working together on areas of common purpose, more areas of shared beliefs emerge. The shared cultural beliefs encourage sub-cultures to bond and form a web of shared beliefs. These webs can become strong, and equally as effective as the tightly woven, singular company culture of the past.

Remember that cultural change initiatives take time to embed – no quick fixes exist. As a leader, getting to grips with organisational culture can be the deciding factor between a strategy's or change initiative's success and failure. Ignore organisational culture at your peril! Be mindful that not all organisational cultures may be to your liking. Unless they're seriously detrimental to the organisation, you need to let go of your personal feelings on the matter and spend your energy on getting the different sub-cultures to work together and establish more and more areas of common ground.

Mindfully discovering common ground

Most researchers believe human beings are more hardwired to cooperate than to compete. Gather together workers from different sub-cultures to work together on areas of common ground. Start the meeting with a three-minute focus break (see Chapter 5), explaining that participants will be working together for the next few hours, you want them to gain the most from this time and that this technique helps them clear their minds and allow them to do so. Get each participant to write down five things they feel need to be worked on – each written on a different piece of paper. Gather the pieces of paper and group them into themes and areas of commonality. These areas of common ground are the things to work on first.

Creating a collective vision for the future

Large organisations generally spend a considerable amount of time and effort on developing organisational visions. Branding and communication experts are drafted in to help the top team define their vision for the future in a manner that will motivate staff and inspire belief, confidence and desire in customers. Smaller organisations sometimes suffer from having no vision, or a vision that is too wordy, difficult to remember and feels unachievable. Visions are intended to paint a vivid picture of the organisation and where it's heading. Less is often more! You need to make your organisational visions memorable and inspiring but also achievable.

Try using the following techniques to help you develop a vision for the future.

Mindfully envisioning the future

Step 1: Centring and visioning

1. Settle yourself in a room where you won't be disturbed. Switch off your mobile phone, your laptop (or at least the volume) and silence any device that may take your attention away from the task in hand.

2. Sit in a comfortable, upright position. Close your eyes or hold them in soft focus.

3. Spend three minutes or so focusing your attention on the sensation of breathing. Really feel the present-moment sensations of the breath entering your body and the breath leaving your body.

4. Spend a further three minutes reconnecting with your body in this moment in time. Check how your feet are feeling in this moment in time, followed by your legs, bottom, shoulders and head.

5. Open your eyes and capture on a piece of paper or your laptop the five key characteristics representing how you'd like your organisation to be in three to five years' time. You can express these characteristics as words, pictures or paragraphs of descriptive text.

Step 2: Identifying things you need to start, stop and continue doing

1. **Refocus your attention on the present-moment experience.** Try to let go of the thoughts that are probably rattling round in your head. Remember, you've jotted them down, so nothing important will be forgotten.

2. **Spend two minutes focusing your** attention on the thoughts in your mind – observing them as mental processes **and then letting them go.**

3. Spend a further two minutes focusing your attention on your breathing, as described above.

4. **Open your eyes.** Read the 'five characteristics' you jotted down and ask yourself, 'In order to achieve this, what do we need to

   • Start doing;

   • Stop doing;

   • Continue doing?'

5. **Jot down what comes to mind.**

Step 3: Checking your gut instinct and intuition

1. **Refocus your attention as in step 2 above.**

2. **Open your eyes again and check what you've jotted down.** Imagine what's on the paper becoming a reality, and hold that thought for a moment.

3. **Close your eyes or hold them in soft focus.** Take five slow breaths. Now focus your attention on your body.

   • How does your body feel in this moment in time? If you feel any tensions or sensations, where in your body are they being held?

   • Do you feel any emotions? What are they?

   • Are any thoughts popping into your head? What are they?

4. **Examine your experiences during this exercise.** If you felt excitement and happiness and your body felt fine, you've probably got it right. If you felt fear or uncertainty, you may need to revisit your strategy.

This activity works well with a group. You can lead the mindfulness exercises and segue into and out of planning activities.

Reading your body

When in approach mode, you're more open to new and innovative ways of doing things. By practising mindfulness for a few minutes at the start, and between, each part of the task, you're more likely to come at the task with fresh ideas and clarity of mind.

Sensations held in your body can have a major impact on the decisions you make. If you're holding anger or fear in your body at an unconscious level, doing so can impact on your decision making and planning, even if you're not aware of it doing so. In a similar way, tapping into your present-moment bodily sensations immediately after making a decision or plan can help you recognise how you really feel about it at an unconscious level. If you're happy, calm or excited, the decision is probably right. If you're fearful, anxious or uncertain, you need to examine why, and probably revisit your plan.

Developing strategies mindfully

Having defined a high-level vision, it's time to develop a strategy to make it happen. You need to gather key information into one place and summarise it into an easy to read format.

You can use the model shown in Figure 15-1 as a discussion tool.

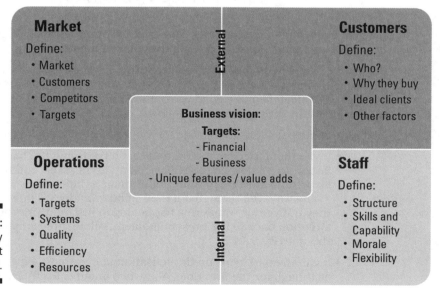

Figure 15-1: Strategy development tool.

Consider conducting a SWOT analysis for each of the segments in the model above, whereby you identify each segment's:

✔ **Strengths**

✔ **Weaknesses**

✔ **Opportunities**

✔ **Threats**

You can take a mindful approach to this task as follows:

Stage 1: Getting ready

1. **Decide on the best people to get the task done and invite them to a meeting.** Identify the mix of skills necessary to create an effective team.

2. **Send a copy of Figure 15-1 (or your own version thereof) to each participant prior to the meeting.** Ask them to come to the meeting with data for their own area relating to each segment.

3. **Create the right environment to enable participants to think out of the box and innovate.** Ensure that hot and cold drinks, slow-energy-release snacks, such as oat-based cereal bars, and fruit are available, even if you have to buy them yourself.

Stage 2: Mindfully preparing for productivity

1. **Ask everyone at the beginning of the meeting to switch off (and not just silence!) all mobile devices so that everyone's complete attention stays on the task.**

2. **Ask everyone to capture any concerns they may have on slips of paper and place these in a filing tray placed near the door.**

3. **Invite everyone to take part in a 'centring' exercise.** You may wish to explain to participants some of the science behind mindfulness exercises and why doing them is a good use of their time. Model mindfulness by leading the centring exercise as follows:

   • Invite participants to close their eyes or hold them in soft focus.

   • Invite them to focus their attention on the thoughts that enter their heads, to acknowledge them as 'mental processes' and to let them go without starting to think about them or interacting with them in any way. Tell them that if their minds wander it's fine and when they notice this wandering happening to just gently escort their attention back to the present moment. Allow three minutes for this activity.

   • Invite them to focus on the sensation of breathing, experiencing it as though for the first time. Allow two minutes for this activity.

- Invite them to focus their attention on any sounds they may be hearing – inside the room, outside the room or even outside the building. Explain that the object of the exercise is to simply observe, not judge or react to the sounds. Allow one minute for this activity.

- Invite them to open their eyes, ready to work on creating a new strategy.

4. **Recap the overall vision that you're all striving to make reality.** This vision should already have been agreed upon in previous meetings.

Ask those participants who do not wish to try the mindfulness exercise to just sit quietly and observe it.

Stage 3: Mindfully establishing the status quo

1. **Appoint five chairpersons – one to focus on each of the five segments.** Split the remaining participants evenly between the five groups.

2. **Explain that everyone will have the opportunity to contribute to all five segments.**

3. **Sound a bell to start the information sharing and capturing process.** After 15 minutes, sound the bell again and ask each group of participants to move to a new chairperson. Repeat until everyone has had the opportunity to visit all five groups.

4. **Lead another short mindfulness exercise.** Use the three-minute focus break from Chapter 5.

Stage 4: Mindfully creating a new strategy

1. **Share the information gathered.** Make sure that you, and the group as a whole, do not start to judge or categorise – just listen and absorb.

2. **Define as a group the strategies needed to achieve the business vision and targets.** Work your way round the segments one at a time.

3. **Thank the group for all their hard work.** Take responsibility for taking away the draft strategy and producing a professional document for sharing and further discussion.

Embedding new values and behaviours

Now that you've a clear idea of your organisation's culture and vision and a clear strategy for the future, you need to make the plan a reality. The vision and strategy may call for staff to embrace new values, and almost certainly to adopt new behaviours.

Be mindful that old ways of working and behaving are likely to be deeply embedded, especially if they worked well in the past and people have enjoyed and been rewarded (by pay, recognition or a sense of achievement) for working in this way. Don't expect staff to embrace your proposed changes with the same enthusiasm as you. For one thing, you have a head start. You've already started to rewire the way your brain thinks about working. As you've worked on creating the strategy, your brain has been busily storing new information and making new connections. You're aware of all the factors that led you to create the new strategy but your team are not.

When you're driving change you're likely to embrace it more quickly, even if you're not wildly enthusiastic about what it involves. Asking people to do things differently can generate all sorts of mental conflicts for them – many of which they may be completely unaware of. If accepted, new ways of doing things are eventually stored by the brain as habits, and these habits in time become more dominant than the work habit circuitry that they're currently using. The process of habit formation can be really slow. The more opportunities that you can create to explore and practise new ways of working, the stronger the brain's neural pathways (circuitry) become.

For some people, the perceived threat of the new way of working may prove too great and they default to old ways of thinking and behaving. Be mindful that they may not defaulting on purpose as an act of anarchy; they may be largely unaware of how their thoughts, emotions and habits are driving their behaviour.

Mindfulness can be invaluable when you're trying to embed new values and behaviours. It helps you to develop awareness of your hidden mental world. It helps you develop the skill to observe your thoughts, emotions and bodily responses. By developing this awareness, you're able to choose a wise response. As a leader, being able to respond to people and situations mindfully helps you manage yourself better when driving through difficult changes. Mindfulness can help you manage your well-being and deal with any personal difficulties or inner conflicts that arise. In addition, you'll be better able to observe when your team members are struggling and can then help them work better with their mind.

In times of change and uncertainty, be kind to yourself and your colleagues. As Chapter 5 describes, self-kindness can help you switch off your fight-or-flight response, making it easier to see things clearly and concentrate.

Remember that how you feel about things is likely to have an impact on your behaviour to others. Your behaviour is likely to have an impact on how others feel, which has an impact on how they behave. By acting as a mindful role model, you make things easier for those around you, and you're likely to feel better too.

If you offer mindfulness training to your staff, it probably won't make an unwelcome change any more palatable. What it can do is help them to become more aware of what's going on in their mental landscape. This awareness gives them the opportunity to bring to the surface thoughts and behaviours that are making them unhappy, stressed or fearful. Knowledge of what's going on in their minds allows them to take control of the situation. They can decide what to do next and focus their energy accordingly.

Creating a More Mindful Organisation

Introducing mindfulness into your organisation can lead to many benefits. Not only is mindfulness likely to improve employees' well-being, it may also make them more productive and creative. But does such a thing as a 'mindful organisation' actually exist?

In the 1990s, the concept of the 'learning organisation' was popular. The idea was that an organisation would facilitate information sharing and learning for all members of staff and in this way continuously transform itself. Knowledge management systems were put in place to capture information and share it, and knowledge managers appointed to oversee the whole thing. The problem was that no one really knew what a 'learning organisation' looked like, so it was virtually impossible for organisations to know when they had metamorphosed into this mythical beast. While the idea was good, it became a never-ending journey – rather like that experienced by the crew in *Star Trek* – boldly going where no organisation had gone before . . . with no clear final destination.

The idea of becoming 'a mindful organisation' may fall into the same trap. You will probably find it easier and more meaningful to focus on incubating pockets of mindfulness within your organisation. Create spaces for staff to go and spend a few minutes in silence to refocus their efforts, and give staff permission to go to this place for short periods when they need to. Let mindfulness evolve within your organisation, and leave the future to sort itself out. Who knows? In a few years' time many aspects of your organisation may be transformed by mindfulness, but it's best to start with the present moment.

Remembering that looking beyond the bottom line is good for the bottom line

Research evidence suggests that mindfulness is likely to be good for your bottom line. Here are a few facts to consider:

- ✔ **Stress is now the top cause of workplace sickness and absence in many countries.** Lost productivity costs money. Studies conducted over the last 40 years conclude that mindfulness is highly effective in reducing stress.

- ✔ **Many workers are now so busy that they're in a constant state of fight or flight.** Practising mindfulness can switch off the brain's fight-or-flight response, improving both well-being and the ability to be productive.

✔ **A lack of focus and concentration can undermine work performance.** Research shows that mindfulness can improve focus and concentration.

✔ **The ability to gain perspective and 'see the bigger picture' is important – especially in times of change.** In recent years, seven independent studies have shown that mindfulness can help you see the bigger picture and set aside personal agendas.

✔ **Research into mindfulness and decision making demonstrates that mindfulness can help you make more rational decisions, not be 'blinded' by past experiences and come up with more creative solutions.**

✔ **Mindfulness has proven effective in helping people manage their emotions better, develop a more positive outlook and prevent burnout.**

The Return On Investment (ROI) of mindfulness

Let's look at some simple mathematics.

An employee on a salary of £25,000 for a five-day week for 47 weeks per year (allowing for five weeks' holiday) costs his company £106 a day. If you add on the cost of National Insurance and additional benefits, the cost is probably more like £133.

Taking a look at a 2013 case study

In 2013, an MBCT based mindfulness pilot took place in a large UK public sector organisation. The organisation was subject to significant change and ongoing uncertainty. The pilot was delivered in-house for two hours per week for eight weeks. The outcomes included the following:

✔ Between 93 and 100 per cent of participants reported that mindfulness had in some way helped them to improve their performance at work, with between 45–59 per cent reporting a great or significant increase in performance.

✔ An increase in positivity when answering staff survey questionnaires.

✔ A decrease in depression, anxiety and stress, with some participants decreasing their levels of depression, anxiety and stress from severe to normal.

✔ Ninety-three per cent of participants planned to continue practising mindfulness, with 93 per cent agreeing that it was a good use of their time.

✔ Participants spent an average of 15 minutes per day practising mindfulness.

Research by the Health and Safety Executive conducted in 2011 demonstrated that, on average, people who were signed off work as a result of stress took 24 days off. Using the example above, the cost of this stress is £3,192.

If the organisation offered mindfulness courses to staff (two hours a week for eight weeks, delivered in-house by an external specialist) at an average cost of £300 per person (assuming a class of 12), and doing so helped reduce or eliminate time off for stress, the savings would be as follows

Cost of two weeks' absence	£3,192
Cost of mindfulness course per person	– £300
Cost of extraction from work per person	– £266
	= £2,626 saving

So, running one mindfulness course for 12 people can potentially save the company £31,512. And that's without taking into account the possible increase in productivity that the mindfulness course can also offer. If, at a conservative estimate, 40 per cent of participants on a mindfulness course for 12 people improve their productivity by 10 per cent, that's equivalent to gaining an additional member of staff for two days a week, which would cost £12,500 per annum.

The above calculations provide a strong argument for promoting and supporting mindfulness in the workplace. Naturally the cost of mindfulness at work consultants varies, as do salaries and average staff absence levels. In addition, levels of productivity can be tricky to measure in many work environments. The question to ask yourself is, 'What is the return on investment for an average training course?' Obviously, this is difficult to calculate.

If we apply the same rules to, for example, a one-day personal effectiveness course delivered by an external consultant, the costs may be as follows:

Trainer costs per person	£70
Extraction costs per person	£133
	= £203 per person

This investment can lead to a 10 per cent increase in productivity, but where is the evidence to support this? Little research evidence suggests that spending on personal effectiveness courses or many of the generic 'interpersonal' skills training actually has any impact on a company's bottom line. In contrast, a significant volume of research demonstrates that mindfulness does improve a wide range of desirable work skills such as relationships with colleagues and customers, focus and concentration, strategic thinking, decision making and overall resilience. It can also increase staff engagement and productivity.

Setting the sums aside, although the bottom line is important, sometimes by looking beyond it and caring for your employees' well-being and making the workplace a great place to be, you gain greater commitment and buy in from your staff. Measuring the value of staff commitment and well-being is clearly impossible, but it cannot fail to produce a positive impact all round.

Mindfully improving employee engagement and retention

'Engaged employees' are fully involved in and enthusiastic about their work. This engagement motivates them to work in harmony with their organisation. An employee's positive or negative emotional attachment to their job, colleagues and the organisation as a whole is important. Employee engagement is distinctively different from employee satisfaction, motivation and organisational culture.

Mindfulness can improve employee engagement and retention. Practising mindfulness leads to improved work engagement because it elicits positive emotions and improves psychological functioning.

Mindfully engaging staff

If your company runs an annual staff survey which includes questions relating to employee engagement , you could use these questions as a baseline. Try running a mindfulness pilot (with the full support of the senior management team and line managers), and compare current responses to those of previous years. You may be surprised at the positivity expressed by staff who have completed the mindfulness course compared with the attitudes of colleagues who did not attend.

Offer staff with a poor attendance record as a result of ill health the opportunity to attend mindfulness training. Transport for London encouraged such staff to undergo mindfulness training in their own time. It resulted in a 51 per cent reduction in sick leave, for a wide range of health conditions. Days off as a result of stress, anxiety and depression dropped by 78 per cent during the four years following the course and 55 per cent of participants reported increased happiness at work.

Creating the right work/life balance for all employees

As this book repeatedly stresses, working long hours does not increase your productivity, it usually decreases it. The same is true for staff members. Some organisations develop a working culture in which long hours are the norm. Employees feel that they need to be seen to be in the office for more hours than they're paid in order to fit in. Emails are often sent late at night, making other employees feel that they're in some way deficient because they're not working at that hour. In a similar way, some organisations expect staff to be in instant contact outside normal working hours.

As a leader, you've the power to support working practices that promote a healthy balance between people's personal and working lives.

Mindfully balancing life and work

Constant connectivity is bad for performance. Try introducing 'no contact times' and encourage staff to switch off their mobile devices when away from work.

Keep an eye on the times that you and other senior managers send emails. If the working style that best suits you involves rest and relaxation after normal working hours and then a little time working in peace late in the evening or first thing in the morning, set your emails to send in normal working hours (you can easily set this system up). By doing so, you're not sending the message to others that they too have to be working late at night or early in the morning.

As Chapter 18 covers, lack of control over workload or working methods can be a major source of stress. Where possible, encourage workers to work in a manner that suits them. Encourage individuality, as long as core work hours are covered, work gets done and targets are met.

Offer staff mindfulness training to examine objectively their current work/life balance and to establish a way of working that is more nourishing and rewarding for them personally.

Offer staff a 'quiet room' to go to when they need 10 minutes of silence to regain their sense of balance and improve their productivity. Doing so sends a positive message to staff that their need for a few minutes of quiet mindfulness is recognised; providing this area is so much better than employees sneaking off to store cupboards or toilet cubicles.

Mindfulness can transform both your own and your employees' perception of change and how to manage it. Fortunately, your organisation can become more mindful while still keeping a keen eye on the bottom line. Maybe you've done your own sums and return on investment calculations. Introducing mindful work practices into your organisation can be difficult when you occupy a junior role, but as a leader you can use your power and influence to change things for the better. You can choose to continue leading as you always have, or start to model some mindful behaviour and start a quiet revolution. You've the power – the choice is yours.

Part V
The Part of Tens

For Dummies can help you get started with a huge range of subjects. Visit www.dummies.com to learn more and do more with *For Dummies*.

In this part . . .

- ✔ Find tips to help you be more personally mindful in the workplace.

- ✔ Understand the ways in which your brain works better with mindfulness.

- ✔ Use mindfulness to overcome stress and tension.

- ✔ Discover ten ways to become mindful in a minute.

- ✔ Learn about the mindfulness resources available to you.

Chapter 16

Ten Ways to Be More Mindful at Work

Mindfulness may seem like a great idea, but how do you become more mindful in the context of a busy work day? You may have emails, phone calls, meetings and presentations to deal with. And, of course, your own work! In the middle of all that, how can you apply the principles of mindfulness so that you feel more alive and present, as well as being productive? This chapter pulls out a few popular and other more radical ways to be mindful at work.

Be Consciously Present

Mindfulness is, above all, about being aware and awake rather than operating unconsciously. When you're consciously present at work, you're aware of two aspects of your moment-to-moment experience – what's going on around you and what's going on within you. To be mindful at work means to be consciously present in what you're doing, while you're doing it, as well as managing your mental and emotional state. If you're writing a report, mindfulness requires you to give that your full attention. Each time your mind wanders to things like Helen's new role or Michael's argument with the boss, just acknowledge the thoughts and bring your attention back to the task in hand. This scenario sounds simple, but many aspects of your experience can get in the way.

Here are some ideas to help you stop being mindless and unconscious at work and more mindful and consciously present:

- Make a clear decision at the start of your workday to be present as best you can. Pause for a few moments before you start your work day to set this intention in your mind.
- Make an effort to work more consciously, even if that means that you need to work a little slower at first – doing so pays in the long run.
- Keep all the advantages of working mindfully in mind to motivate you.
- Connect with your senses rather than getting lost in trains of thought when you're doing a task.
- Give your full attention to seemingly mundane tasks like washing your hands, opening doors, dialling phone numbers and even just feeling your breathing as you're waiting in a meeting room. These little moments add up to make the day a more mindful one.

Use Short Mindful Exercises at Work

Mindful exercises train your brain to be more mindful. The more mindful exercises you do, the easier your brain finds it to drop into a mindful state, thus optimising your brain function.

In the busy workplace, finding time for a 30-minute mindful exercise can be difficult. So does that mean you can't be mindful at all at work? Nope. Mindful exercises can be as short as you wish. Even one minute of consciously connecting with one of your senses can be classified as a mindful exercise.

Two of the simplest mindful exercises to get you started are a mindful minute (see Chapter 7) or the three step body check (see Chapter 6). You don't need to close your eyes. You don't even need to be sitting down.

Be creative about finding slots in the day to practice mindfulness exercises. At times of excessive pressure at work, practising a short mindfulness exercise can be a saviour. The process helps to rebalance your nervous system, toning down the fight-or-flight response and engaging the wise part of your brain, so that you make reasoned decisions rather than automatically react to situations.

Be a Single-Tasker

Single-tasking is doing one thing at a time. Multi-tasking is trying to do two or more tasks at the same time or switching back and forth between tasks. Nobody can actually multi-task. In reality, your brain is madly switching from one thing to the next, often losing data in the process.

Most people know multitasking is ineffective nowadays. If multi-tasking is so inefficient, why do people still do it? The reason was uncovered in a study by Zheng Wang at Ohio State University. She tracked students and found that when they multi-tasked, it made them *feel* more productive, even though in reality they were being unproductive. Other studies found that the more you multitask, the more addicted you get to it.

Here are a few ways to kick the multi-tasking habit and become a mindfulness superhero:

- ✔ Keep a time journal of what you achieve in a block of time. Work out when you're single-tasking and when you're multi-tasking. Note down what you achieved in that time block and how mindful you were.

- ✔ See whether you can notice your productivity going up when you single-task – noticing the benefits can motivate you to do one thing at a time in a mindful way.

- ✔ Group tasks in categories. For example, put together emails, phone calls, errands and meetings. Then you can do them all together in one block of time rather than switching from emails to calls to running an errand.

- ✔ Switch off as many distractions as you can. Silence your phone, log off from your email account and so on. Then set a timer for the amount of time you need to work, and record how much you get done. Do what works for you to focus on one task for a fixed period of time.

- ✔ Practise mindfulness in your breaks between tasks. Stretch, take deep breaks or go for a mindful walk.

Use Mindful Reminders

The word 'mindful' means to remember. Most people who've read about or undertaken training in mindfulness appreciate the benefits of mindful living. Unfortunately, they keep forgetting to be mindful!

The reason you forget to be mindful is because your brain's normal (default) mode is to be habitually lost in your own thoughts – running a sort of internal narrative. When you're going about your usual daily activities, your brain switches you into this low energy state, which is unmindful, almost dreamy. Doing some things automatically, without thinking, is fine but research undertaken at Harvard University showed that 47 per cent of a person's day can be spent lost in thoughts. The same research found that day dreaming can have a negative impact on well-being. Being on auto-pilot means that you're not fully present and awake to the opportunities and choices around you. You can't be creative, plan something new or respond appropriately if you're operating mechanically.

By using some form of reminder, you can be mindful again. The reminder shakes you out of auto-pilot mode. Try these reminders:

- Setting an alarm on the phone – even a vibrating alarm that doesn't disturb others can work well.

- Putting mindfulness in your calendar – setting an appointment with yourself!

- A small note or picture on your desk to remind you to be mindful.

- Associating certain activities with mindfulness, such as meal times or meetings or when finishing one task and starting another.

- Using the sound of bells and rings in the workplace as 'bells of mindfulness'. So, every time your phone rings, you take a mindful breath. Every time you hear the ping of a text message, you pause to be mindful of your surroundings rather than immediately reacting by checking the message.

All these things are opportunities to come back into the present moment, to see yourself and your surroundings afresh. You take a small step back and reflect rather than automatically react to what's coming at you in the form of demands, tasks and challenges.

Slow Down To Speed Up

Mindfulness at work does seem counter-intuitive. You're considering the fact that, by stopping or slowing down, you can become more efficient, productive, happy, resilient and healthy at work. You may not think that slowing down and being conscious can have such an effect.

Imagine being asked to stop sleeping for a week. Sleeping is resting – and resting isn't work. So, simply stop sleeping and just keep working. Maybe you've experienced this when studying for exams or trying to meet a deadline at work. Eventually your efficiency drops to almost zero; you're completely living out of the present moment and perhaps even hallucinating! You need to sleep at least seven hours every night to be able to function effectively.

Clearly, rest can increase efficiency. If you do manage to get about seven hours of sleep and achieve a certain amount of work, imagine what would happen if you also did a few mini-mindfulness exercises during the day? Your brain would become even more efficient, focused, effective at communicating with others and better at learning new skills.

Being in a panicky rush leads to bad decisions and is a misuse of energy. Instead, pause, focus on listening, stroll rather than run and generally take your time when at work. Effective leaders, workers and entrepreneurs slow down and reflect to make the best decisions and actions – they slow down to speed up. That's a mindful way of working.

Make Stress Your Friend

Recent research conducted at the University of Wisconsin-Madison, asked 30,000 people the same question: 'Does the perception that stress affects health matter?' The results were astonishing.

The researchers found that people experiencing high levels of stress but who believed that stress was good for them *had among the lowest mortality rates*. Whereas highly stressed people who believed that stress was bad for their health had the highest chance of dying. Your *beliefs* about stress clearly affect how they impact on your health and well-being. Another study even found that the blood vessels constricted (as is seen in those with heart disease) in people who believed that stress was bad for them, but stayed open and healthy in those who believed that stress was good for them.

If reading this didn't make you go 'wow', try reading it again. It's the most exciting research I've (Shamash) read this year!

So if you want to make stress your friend, you need to change the way you think about it and, in turn, your body's response to it.

Mindfulness can help you achieve this change in perception. The next time you're facing a challenge at work, notice how your heart rate speeds up and your breathing accelerates. Observe these responses and then switch your attitude – respond to your stress creatively rather than negatively. Be grateful that the stress response is energising you. Note that your body is preparing you for your upcoming challenge and that a faster heart rate is sending more oxygen around your body. Be grateful that the process is sharpening your senses and boosting your immune system. By viewing the stress response from this perspective, you see your upcoming problem as a positive challenge and recognise your body preparing to meet it. This small change in attitude can literally add years to your life and improve your productivity and achievements in the workplace.

Feel Gratitude

Humans have a 'negativity bias' (see Chapter 5 for more on this). Essentially, this means that you're much more likely to focus and dwell on something that's gone wrong than on things that have gone well. Behaving in this way every day means that you ultimately adopt an excessively negative and unbalanced way of thinking.

Gratitude is the antidote. Plenty of evidence suggests that actively practising gratitude makes you feel better and has a positive impact on your creativity, health, working relationships and quality of work. Gratitude makes being at both work and home more positive experiences.

If you feel like you're stuck in a job you don't enjoy, the first step is to practise gratitude. What's going well in your job? Maybe you're grateful for the money? Even though it may be less than you'd like, you probably prefer it to having no salary at all. You may not like your manager, but maybe you're friends with a couple of colleagues? You hate the office politics, but they give you insight into what you don't like in a job, so in the future you know what to look for. After practising gratitude, you can then consider whether you want to continue in that role or need to find another job.

Being mindful of what's going well at work helps to improve your resilience. Rather than allowing your mind to spiral into anxiety or dip into low moods as you brood over all the aspects of the job you don't like, you can feed your mind with thoughts of gratitude to raise your well-being. Then, if you do decide to find another job, your positive mental state can help you select an appropriate position and optimise your performance in the interview. People hire positive people, not those who just complain about what's going wrong. Use gratitude to neutralise your brain's natural negativity bias.

Cultivate Humility

Humility comes from the Latin *humilis,* meaning grounded. Humble people have a quiet confidence about themselves and don't feel the need to continuously remind others of their achievements. Humility may seem counter to our culture of glorifying those who make the most noise about themselves, grabbing our attention. But actually, humility is attractive – no one enjoys being around those who continually sing their own praises, and most people enjoy the company of those who are willing to listen to them rather than talk about themselves all the time.

In Jim Collin's hugely popular book *Good to Great,* he identified leaders who turned good companies into great ones. He found that the companies exhibiting the greatest long-term success (at least 15 years of exceptional growth) had leaders demonstrating all the skills of your standard leader but with one extra quality – personal humility. They were willing to work hard, but not for themselves – for the company. If things went wrong, they didn't seek to blame other to protect themselves. And if things went well, they immediately looked outside of themselves to congratulate others. They didn't have an inflated ego that needed protecting all the time.

Humility is often confused with meekness or timidity but they're not the same. Humility does not mean seeing yourself as inferior; rather, it means being aware of your natural dependence on and equity with those around you.

How is humility linked to mindfulness? Mindfulness is about accepting yourself just as you are, and being open to listening to and learning from others. Mindfulness is also synonymous with gratitude – you appreciate how others have helped you. And someone who is grateful for the contribution of others is naturally humble.

To develop a little more humility, try the following:

- ✔ **Undertake mindful exercises:** Mindfulness reduces activity in the part of the brain that generates the story of your self – sometimes called the narrative self. Giving too much attention to you and your own story is unhealthy. Mindfulness practice helps you to be more connected with your senses – the present self. Your attention widens and you can see how much others contribute to your everyday successes.

- ✔ **Consider who has helped you right now:** Spend a few minutes thinking about the number of people who have enabled you to read this page: your parents, guardians or teachers who taught you to read: your employers who help you afford to pay for it; the people involved in writing, editing and producing the copy; the distributors, sales people, providers of ink; the trees that were used to make the paper. We could go on. Think in this way from time to time to identify just how many people help you every day.

- ✔ **Show appreciation:** When someone helps you out, in whatever way, show appreciation. It sounds obvious, but doing so is an act of humility and reminds you to value the contribution of others: the driver who let you into her lane; the postman who delivered your letters; the person who held the door open and the cleaner who vacuumed your office – they all count.

- ✔ **Value other people's opinions:** If someone makes a point that challenges yours, suspend judgement. You can easily jump in and argue – but that implies that they're wrong and you're right. How can you be so sure? Stop and consider in what ways they may be right, too. This is true mindfulness in action – non-judgemental awareness together with curiosity and respect.

Accept What You Can't Change

Acceptance lies at the heart of mindfulness. To be mindful means to accept this present moment just as it is. And it means to accept yourself, just as you are now. It doesn't mean resignation or giving up. But it does mean acknowledging the truth of how things are at this time before trying to change anything.

Here's a workplace example. If you went £20,000 over budget, that's a fact. It's already happened. As soon as you accept that, you can move forward and try to deal with the situation. Lack of acceptance can lead to denial of the fact (maybe causing you to go even more over budget) or avoidance (you keep skipping meetings with your boss) or aggression (you vent your anger at your team unnecessarily, adversely affecting relationships and motivation). Instead, you can accept the situation, talk to the necessary people, learn from your mistakes and move on. Acceptance actually leads to change.

Personal acceptance is even more powerful. Self-acceptance is embracing all facets of yourself – your weaknesses, shortcomings, aspects you don't like and those you admire. When you accept yourself, you cut down on energy-draining self-criticism. You're then much better able to enjoy your successes and smile at your shortcomings. Through self-acceptance, you can create a clarity of mind that allows you to work on those aspects of yourself you wish to improve. The starting point of self-improvement and personal development is self-acceptance.

Adopt a Growth Mindset

According to Carol Dweck and her team at Stanford University researcher, people essentially adhere to one of two mindsets – a growth or a fixed mindset.

People with a fixed mindset believe that their basic qualities, such as their intelligence and talents, are fixed traits. Instead of developing their intelligence and talents, they spend their time hoping their traits will lead to success. They don't seek to develop themselves, because they think that talent alone leads to success. They turn out to be wrong – brain science has proved otherwise.

People with a growth mindset believe that they can improve their intelligence and talents with effort. By applying themselves, they think that they can get better. They see brains and talent as just the starting point, and build on them with hard work and determination. Brain scans have actually revealed that effort does lead to growth in intelligence and enhancement of initial talent over time. People with this mindset have a love of learning and demonstrate greater resilience. Success at work depends on having a growth mindset.

Mindfulness is about adopting a growth mindset. Mindfulness is about giving attention to the present moment and not judging your innate talent or intelligence, but being open to new possibilities. When you adopt a growth mindset at work, you don't mind getting negative feedback as you view it as a chance to discover something new. You don't mind taking on new responsibilities because you're curious about how you'll cope. You expect and move towards challenges, seeing them as opportunities for inner growth. That's the essence of mindfulness at work – believing that you can improve and grow with experience, moving towards challenges, living in the moment and discovering new things about yourself and others.

Use the following four steps to develop a growth mindset, based on research by Dweck and colleagues:

1. **Listen to the voice of a fixed mindset in your head.** This is about being mindful of your own thoughts when faced with a challenge. Notice if the thoughts are telling you that you don't have the talent, the intelligence or if you find yourself reacting with anxiety or anger when someone offers feedback to you.

2. **Notice that you have a choice.** You can accept those fixed mindset thoughts or question them. Take a few moments to practice a mindful pause.

3. **Question the fixed mindset attitudes.** When your fixed mindset says 'What if I fail? I'll be a failure', you can ask yourself 'Is that true? Most successful people fail. That's how they learn.' Or if fixed mindset says 'What if I can't do this project? I don't have the skills' reply with 'Can I be absolutely sure I don't have the skills? In truth, I can only know if I try. And if I don't have the skills, doing this will help me to learn them.'

4. **Take action on the growth mindset.** This will make you enjoy the challenges in the workplace, seeing them as opportunity to grow rather than avoid. Use the above system if you mind starts leaning towards the fixed mindset.

Over time, you'll find yourself habitually of a growth rather than fixed mindset, leading to greater success and personal mastery that before.

Chapter 17

Ten Ways to Improve Your Brain with Mindfulness

*B*rain scans show that practising mindfulness has a physical impact on specific areas of the brain, such as those shown in Figure 17-1.

Forget brain-training games! Mindfulness is an opportunity for the brain to strengthen and enhance itself.

Mindfulness can help you become more healthy and happy; it can even boost your social life. It can improve your sense of self-control, productivity and some say it can even make you wiser. Mindfulness is like taking your brain to the gym.

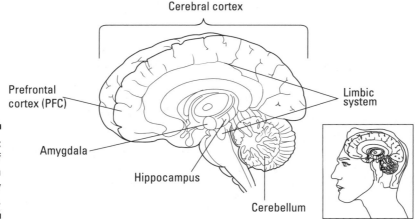

Figure 17-1: Areas of the brain affected by mindfulness.

Increase the Strength of Your Brain

Did you know that practising mindfulness can strengthen your brain? Research conducted by the University of California in 2012 concluded that meditation strengthens the connections between brain cells, and that the more you practise the more you benefit.

The cerebral cortex is the outermost layer of brain tissue. It plays a key role in memory, attention, thought and consciousness. People who've been practising mindfulness for long periods of time have increased gyrification ('folding' of the cortex – see Figure 17-2), which may allow the brain to process information faster.

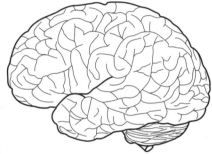

Figure 17-2:
Brain
gyrification.

Experts believe that the more 'folding' that occurs, the better the brain is at processing information, prioritising and making decisions.

So, to turbo charge your brain you need to help it increase its gyrification so that it can squeeze more grey matter into your skull. Your regular mindfulness practice can aid this process.

Alter the Structure of Your Brain

Practising mindfulness can help you change the structure of your brain for the better. Magnetic resonance imaging (MRI) was used to assess cortical thickness in research volunteers who were highly experienced meditators. Brain regions associated with attention, interception, emotion regulation and sensory processing (including the prefrontal cortex (see Figure 17-1) and right anterior insula) were thicker in meditation participants than matched controls, This research also suggests that regular mindfulness practice may slow age-related thinning of the frontal cortex.

Research in 2009 demonstrated that meditators have larger hippocampi (the area of the brain responsible for learning and memory – see Figure 17-1) than non-meditators.

In another academic study involving healthy people who had never practised mindfulness, changes to the brain's grey matter were measured before and after an eight-week MBSR course. Grey matter can be found in the brain in the surface cerebral cortex, in the depths of the cerebrum and in parts of the limbic system (see Figure 17-1). MRI scans of the MBSR group revealed increases in grey matter in many areas of the brain, including the left hippocampus and the cerebellum. The results suggest that practising mindfulness results in tangible changes in grey matter concentration in brain regions involved in learning and memory processes, emotion regulation, self-referential processing and perspective taking.

Improve Your Ability to Learn

If you want to improve your ability to learn, stop what you're doing and start practising mindfulness. Recent research demonstrates that practising mindfulness can develop areas of your brain connected with learning and memory, and even help you do better in tests.

Mindfulness practice can improve your working memory in as little as two weeks. University of California Santa Barbara researchers conducted rigorous research that demonstrated that mindfulness can reduce mind-wandering and improve working memory. Undergraduate students were given a graduate record examination (GRE) and a working memory capacity test. After two weeks of mindfulness training with an experienced instructor, those who took part saw a marked improvement in their GRE score.

A study assessing the impact of a five-week mindfulness course for adults with learning difficulties demonstrated that, among other benefits, the mindfulness training resulted in improved academic performance.

Gain More Cognitive Control

Humans have a unique ability to focus their attention on something other than the present moment. This ability allows you to learn, plan and reason, but it can also make you unhappy. Recent research used the 'Track Your Happiness' app to ask people to record their feelings on a moment-by-moment basis. Throughout the day the app gave users random pings, asking them to share their current activity and note their mood. Data was gathered from 15,000 people in 80 countries, with a wide range of ages, education levels and occupations. The research showed that when the mind was wandering it was less happy. Apparently the mind wanders most when in the shower and least when having sex! But, still, mind-wandering is a constant. Overall, people's minds wander 47 per cent of the time.

It stands to reason that the less your brain wanders, the happier you'll be. Mindfulness helps you train your brain to be more in the present moment and to respond less on auto-pilot.

The more you live your life based on direct experience (present-moment facts), the less likely you are to default to habits and unconscious auto-pilot responses. The more 'present' you are in your own life, the less time you spend on auto-pilot and the more in control and happy you'll be.

Improve Your Health and Well-Being without Going to the Gym!

Did you know that mindfulness is good for your health? Research described in the *American Journal of Health Promotion* suggests that practices such as mindfulness are linked with lower annual health costs in the USA. While this connection may be explained by mindfulness producing an improved sense of positivity and reducing stress and depression, it may also be that mindfulness can actively boost your immunity. The better your immunity, the less likely you are to fall prey to bugs doing the rounds. In fact, mindfulness may even reduce your risk of developing serious illnesses.

The 'fight-or-flight' response evolved to keep our ancient ancestors safe from harm. When they encountered something life-threatening, their brains triggered a number of responses in their bodies. Blood flow, heart rate and breathing increased in order to rapidly pump energy to the muscles to help them sprint away from danger. Blood sugar levels increased to provide more energy. Blood clotting agents were released in case of injury, to stop them bleeding to death. Simultaneously, the digestive system, cell growth and repair, and the immune function also slowed down. These physiological changes make sense: if you're facing the possibility of death, digesting food and routine body repair and maintenance are unimportant.

The human fight-or-flight response is marvellous if you need to evade short-term mortal danger. The response isn't so good if, like many people, the greatest threat you face is crossing a road or driving on a busy motor-way. Worrying about your job, family or money can lead to you living life in a permanent state of heightened arousal. While in this state, normal bodily repair and the immune function are reduced. Mindfulness is very effective in reducing stress levels. When your stress levels are reduced and your normal bodily functions resume, the immune system starts working properly again, and you're much less likely to fall ill.

Too busy to practise mindfulness? Remember, your mind wanders for around half of your waking hours. Mindfulness can help you reduce this mind-wandering. In the time you save, you can practise mindfulness and improve your health and well-being. Just 15 minutes of mindfulness practice a day can make all the difference. You do the sums: you're awake for roughly 15 hours a day, seven days a week – that's 105 hours; your brain wanders 47 per cent of the time – that's 49 hours. So, if mindfulness can help your brain wander less, for example by 10 per cent, you save five hours. With five hours extra a week, you can easily fit in 15 minutes of mindfulness a day and still have more than three additional hours to do with as you wish. If you're off work with a bug for three days, you waste 45 waking hours. Practising mindfulness for 15 minutes a day for half a year takes less time!

Many people stagger through the working week, then flop on the sofa and succumb to illness at the weekend. Just 15 minutes of mindfulness practice a day can prevent this pattern. In bed with flu or out with friends having fun? Surely it's a no-brainer!

Mindfulness is also good for your health because it can help you sleep better. A University of Utah study found that those with higher levels of mindfulness had lower levels of brain activation at bedtime – in other words, their brains weren't full of random thoughts, fears and concerns. A good night's sleep is vital if you want to work effectively the next day.

Live Life with Less Fear

Did you know that mindfulness practice has been proven to reduce the fear centre of the brain – the amygdala? The amygdala (see Figure 17-1) triggers your fight-or-flight response when things happen that your brain regards as threatening.

Mindfulness makes you more aware of your thoughts as they arise. This awareness helps you to reduce your brain's auto-pilot response, allowing you to consciously decide how you react to threat. In approach mode of mind, your brain approaches what's going on in your life with openness and curiosity. In avoidance mode of mind, your brain's primary motivation is to avoid something bad happening.

Imagine that you've just been told that your small, UK-based company is being bought out by a large multinational organisation. In approach mode of mind you look at all the possibilities this buy-out offers, good and bad, with open-ness and interest. In avoidance mode of mind, you're driven by fear and your primary motivation is to avoid harm. This perceived harm may be a loss of reputation, a reduction in status or damage to your financial well-being. In avoidance mode of mind, you're less able to look at the situation objectively and more likely to identify the negative things that may happen as a result of the buy-out, such as job loss, demotion and the threat to your home life.

When you feel threatened, your primitive brain may take control and your rational brain is thus less engaged. Mindfulness helps you to adopt an approach mode of mind that is less likely to trigger your threat system. By finding out how to approach rather than avoid challenging situations, the perceived threat is usually reduced. Your rational brain then remains in control, helping you to respond in a wiser, less fear-driven way.

Two final things to consider when exploring the brain's response to fear are empathy and compassion. Mindfulness can help you to become less judgemental and hard on yourself, which can improve your self-compassion. Self-kindness can reduce or even de-activate your brain's threat response. The simple act of saying to yourself, 'It's okay, I'm human, I'm doing the best I can' can help you to relax and let go, and make everything feel less threatening. When you let go, you're better able to stand back and look at what's going on calmly and rationally.

Make Yourself Happier

It's official! Mindfulness can make you happier. Studies into depression and low mood suggest that the right brain of people who are depressed becomes more active. The right brain tends to react more emotionally than the left brain. The right brain is great for spotting patterns and connections, and is highly creative but needs input and guidance from the left brain. Over-reliance on the right brain can lead you into an emotional fog, which seems endless and difficult to break out of.

Depression often starts with a sense of prolonged uncontrolled stress. In this situation, your brain releases the stress hormone, cortisol. At this stage, your left brain usually kicks in to balance things out, but in depressed people this kicking in doesn't always happen. When your cortisol levels are high for prolonged periods, your right brain becomes much more active than your left brain. With an underactive left brain, it becomes difficult to be cheerful, positive or socially outgoing. Without the left brain coming to the rescue with a present-moment reality check, you can easily feel pulled into a downward spiral of negativity and helplessness.

Brain scans show that, when people practise mindfulness, their left brain becomes more active. The left brain is associated with logical thought and current reality. It also plays an important role in making plans for the future. Increased left-brain activation is associated with better mood and increased objectivity.

So, if you're feeling down, stop what you're doing, sit down and practise mindfulness. Doing so can help you put things into perspective and regain your equilibrium.

Regulate Your Emotions More Effectively

A 2011 study published in *Psychiatry Research: Neuroimaging* concluded that mindfulness can induce emotional regulation, clear thinking and brain plasticity (see Chapter 1). In a randomised trial, the MRI scans of those participants who practised mindfulness showed increases in grey matter/nerve cells in the hippocampus (see Figure 17-1). Participants in the control group showed no change in grey matter.

So why would you want to increase hippocampus grey matter? The hippocampus is associated with emotional regulation. The better able you are to regulate your emotions, the more you gain a sense of well-being. Feeling that everything is okay clearly leads to experiencing a higher quality of life.

Mindfulness training can also have a progressive impact on the limbic system, the area of the brain associated with emotions. Mindfulness has been shown to reduce activity in the amygdala, an area of the brain that helps you to modulate your response to fear. People with an active amygdala tend to experience more depression and anxiety. Practising mindfulness can actually reduce the size of the amygdala. One study conducted with stressed executives found that eight weeks of mindfulness training resulted in a reduction in the size of the amygdala. This reduction was correlated with less perceived stress. Can you believe it that just eight weeks' training can change your brain forever?

Improve Your Life without Even Trying

Throughout this book we encourage you to make mindfulness part of your life, and emphasise the importance of practice to embed your skills and reshape your brain.

Findings from a recent study reported in the *Frontiers in Human Neuroscience* journal demonstrate that you don't actually need to be practising mindfulness to benefit from it! Practices like mindfulness change the way your brain processes emotions, and help you step away from habitual responses and behaviours. Regular mindfulness practice changes how your amygdala (the brain's fear centre) responds to emotional stimuli. This change is maintained even when you're not actively sitting down practising.

So, a little mindfulness practice on a regular basis has long-lasting positive benefits that continue even when you're not doing it!

Improve Your Attention Span

In 2012, researchers from the University of Washington examined the effects of mindfulness on multi-tasking in a real-world setting. A group of human resources professionals were placed in a one-person office, with a laptop and a phone, and asked to complete several typical tasks: schedule a meeting for multiple attendees, locate a free conference room and write the agenda. They were allowed to use email, instant messaging and the phone as they normally would, and were given 20 minutes to complete the multiple tasks.

Half of the group was then given mindfulness training, and the other relaxation classes. Everyone was then asked to multi-task again.

Only the mindfulness participants showed improvement. Their ability to concentrate had improved significantly. They were able to stay on task longer and they switched between tasks less frequently. The overall time they took to complete the tasks did not change; they just spent it more efficiently. They also remembered what they did better than the other participants in the study.

The concentration benefits of mindfulness training aren't just behavioural; they're physical too. Mindfulness has been shown to improve connectivity inside your brain's attentional networks, which results in reduced distractions. Practising mindfulness can help your brain's attention networks communicate better and with fewer interruptions than they otherwise would. Good news indeed!

Chapter 18

Ten Ways to Mindfully Manage Work Pressures

*H*owever good you are at your job or happy you are in your work, at some time or other you'll feel under pressure. This chapter looks at some of the most commonly experienced pressures and some ways that mindfulness can help you deal with them.

The UK Health and Safety Executive (HSE) defines workplace stress as 'the adverse reaction people have to excessive pressures or other types of demand placed on them at work'. In 2012, it identified six factors that can lead to work-related stress if they're not managed properly: demands, control, support, relationships, role and change. This chapter starts by exploring these six in turn before moving on to some more general pressures you may encounter at some time or other.

Mindfully Coping with Inappropriate Work Demands

In the current economic climate, many organisations are looking at ways to cut costs. Making people redundant is often an obvious solution. Unfortunately for those left behind, fewer staff mean greater workloads and increased responsibilities for them. While some people may thrive in this situation, seeing it as a way to acquire new experience and improve their prospects for promotion, others may struggle to meet the new demands of their jobs.

At the other end of the spectrum, some job roles are being de-skilled. This situation too can be a source of pressure as work becomes less stimulating and meaningful, and fewer opportunities for promotion exist.

 When you're next feeling overwhelmed by your workload, step away from it for a short while. Spend a few minutes practising mindfulness to help put things back in perspective. Doing so will save you time in the long run because you'll return to the task in hand feeling more focused and your stress level declines.

Spend ten or more minutes practising your favourite mindfulness exercise. Try mindfulness of breath, a body scan or using thoughts or sounds as the focus for your attention. Immediately afterwards, choose something to work on that gives you a sense of personal satisfaction or a feeling of control over your work.

If doing a spot of mindfulness isn't possible, try giving your full attention to just one task and aim to get it finished. If you catch your mind wandering onto other things you need to do, kindly and gently escort your attention back to the task you're working on. When you've finished the task, acknowledge its completion and congratulate yourself on a job well done. Now you can go on to your next job.

Single-tasking in this manner works as follows. First, it helps you to recognise just how much you achieve each day. By consciously celebrating each little success, you benefit from the release of lots of short bursts of feel- good hormones into your bloodstream, which help lift your mood. Second, the act of focusing on just one task at a time helps you get through your work more quickly and efficiently. Third, single-tasking reduces the feeling of being out of control, which means that you can then deal with your workload more calmly – one task at a time.

Mindfully Dealing with a Lack of Control over Your Work

Lots of research demonstrates that feeling a lack of control over your work can rapidly lead to stress and poor performance. This situation is true whatever your job role – from senior executive to manual worker. Workplace health and safety organisations all over the world agree that having no power to decide on how a job is done is a major cause of workplace stress and frequently makes employees, at all levels in the organisation, unwell.

Try this exercise when your thoughts are whirling or you're feeling angry or frustrated:

1. **Spend a minute observing your emotions.** What are they? What impact (if any) are they having on your body? Are you holding any tension? If so, where? Are your emotions triggering any thoughts? Try to just observe what's happing in this present moment; don't try to start fixing things!

2. **Spend a minute observing your thoughts.** Remember to observe them with openness and curiosity. You don't need to change them or make them go away. Just observe them as they come and go.

3. **Spend a minute focusing on the present-moment sensation of breathing.** Feel the breath coming in and the breath going out.

4. **Ask yourself what, in this present moment, you do *have control* over.** Write these things down or record them on your smart phone.

Focus on the things that you're able to control – there may be more of them than you think! Stop wasting energy on things you simply can't control in this moment in time and mindfully accept them instead. Letting go of them can be a great source of relief.

Mindfully Managing a Lack of, or Inappropriate, Support

If you're offered a promotion, you'll probably be very pleased won't you? But a promotion can turn into nightmare if you receive inadequate support from colleagues, peers and senior staff. This situation is true for all staff, from the most senior to the most junior.

For a trainee or apprentice, their first role can be daunting if no one introduces them to the organisation, its culture and unwritten rules. Without adequate instructions or guidance, making mistakes is all too easy, which can be highly stressful. At a more senior level, if you receive no guidance on your key objectives and fail to meet unspecified expectations, you may damage both your reputation and long-term career prospects.

Get mindful. Identify the help you really need at this moment in time. If you can't see the wood for the trees, stop what you're doing and practise some mindfulness. Don't worry about the bigger picture – you can fix that later. Ask for the guidance or support you need. Don't waste energy worrying about what people might think; doing so usually causes more suffering and wastes more time than actually asking the question! If you still don't get the clear guidance you need, ask in writing via a letter or email. Be polite and concise – keep it short to read and short to answer.

If you receive a vague or unclear response, take control. Write down what you think you should be doing and what you think your priorities are, and state them in a short and professional email. Politely point out that this list is what you think you should be getting on with, and will do so unless you hear otherwise. Rest assured that if you've got it wrong in any way, this email should prompt a response. It may also help your boss to articulate more clearly what you should be doing – so either way should produce a win–win situation.

Mindfully Managing Difficult Working Relationships

Whatever your job role, a big part of working life is interacting with your colleagues. For many people, this chance to socialise can be a source of enjoyment, learning and fulfilment. It can transform a dull, low-paid job into something that makes you feel good about yourself and to which you look forward every day.

On the flip side, some people are subjected to unacceptable behaviour from colleagues ranging from bullying to discrimination in all its forms. If you were treated badly outside work, you'd probably walk away. You'd probably also take appropriate action to stop people from making you unhappy. Unfortunately, things aren't so simple at work.

Try a befriending exercise (see Chapter 5). It may help you see things in a different way or reduce the level of tension induced by the people you find difficult.

If things don't get easier, practising mindfulness regularly will help ease tension and emotional reactivity. It may also help you stand back and gain a greater perspective. If fixing things or finding a different way to relate to the difficult person are impossible, take steps to regain control over the situation. Speak in confidence to someone in the human resources department. Talk to your boss, or even your boss's boss. If things can't be made better, start looking for a new job and, for your remaining time in the company, keep reminding yourself that this problem isn't forever, it will pass. Life's too short to remain unhappy.

Mindfully Gaining Clarity about Your Job Role

In most roles, you're judged based on your ability to do your job to the required standard. But what if you have no job description? What if you don't understand what your job description really means in terms of expected outcomes? What if your job description doesn't match the job you're being asked to do? What if the rules keep changing but nobody tells you?

These scenarios are all too common. We know of many people who have no job description, despite having asked for one. This situation can lead to them missing out work that their managers deem important (despite not telling them so!), or working hard on things that the organisation doesn't value. We know of other employees who do have clearly defined job descriptions but they're not updated in line with organisational changes.

If you find yourself in any of these situations, decide for yourself what your work priorities should be and tactfully let your boss know. If you are unsure, try practising mindfulness. Doing so may help you gain perspective and decide what you really need in the present moment.

Mindfully Navigating the Bumpy Road of Frequent Organisational Change

As Chapter 5 discusses, many employees are now subjected to constant, ongoing change. While change may now be the norm, humans dislike uncertainty, and change creates uncertainty. When you're faced with an uncertain future, your threat system almost certainly kicks in, putting your primitive brain in control (see Chapter 1).

Mindfulness can help you reduce your sense of being under threat, and put your higher brain back in control. Use mindfulness of breath on a regular basis. When your mind wanders and you start thinking, observe the thoughts that arise in a detached manner. After your mindfulness practice, reflect on any patterns or common themes that emerged. Try to bring some conscious attention to what specific thoughts are unsettling you. Reflect on how much of the discomfort or suffering you're experiencing is self-induced – self-generated by your attempts to predict the future. Make a wise decision on what to do next.

Even when you know logically that the change is necessary and unavoidable, your primitive brain may kick in and you'll find yourself retreating to your place of safety – old habits and behaviours that have worked well in the past.

Changing the way you work (even when you really want to!) is often a slow process. Mindfulness can help you to bring conscious awareness to what you're thinking and feeling, and to recognise how your thoughts and feelings impact on your behaviour. With a little regular mindfulness practice, you'll be able to more quickly identify when you're falling into old patterns of thoughts and behaviours, and consciously decide on a skilful course of action.

Mindfully Dealing with Difficult One-to-One Meetings

Other people can be the most challenging aspect of your working day! You might be faced with a colleague who agrees with a plan of action, then goes off and does her own thing. You may experience conflict with a peer over a difference of opinion; this situation can turn ugly and be harmful to working relationships. Maybe you're one of those people who try to avoid conflict whenever possible? Conflict avoidance is very common in workplaces. Unfortunately, steering clear of disagreement and conflict or leaving things unsaid often results in anxiety and further tension.

Mindfulness can be really valuable when dealing with conflict in one-to-one meetings. Bear these tips in mind:

- ✔ **Try to resist the urge to judge or make assumptions.** Step back, freeing yourself from past baggage and stepping into the present moment with an open mind. Deal with any issues that arise if and when they actually do so.

- ✔ **Manage your emotional response to the situation.** Anger and frustration are very human responses when you're experiencing difficulty with others. Unfortunately, they're unlikely to help and may make things a whole lot worse. While you can't manage the emotional responses of other people – you can manage your own. Practising mindfulness makes you more consciously aware of your own emotional state, and thus better able to regulate and manage it.

- ✔ **Tuning in to the present moment.** You'll be able to respond more skilfully to the situation instead of reacting based on old mental programming that may be inappropriate.

Mindfully Coping with the Threat of Redundancy

A number of different research studies have revealed that one in three people has been faced with redundancy at some point in their career. Worryingly, over 40 per cent of people in one study believed that they could not survive financially for longer than a month. Threat of redundancy can be a very worrying time. While you may not have any control over whether you're made redundant or not, you do have control over how much you suffer.

Naturally, being under threat of redundancy is a cause of anxiety, but if you step back and think about it, losing sleep at night and worrying yourself sick don't actually help matters. First and foremost, be kind to yourself. It's okay to feel worried or frightened – acknowledge that that's how you feel, and then get on with something else.

Take time out to linger and appreciate the good things in your life. They may be as simple as a car with a tank of fuel that safely and comfortably gets you from A to B. It may be coffee with a good friend or a hug from your child. Really pause to soak up the good from these moments.

When you do realise that you're spiralling into negative thoughts, don't get angry with yourself – it only adds fuel to the fire. Just acknowledge that you're starting to spiral, bring yourself back to the present moment and get on with what you need to do.

Mindfully Coping with Redundancy Survivor Syndrome

If you're 'lucky' enough to survive a round of redundancies, you may fall victim to redundancy survivor syndrome.

Redundancies make things uncomfortable for all employees. Many employers make great efforts to support and care for staff facing redundancy. Few plan for the survivors who keep their jobs – assuming that they're just pleased and relieved to still have a job. Employees who survive redundancy may experience initial relief, but this relief can quickly turn into guilt because they've kept their jobs while others have been forced to leave. They can even feel envious of their colleagues' redundancy payments and their chance to embark on a new life. A few months down the line, the survivors may ultimately feel resentful about the extra work they have to do to cover the work of those who have left.

As in the previous section, just remember to be kind to yourself. Experiencing these sorts of feelings is completely natural (even if they're unhelpful at times!). Accepting your feelings without trying to change them often reduces their grip on you and can provide welcome relief.

Using Mindfulness to Reduce Stress

Some stress is necessary – this stress is what makes you get out of bed in the morning and motivates you to do your best. However, excessive stress is bad both for the individual and in terms of a firm's productivity. Work-related stress is a widespread problem, and isn't confined to specific sectors or job roles. Stress can affect anyone at any time in any business. Stress is also a major cause of sickness absence and staff turnover. If you're very stressed, you may make errors at work and your inability to focus may mean that you waste lots of time.

Mindfulness is proven to reduce stress. A little mindfulness practised daily can reduce your tendency to feel stressed out or depressed. It can also enable you to recognise when you're starting to feel excessively stressed, and to take steps to get things back in balance. Spotting the symptoms of stress early enables you to take the mindful steps necessary to regain equilibrium. As little as three minutes of mindfulness may be all it takes. If you ignore the early warning signals, it may take you much longer to return to peak performance – you might have to take time off work or even use medication. Suffering from stress at times is inevitable, how long you suffer for is up to you. Mindfulness puts this choice in your hands.

Chapter 19

Ten Ways to be Mindful in a Minute

Start Your Day with an Energising, Mindful Shower

A busy woman, attending one of my (Juliet's) eight-week mindfulness courses told me that she starts each day with a shower. As soon as she steps in the shower her mind starts to race. She overthinks interactions with staff and clients that haven't gone to plan. She tries to plan her day, anticipating what may happen and how she should respond. The more she tries to make sense of her thoughts, the less clear things become, inducing a mild state of panic. As she steps out of the shower and dries herself, she continues to mull over the day ahead and worry. She arrives at work primed to deal with possible problems and conflicts, with a knotted feeling in her stomach.

I asked her what she remembered about her shower, the shampoo she had used, the scent of the body wash and the feeling of water on her skin – she couldn't recall any of it! She spends her time in the shower in the past and future, and completely misses out on the present-moment experience.

Try starting your day with a minute of mindful showering because mindful showering:

✔ Is good way to give your brain a short break from overthinking

✔ Helps you relax and see things more clearly

✔ Feels good!

The mindful element of your shower can last for as little as a minute or for the full duration. Follow these steps:

1. **Get in the shower.**

2. **Notice how your skin feels as the water pours over it.** Is it tingling? Is it hot or cold?

3. **Observe any emotions you experience.** Maybe you feel a sense of pleasure as you start to relax; maybe shock if the water is too cold. Possibly you feel tense if you're in a hurry to get to work or perhaps all this extra attention you're paying to the present-moment experience of showering makes you feel uncomfortable. Just notice what's there – no need to fix it or change it – just experience everything that's going on in this present moment.

4. **Pause to notice the texture of the products you apply to your skin or hair.** Notice their scent. Explore the experience as a scientist may, with openness and curiosity. Is the sensation of washing your hair pleasurable? Does the smell of the shampoo evoke any memories? Does the texture of the shower gel feel good on your skin?

5. **Leave the shower feeling refreshed in mind and body, ready to face your day.**

Begin with a Mindful Moment

Do you commute to work by car or public transport? At times the journey can be slow and frustrating. As a result, you enter work holding tension in your body. Not a great start to the day!

When discussing mindful working practices on my (Juliet's) mindfulness at work courses, participants often struggle to think of ways that they can incorporate mindfulness into their busy working day. In large organisations, most people have networked computers. These often seem to take an age to boot up first thing in the morning, which can be another source of frustration.

Waiting for the computer to boot up can be a great excuse for a minute (or more!) of mindfulness. If you're sitting in an office chair facing your PC, your colleagues probably won't even notice that you're practising mindfulness. Bonus! Starting the day with a mindful moment helps you let go of any tension or negativity you've brought into the building with you.

1. **Switch on your computer.**

2. **Sit on your chair facing your computer in a comfortable, upright position.** Place your feet on the floor and rest your arms comfortably.

3. **Shut your eyes or hold them in soft focus.**

4. **Do one or all the following, depending on how much time you've available:**

   • Observe any thoughts going around in your head as 'just mental processes'.

   • Identify any bodily tension you may be holding. If you find any, try relaxing the area and letting the tension go.

   • Notice any emotions you're experiencing. Remember that emotions, just like thoughts, are simply mental processes. Notice the emotions but don't try to make them go away or change; just accept that this state is where your emotions are at the present moment.

5. **Open your eyes and start your working day afresh.**

Enjoy a Mindful Coffee

At present, no one has brought to market a 'mindful coffee' – or 'mindful tea' for that matter! Maybe it's only a matter of time.

Whatever you like to drink at work, it can be a great excuse for bringing some mindfulness as well as hydration into your day. In the same way as taking a mindful pause when switching on your PC, you can take a mindful pause when drinking your favourite hot or cold drink – no one will notice and you'll feel the benefits.

Why drink mindfully? Well, drinking mindfully:

✔ Trains your brain to focus a spotlight of attention on exactly where you want it to be (in this case, your cuppa!)

✔ Slows down or stops excessive thinking and brain chatter

✔ Helps you step back and see things more clearly

✔ Makes the coffee (or tea or fruit juice) more enjoyable

✔ Is quick and easy to do

A big part of mindfulness is paying present-moment attention to what you're doing. Simply apply this principle to the first minute of drinking your drink. Observe the aroma, texture, temperature and taste. Notice what's going on in your mouth and throat as you swallow; how your hand holds and brings the cup to your lips; and the movement of your lips and tongue as you drink.

If you find this little exercise a bit tricky, try using your other hand to hold and lift the cup to your lips. Because it feels unnatural, the experience is completely different – do watch out for drips and spills, though!

Use your Phone to Become More Mindful

Smart phones are great. You can use them to surf the net, check emails, take photos, order a pizza, watch TV or even make a phone call. This kind of technology is supposed to make life easier but can actually make it harder than it needs to be. In mindfulness classes, I (Juliet) often hear people saying they're on sites like Facebook into the early hours and then feel tired the next morning when they get up for work. Others find it hard to sleep after getting wound up and stressed over friends' comments posted online. I was bemoaning the dangers of Facebook to a psychotherapist friend recently and her response was, 'Facebook is great! It brings me so much work!'

So how can your mobile phone make you more mindful? Simple – find a mindfulness app that works for you.

The Mindfulness Bell is a simple app. You just set it to go off at various intervals during the day (every 30 minutes, every hour or two hours – whatever suits). When the bell rings, you simply stop what you're doing and pause for a minute's mindfulness. Simple as that! Breaking up your day in this way helps train your brain to become more mindful, and can have a transformative effect on your working day.

You can select the bell or gong you like or, if you work in a quiet environment, a 'vibrate only' option is available. Download the Mindfulness Bell from: `https://play.google.com/store/apps/details?id=com.googlecode.mindbell`

Eat Lunch Mindfully

As you approach the middle of your working day, lunch is a wonderful opportunity for a minute or more of mindfulness. It makes no difference what your lunch is or where you eat it, you can always sneak in mindfulness.

1. **Spend a few seconds observing your lunch.** Identify the colours, textures and aromas.

2. **Observe the impact of this observation on your body or emotions.** Are you starting to salivate in anticipation of tucking in or does your lunch leave you unexcited?

3. **Notice and explore the textures and flavours of the food as you chew and swallow.** Spend a few moments more than you usually do on this activity.

4. **Check whether you're actually still hungry from time to time or if you're just eating for eating's sake.** This simple mindful check can save you both money and inches.

Try to make a few moments of each meal a journey of discovery into the present-moment enjoyment of food.

Be Mindful of Sounds

Lunchtime, or any other time of the day in fact, is a great opportunity to train your brain to notice sounds and the impact that they have on you. Sounds are all around you at work – in the room, elsewhere in the building, outside and even from time to time in your body.

In *A Book of Silence*, Sara Maitland describes her quest to find just that. She visited Skye in the Inner Hebrides, the Sinai desert, forests and mountains. She bobbed about in a flotation tank, stayed in monasteries and sat in libraries. She discovered that, even in these quiet places, she was still surrounded by sounds.

Although some sounds can be frustrating at times, they provide great every-day opportunities for mindfulness. I (Juliet) once started a workshop with a mindful pause, at the end of which one delegate commented, 'You know I've been coming to meetings in this room for the last six years and I've never noticed that the clock on the wall ticks!' You'll be amazed at what you notice when you really focus your attention on what's around you.

1. **Close your eyes or hold them in soft focus.**

2. **Focus on the sounds around you.** Try to just observe them as sounds without attaching meaning to them or judging them as good or bad.

3. **Notice new sounds as they appear and vanish.** Also observe the pauses between them.

4. **Observe any thoughts that pop into your head.** Acknowledge them, let them go and refocus on sounds.

5. **Notice your emotional responses.** Do certain sounds induce tension or anxiety? Observe where you hold this tension and anxiety in your body and try to let it go.

6. **Open your eyes and start work newly refreshed when your minute is up.** Set a timer at the start if you feel the need.

Appreciate the Good

Humans tend to have an inbuilt negativity bias. As a result, we're much quicker to spot potential problems than opportunities. We tend to focus on the negative rather than the positive.

On a recent eight-week mindfulness at work course for NHS staff, I (Juliet) asked participants to think of some good things that had happened to them at work in the previous week. I was met with a wall of silence. One woman told me that she felt like a brain plugged into her computer. I asked the participants if their actions or expertise had been able to help any of their patients. Some great examples then emerged. I asked them if these experiences gave any of them a sense of personal achievement or mastery, and they started to realise that many of their encounters with patients did indeed make a real difference and made them feel good about their work. Until that point they had rarely allowed themselves to stop and appreciate those precious moments.

As we discussed other aspects of their work, the participants started to recognise that, although their current work environment was tough and they were dealing with constant change, there were many things to feel good about. They just hadn't noticed them. As home practice, I asked them to try to notice things that made them feel good at work and home. I suggested that they should pause to mindfully appreciate them and derive as much benefit from these moments as possible.

Why did I ask them to do this activity? When you feel negative, or blame yourself for something, you tend to activate your body's fight or flight response. As a result, you may find it increasingly difficult to step back and see the bigger picture. When you do something you really enjoy and that makes you feel good, you activate your body's rest and relaxation response, which decreases or switches off your threat response. You can then regain your equilibrium.

Next week one participant told me that for years her kids came down each morning and asked for a hug, which she found mildly irritating as she was in a rush to get them fed and ready for school. The next week she paused to appreciate that hug moment. She said 'it felt sooo good, and it did not delay my morning in any way'.

The next time you encounter something good or pleasurable (however small or trivial), pause for a moment to fully experience it. Notice how it makes you feel. If it makes you smile, explore how smiling feels. When you actively seek them out, you'll start to notice these little feel- good incidents throughout your day. If you take a few moments to fully appreciate each one, you'll be amazed by how much your outlook on life changes.

Notice the Interplay between Your Thoughts, Emotions and Physiology

Thoughts, emotions and bodily sensations (physiology) are tightly linked and have a huge impact on one another. If your body is feeling tense, it is going to have an impact on your behaviour and the decisions you make. If you feel unhappy, you may find it difficult to think positive thoughts. If the hour is late and you're feeling tired, you may not be doing your best work. In fact you may be working in the zone of delusion (see Chapter 5) – working harder and harder to get things done but achieving little.

If you're struggling to get things done, just stop and practice a little mindfulness. It may feel counter-intuitive at first, but it really works!

Become More Body Aware

You may feel disconnected from your body at times. Many people treat their body as an enemy – getting annoyed because it won't always do what they want it to do. This situation may be even worse if, like many people, you don't like the way your body looks.

Work can feel so all-consuming and important that you neglect or forget your body. Quite a number of people on my (Juliet) mindfulness at work courses have told me that they often put off going to the toilet because their work seems more important. They later end up sprinting to the toilet, legs crossed and desperately hoping that a cubicle is free.

If your body feels okay, it's one less thing for your mind to subconsciously worry about. If your body feels good, you'll find it easier to focus and concentrate and you may also feel more positive.

At regular intervals in the day pause to see how your body feels. Mindfully stretch your legs under the table, stand up or make an excuse to take a short walk somewhere. Re-learn how to listen to your body and start to work with it rather than against it.

Move Mindfully

Plenty of opportunities for mindful movement present themselves each day. Many people find the act of focusing on their body in the present moment an effective way of remaining focused. Below are a few tips to help you spend a mindful moment focused on body movement.

✔ As you arrive home at night, really observe and notice your last few steps as you approach your front door. Notice all the muscles and movements involved in opening your door, stepping through it and closing it behind you.

✔ As you get changed, really observe and notice the movements your body is making. What parts of your body are involved? How do they move? How do your clothes feel? Can you identify the different textures?

✔ As you cook supper, spend a moment noticing the movements involved as you reach up and grab things, use utensils and handle food.

✔ If you go to the gym, really notice the muscles you use when you stretch. Observe your body's movements when you use the running machine or cross-trainer.

✔ If you go swimming, really notice the experience as your body moves through the water. What are your hands, legs and feet doing? How does the water feel as you glide through it?

✔ If you take your dog for a walk, take ten mindful steps. Really notice how you're walking, how your weight shifts and how your feet feel on different surfaces.

Hopefully this chapter has given you plenty of ideas about how you can practise mindfulness in a minute throughout your day. Try a few and see what works best for you. A little mindfulness can go a long way!

Chapter 20

About Ten Resources for Further Study

*T*his chapter points you towards a host of resources which can help you develop mindfulness in your daily working life. Whether you're a dedicated online surfer, a bookworm or in search of some face-to-face guidance and training, dive in: There's something here for you.

Whizzing through Websites

Websites devoted to the subject of mindfulness abound. To make your web surfing easier, here are a few good ones.

Mindfulnet.org

Juliet launched Mindfulnet.org in 2010 to provide easy access to a wide range of information on mindfulness. Its packed with free resources and information. Site users tell me Mindfulnet .org is a good first port of call if you're trying to find out more on the subject. Its and is designed to be accessible to newcomers and mindfulness professionals alike. The website includes informationon the following:

✔ How mindfulness can be applied in the workplace, schools and medical practice

✔ Research into mindfulness

✔ Making the business case for mindfulness

✔ The bi-annual Mindfulness at Work Conference

✔ Teachers (finding one and training to be one)

✔ The neuro-science underpinning mindfulness

Check out Mindfulnet at www.mindfulnet.org

Mindful.org

Mindful.org covers all aspects of mindfulness in daily living, including work. It provides information via its website, monthly magazine and social media.

Mindful.org offers new ideas from leaders in the field about mindfulness as it applies to health, happiness, family, career, society and more – and explores the science proving the techniques work. The content on the website continues to grow everyday, and the creative and intelligent ways of offering mindfulness in different settings is impressive. If you want to know more about mindful leadership, mindfulness in the workplace, or just being more mindful in your own life, check out the website from time to time for the latest research and ideas in this exciting, growing field.

Take a look at http://mindful.org

ShamashAlidina.com

When you sign up to Shamash's site, you can listen to free interviews with leading experts in the field of mindfulness in the workplace, including Chade-Meng Tan, Dan Goleman, Dan Siegel, Frank Bond, Elisha Goldstein and Mirabai Bush. You can also try out his 21 day e-course in mindfulness for free, completed by thousands of people.

Check out shamashalidina.com

Benefitting from Books

Secular books on mindfulness mainly fall into two camps, those on mindfulness-based stress reduction (MSBR) and those on mindfulness-based cognitive therapy (MBCT).

MBSR

Jon Kabat-Zinn is regarded as the founder of modern-day mindfulness. Jon developed MBSR in the 1970s and his work was the catalyst for a huge volume of research into the applications of mindfulness. We have met him on a number of occasions and warmly recommend him to you.

Jon has written a number of highly regarded books on mindfulness, including *Wherever You Go, There You Are: Mindfulness Meditation in Everyday Life,* now in its tenth edition and *Full Catastrophe Living: Using the Wisdom of Your Body and Mind to Face Stress, Pain, and Illness*, updated in 2013.

MBCT

Mark Williams is Professor of Clinical Psychology at the University of Oxford. He co-developed MBCT and was founding director of the Oxford Mindfulness Centre. Mark is one of the premier researchers in the field of mindfulness worldwide, and has been a pioneer in its development and dissemination. Check out *Mindfulness: A Practical Guide to Finding Peace in a Frantic World* (co-authored with journalist, Danny Penman, 2011) which, unlike many other mindfulness tomes, is a self-help book for a *healthy* population; it includes lots of real-life examples and is an easy read.

Other books worth a read

We could list hundreds of books in this section but manage to restrict ourselves to just four:

- ✔ *Mindfulness For Dummies:* by Shamash Alidina: This was Shamash's first book on mindfulness and is a good general introduction to the whole field of mindfulness, both at home and work, and includes many ways to develop mindful awareness. If you liked the style of this book, you'll probably enjoy *Mindfulness For Dummies* too.

- ✔ *The Mindful workplace: Developing Resilient Individuals and Resonant Organisations with MBSR* (Michael Chaskalson) This book, published in 2011 is one of the first books published on mindfulness at work and is full of practical ideas and workplace examples.

- ✔ *The Mindful Brain: Reflection and Attunement in the Cultivation of Well-Being* (Daniel J. Siegel) – this author is co-director of the Mindful Awareness Research Center and executive director of the Mindsight Institute. This book integrates neuro-science research with the ancient art of mindfulness. It describes how personal awareness and attunement can actually stimulate emotional circuits in the brain, leading to a host of benefits.

✔ *Your Brain at Work: Strategies for Overcoming Distraction, Regaining Focus, and Working Smarter All Day Long* (David Rock) – although not specifically a mindfulness book, mindfulness is at its heart. The book is all about understanding how your brain functions and applying this knowledge to your work to help you become more productive and resilient.

Practising with Audios

Mindfulness must be practised – not just read about. And guided mindfulness audios are perfect for the job. Here are two that you may like to try out, in addition to the CD that comes with this book:

✔ **Working with Mindfulness:** Developed and narrated by Mirabai Bush – a key contributor to Google's 'Search Inside Yourself' course – this is a set of guided mindfulness exercises that are ideal for use at work. Access them at www.morethansound.net.

✔ **Practicing Mindfulness:** In 24 detailed lectures, including guided mindfulness exercises, Professor Mark Muesse teaches the principles and techniques of mindful sitting, the related practice of mindful walking and the highly beneficial use of mindful awareness in many important activities, including eating and driving.

This programme is a thorough one for anyone who enjoys the lecture format and wants to gain an in-depth understanding of the art of mindfulness. Access at www.thegreatcourses.com.

Reading Up on the Research

Research into mindfulness has grown exponentially in recent years. Finding out how to be more mindful in your approach to work can have a number of benefits from both the individual and corporate perspective, as the research studies described below prove.

✔ Dane, E. and Brummel, B.J. 2013. Examining workplace mindfulness and its relations to job performance and turnover intention. *Human Relations,* June – The results of this research conducted in the service industry suggest that, in a dynamic work environment, workplace mindfulness improves job performance and reduces staff turnover.

✔ Ostafin, B.D. and Kassman, K.T. 2012. Stepping out of history: Mindfulness improves insight problem solving. *Consciousness and Cognition,* 21(2): 1031–36 – These researchers studied the impact of mindfulness on problem solving and were the first to document a direct relation between mindfulness and creativity.

✔ Reb, J., Narayanan, J. and Chaturvedi, S. 2012. Leading mindfully: Two studies of the influence of supervisor trait mindfulness on employee well-being and performance (*Mindfulness,* 2012). This research examines the influence of leaders' mindfulness on employee well-being and performance. Supervisor mindfulness was positively related to employee job satisfaction and psychological need satisfaction. Furthermore, leader mindfulness was positively related to both overall job performance and organisational citizenship behaviours. The results suggest the potentially important role of leading mindfully in organisations.

✔ Reb, J., Narayanan, J. and Ho, Z.W. 2013. Mindfulness at work: Antecedents and consequences of employee awareness and absent-mindedness. *Mindfulness,* (2013) This study examined two aspects of mindfulness in a work setting: employee awareness and employee absent-mindedness. Using two samples, the study found that these two aspects of mindfulness were beneficially associated with employee well-being, as measured by emotional exhaustion, job satisfaction and psychological need satisfaction, and with job performance, as measured by task performance, organisational citizenship behaviours and deviance.

Accessing Apps

Lots of mindfulness apps are available for smart phones – some good, some not so good! In some ways, frequent use of mobile devices is bad for mindfulness, but used selectively and not slavishly, they can be a real help.

✔ ***Mindfulness Meditation:*** This app is an eight-week set of daily activities that help you establish and maintain regular mindfulness practice. It includes six guided meditations of varying length, from 5 to 40 minutes and eight talks on integrating mindfulness into everyday life. Available from `www.mentalworkout.com/store/programs/mindfulness-meditation`

✔ ***Insight Timer:*** This free app includes a range of lovely Tibetan singing bowl sounds to guide you through your practice. You can use it as a timer and to record your experiences if you wish to. Recent updates include guided meditations by teachers. The upgrade version (paid) includes interval bells, a wider variety of bells and an optional daily meditation reminder. The app is available from Google Play and iTunes.

✔ *Mindfulness Bell:* This app is a nice simple one that costs less than £1. You can set it to ring periodically during the day to give you the opportunity to consider what you're currently doing your state of mind while you're doing it. Available from Google Play and iTunes.

✔ *Walking Meditations:* This app is designed to lead you through walking meditation. You can set the duration of and your intent for the walk. You receive instructions and reminders as you're walking. Available from Google Play and iTunes.

Locating Training Providers

You can find mindfulness training providers the length and breadth of the UK, but here are three we particularly recommend – including our own, of course!

Mindfulness at Work Training

Mindfulness at Work Training (MAWT) delivers the six-week workplace course outlined in this book, developed and delivered by Juliet and Shamash. It combines scientifically proven core elements of the eight-week MBCT syllabus with practical everyday practical applications of mindfulness at work such as mindful meetings, mindful emailing and mindful communication. The mindfulness techniques taught are shorter than those used on traditional courses, but have been proven to be highly effective. For more information, visit http://mawt.co.uk

The Mindfulness Exchange

The Mindfulness Exchange (TME) is a spin-off from the Oxford Mindfulness Centre. It provides mindfulness programmes for the workplace using cognitive scientific principles based on Williams and Penman's book *Mindfulness: A Practical Guide to Finding Peace in a Frantic World* (see the 'Benefitting from Books' section earlier in this chapter for details). The programmes TME offers are scientifically based, but take half the amount of time of standard mindfulness training. TME takes best practice from mindfulness-based research and training in clinical fields and applies it to a business paradigm. Check out http://mindfulness-exchange.com

Mindfulness Works

Michael Chaskalson teaches MBSR in London and at client premises across the UK and internationally. He is the founder and chief executive of Mindfulness Works. Michael coaches senior executives and teaches mindfulness in corporate settings. For more information, visit www.mindfulness-works.com

Identifying Universities and Management Schools Utilising Mindfulness

An increasing number of business schools are embracing mindfulness, offering it within modules or as stand-alone courses, or incorporating it into MBA programmes.

Ashridge Business School incorporates mindfulness into elective modules forming part of the MBA and Diploma leadership programmes. Its 'The Leader as Coach and Facilitator' module aims to help leaders to engage with and lead in complex and uncertain environments.

Since 2012 full-time MBA students at Cranfield University's School of Management have been learning about and applying mindfulness to improve their resilience and personal effectiveness. Mindfulness training forms part of the core curriculum in applied evidence-based personal and leadership development techniques at Cranfield. Anecdotal evidence from its recent MBA graduates suggests that these mindfulness-based techniques have helped them lead more effectively back in the workplace.

On the leadership course at Harvard Business School in the USA, Professor of Management Practice William George focuses on helping business people to better understand their emotions. According to him, 'It isn't a lack of intelligence that causes executives to make poor decisions, but a lack of awareness of the feelings that drive their reactions.'

Reflecting on Retreats

If you want to deepen your mindfulness skills, consider attending a mindfulness retreat. Here are a couple:

✔ Gaia House Meditation Retreat Centre offers silent meditation in the Buddhist tradition. Located within the peaceful beauty of South Devon, check out Gaia House at http://gaiahouse.co.uk

✔ The Mindful Leadership Foundation exists to support, nurture and develop leaders grappling with the big issues. It runs Mindful Leadership Retreats for people working in the public and voluntary sectors, in the beautiful setting of Parcevall Hall in North Yorkshire. Visit www.themindfulleadershipfoundation.com

Training to be a Mindfulness Teacher

No worldwide recognised qualifications in mindfulness teaching currently exist. In 2010, the UK Mindfulness Trainers' Network developed some good practice guidance for teaching mindfulness-based courses, which the main teaching institutions in the UK now adhere to. Institutions offering mindfulness teacher qualifications in the UK include Aberdeen, Exeter and Bangor Universities and the Oxford Mindfulness Centre.

The Oxford Mindfulness Centre is an international centre of excellence within the University the Oxford's Department of Psychiatry. It offers a range of mindfulness courses, including an MSc in Mindfulness-Based Cognitive Therapy. Visit http://oxfordmindfulness.org/train.

Enter Mindfulness is one of the few independent mindfulness teacher training providers in the UK. It offers a two-stage approach to mindfulness teacher training that broadly follows the UK good practice guidelines. Visit www.entermindfulness.com/workshops.

Shamash runs a professional certified 10-week teacher training programme, Teach Mindfulness, for people who cannot access courses in person. The training is based on the MBSR and MBCT syllabus but can be adapted to meet the needs of your client group. Contact him via shamashalidina.com or visit www.teachmindfulnessonline.com for further details.

Part VI
The Appendixes

In this part . . .

✔ Check out the answers to the learning check questions.

✔ Get the lowdown on the research underpinning mindfulness.

Appendix A

Answers to Learning Check Questions

• •

*T*his appendix presents the answers to the Mindfulness at Work Training (MAWT) learning check questions in Chapter 6.

Week 1 Learning Check

The answers to the week 1 learning check are as follow:

1. Mindfulness is 'paying attention, on purpose, to the present moment without judgement'. Mindfulness is all about training your brain to become more aware of what is happening as it is happening. It cultivates awareness of your thoughts, emotions and body, and the interplay between them. Mindfulness is experiencing the present moment with openness and curiosity, without judging it as good or bad or trying to categorise it.

2. Mindfulness:

   • Can thicken those parts of the brain's cerebral cortex responsible for decision making, attention and memory.

   • Reduces the tendency for the brain to default to habits and ways of thinking based on past experiences.

   • Helps you balance left- and right-brain activity.

3. The brain's tendency to work on auto-pilot is a good thing because it frees your working memory to do more things. However, the brain working on auto-pilot is also a bad thing because people make decisions and act based on old information, which may or may not be relevant or appropriate.

4. Being in the present allows you to see things as they really are in this moment rather than how you *think* they are, which may be inaccurate. It allows you to make wiser decisions based on facts rather than passing thoughts.

Week 2 Learning Check

The answers to the week 2 learning check are as follow:

1. True. My body really can detect my thoughts before I have consciously registered them myself.

2. Approach mode is when you approach and explore things in the present moment with an open mind. It creates a happier, more open approach to work.

3. Avoidance mode is when you expend energy in trying to avoid thinking about or exploring emotions or situations, especially those you find difficult or challenging. Working in avoidance mode can lead to a downward mood spiral.

   Avoidance mode is the human brain's default mode for most people – your brain tries to maximise reward and minimise threat so you may often avoid approaching things you find difficult or challenging.

4. False. At times many people become bored or frustrated with mindfulness practice. That's fine; just keep working at it. Each time you practise, you're strengthening your brain's ability to be mindful. Doing exercises in the gym may feel boring but you still get results – the same goes for mindfulness.

5. False. The sensations you feel can vary from day to day, minute to minute. Some people never feel any sensations in certain parts of their body, which is fine. Focusing your attention on a specific part of the body and seeing what (if anything) you notice is what's important, not the feeling itself.

Appendix B

Summary of Research

· ·

*T*he following table summarises a small selection of research into the impacts of practicing mindfulness.

Research paper	*Summary*
Dane E, 2010. Paying Attention to Mindfulness and its effect on Task Performance in the Workplace. *Journal of Management* 37(4), 997-1018.	This research into mindfulness in a work context suggests that mindfulness widens your attentional breadth', allowing you to be aware of a lot of things simultaneously.
Dane E, Brummel BJ ,2013. Examining workplace mindfulness and its relations to job performance and turnover intention. *Human Relations*	This research conducted in a dynamic the service Industry environment suggests workplace mindfulness improves job performance and reduces staff turnover.
Ostafin BD & Kassman KT, 2012. Stepping out of History: Mindfulness improves insight problem solving. *Consciousness and cognition,* 4(5).	Researchers studied the impact of mindfulness in problem solving. The findings are the first to document a direct relation between mindfulness and increased creativity.
Reb J, Narayanan J, & Chaturvedi S, 2012. Leading mindfully: Two studies of the influence of supervisor trait mindfulness on employee well-being and performance. *Mindfulness.*	This research examines the influence of leaders' mindfulness on employee well-being and performance. Mindfulness training reduced employee emotional exhaustion and increased employee work–life balance. It improved employee performance and staff engagement. It improved job satisfaction and overall job performance.
Reb J, Narayanan, J, & Ho ZW, 2013. Mindfulness at Work: Antecedents and Consequences of Employee Awareness and Absent-mindedness. *Mindfulness,* forthcoming.	Using two samples, the study suggests that mindfulness improves employee well-being, job satisfaction, and job performance.

(continued)

(continued)

Research paper	Summary
Zhang J, Ding W, Li Y, & Wu C, 2013. Task complexity matters: The influence of trait mindfulness on task and safety performance of nuclear power plant operators. *Personality and Individual Differences* 55, 433-439.	This study involving 136 Chinese nuclear power plant operators concluded that people who practice mindfulness are more likely to maintain an open and present-focused awareness and attention.
Davidson, R.J., Kabat-Zinn, J., Schumacher, J., et al. (2003) Alterations in brain and immune function produced by mindfulness meditation. *Psychosomatic Medicine,* 65, 564–570	This research involved employees at a biotech company who had their brains scanned to investigate the effects of mindfulness training on their brain. The study showed significant increases in left Prefrontal Cortex activation, an area of the brain associated with approach mode of mind. They also found significant increases in immunity. The course resulted in participants feeling more positive, more energetic, more engaged in their work and less stressed.
Stanley and Jha (2009) Mind fitness: Improving operational effectiveness and building warrior resilience. *Joint Force Quarterly,* 55, 144-151.	31 US Marines took part in 8 weeks of mindfulness based mind fitness. The research suggests mindfulness training improves well-being, and reduces negativity and rumination. It also reduces emotional reactivity.
Bostoket et al (2013) Can finding headspace reduce work stress? Randomised controlled workplace trial of mindfulness app. *Psychosomatic Medicine* 75 (3) A36-A37	120 employees used a self-administered mindfulness training app 45 day programme of 10-20 minutes practice. This resulted in significant improvements in job control, reduced anxiety and depression.
Beckman, H. B., Wendland, M., Mooney, C., Krasner, M. S., et al. (2012). The impact of a program in mindful communication on primary care physicians. *Academic Medicine,* 87(6), 1-5.	This research conducted on physicians suggests that training in mindfulness can significantly reduce exhaustion and burnout experienced by many physicians and can improve their well-being and empathy with others.
Smith et al (2011) Mindfulness is associated with fewer PTSD symptoms. . . In urban fire-fighters. *Journal of Consulting and Clinical Psychology* 79(5) 613-617	This research involved 124 fire fighters who were taught mindfulness. It suggests that mindfulness reduced PTSD, and depression, and increases well-being and resilience.

Research paper	*Summary*
Limm, H., Gundel, H., Heinmuller, M., Marten-Mittag, B., Nater, U. M.,Siegrist, J., & Angerer, P. (2011). Stress management interventions in the workplace improve stress reactivity: A randomized controlled trial. *Occupational and Environmental Medicine,* 68, 126 –133. doi:10.1136/oem.2009.054148174	This study involved lower or middle management employees. It suggests that mindfulness can decrease stress reactivity and sympathetic nervous system (fight or flight) activation.
Hölzel, B.K., Carmody, J., Vangel, M., Congleton, C., Yerramsetti, S.M., Gard, T., and Lazar, S.W. (2011) Mindfulness practice leads to increases in regional brain grey matter density. *Psychiatry Resource* 2011 2011 Jan 30;191(1):36-43. Epub 2010 Nov 10.	This research involved scanning the brains of participants of an 8-week mindfulness training course. Results included changes in participant's brain areas that are associated with attention, learning and memory processes, emotion regulation and perspective taking.
Gaëlle Desbordes, Lobsang T. Negi, Thaddeus W. W. Pace, B. Alan Wallace, Charles L. Raison and Eric L. Schwartz (2012) Effects of mindful-attention and compassion meditation training on amygdala response to emotional stimuli in an ordinary, non-meditative state	A 2102 Massachusetts General Hospital study showed that eight weeks of mindfulness training shrunk the amygdala, the portion of the brain modulating response to fear and stress. These effects continued even when not actively practising mindfulness.

Index

• **F** •

• **G** •

• *N* •

About the Authors

Shamash Alidina, MEng MA PGCE, is CEO of Learn Mindfulness International, offering training and teacher training in mindfulness for both the general public, as well as life and executive coaches, yoga teachers, doctors, nurses, and other health professionals. His website offers online mindfulness courses and online mindfulness teacher training. He continues to grow his offers of audio CDs, books and more.

Shamash offers mindfulness workshops several times a year around the world and offers a limited number of one-to-one mindfulness coaching in person in London, or via phone/Skype.

Shamash has trained extensively in mindfulness at Bangor University's Centre for Mindfulness in the UK, and with Dr Jon Kabat-Zinn and Dr Saki Santorelli in New York. He holds a Masters Degree in Engineering (Imperial College) and a Masters Degree in Education (Open University), with a focus on Brain and Behaviour.

Shamash has appeared on television, radio and in magazines and newspapers including on the BBC and in the *Daily Express*. He hosts a mindfulness radio show at www.mindfulnessradio.com which has had several thousand listeners. He is an international speaker, addressing audiences at places like Cambridge University's conference on Mindfulness in the Workplace, the Mind and its Potential conference in Sydney and the Healthy Living Show in Auckland.

Shamash is the author of the international bestsellers *Mindfulness For Dummies* and *Relaxation For Dummies*.

See all Shamash's courses and workshops at www.learnmindfulness.co.uk or email him directly at shamash@learnmindfulness.co.uk.

Catch Shamash on the social networks at: www.twitter.com/shamashalidina, www.facebook.com/learnmindfulness and www.linkedin.com/in/learnmindfulness.

Juliet Adams has spent most of her career working with organisations on leadership and strategic learning programmes, organisational development, and change projects. She has worked on national projects for the police and several standards setting bodies. She now runs her own successful consultancy 'A Head for Work' specialising new approaches to leadership, where she develops programmes and e-learning content for leading organisations.

In recent years Juliet has become increasingly involved in bringing mindfulness to the world of work. She is the founder of Mindfulnet.org, a leading web-based independent mindfulness information resource. She arranged the first Mindfulness at work conference at Robinson College Cambridge in 2012, and is currently working with a leading University to arrange the 2014 conference. She is author of *Making the business case for mindfulness*. She teaches mindfulness to groups of staff in the workplace and coaches one-to-one with senior staff.

Juliet has been interviewed by the Daily Telegraph, BBC and Personnel Today and is a regular commentator on mindfulness at work. She lives in Cambridgeshire near the beautiful City of Ely.

Dedication

This book is dedicated to you, the reader, in your journey towards a more mindful way of working, and more balanced, enjoyable life.

Authors' Acknowledgments

From Juliet: I would like to personally thank Shamash for getting me involved in writing this book, and all the staff at Wiley who assisted me in the journey. My special thanks go also to Mark Leonard and Dr Patrizia Collard for their encouragement, support, along with other members of the mindfulness training community. Closer to home, my thanks go also to Sophie and Marta at Samovar Tea House Ely for all the wonderful tea and homemade cake. Last, but most importantly, my heartfelt thanks go to my partner Jim for supporting me in so many ways while I tapped away at the keyboard for hours on end.

Publisher's Acknowledgments

We're proud of this book; please send us your comments at http://dummies.custhelp.com. For other comments, please contact our Customer Care Department within the U.S. at 877-762-2974, outside the U.S. at (001) 317-572-3993, or fax 317-572-4002.

Some of the people who helped bring this book to market include the following:

Acquisitions, Editorial, and Vertical Websites

Project Editor: Simon Bell

Commissioning Editors: Sarah Blankfield, Drew Kennerley

Assistant Editor: Ben Kemble

Development Editor: Kate O'Leary

Copy Editor: Kim Vernon

Proofreader: Mary White

Publisher: Miles Kendall

Audio Production: Heavy Entertainment

Vertical Websites: Rich Graves

Cover Photos: ©iStockphoto.com/Don Bayley

Project Coordinator: Sheree Montgomery

Take Dummies with you everywhere you go!

Whether you're excited about e-books, want more from the web, must have your mobile apps, or swept up in social media, Dummies makes everything easier .

FOR DUMMIES®

A Wiley Brand

BUSINESS

978-1-118-73077-5

978-1-118-44349-1

978-1-119-97527-4

MUSIC

978-1-119-94276-4

978-0-470-97799-6

978-0-470-49644-2

DIGITAL PHOTOGRAPHY

978-1-118-09203-3

978-0-470-76878-5

978-1-118-00472-2

Algebra I For Dummies
978-0-470-55964-2

Anatomy & Physiology For Dummies, 2nd Edition
978-0-470-92326-9

Asperger's Syndrome For Dummies
978-0-470-66087-4

Basic Maths For Dummies
978-1-119-97452-9

Body Language For Dummies, 2nd Edition
978-1-119-95351-7

Bookkeeping For Dummies, 3rd Edition
978-1-118-34689-1

British Sign Language For Dummies
978-0-470-69477-0

Cricket for Dummies, 2nd Edition
978-1-118-48032-8

Currency Trading For Dummies, 2nd Edition
978-1-118-01851-4

Cycling For Dummies
978-1-118-36435-2

Diabetes For Dummies, 3rd Edition
978-0-470-97711-8

eBay For Dummies, 3rd Edition
978-1-119-94122-4

Electronics For Dummies All-in-One For Dummies
978-1-118-58973-1

English Grammar For Dummies
978-0-470-05752-0

French For Dummies, 2nd Edition
978-1-118-00464-7

Guitar For Dummies, 3rd Edition
978-1-118-11554-1

IBS For Dummies
978-0-470-51737-6

Keeping Chickens For Dummies
978-1-119-99417-6

Knitting For Dummies, 3rd Edition
978-1-118-66151-2

FOR DUMMIES®

A Wiley Brand

SELF-HELP

978-0-470-66541-1

978-1-119-99264-6

978-0-470-66086-7

LANGUAGES

978-0-470-68815-1

978-1-119-97959-3

978-0-470-69477-0

HISTORY

978-0-470-68792-5

978-0-470-74783-4

978-0-470-97819-1

Laptops For Dummies 5th Edition
978-1-118-11533-6

Management For Dummies, 2nd Edition
978-0-470-97769-9

Nutrition For Dummies, 2nd Edition
978-0-470-97276-2

Office 2013 For Dummies
978-1-118-49715-9

Organic Gardening For Dummies
978-1-119-97706-3

Origami Kit For Dummies
978-0-470-75857-1

Overcoming Depression For Dummies
978-0-470-69430-5

Physics I For Dummies
978-0-470-90324-7

Project Management For Dummies
978-0-470-71119-4

Psychology Statistics For Dummies
978-1-119-95287-9

Renting Out Your Property For Dummies, 3rd Edition
978-1-119-97640-0

Rugby Union For Dummies, 3rd Edition
978-1-119-99092-5

Stargazing For Dummies
978-1-118-41156-8

Teaching English as a Foreign Language For Dummies
978-0-470-74576-2

Time Management For Dummies
978-0-470-77765-7

Training Your Brain For Dummies
978-0-470-97449-0

Voice and Speaking Skills For Dummies
978-1-119-94512-3

Wedding Planning For Dummies
978-1-118-69951-5

WordPress For Dummies, 5th Edition
978-1-118-38318-6

Think you can't learn it in a day? Think again!

The **In a Day** e-book series from **For Dummies** gives you quick and easy access to learn a new skill, brush up on a hobby, or enhance your personal or professional life — all in a day. Easy!

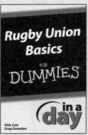

Available as PDF, eMobi and Kindle